Keywords in Chinese Culture

KEYWORDS IN CHINESE CULTURE

EDITED BY

Wai-yee Li

Yuri Pines

The Chinese University of Hong Kong Press

Keywords in Chinese Culture

Edited by Wai-yee Li and Yuri Pines

ISBN: 978-988-237-119-4

Published by The Chinese University of Hong Kong Press
             The Chinese University of Hong Kong
             Sha Tin, N.T., Hong Kong
             Fax: +852 2603 7355
             Email: cup@cuhk.edu.hk
             Website: cup.cuhk.edu.hk

Printed in Hong Kong

Contents

Virtue Keywords

Keywords of the Self

Afterword

Acknowledgements

This volume is based on the papers presented at the symposium *Keywords in Chinese Thought and Literature* held in June 2016 at the Hebrew University of Jerusalem. We organized the symposium to celebrate the achievements of our teacher and friend, Andrew Plaks, whose interests span literature, philosophy and philology from pre-imperial to late imperial China. Andy's example inspired us to seek possibilities of transcending period and disciplinary confines and to create common ground among scholars working on topics as divergent as early Chinese political thought and late imperial fiction and drama. The results of these efforts are presented in the current volume.

We are delighted to thank all those who generously supported the symposium: the Hebrew University, the Confucius Institute at the Hebrew University (HUJI), and the Louis Frieberg Center for East Asian Studies. We are grateful to our contributors as well as those conference participants (Wolfgang Behr and Amira Katz-Goehr) who opted not to submit their papers for the final publication. Many other colleagues, too numerous to be named individually here, contributed to the discussions at the conference and helped the symposium participants advance their arguments. The comments from the anonymous readers have been extremely helpful. We thank Roberta Raine for her careful editorial work, Ye Minlei for her commitment to our project, and Rachel Pang for her design of the cover and for steering the book through production.

Research leave made possible by the Guggenheim Foundation and the American Council of Learned Societies (Wai-yee Li) and support by the Israel Science Foundation (Grant 240/15) and the Michael William Lipson Chair in Chinese Studies (Yuri Pines) facilitated our work for this volume. We gratefully acknowledge their support.

W. Y. L., Y. P.

Introduction

Wai-yee Li

In his influential study, *Keywords: A Vocabulary of Culture and Society*, originally published in 1976, Raymond Williams defined keywords as "significant, binding words in certain activities and their interpretation" and "significant, indicative words in certain forms of thought." Keywords are the "words in which both continuity and discontinuity, and also deep conflicts of value and belief, are ... engaged."[1] Responding to cultural changes in the postwar period, Williams was intent on raising awareness of how specific social and historical conditions determined our vocabulary. To show how keywords shape us and are being reshaped by us is to demystify their "natural" authority and to heighten our agency.

This book departs from Williams' agenda of contemporary social and political intervention and his focus on modernity, although we do follow his cue on how keywords offer precious clues about "conflicts of value and belief." Like every major culture, Chinese has its set of "keywords": pivotal

---

[1] Williams 1985: 15, 23. See also a brief analysis in Rodgers 1988. Among the many works inspired by Williams' *Keywords* is *Keywords Re-Oriented* (Gentz et al., 2009), which explores the implications of using Western theoretical keywords as analytic tools in Chinese contexts. At the other end of the temporal spectrum, Bergeton attempts to examine the emergence of civilizational consciousness in early China by focusing on "how words are used in pre-Qin texts to construct identities and negotiate relationships between a 'civilized self' and 'uncivilized others'" (2019, front matter).

terms of political, ethical, literary and philosophical discourse. Tracing the origins, development, polysemy, and usages of keywords is one of the best ways to chart cultural and historical changes. What elevates a mere word to the status of "keyword"? The answer seems both self-evident and elusive. There is general consensus on how certain words recur and play a central role in discussions of reality, morality, society, knowledge, human experience and so on.[2] Yet a hard and fast definition would be difficult to nail down. Indeed, the challenges of defining what constitutes a keyword may be itself a window into the multi-dimensionality of keywords. One can focus on keywords in a text, a textual tradition, or a school of thought, but the rewards of thinking through keywords are most apparent when one takes a more sweeping overview. Temporal continuities and transformations, as well as the connections between different intellectual traditions and supposedly disparate categories of knowledge and experience, can only emerge when we examine how the semantic range of a keyword explains the different kinds of arguments it generates.

Questions of "how to do things with words" and "what words do" align with the "linguistic turn" in various intellectual trends, including lexicometry, discourse analysis, historical semantics focused on "intentional speech acts" and rhetorical contexts,[3] and conceptual history that seeks to integrate the emergence and development of concepts with their socio-political contexts and treats the linguistic transformation of concepts as both the agent unleashing historical forces and their inevitable product.[4] In such directions of enquiry, "concept" and "word" sometimes overlap.

---

2   See, e.g., Zhang Dainian's 張岱年 (2005: 8–11) list of keywords—what he calls "philosophical categories" (*zhexue fanchou* 哲學範疇)—in different periods in Chinese thought.

3   See Skinner 1969.

4   For an introduction to conceptual history, see Koselleck 1989; Lehmann and Richter 1996. On conceptual history in the East Asian context, see Lackner et al. 2001; Jin Guantao and Liu Qingfeng 2008; Vogelsang 2012; Harbsmeier 2013; *Dongya guannian shi jikan*; Harbsemeier, *Thesaurus Linguae Sericae*, an attempt to create a taxonomic grid for understanding Chinese concepts (http://tls.uni-hd.de/home_en.lasso), and the "Afterword" in this volume by Harbsemeier.

Vogelsang helpfully defines a concept as "a generic mental image abstracted from precepts or directly intuited from thought," and also laments that the strong philological tradition in China might have obscured the difference between concepts and words.[5] I submit that this apparent "confusion" is precisely why the study of words holds such promise in the Chinese case. For example, Vogelsang is certainly correct in noting that "the appearance of the character 史 (or its precursor) in oracle bone inscriptions does not mean that the Shang had a concept of history,"[6] but the ways that character is embedded in the social, political, and ritual contexts of Shang history, plus all its shifting frames of reference in subsequent periods, are precisely what allow us to reconstruct the modes of reasoning that may or may not justify the character's connection with "a concept of history."[7] The very proposition of "a concept of history" in turn implies a level of abstraction and generalization that alerts us to how changes in word use negotiate the divide between modern times and antecedent eras. (*Gainian* 概念, the term usually used to translate "concept," came to China via Japan and was coined by Nishi Amane 西周 [1829–1897].[8] Another common translation, *guannian* 觀念, arose first in Buddhist discourse and meant "the observation and contemplation of one's thoughts or of Buddhist teachings" from Tang to late Qing.[9])

One brief and well-known example suffices to demonstrate the importance of a keyword-oriented approach. Three decades ago, Angus C. Graham called his major study of early Chinese thought *Disputers of the Tao*.[10] Graham, of course, did not confine his study of intellectual

---

5   Vogelsang 2012: 14. Vogelsang is trying to explain "why East Asian scholarship has been reluctant to embrace conceptual history."

6   Ibid.

7   See Durrant, Chapter 3 in this volume.

8   Zhong Shaohua 2012: 27. In the writings of 17th-century Jesuits and their Chinese collaborators, the Latin word *concetpum* was translated as *yi* 臆 and *yixiang* 意想; see Zhong Shaohua 2012: 25–32.

9   See, e.g., Song Zhiwen 宋之問, "You Fahua si" 遊法華寺, in *Quan Tang shi*, 51.622.

10   Graham 1989.

developments in pre-imperial (pre-221 BCE) and early imperial China to the changing definitions of the word Dao (道, "Way"), but he implies that debates built on that keyword yield a road map to the world of thought in early China. Dao can mean governing principles of political and ethical relations—as in *Zuozhuan* 左傳 (The Zuo tradition), *Lunyu* 論語 (Analects), or the early layers of *Mozi* 墨子. It is linked to the ineffable "Way of Heaven" in *Laozi* 老子 and *Zhuangzi* 莊子.[11] Xunzi's 荀子 reorientation of the word addresses competing arguments in texts like *Laozi* and *Zhuangzi*:

> 道者，非天之道，非地之道，人之所以道也，君子之所道也。
>
> The Way is neither the Way of Heaven nor the Way of Earth. It is that which humans try to follow as their way, and what the noble man realizes as his way.[12]

Tracing shades of meanings and range of reference for *Dao* can thus help us navigate the relationship between different positions, investigate the connection between intra- and inter-textual components, and reimagine textual transmission and the dissemination of ideas. The variants of the graph in excavated texts enrich our understanding of its early formative associations. Forays further afield take us to subsequent attempts by thinkers and religious leaders who sought to imbue this word with new meanings, allowing fresh departures in politics, ethics, aesthetics, metaphysics, religion, and so on. Indeed, throughout Chinese history,

---

11 See *Laozi* paragraphs 9, 47, 73, 77, 81. The phrase "Way of Heaven" (*tiandao* 天道, *tian zhi dao* 天之道) also appears several times in *Zuozhuan*. Sometimes it refers to the movements of asterisms and their possible effect on human affairs (*Zuozhuan*, Xiang 9.1: 963; Xiang 18.4: 1043; Zhao 9.4: 1310; Zhao 11.2: 1322; Zhao 18.3: 1395); on other occasions it designates the ethical or politically acceptable course (*Zuozhuan*, Zhuang 4.1: 163; Wen 15.11: 614; Xuan 15.2: 759; Xiang 22.3: 1068; Ai 11.4: 1665) or even predestination (Zhao 27.4: 1486). As something Confucius is said to have been reluctant to talk about in the *Analects* (*Lunyu* 5. 13: 46), *tiandao* 天道 implies something lofty and mysterious.

12 *Xunzi* 8:122 ("Ru xiao" 儒效). All translations are my own.

new ideas and new approaches often mean reinterpreting important words; rupture, continuities, and inflection points are inseparable from the linguistic history of specific terms. It behooves us, therefore, to take stock of significant moments in the word-centered intellectual endeavors in the Chinese tradition before proceeding to our attempts to investigate keywords in this volume.

1. Discourse on Keywords in the Chinese Tradition

1.1 Lexicography and Philology

Early Chinese lexicographical works are not merely dictionaries; they reflect and embody the persistent concern with naming in Chinese thought.[13] Acts of naming are ways of articulating worldviews; categorization and definition of names are often implicit arguments on how the world should be ordered. A brief look at *Erya* 爾雅 (Approaching correct meanings; ca. 3rd–2nd century BCE), the earliest of such works, makes this clear. Its 2,091 entries are grouped as categories of synonymous or analogous words. Many commentators have emphasized *Erya*'s exegetical function. Wang Chong 王充 (27–100) characterizes it as "glosses on the Five Classics" 五經之訓詁.[14] Guo Pu 郭璞 (276–324) declares in his preface to *Erya*: "For it is through *Erya* that one understands the purpose of glosses, sets forth the poet's expressive chanting, collects variant words from distant generations, and distinguishes different names for a shared reality" 所以通詁訓之指歸，敘詩人之興詠，揔絕代之離詞，辯同實而殊號者也.[15] Shao Jinhan 邵晉涵 (1743–1796) lauds *Erya* for "rectifying names and matching meanings,

---

13   On this issue, see Defoort, Chapter 1 in this volume.

14   *Lunheng jiaoshi*, 52.765.

15   Guo Pu, "*Erya xu*" 爾雅序, in *Erya zhushu* 爾雅註疏 1.4. "Poets" here refer specifically to the authors of *Shijing* (詩經 *Classic of Odes*). For a full translation of Guo Pu's preface, see O'Neill 2010: 392–394.

fully illuminating the subtle teachings of the sages" 正名協義，究洞聖人之微旨.[16]

Erya was briefly instated as official learning during the reign of Emperor Wen of Han 漢文帝 (r. 180–157 BCE). It came under "Six Arts" in "Yiwen zhi" 藝文志 ("Treatise on arts and writings") in *Hanshu* 漢書 (History of the Han dynasty; 1st century) and was included in the category of "Classics" (經 *jing*) in Ruan Xiaoxu's 阮孝緒 (479–536) *Qi lu* 七錄 (Seven lists) and in "Jingji zhi" 經籍志 ("Treatise on bibliography") in *Suishu* 隋書 (History of the Sui dynasty; 7th century). In other words, even before *Erya* became part of the "Twelve Classics" carved on stelae in 837 under imperial auspices, it enjoyed the de facto status of a canonical classic. Notwithstanding oft-repeated claims that it is a "key" or "ladder" for understanding the Classics, academicians compiling and editing *Siku quanshu* 四庫全書 (Complete library of the four treasuries, 1773–1782) pointed out that only about 30–40% of *Erya* are glosses related to the Five Classics.[17] Perhaps a deeper reason for its elevation is its implicit claim to explain and order the world through words by bringing together entries from different time periods, regions, and sources and categorizing them for mutual illumination.

For example, the first group of entries in the first section of *Erya*, "Explaining glosses" (釋詁 "Shi gu"), approaches the notion of "beginning" (*shi* 始) from different contexts. Paraphrasing Xing Bing's 刑昺 (932–1010) sub-commentary, we have *chu* 初 (the start of tailoring), *zai* 哉 or *cai* 才 (the sprouting of vegetation), *shou* 首 (head, the top of the body), *ji* 基 (the foundation of a wall), *zhao* 肇 (to begin, to open), *zu* 祖 (ancestor, the beginning of the ancestral temple), *yuan* 元 (prime, the excellence or beginning of goodness), *tai* 胎 (fetus, the beginning of a human taking form), *shu* 俶 (the beginning of movement), *luo* 落 (to fall, the beginning of leaves withering), and *quanyu* 權輿 (the beginning of heaven and earth),

---

16   Shao wrote *Erya zhengyi* 爾雅正義. Cited in Dou Xiuyan 2004: 238–239.

17   *Siku quanshu zongmu* 四庫全書總目, in *Erya zhushu* 1.

all summed up as "[meaning] the beginning" 始也.[18] In the semantic field implied by this list, what matters is "the practical use of words according to proper linguistic and social order."[19] Perhaps the most surprising word included here is *luo*, glossed elsewhere in *Erya* as "death."[20] Hao Yixing 郝懿行 (1757–1825) explained:

此訓始者，始終代嬗，榮落互根⋯⋯落之訓死，又訓始，名若相反，而義實相通矣。

> This (*luo*) is glossed as "beginning" because beginnings and endings succeed each other, and flourishing and withering have their roots in each other ... Luo is glossed as "death" and also as "beginning": the names appear to be opposite but their meanings are in fact connected.[21]

Through a web of associations with other words, the word "beginning" organizes our thinking about origins, gestation, foundation, time, sequence, and the mutuality of opposites.

Categorical and associative reasoning, the use of an act of naming to explain another, and the ambition to order the world through words in *Erya* are the hallmarks of other early lexicographical works, the most famous being Xu Shen's 許慎 (d. ca. 147) *Shuowen jiezi* 説文解字 (Explanation of simple graphs and analysis of composite characters), "a dictionary of graphic etymology"[22] compiled around 100 CE. Liu Xi 劉熙 (late 2nd–early 3rd century) in *Shiming* 釋名 (Elucidation of names) chose twenty-seven categories of meaning units or names (concepts, linguistic usages, things, rituals, etc.), each encompassing entries that Liu glossed through homophones or close homophones, a mode of phonetic exegesis (*shengxun*

---

18 *Erya zhushu* 1.6. As Guo Pu noted, *zai* appears in *Shangshu* (尚書 *Book of Documents*), and *shu*, *luo*, and *quanyu* are found in *Shijing*.

19 O'Neill 2010: 412.

20 *Erya zhushu* 2.29.

21 Hao Yixing, *Erya yishu* 爾雅義疏, cited in Gao Ming 1978: 473.

22 Bottéro and Harbsmeier 2008: 429.

聲訓) that assumes sounds generate meanings.[23] Yang Xiong's 揚雄 (53 BCE–18 CE) *Fangyan* 方言 (Words from different regions) offers regional variations of clusters of semantically related words. (*Fangyan* contributes to our thinking about keywords by omission—since it is concerned with regional differences, it excludes words that are important enough to have universal application across regions despite, or because of, built-in polysemy.)

Shuowen, comprising 9,353 entries, is frequently cited in later discussions of keywords. Even though its graphic etymology may now seem inaccurate in light of evidence from oracle bones and bronze inscriptions, it still offers major insights into the reasoning inspired by words. For example, in glossing the word *wu* 武 (martial), *Shuowen* quotes *Zuozhuan*: "In writing, 'stop' and 'dagger axe' form 'martial.'" 夫文，止戈為武.[24] The graph *wu* appears as 𢎵 in oracle bones and is supposed to represent a man walking (or marching) with a weapon. The "rationalization" of the word in *Zuozhuan*, subsequently adopted in *Shuowen*, shows the appeal of the idea of "using a war to end wars" or "stopping violence as true martial power." Xu Shen's gloss of *shi* 史 as having *zhong* 中 (center, correct) and *you* 又 (hand) as its constitutive components (Durrant, Chapter 3) is another suggestive example of etymological reasoning. While his reading may not be borne out by the earliest forms of this character, it points rightly to the association of *shi* with scribal tradition and accurate record keeping.

---

23 Phonetic gloss is also sometimes tied to semantic explanations in *Shuowen jiezi*. See Zhu Junsheng 朱駿聲 (1788–1858), *Shuowen tongxun dingsheng* 説文通訓定聲. Ruan Yuan 阮元 (1764–1849) argues that "meanings arise from sounds, and words are created from phonetic meanings" (義從音生也，字從音義造也.) (*Yanjing shi ji*, 1: 18). Cf. Liu Shipei 劉師培 (1884–1919), "Ziyi qiyu ziyin shuo" 字義起於字音説 (2004: 147–151); Chen Xionggen 2005.

24 *Zuozhuan*, Xuan 12.2: 744; *Zuo Tradition* 1: 660–661; *Shuowen jiezi zhu* 12B.633. *Shuowen jiezi zhu* (2B.69) also adopts the reading of *fa* 乏 (lack) in *Zuozhuan* (Xuan 15.3: 763; *Zuo Tradition*, 1: 680–681): "The reverse of 'correct' is 'lack'" 反正為乏. In seal script, the two graphs for *zheng* 正 (correct) and *fa* seem to be mirror images. In bronze inscriptions, where *fa* has a slanted top stroke in place of the horizontal one for *zheng*, the logic does not apply. According to He Leshi (2010: 72–79), about one-fifth (213 out of 1,085) of the references to pre-Han texts in *Shuowen jiezi* come from *Zuozhuan*.

More to the point, *Shuowen* and other lexicographical works train us to think in terms of semantic fields and contextual transformations. The issue is not establishing hard and fast definitions or logical equivalents, but why something can be called by a certain word in a particular context. For example, the word *ren* 仁 (humaneness) is glossed as *qin* 親 (kin and by extension the feelings one has for one's kin), but it is also offered as explanations for *wen* 盈 (to feed a prisoner), *hui* 惠 (to benefit another), and *shu* 恕 (forgiveness and empathy).[25] The word *luan* 亂 (disorder) is used to explain (among other things) mental states of bewilderment, delusion, stupidity, confusion (*huo* 惑, *nu* 恘, *chun* 惷, *kui* 憒), muddied water (*hun* 潤), the act of stirring (*jiao* 攪), deception (*wang* 妄), and various states of entanglement for silk threads (*suo* 縮, *wen* 紊, *fu* 紼), but the word *luan* itself is glossed as *zhi* 治 (order).[26] While phonetic borrowing might have explained this apparent example of "glossing a word by its opposite meaning" (*fanxun* 反訓),[27] it has inspired reflections on how a word can encompass opposite meanings. Thus Xu Hao 徐灝 (1810–1879) stated: "Pertaining to the essential situation, it is disorder; pertaining to the functional manifestation (i.e., proper reaction), it is order. That is why 'disorder' is also glossed as 'order.'" 自其體言則為亂，以其用言則為治，故亂亦訓治也.[28]

In that sense, glosses in lexicographical works are not structurally or functionally different from philosophical reasoning by way of defining terms in other texts. *Chunqiu fanlu* 春秋繁露 (Luxuriant dew of the *Spring and Autumn Annals*), for example, speaks of the five aspects (*wuke* 五科)

---

25 *Shuowen jiezi zhu*, 8A.365, 5A.213, 10B.504.

26 *Shuowen jiezi zhu*, 10B.511, 11A.550, 12B.623, 13A.646, 662, 14B.740. Duan changed the gloss "(meaning) order" to "the negation of order" 不治 (14B.740).

27 See Fang Yizhi 方以智 (1611–1671), *Tong ya* 通雅: "The graph *luan* has the sound of *ci*, *zhi*, and *luan*" 鑾有辭治變之音 (*luan* 鑾 is glossed as *luan* 亂 in *Shuowen*), cited in Qi Peirong 2015: 176. *Luan* and *zhi* are also grouped together as analogous and semantically related in *Erya*. Examples of *luan* meaning *zhi* are found in *Shangshu* and *Zuozhuan*.

28 Xu Hao, *Shuowen jiezi zhujian* 説文解字注箋, cited in Qi Peirong 2015: 176.

of the name "ruler" (君 *jun*): prime (元 *yuan*), origins (原 *yuan*), judicious expediency (權 *quan*), moderation (溫 *wen*), and (creating cohesion for) the multitude (群 *qun*).[29] The reasoning is similar to the grouping of terms in *Erya*, *Shiming*, and sometimes *Shuowen*. Their glosses are less "dictionary definitions" than "thinking with words" and participation in ongoing generation of and debates about meanings. For example, *Shuowen* glosses *shi* 詩 (poetry) as "intent" (*zhi*) 志也. *Shiming* glosses it as "to go" (*zhi*) 之也.[30] Both are related to the definition of poetry in the Mao Preface to *Shijing*: "Poetry is where the intent goes" 詩者，志之所之也.[31] The sense of movement here is the opposite of the emphasis on restraint in *Xunzi*, which defines the poems in *Shijing* as "stopping (*zhi*) at concordant sounds" 中聲之所止也.[32] Liu Xie 劉勰 (ca. 465–532) in *Wenxin diaolong* 文心雕龍 (Literary mind and carvings of dragons) follows a similar logic with a different phonetic association: "poetry means 'to hold' (*chi*) because it upholds a person's emotions and innate nature" 詩者，持也，持人情性.[33] Kong Yingda 孔穎達 (574–648) combines different meanings into a logical sequence:

詩有三訓。承也、志也、持也。作者承君政之善惡，述己志而作詩，所以持人之行，故一名而三訓也。

The word poetry has three glosses: to receive, intent, to hold. The authors receive the good and bad consequences of the ruler's government, tell of their intent and compose poems, with a view to upholding people's conduct. That is why one name has three glosses. [34]

---

29   *Chunqiu fanlu yizheng*, 35.290.

30   What is translated as "poetry" refers specifically to poems in *Shijing*. Lexicographical works sometimes gloss the same words differently, and even the same gloss can generate totally different explanations (Gong Pengcheng 1992).

31   *Maoshi zhushu*, 1.13.

32   *Xunzi jijie* 1.11 ("Quanxue" 勸學).

33   *Wenxin diaolong zhu* 6.65.

34   *Maoshi zhushu* 4.

Since early lexicographical works were designed to complement and supplement exegetical scholarship on the canonical classics, they establish the crucial role of words as the venue for understanding the sages' intent. The postface of *Shuowen jiezi* (submitted to the emperor in 121 CE), linking the text to ancient script (*guwen* 古文) learning, elaborates this point:

> 蓋文字者，經藝之本，王政之始。前人所以垂後，後人所以識古。
>
> For graphs and characters are fundamental to the classics and letters; they are the beginnings of royal governance. Through them the ancients leave traces for posterity, by them those born later learn about the ancients.[35]

In addition, later discussions of keywords draw on these early sources, turning etymology and constituent graphemes into endemic meanings. The sense of system in such works also encourages the exploration of the functions of keywords through their graphological, semantic, and phonetic connections with other words. Furthermore, the very notion of system is tied to the claims of words to order reality. The nineteen lexical groups in *Erya* move from human civilization to nature, while the twenty-seven categories in *Shiming* reverse the order and move from nature to human existence, starting with heaven and ending with death and funeral rites. The structure of *Shuowen* has clear ties with Han cosmology, as Xu Shen explains in the postface:

> 其建首也，立一為端。「方以類聚，物以群分」。同條牽屬，共理相貫。「襍而不越」，據形系聯。引而申之，以究萬原。畢終於亥，知化窮冥。
>
> In building the top category, this work establishes "one" as the beginning. "Affairs are brought together as categories, and all things divided according to groups."[36] They are linked together in the same entry; the same principle goes through them. They are "various but do not exceed

35   *Shuowen jiezi zhu*, 15A.763. For a complete translation of the postface, see O'Neill 2013.

36   These lines appear in "Xici" 繫辭 commentary on the *Classic of Changes* (*Zhouyi zhushu*, 143) and "Records of Music" ("Yueji" 樂記) in the *Records of the Rites* (*Liji zhushu* 禮記注疏, 271).

proper boundaries,"[37] and are connected according to form. This work draws on all forms and extends their application to investigate myriad causes. It ends with *hai* to let us understand transformations and exhaust the deepest mysteries.[38]

1.2 Lexicography and Power

Lexicographical works are traditionally classified as *xiaoxue* 小學 or "foundational learning," the groundwork for other branches of learning. Han experts of classical texts transmitted in ancient script were de facto masters of lexicography.[39] But while this connection was cemented by the challenge of decipherment during the Han dynasty, later attempts to tie the exegesis of canonical classics with the study of characters are sometimes based on their respective sacralization. *Zishuo* 字説 (Disquisition of characters) by the Song-dynasty reformer, scholar, and poet Wang Anshi 王安石 (1021–1086) is a case in point. The text is no longer extant, but fragments have been preserved in other texts.[40] In his preface to *Zishuo* (dated 1080), Wang argues for the analogy between characters and symbols in the *Yijing* 易經 (Classic of changes):

> 字者，始於一，一而生於無窮，[41] 如母之字子，故謂之字……皆有義，皆出於自然……與伏羲八卦，文王六十四，異用而同制，相待而成易。

---

37 "Xici" (*Zhouyi zhushu*, 172).

38 *Shuowen jiezi zhu*, 15.B.782. *Hai* is the last of the twelve "Heavenly stems." I have substituted standard characters for variant characters in the original woodblock print edition.

39 See Wang Guowei 王國維 (1877–1927), "Liang Han guwen xue jia duo xiaoxue jia shuo" 兩漢古文學家多小學家説 (Wang Guowei 2003: 163–166).

40 See *Wang Anshi "Zishuo" ji*; Huang Fushan 2008. Wang Anshi was interested in *Shuowen jiezi*, for which there was a new wave of attention with the commentaries by Xu Xuan 徐鉉 (916–991) and Xu Kai 徐鍇 (920–974).

41 Two other editions have "beginning with one or two, they multiply until reaching infinite multitude" 始於一二，而生生至於無窮.

Characters originate in oneness, and oneness gives rise to infinite multiplicity, just like a mother giving birth (*zi*) to children, that is why it is called *zi* ... [The sounds and shapes of characters] all have meanings; they all come from nature ... Compared to Fuxi's eight trigrams and King Wen's sixty-four hexagrams, the application is different but the principle is the same, and each depend on the other to form the *Changes*.[42]

By Wang's reasoning, characters embody an organic life force. The idea of "natural meaning" also goes further than the story, told in Xu Shen's postface, that the legendary figure Canjie 倉頡 took inspiration from the tracks of birds and beasts in creating characters. Here words are fashioned by nature and hold the mysteries of the Way, and they can be treated as symbolic, like components of hexagrams.

In his explanation of words, Wang Anshi endows all constituent graphemes with semantic content and uses them to make broad historical, political, or metaphysical arguments. This exegetical penchant was already evident in his *San jing xin yi* 三經新義 (New interpretations of the three classics), and many of the items included in the modern edition of the reconstituted fragments of *Zishuo* are taken from his exegetical comments on the canonical classics.[43] For example, this is how he glosses the word *shi* 史 in *Zhou li* 周禮 (Zhou rituals):

史之字从中从又，設官分職，以為民中，史則所執在下，助之而已。

The word *shi* has *zhong* (center) and *you* (hand) as the main constituent components. Official ranks are established and duties apportioned to create what is central for the people. As for the scribe, what he holds on to lies below; he serves only to assist.[44]

---

42 *Wang Anshi quanji*, 322–323. Wang elaborates the same point in the memorial wherewith he submitted *Zishuo* to Emperor Shenzong 宋神宗 in 1080 ("Jin *Zishuo* biao" 進字說表), see idem, 175.

43 The original titles were *Zhouli yi* 周禮義, *Shi yi* 詩義, and *Shu yi* 書義. Fragments of these works (no longer extant) are collected and collated in *San jing xinyi jikao huiping*.

44 *San jing xin yi jikao huiping*, 2:7; *Wang Anshi "Zishuo" ji*, 79.

In other words, for Wang the word *shi* bears the burden of illuminating the whole Zhou bureaucratic system. *Zishuo* includes this explanation of *tong* 同 (same):

> 彼亦一是非也，此亦一是非也，物之所以不同。門一口，則是非同矣。[45]

> That offers one set of affirmation and negation. This also offers one such set. That is why things are not the same. When even in the wilds there is one opinion [literally, one mouth], then there will be the same affirmation and negation. [46]

We see an implied desire to reject dissent in the polity. The same predilections thus underlie his exegetical commentary and explanation of words.[47] Constituent components (of a text or of a word) are seen as always symbolic and supportive of an overarching structure. Both the canon and words are intimations of the Way and in that sense sacral, but the will to system also means arbitrary interventions in the service of imagined absolutes.

Wang Anshi has often been criticized for being speculative and cavalier in his interpretations of words. *Zishuo*, together with Wang's interpretations of the classics, gained wide currency when he was in power but eventually fell into oblivion. He favored the principle of "combined meanings" (*huiyi* 會意) in constructing the relationship between constituent graphemes, and the fanciful combinations he is alleged to have justified sometimes become the butt of jokes in Song miscellanies.[48] Despite the chorus of

---

45   *Wang Anshi "Zishuo" ji*, 6.

46   These two lines are from the "Qi wu lun" 齊物論 chapter of *Zhuangzi* (*Zhuangzi jinzhu*, 54). Note that the original *Zhuangzi* lines may be translated in several ways that are not consistent with Wang Anshi's usage.

47   See Hu Jinwang 2015: 98–110.

48   See, e.g., Zeng Minxing 曾敏行 (1118–1175), *Duxing zazhi* 讀醒雜志; Shao Bo 邵博 (12th century), *Henan Shaoshi wenjian hou lu* 河南邵氏聞見後錄 (both cited in Zhang Yu 2012: 236–37); *Ting shi*, 14; Zeng Zao 曾慥 (12th century), *Gaozhai manlu* 高齋漫錄 (cited in Niu Baotong 2016: 1004). See also Feng Menglong 馮夢龍 (1574–1646), *Jingshi tongyan* 3, "Wang Anshi san nan Su xueshi" 王安石三難蘇學士 (*Feng Menglong quanji*, 2: 24–37).

critics, creative application of the principle of "combined meanings" has a distinctive appeal. [49] Thus, although Zhu Xi 朱熹 (1130–1200) dismisses *Zishuo* as wrong-headed,[50] his influential definition of *shu* 恕 (kindness, forgiveness) as "being of the same heart" 如心 (i.e., the components that make up the character *shu*)—the empathy that overcomes boundaries between people—is supposedly taken from *Zishuo*.[51]

1.3 Philology and Philosophy

Wang Anshi's attempt to propagate *Zishuo* and his interpretation of the classics, though ultimately rejected, highlights how the study of words can underwrite grand political and philosophical goals. More often, we see the systematic studies of keywords serving pedagogical and exegetical imperatives. One of the most famous examples is *Beixi ziyi* 北溪字義 (Beixi on the meanings of words) by Zhu Xi's disciple Chen Chun 陳淳 (sobriquet Beixi, 1159–1223).[52] Comprising exposition of twenty-six keywords, including words on interiority such as *xing* 性 (innate nature), *xin* 心 (heart/mind), *qing* 情 (emotions), *zhi* (intent), words on virtue such as *ren* 仁 (humaneness), *yi* 義 (dutifulness, righteousness), *zhongshu*

---

49   Although the phrase "looking at the graph to generate meanings" (*wangwen shengyi* 望文生義) is often used to convey criticism, the practice is pervasive in the definition of words in all kinds of texts. One may argue that the principle of generating meanings by phonetic connection can be similarly "creative."

50   *Zhuzi yulei*, 140.3336.

51   *Kaogu zhiyi*, 3.16a; *Wang Anshi "Zishuo" ji*, 112. On Zhu Xi's discussion of *ru xin wei shu* 如心為恕, see *Zhuzi yulei*, 27.689–90. Note that early texts (including Xu Shen) also apply the principle of "combined meanings" according to contemporary intellectual trends and understanding of graphology, as shown in our earlier discussion of the words *wu* 武, *shi* 史, and *fa* 乏. Wang Fuzhi's 王夫之 (1619–1692) *Shuowen guangyi* is also full of such examples. *The Chinese Written Character as a Medium for Poetry* by Fenellosa (1853–1908) and Pound (1885–1972) (2008) includes many creative misreadings based on the principle of "combined meanings."

52   *Beixi ziyi* also bears the alternative titles *Ziyi xiangjiang* 字義詳講 (Detailed exposition of the meanings of words), *Sishu xing li ziyi* 四書性理字義 (The meanings of words on nature and reason from the Four Books), *Sishu ziyi* 四書字義 (Meanings of words from the Four Books).

忠恕 (loyalty or self-exertion, forgiveness or empathy),[53] and words on ultimate truth such as *dao* and *li* 理 (principle), it purports to explain words from the Four Books by drawing on the teachings of Zhou Dunyi 周敦頤 (1017–1073), Cheng Hao 程顥 (1032–1085), Cheng Yi 程頤 (1033–1107), Zhang Zai 張載 (1020–1077) and Zhu Xi.[54] Compiled from lecture notes, the creation of *Beixi ziyi* is embedded in a pedagogical context. That Chen Chun made his living as a tutor, discoursed on Zhu Xi's teachings to a large number of followers, and strove for plain expression also implied its usefulness for teaching. According to Chen Chun's biography in the *Song shi* 宋史 (History of the Song dynasty), Chen adopted this approach in reaction to the emphasis on inwardness in Lu Jiuyuan's 陸九淵 (1139–1193) teachings, which "fully adopted the mainstays of Chan Buddhism, and took the ineffable, spiritual awareness of form and of animating force as the greatest marvel of heavenly principle" 全用禪家宗旨，認形氣之虛靈知覺為天理之妙.[55]

In assailing Lu Jiuyuan's emphasis on intuitive understanding and parleying the precise meanings of words, Chen Chun seems to follow the path of self-cultivation through exegetical and philological glosses (*xungu* 訓詁) of words in the classics. In practice, however, Chen Chun's expositions fashion a sense of system and internal coherence from Zhu Xi's arguments, drawing from Zhu Xi's ideas as he expands the basic meanings of words. For example, the beginning entry, *ming* 命, is glossed as being "just the same as command" 猶令也.[56] This is close to the explanation in *Shuowen*: "This means to order. It has as crucial constitutive components

---

53   See Zhu Xi's gloss on *Lunyu* 4.15: "To fully exert oneself is *zhong*, to extend to others what one feels for oneself is *shu*" 盡己之謂忠，推己之謂恕 (*Dianjiao Sishu zhangju jizhu*, 72).

54   Zhu Xi elevated the *Analects*, *Mengzi*, *Daxue* 大學 (Great learning), and *Zhongyong* 中庸 (Doctrine of the mean)—the latter two are chapters in *Liji* 禮記 (Records of ritual)—as the Four Books. The Four Books with Zhu Xi's commentary became the basic texts for the civil service examination after 1313.

55   "Chen Chun zhuan" 陳淳傳, *Song shi*, included in *Beixi ziyi*, 86.

56   This follows Zhu Xi's gloss of *ming* in *Zhongyong zhangju*, 4.

'mouth' and 'command'" 使也，从口从令. But Chen goes on to explain it as something universal and inevitable:

> 天無言做，如何命？只是大化流行，氣到這物便生這物，氣到那物便生那物，便是分付命令他一般。
>
> Heaven does not speak, so how does it command? This is nothing but the flowing course of the Great Transformation: where the animating force (*qi*) reaches this thing, this thing comes into being; where the animating force reaches that thing, that thing also comes into being—as if they are receiving commands and orders.[57]

Immanent in *ming* is *qi* 氣 (animating force) and *li* 理 (principle), the reason for being of all things and the moral imperatives governing them. In other words, in explaining the word *ming*, with its dual aspect of "fate" and "the allotment or endowment of heaven" versus the "command" underwriting moral existence, Chen relies on key concepts like *qi* and *li* that are fundamental to the neo-Confucian worldview.[58]

Whereas Chen Chun builds a philosophical system with his chosen words, Dai Zhen 戴震 (1724–1777) in his *Mengzi ziyi shuzheng* 孟子字義疏證 (Exegetical exposition of words in *Mengzi*) claims to focus on source texts rather than later elaborations. In discussing the word *li* (principle), for example, he takes aim at Song neo-Confucians who elevate it as the absolute principle of truth and posit human feelings and desires as its opposite, accusing them of unconsciously borrowing from Daoist and Buddhist ideas such as the "true arbiter" (*zhenzai* 真宰) or "true void" (*zhenkong* 真空).[59] In contradistinction to the emphasis on absolute truth, transcendence, indivisibility, and a propensity to absorb other key terms such as *xing* (innate nature) or *tian* 天 (heaven) in the neo-Confucian

---

57   *Beixi ziyi*, 1.

58   *Beixi ziyi*, 1–6. Chen Chun's choice of *ming* as the beginning entry (signaling its importance) departs from the relative neglect of that word in Zhu Xi's writings. There is no special discussion of *ming* in *Zhuzi yulei* or *Zhuzi quanshu* 朱子全書 (Chan Wing-tsit 1988: 455).

59   *Mengzi ziyi shuzheng*, 14–19.

discourse on *li*, Dai Zhen parses its meanings as division, pattern, order, and structure in early texts (especially *Mengzi*, *Liji* 禮記, and *Shuowen*). Dai defines *li* as "that which, upon observation, yields distinctions even for what is minute and incipient" 理者，察之而幾微必區以別之名也,[60] hence its association with order (*tiaoli* 條理), patterns of distinctions (*fenli* 分理),[61] musculature (*jili* 肌理, *couli* 腠理), stylistic structure and literary organization (*wenli* 文理). Keeping *li* within the compass of more mundane considerations neutralizes its supposed opposition with human feelings. *Li* is but the optimal existence of human feelings, where their emergence and expression cause no harm or error. He defines *tianli* 天理 (heavenly principle) as "natural principles of distinction" 自然之分理, whereby "one can use one's own feelings to measure those of others, and without fail obtains the state of fairness and equanimity" 以我之情絜人之情，而無不得其平是也.[62] The hallmark of *li* is thus its regulatory function in establishing optimal relations between the self and larger socio-political entities.[63]

It is customary to contrast the broad disquisition on fundamental principles (*yili* 義理), sometimes veering into the realm of metaphysics, in "Song learning" (*Song xue* 宋學) with the focus on philological exegesis (*xungu*) on canonical classics in "Han learning" (*Han xue* 漢學), especially its florescence and reinvention in the Qing dynasty (1636/1644–1912). The latter is more commonly associated with the analysis of words, especially

---

60   Ibid., 1.

61   Dai Zhen cites the *Shuowen* postface on the creation of the Chinese script: Cangjie, seeing the traces and tracks of birds and beasts, "understood that patterns of distinctions can be differentiated from each other" 知分理之可相別異也 (*Mengzi ziyi shuzheng*, 1). Zheng Xuan 鄭玄 (127–200) glosses *li* as *fen* 分 (distinctions) (*Liji zhushu*, 37.665).

62   *Mengzi ziyi shuzheng*, 2. Cf. Dai's definition of *li* as "(the condition) whereby feelings are neither excessive nor inadequate" 無過情無不及情之謂理 (ibid., 2).

63   Dai Zhen draws an important distinction between the principle (*li*) shared by many and the opinion (*yijian* 意見) held by the individual. Cf. Zheng Jixiong 2008a: 56–59, 140–142.

since Qing learning is so bound up with philology.[64] Dai Zhen sums up the faith in the promise of words:

由文字以通乎語言，由語言以通乎古聖賢之心志，譬之適堂壇之必循其階，而不可以躐等。

From words one gains access to language, from language one gains access to the heart and intent of ancient sages. Just as one has to follow the stairs in order to reach the altar in the hall, there is no skipping over the gradation of steps.[65]

As we have seen from the examples of Chen Chun and Dai Zhen, however, both sweeping philosophical claims and painstaking philological analysis devolve on what one can do with words. The will to system and the engagement with details can be polarized, but more often than not scholars and thinkers move along the spectrum as they stake different or evolving positions. Sweeping assertions about the nature of reality or moral self-cultivation are often presented as exegesis of the classics. Thus Zhu Xi (as recorded by Chen Chun): "The Four Books are the stairs to the Six Classics. *Reflections on Things at Hand* constitutes the stairs to the Four Books" 四子，六經之階梯。近思錄，四子之階梯。[66] Chen Chun's *Beixi ziyi* has also been characterized as "the stairs" to Zhu Xi's *Sishu zhangju jizhu* 四書章句集註 (Commentaries on the Four Books by sections and

---

64   This is the consensual view in accounts of Qing thought. See, e.g., Liang Qichao's 梁啟超 (1873–1929) *Qingdai xueshu gailun* 清代學術概論 (1920, rpt. 2003) and *Zhongguo jin sanbai nian xueshu shi* 中國近三百年學術史 (written ca. 1923–1925, rpt. 2011); Yu Ying-shih 1976; Elman 1984; Ge Zhaoguang 2013.

65   Dai Zhen, "Gu jingjie gouchen xu" 古經解鈎沈序, in *Dai Zhen quanji*, 2630–2631. He is especially disdainful of Lu Jiuyuan and Ming followers of *xinxue* 心學 (learning of the heart-mind), accusing them of "honoring (the cultivation of) moral nature" 尊德性 without "paying attention to concrete learning" 道問學 ("Yu Shi Zhongming lun xue shu" 與是仲明論學書, in *Dai Zhen quanji*, 2587–2588).

66   *Zhuzi yulei*, 105.2629. *Jin si lu* 近思錄 (Reflections on things at hand) by Zhu Xi and Lü Zuqian 呂祖謙 (1137–1181) expounds on key Confucian ideas by categorizing selected sayings of Zhou Dunyi, Cheng Hao, Cheng Yi, and Zhang Zai.

sentences).[67] Conversely, exegesis easily broadens into arguments about philosophical systems and intellectual history (as evinced by changes in interpretations over time).[68] More importantly, the preoccupation with defining words transcends arguments on whether exegesis is the necessary step for disquisition on fundamental principles or vice versa.[69] Liu Shipei 劉師培 (1884–1919) implicitly made this point when he drew on both Song neo-Confucian discourse and Qing philological scholarship to discuss keywords in neo-Confucian thought.[70]

1.4 The Meaning of Meaning

Definitions inevitably raise questions on the meaning of meaning. Starting with "Teachings on the Original Way" ("Yuan Dao xun" 原道訓) in *Huainanzi* 淮南子 (2nd century BCE), we have numerous disquisitions with the word *yuan* 原 (the original, the fundamental) in their titles.[71] Sometimes the stance is polemical, implying the assertion of orthodoxy and rejection of heterodox ideas in reclaiming meanings, as with Han Yu's 韓愈 (768–824) essays "Original Way" ("Yuan Dao" 原道) and "Original Nature" (*Yuan xing* 原性).[72] As noted above, tracing "original meanings"

---

67   See Shi Yuanxun's 施元勳 preface (dated 1695) to *Beixi ziyi* (*Beixi ziyi*, 92).

68   See Zheng Jixiong 2008b.

69   See Zheng Jixiong 2009: iii. Qing scholars upheld the position that "fundamental principles are elucidated when exegesis is elucidated" 訓詁明而後義理明. Twentieth-century New Confucians 新儒家 reversed the priorities. Tang Junyi 唐君毅 (1909–1978), for example, maintained that disquisition on ideas would illuminate exegetical problems (Tang Junyi 1986: 4; cited in Zheng Jixiong 2009: ii).

70   Liu Shipei, "Lixue ziyi tongshi" 理學字義通釋, first published in issues no. 8, 9, 10 (Sep. to Dec. 1905) of *Guocui xuebao* 國粹學報 (2004: 111–146).

71   Note that in all these cases, *yuan* can be read as a verb: "tracing something to its origins." Thus, for example, the first chapter of Liu Xie's *Wenxin diaolong*, "Yuan dao," should be read as "Having Origins in the Way."

72   *Han Changli wenji jiaozhu*, 14–25. Han Yu's other three essays with the word *yuan* in their titles ("Yuan hui" 原毀, "Yuan ren" 原人, "Yuan gui" 原鬼) are less explicitly concerned with philosophical issues.

can be one way to build a new philosophical system, as is arguably the case with Dai Zhen's discussion of keywords from *Mengzi* and his essay titled "Original Goodness" ("Yuan shan" 原善).[73] By contrast, Ruan Yuan's 阮元 (1764–1849) analysis of the words *xing* and *ming* in ancient texts ("Xing ming gu xun" 性命古訓) or of the word *ren* in the *Analects* and *Mengzi* does not venture far beyond contextualizing the earliest meanings of these words.[74] His recurrent refrain is "original meaning" (*benyi* 本義), which he often tries to establish through his phonological learning.

This implicit dichotomy between "seeking what is ancient" 求其古 (i.e., the emphasis is on the reconstruction of the historical meanings of words) and "seeking what is right" 求其是 (i.e., the goal is to seek fundamental truths through words) also informs the modern retrospection on the history of Chinese thought.[75] The analysis of keywords (and in some cases new categories and concepts introduced in the 20th century) is one way to impose order on the history of Chinese thought. Often the approach remains largely historical, as when Xu Fuguan 徐復觀 (1904–1982) discusses "The Original Meanings of History" ("Yuan shi" 原史).[76] In some cases, however, the search for sources of ideas and "original meanings" morphs into a discourse on fundamental truths and the values of Chinese civilization. This ambition is evident in Feng Youlan's 馮友蘭 (1895–1990) *Xin yuan ren* 新原人 (New original human, 1943) and *Xin yuan dao* 新原道 (New original way, 1944), part of his attempt to forge a new

---

73   *Mengzi ziyi shuzheng*, 61–78.

74   *Yanjing shi ji*, 1: 176–237 (*juan 8–juan* 10). Cf. Fu Sinian 傅斯年 (1896–1950), "Xing ming gu xun bianzheng" 性命古訓辯證 (2009: 194–354). Ruan Yuan also devotes most of *juan* 1 of *Yanjing shi ji* (5–36) to explanation of words.

75   Hong Bang 洪榜, in his biography of Dai Zhen ("Dai xiansheng xingzhuang" 戴先生行狀, in *Dai Zhen quanji*, 3379–3388), quotes Wang Mingsheng 王鳴盛 (1722–1797), who characterizes Hui Dong 惠棟 (1697–1758) as one who "seeks what's ancient" and Dai Zhen as one "seeks what's right" (*Dai Zhen quanji*, 3383).

76   Xu Fuguan 1989, 3: 217–304.

philosophical system based on Confucian thought.[77] The same impetus informs the discourse on "original nature," "original Way," and "original teachings" (*yuan jiao* 原教) in Tang Junyi's 唐君毅 (1909–1978) *Zhongguo zhexue yuanlun* 中國哲學原論 (The fundaments of Chinese philosophy), even though it is presented as historical reconstruction.[78] In comparison, more recent scholarship on keywords in the Chinese tradition, in Chinese as well as other languages, has focused on fluid transitions and layers of meanings, drawing attention to the historical contexts shaping the debates traceable through the study of keywords.[79]

2. The Making of Keywords

Formulations about naming, calling, or considering the description of an action, a story, a quality, or an attitude of mind by specific words are ubiquitous in the Chinese tradition.[80] As Defoort points out, "to name" or "to call" often becomes a "to be" in translation, turning a supposedly unique utterance or specific instantiation into a matter of "definition." Irrespective of possible ways to make sense of this phenomenon (see Chapter 1), its prevalence foregrounds the meanings and usages of words

---

[77] *Xin yuan ren* and *Xin yuan dao* are two of the six books that Feng published between 1937 and 1946 (the so-called *Zhen yuan liu shu* 貞元六書; Feng Youlan 1996). After completing *Zhongguo zhexue shi* 中國哲學史 (The history of Chinese philosophy) (1930–1934), Feng sought to leave the historical framework behind and redefine concepts such as *li*, *qi*, and *Dao* as abstract philosophical categories.

[78] Tang Junyi 1986.

[79] It is impossible in the context of this introduction to address even a small fraction of relevant studies in China and in the West. For just a sample, see the studies of the keyword *ren* 仁 in Western languages: Chan Wing-tsit 1955; Lin Yü-sheng 1974; Nikkilä 1982 and 1992; Zhang Qianfan 2010; Behr 2015.

[80] Terms such as *kewei* 可謂, *weizhi* 謂之, *zhiwei* 之謂, or *yiwei* 以為 are often understood as synonymous. Dai Zhen argues, however, that there is an important distinction between *zhiwei* and *weizhi*: for the former, the first named entity explains what follows, for the latter, the first named entity is explained by what follows (*Mengzi ziyi shuzheng*, 22).

as the focal point of enquiry. As mentioned above, there are moments in the history of Chinese thought when attempts to parse keywords in a more sustained and systematic fashion became particularly important. But keywords matter in a more pervasive way: developments in the history of Chinese thought and literature almost always hinge on creating or redefining keywords. In some cases, tracing the emergence, changing meanings, and evolving reverberations of a keyword can encapsulate much broader trends in cultural and intellectual history.

Cultural encounters are often decisive in shaping keywords. The words for non-being (*wu* 無) and emptiness (*kong* 空, *xukong* 虛空) in Daoist texts are used to translate the concept of śūnyatā in Buddhism, and they acquire new dimensions of negating experience and existence. The advent of Buddhism also brought a new urgency to the perceived need to transcend desires and emotions, embedded in the use of such words of negation. This became the premise of Qing critique of neo-Confucian thought, whose suspicion of human feelings is traced to Buddhist influence. Indeed, one of the most common reproaches that Qing critics (e.g., Gu Yanwu 顧炎武 [1613–1682], Wang Fuzhi 王夫之 [1619–1692] and Dai Zhen, among others) launched against Song and Ming Confucians is that their understanding of words like *xin* 心 and *xing* 性 in the sage's teachings have been beclouded by Buddhism.

China's encounter with the West and transition to modernity created new keywords from old expressions.[81] Thus *geming* 革命, which in early texts means "the change of heavenly mandate (in the founding of a dynasty)" and often refers to the rise to power of the first Shang and Zhou kings (Cheng Tang 成湯 and King Wu 武王), comes to mean "revolution" in the 20th century. Ding 鼎 and Ge 革, the names of hexagrams number 49 and 50 in the *Yijing* 易經 respectively, combine to form the expression *dingge*, which means "change of dynasty" in classical Chinese. But whereas *geming* enters the lexicon as the term for political revolution, *dingge* or *yiding* 易

---

81   Many of these were coined in Meiji Japan and imported into China. See Lydia Liu 1995.

鼎 (literally "change of cauldrons") is relegated to historical discussions of past dynastic changes. (It may be because *ding*, or the cauldron, as the symbol of political power, is too concrete, while *ming*, implying mandate and destiny, is more abstract and resonant.) *Quanli* 權利, which means "to weigh the profit" or "power and profit" in pre-modern usage, has been used to translate the idea of "rights" since the early 20th century.[82] *Duli* 獨立, meaning "to stand alone (physically and metaphorically)" in texts before the late Qing, comes to mean political independence (often by reclaiming sovereignty from foreign government or an alien ruling ethnic group) and the individual's rebellion against the pressure to conform. *Ziyou* 自由 has the dual sense of "self-willed" and "carefree" in pre-modern texts, but comes to be understood as the equivalent of "freedom" or "liberty," the individual's defense against encroachment of his or her rights.[83] The word *min* 民 ("the people") is elevated as a new keyword. References to "the people" as "the master of the spirits" 神之主也[84] and assertions that they matter more than the altars of state and the ruler[85] come to be interpreted as the nascent conception of a political ethos based on the rights of the people (or even some version of "democracy").[86] One self-conscious effort to systematically introduce new social, political, philosophical, and scientific terms, many of them European in origin, was *Xin Erya* 新爾雅 (Approaching correct meanings, a new version) compiled by

---

82 See, for example, Liu Shipei's gloss (1905) of *keji* 克己 ("overcoming selfish desires") as "controlling one's desires and no longer encroaching upon the rights of others" 抑制己情而不復侵他人之權利也 (Liu Shipei 2004: 121). Cf. Angle 1998.

83 There was considerable anxiety about the scope for individual agency and freedom in late Qing thought. Hence Yan Fu 嚴復 (1854–1921) translated J. S. Mill's *On Liberty* as *Qun ji quanjie lun* 群己權界論 (On the boundary of power between the self and the multitude), emphasizing the negotiation and balance of power between the self and larger social and political entities. Cf. Huang Kewu 1995.

84 *Zuozhuan*, Huan 6.2: 111, Xi 19.3: 382; *Zuo Tradition*, 1: 96–97, 1: 342–343.

85 *Mengzi* 14.14: 328.

86 For this point and related debates, see, for instance, Xu Fuguan 1994: 51–61; Xiao Gongquan 1983, 1: 91 (Hsiao 1979: 161); Murthy 2000; Xu Keqian 2006; Bai Tongdong 2008.

Wang Rongbao 汪榮寶 (1878–1933) and Ye Lan 葉瀾 (ca. late 19th–early 20th century) in 1903.

Twentieth-century retrospection on the history of Chinese thought brought new scrutiny to long-standing keywords. After completing his *Zhongguo zhexue shi* 中國哲學史 (A history of Chinese philosophy, 1931–1934), Feng Youlan tried to reorganize aspects of that history through keywords in *Xin lixue* 新理學 (New Neo-Confucianism, 1937).[87] The search for terms commensurate with Western categories of knowledge—e.g., philosophy—led to new ways of conceptualizing China's intellectual heritage.[88] Conversely, the encounter with European philosophy also encouraged the definition of "the quintessentially Chinese" perspective. The convergence of these factors could explain the prominence of *zhengming* 正名 (rectification of names) in the modern discourse on early Chinese thought—the perceived need to locate a "philosophy of language" as well as a uniquely Chinese discourse on normative control might have led Hu Shi 胡適 (1891–1962) and others to single it out for emphasis (Defoort, Chapter 1).

Keywords also rise to prominence through the prism of cross-cultural perception. The emergence of "harmony" as a dominant concept in Chinese thought is in part explained by trends in European cultural and intellectual history and the projection of non-dualistic ideals onto a cultural other (Gentz, Chapter 2). While there are indigenous roots for this view—most prominently expressed in the *Zhongyong* and therefore imbibed as part of elementary education since the elevation of the Four

---

87   In *Xin lixue*, Feng proposed seventeen keywords: *li* 理 (principle), *taiji* 太極 (supreme polarity), *liangyi* 兩儀 (two modes), *sixiang* 四象 (four manifestations), *dao* 道 (way), *tiandao* 天道 (heavenly way), *xing* 性 (nature), *xin* 心 (heart/mind), *daode* 道德 (the power of the way), *rendao* 人道 (the human way), *shi* 勢 (momentum), *lishi* 歷史 (history), *yili* 義理 (meaning and principle), *yishu* 藝術 (the arts), *guishen* 鬼神 (spirits), *shengren* 聖人 (sages).

88   On the idea of "Chinese philosophy," see Defoort 2001, 2006; Denecke 2010: 4–31.

Books[89]—Gentz argues that the European perspective is instrumental in elevating "harmony" as a keyword for understanding Chinese civilization. The implied contrast between East and West in turn underwrites some Chinese accounts of cross-cultural comparisons. Emphasis on the unique importance of *he* 和 is heightened through assimilation of other ethical categories within its compass. Harmony becomes the prism through which distinctive traits of Chinese thought (such as monism and non-duality) can be explained. The case of *he* and harmony also reminds us of what is gained and lost through translation. While harmony is rooted in the idea of conjoining or reconciling differences, *he* is often explained as optimal expression and inherent order.[90]

All of the essays in this volume deal with issues of translation: mapping the range of associations of a keyword against its close equivalent in another language leads to reflections on the contexts shaping its meanings. For example, reflecting on the juxtaposition of *shi* 史 with the English word "history" and its Greek root *historia* (systematic investigation), Durrant uses the obvious divergence as the premise for exploring *shi* as an office (or bureaucratic function) and as a bibliographic category. Taking *shi* as a keyword and tracing its etymology and changing meanings over time have the salutary effect of illuminating the "layering effect, with later conceptions projected into the past and reshaping what had happened before" and drawing attention to the problems with a unified translation. Government institutions, political practice, and the categorization of knowledge and of books shape the meanings of *shi*. We elevate *shi* as a

---

89 There are many discussions of *zhonghe* 中和 in *Zhuzi yulei*, especially *juan* 62. Chen Chun expounds on the meanings of *zhonghe* in *Beixi ziyi*, 47–48.

90 See, for example, Zhu Xi's explanation of the phrase *zhi zhong he* 致中和 from *Zhongyong* (*Zhuzi yulei*, 62: 1516–1520). However, the importance of reconciling or tolerating differences is emphasized in some passages, notably the discussion of "harmony" (*he* 和) and "sameness" (*tong* 同) in *Zuozhuan* (*Zuozhuan* Zhao 20.8: 1419–1420; *Zuo Tradition* 3: 1586–1589) and *Yanzi chunqiu* (*Yanzi chunqiu jishi*, "Wai pian" 7, 442–443). Cf. discussion of this issue in Gentz's chapter in this volume (Chapter 2).

keyword because historical understanding and writing about the past seem to be persistent concerns in Chinese civilization, but it is by exploring its socio-political contextualization that we can understand its making as a keyword (Chapter 3).

3. Keywords in Action

To speak of "the making of keywords" and "keywords in action" imply different temporal perspectives: we imagine causes and consequences, formative factors and historical reverberations. The two processes, however, are sometimes intertwined. For example, in Graziani's discussion of how the slogan "enrich the state" (*fuguo* 富國) gathered momentum in early China, he shows the mutual implication of the economic and technological advances that generated the slogan and its policy implications (Chapter 4). Likewise, Pines demonstrates how *ming* 名, in the sense of "name" or "reputation," emerges as a keyword in stories and arguments about meaningful existence in Warring States texts, and these materials in turn provide moral motivation and define political visions determining how people act (Chapter 5).

The most tangible manifestation of "keywords in action" is the political slogan. Graziani parses the debates surrounding the injunction to "enrich the state"—and its frequent corollary "strengthen the army" (*qiangbing* 強兵)—based on divergent interpretations of the word "state" (*guo* 國) (as designating the ruler, the ruled, the elite or the commoners), and of resources (as something to be exploited, conserved, or allocated) and expenditures (as something to be limited or justified), that unfold in texts such as *Mozi* 墨子, *Xunzi* 荀子, *Guanzi* 管子, and *Shangjunshu* 商君書 (*The Book of Lord Shang*). The balance and tension between limiting spending and enhancing resources, between frugality and expenditure, between state wealth and wealth for its constituent groups, are constants in economic thought that translate into arguments in economic policy throughout Chinese history (Chapter 4).

At first glance, the discourse "about the quest for a name, its legitimacy, and its social and political desirability" (Chapter 5), the focus of Pines' study, may seem more a question of personal motivation, as distinct from the political slogan discussed in the previous chapter. Inasmuch as leaving a good (or bad) name in historical records motivates political choices, however, the issue of name is an intrinsically political one. The power of the state to confer "ranks of merit" and other forms of social prestige based on the recognition of a person's "name" can also become the basis of "social engineering." At the same time, *ming* becomes the venue for affirmation outside the system, the compensatory consolation for lack of recognition, failure, and futility (Chapter 5). Even followers of Laozi or Zhuangzi, who claim to "wander beyond boundaries" (*you fang zhi wai* 遊方之外) and disdain fame, end up leaving their names in literati writings and official historiography.

The dual dynamics of *ming* as a force working both within and outside the socio-political system in part accounts for its resonance. Many of the keywords explored in this volume show this potential to generate divergent or even opposite arguments. Thus "loyalty" (*zhong* 忠) can describe simple fealty or justify opposition to a lord or ruler. The potentially adversarial element in loyal remonstrance and its implications for the power balance between ruler and subject turn it into a major topic. Elevated to an almost metaphysical level as foundational morality and ultimate political efficacy in *Zhongjing* 忠經 (The classic of loyalty; ca. 9th–12th century), *zhong* points to different directions through concerns with emotional engagement and pedagogical imperatives in popular story compendia from about the 13th century onwards, as Liu demonstrates (Chapter 6). By focusing on pedagogical texts and drama in the late imperial period, Liu also shows how *zhong* operates across linguistic registers and cultural levels. The strategic use of violent and sensationalist details, the complex emotional range of loyalty, as well as the new prominence of the loyal commoner underline how the earlier discourse of loyalty is concretized and popularized to mold hearts and minds.

The contrast between the metaphysical turn and grand claims in *Zhongjing* and the focus on particularities and emotional details in elaborations of the idea of loyalty in late imperial literature obtains in the analogous relationship between *Xiaojing* 孝經 (The classic of filial piety) and Ming-Qing iterations of filial conduct. (In structure and wording, *Zhongjing* echoes the earlier *Xiaojing*: both consist of eighteen sections, and both seek to turn one virtue into *the* foundational virtue underlying all moral behavior.) Although *Xiaojing* includes injunctions on the need to remonstrate with errant parents, the oppositional potential in the discourse of loyalty has no real counterpart in that of filial piety. Instead the range of meanings encompassed by *xiao* pertain more to the balance or tension between genuine emotions and ritual prescriptions, between the child-parent bond and its political ramifications, as Epstein explains. Filial piety emerges as "a core expression of the ethical and affective self" as she examines how it works in Qing court documents, fiction, and local gazetteer (Chapter 7).

Both loyalty and filial piety are hierarchical virtues—that is, they are role-determined and embedded within the hierarchical relationships between ruler and ruled, parent and child. To think about these "keywords in action," especially in the Ming-Qing period (the focus of Chapters 6 and 7), is to turn our attention to how such words influence perceptions and actions through explicit didacticism or performative twists. In some ways they form a convenient contrast with the words explored in Chapters 8 and 9: *qing* 情 (nature, actuality, truth, feelings, desire, among other usual renderings) and *zhen* 真 (genuine, true, authentic), while encompassing meanings of an objective truth or reality, both pertain to a discourse of interiority, and as such answer the interest in a selfhood more fundamental than (or even beyond the call of) duty or moral obligation. Such a concern may seem anachronistically modern, but it is in fact rooted in vibrant discussions of the nature of inner life in the Chinese tradition.

The fact that the word *qing* refers both to "essential nature, actual conditions, reality, or even truth" and to emotions or desire prompts Plaks to explore the common ground of meaning underlying apparently divergent arguments. There is no simple trajectory of evolving meanings from an emphasis on actuality in early thought to dominant implications of feelings or desire in fiction and drama from Yuan through Qing. Counterexamples on both ends of the temporal spectrum abound. Supposed boundaries between these different meanings also become more uncertain upon closer inspection. *Qing* can mean the basic condition of things or of the world, but such meanings can encompass the ground of the human condition and by extension the emotional core of human experience. Late imperial masterpieces of fiction and drama, such as *Mudan ting* 牡丹亭 (Peony pavilion) by Tang Xianzu 湯顯祖 (1550–1616) and *Honglou meng* 紅樓夢 (The Story of the Stone or The Dream of the Red Chamber) by Cao Xueqin 曹雪芹 (1715?–1763?), are often said to glorify love. Yet they are no less concerned with the essential reality of human experience, which may involve questioning the claims of desire or pitting it against versions of truth or transcendence (Chapter 8).

If the dual signification of *qing* promises the unity or continuity between experiential reality and essential reality, the quest for the "true self" (*zhenwo* 真我) opens up fissures and discontinuities. Li explores how the word *zhen* is central to the contradictions of late Ming sensibility and to its critique after the Ming-Qing dynastic transition. Thus the thinker and scholar Gu Yanwu laments that the obsession with being genuine or authentic is one index to Ming dynastic decline. The word *zhen,* so prevalent in late Ming (late 16th–mid-17th century) writings, does not appear in the Five Classics, but instead recurs in *Zhuangzi* and *Laozi*, where it carries implications of Daoist transcendence and immortality. The cultural roots of the tensions and ambivalence in the quest for "the genuine core" of a person may indeed be traceable to the valence of the word *zhen* in *Zhuangzi*, where questions on the limits of knowledge are explored through notions of *zhenren* 真人 (true being) and *zhenzhi* 真知 (true knowledge). *Zhen* seems to inspire as a cultural ideal especially during periods when orthodoxy is challenged (Chapter 9).

Finally, as a kind of counterpoint to the essays in this volume, we have Christoph Harbsmeier's "Afterword" entitled "Philological Reflections on Chinese Conceptual History." In this essay, adapted from his earlier publication,[91] Harbsmeier explores the possibility of a

---

91   Harbsmeier 2013.

taxonomic and mereonomic grid of abstract concepts. Harbsmeier regards the understanding of such transparently and analytically defined concepts less as an end in itself than as common reference points facilitating "a comparative archeology and history of cultural imagination." The issue is the translation and translatability of words across historical periods and cultures, a question taken up in all the chapters in this book.

Most studies of keywords and key concepts have a more focused agenda. Thus Reinhart Koselleck focused on how social and political language underwent a fundamental transformation from 1750 to 1850, a period he termed the "Sattelzeit" (a "saddle time" or "threshold time").[92] Raymond Williams' *Keywords* was primarily interested in the vocabulary of culture and society from the 19th to the 20th century, although he discussed its earlier sources and transformations.[93] Jin Guantao 金觀濤 and Liu Qingfeng 劉青峰, in their study of key concepts in modern Chinese political discourse, *Guannian shi yanjiu: Zhongguo xiandai zhongyao zhengzhi shuyu de xingcheng* 觀念史研究：中國現代重要政治術語的形成 (History of concepts: The formation of important modern Chinese political terms),[94] focused on the period from 1830 to 1930. Often a more limited timespan facilitates sustained attention on a phase of momentous transformation. The premise of our volume is that taking the long view and encompassing different disciplines yield new insights and unexpected connections. The contributors to this volume—who come from the fields of history, philosophy, and literature—explore keywords in different genres and illuminate their multiple dimensions in various contexts. Moreover, despite their different temporal focus, the contributors take into consideration the development of selected keywords from the Warring States to the late imperial period, sometimes adding excurses that extend to contemporary usage. This allows us to transcend the usual division of

---

92   Koselleck 1989; see also Koselleck 2002.
93   Williams 1985.
94   Jin Guantao and Liu Qingfeng 2008.

pre-20th century Chinese studies into "early China," "middle period," and "late imperial period." Obviously there are many more examples we can use to illustrate how keywords come into being and influence actions and discourse. The small sample provided here will hopefully set forth the promise and provide some of the rewards of thinking through keywords.

Bibliography

Angle, Stephen. 1996. "Did Someone Say 'Rights'? Liu Shipei's Concept of *Quanli*." *Philosophy East and West* 48.4: 623–651.

Bai Tongdong. 2008. "A Mencian Version of Limited Democracy." *Res Publica* 14. 1: 19–34.

Behr, Wolfgang. 2015. "Der gegenwärtige Forschungsstand zur Etymologie von *rén* 仁 im Überblick." *Bochumer Jahrbuch zur Ostasienforschung* 38: 199–224.

Bergeton, Uffe. 2019. *The Emergence of Civilizational Consciousness in Early China: History Word by Word*. London and New York: Routledge.

Bottéro, Francoise and Christoph Harbsmeier. 2008. "The 'Shuowen jiezi' Dictionary and the Human Sciences in China." *Asia Major* (Third series) 21.1: 249–271.

Chan Wing-tsit (Chen Rongjie 陳榮捷). 1955. "The Evolution of the Confucian Concept *Jen*." *Philosophy East and West* 4.4: 295–319.

———. 1988. *Zhuzi xin tansuo* 朱子新探索. Taipei: Xuesheng shuju.

Chen Xionggen (Chan Hung Kan) 陳雄根. 2005. "*Shuowen jiezi* tongxun yanjiu" 《说文解字》通訓研究. *The Journal of Oriental Studies*, 39.2: 165–204.

Chongkan Song ben Shisan jing zhushu fu jiaokan ji 重刊宋本十三經注疏附校勘記. 1973. Edited by Ruan Yuan 阮元 (1764–1849) et al. 8 vols. Taipei: Yiwen yinshu guan.

Chunqiu fanlu yizheng 春秋繁露義證. 1992. Annotated by Su Yu 蘇輿. Edited by Zhong Zhe 鐘哲. Beijing: Zhonghua shuju.

Chunqiu Zuozhuan zhu 春秋左傳注. 1990. 4 vols. Commentaries and annotations by Yang Bojun 楊伯峻. Beijing: Zhonghua shuju.

Dai Zhen quanji 戴震全集. 1991. By Dai Zhen 戴震 (1724–1777). Edited by Dai Zhen yanjiu hui 戴震研究會 et al. Beijing: Qinghua daxue chubanshe.

Defoort, Carine. 2001. "Is There Such a Thing as Chinese Philosophy? Arguments of an Implicit Debate." *Philosophy East and West* 51.3: 393–413.

———. 2006. "Is 'Chinese Philosophy' a Proper Name? A Response to Rein Raud." *Philosophy East and West* 56.4: 625–660.

Denecke, Wiebke. 2010. *The Dynamics of Masters Literature: Early Chinese Thought from Confucius to Han Feizi. Cambridge*, MA: Harvard University Asia Center.

Dianjiao Sishu zhangju jizhu 點校四書章句集注. 2003. Annotated by Zhu Xi 朱熹 (1130–1200). Beijing: Zhonghua shuju.

Dongya guannian shi jikan 東亞觀念史集刊. 2011. Taipei: Zheng da chubanshe.

Dou Xiuyan 竇秀豔. 2004. *Zhongguo ya xue shi* 中國雅學史. Jinan: Qi Lu shushe.

Elman, Benjamin. 1984. *From Philosophy to Philology: Intellectual and Social Aspects of Change in Late Imperial China*. Cambridge, MA: Council on East Asian Studies, Harvard University.

Erya zhushu 爾雅注疏. Commentaries by Guo Pu 郭璞 (276–342) and Xing Bing 邢 昺 (932–1010). In *Chongkan Song ben Shisan jing zhushu fu jiaokan ji*.

Fenellosa, Ernst and Ezra Pound. 2008. *The Chinese Written Character as a Medium for Poetry*. New York: Fordham University Press.

Feng Menglong quanji 馮夢龍全集. 2007. By Feng Menglong 馮夢龍 (1574–1646). Edited by Wei Tongxian 魏同賢 et al. 18 vols. Nanjing: Fenghuang chubanshe.

Feng Youlan 馮友蘭 (1895–1990). 1996. *Zhen yuan liu shu* 貞元六書. Shanghai: Huadong shifan daxue chubanshe.

———. *Zhongguo zhexue shi* 中國哲學史. Shanghai: Huadong shifan daxue chubanshe, 2000.

Fu Sinian 傅斯年 (1896–1950). 2009. "Xing ming guxun bianzheng" 性命古訓辯 證. In *Dajia guoxue: Fu Sinian juan* 大家國學：傅斯年卷, 194–354. Tianjin: Tianjin renmin chubanshe.

Gao Ming 高明. 1978. *Gao Ming wenji* 高明文輯. Taipei: Liming wenhua shiye gongsi.

Ge Zhaoguang 葛兆光. 2013. *Zhongguo sixiang shi* 中國思想史. Shanghai: Fudan daxue chubanshe.

Gentz, Joachim. 2009. With the collaboration of Ella Chmielewska, Hannah Sommerseth, and Jack Burton. *Keywords Re Oriented*. Göttingen: Universitätsverlag Göttingen.

Gong Pengcheng 龔鵬程. 1992. *Wenhua fuhao xue* 文化符號學. Taipei: Xuesheng shuju.

Graham, Angus C. 1989. *Disputers of the Tao: Philosophical Argument in Ancient China*. La Salle, IL: Open Court.

Han Changli wenji jiaozhu 韓昌黎文集校注. 1986. By Han Yu 韓愈 (768–824). Annotated by Ma Qichang 馬其昶 (1855–1930). Edited by Ma Maoyuan 馬茂 元. Shanghai: Shanghai guji chubanshe.

Harbsmeier, Christoph. 2013. "Concepts that Make Multiple Modernities: The Conceptual Modernisation of China in a Historical and Critical Perspective." In *Institute of Chinese Studies Visiting Professor Lecture Series* (III), edited by Shun Kwong-loi, 23–46. Hong Kong: Institute of Chinese Studies.

He Leshi 何樂士. 2010. *Sui jin ji shi: He Leshi gu Hanyu zhuyi wengao* 碎金集拾：何 樂士古漢語著譯文稿. Beijing: Shangwu yinshuguan.

Hsiao Kung-chuan (Xiao Gongquan). 1979. *A History of Chinese Political Thought. Vol. I: From the Beginnings to the Sixth Century A.D.* Translated by F. W. Mote. Princeton: Princeton University Press.

Hu Jinwang 胡金旺. 2015. *Su Shi, Wang Anshi de zhexue jiangou yu fo dao sixiang* 蘇軾王安石的哲學建構與佛道思想. Beijing: Zhongyang bianyi chubanshe.

Huang Fushan 黃復山. 2008. *Wang Anshi "Zishuo" zhi yanjiu* 王安石《字説》之研究. Taipei: Hua Mulan wenhua gongzuo fang.

Huang Kewu 黃克武. 1995. "Yan Fu dui Yuehan Mi'er ziyou sixiang de renshi—yi Yan Fu '*Qun ji quanjie lun*' wei zhongxin de fenxi." 嚴復對約翰彌爾自由思想的認識——以嚴復《群己權界論》(On Liberty) 為中心的分析. *Zhongyang yanjiu yuan jindai shi yanjiu suo jikan* 中央研究院近代史研究所集刊 24.1: 83–148.

Jin Guantao 金觀濤 and Liu Qingfeng 劉青峰. 2008. *Guannian shi yanjiu: Zhongguo xiandai zhongyao zhengzhi shuyu de xingcheng* 觀念史研究：中國現代重要政治術語的形成. Hong Kong: Chinese University Press.

Jin si lu jizhu 近思錄集註. 1994. By Zhu Xi 朱熹 (1130–1200) and Lü Zuqian 呂祖謙 (1137–1181). Commentaries and annotations compiled by Jiang Yong 江永 (1681–1762). Shanghai: Shanghai guji chubanshe.

Kaogu zhiyi 考古質疑. 1983. By Ye Daqing 葉大慶 (jinshi 1205). In *Yingyin Wenyuan ge Siku quanshu* 景印文淵閣四庫全書, Volume 853. Taipei: Shangwu yinshuguan.

Koselleck, Reinhart. 1989. "Social History and Conceptual History." *International Journal of Politics, Culture, and Society* 2.3: 308–325.

———. 2002. *The Practice of Conceptual History: Timing History, Spacing Concepts.* Translated by Todd Samuel Presner et al. Stanford: Stanford University Press.

Lackner, Michael, Iwo Amelung, and Joachim Kurtz, eds. 2001. *New Terms for New Ideas: Western Knowledge and Lexical Change in Late Imperial China.* Leiden: Brill.

Lehmann, Hartmut and Melvin Richter. 1996. *The Meaning of Historical Terms and Concepts: New Studies on Begriffsgeschichte.* Washington: German Historical Institute.

Liang Qichao 梁啟超 (1873–1929). 2003. *Qingdai xueshu gailun* 清代學術概論. Tianjin: Tianjin guji chubanshe.

———. 2011. *Zhongguo jin sanbai nian xueshu shi (xin jiaoben)* 中國近三百年學術史 (新校本). Beijing: Shangwu yinshuguan.

Liji zhushu 禮記注疏. Commentaries by Zheng Xuan 鄭玄 (127–200) and Kong Yingda 孔穎達 (574–648). In *Chongkan Song ben Shisan jing zhushu fu jiaokan ji.*

Lin Yü-sheng (Lin Yusheng 林毓生). 1974/75. "The evolution of the pre-Confucian meaning of *jen* 仁 and the Confucian concept of moral autonomy." *Monumenta Serica* 31: 172–204.

Liu, Lydia. 1995. *Translingual Practice: Literature, National Culture, and Translated Modernity.* Stanford: Stanford University Press.

Liu Shipei 劉師培 (1884–1919). 2004. *Qing ru deshi lun: Liu Shipei lunxue zagao* 清儒得失論：劉師培論學雜稿. Beijing: Zhongguo renmin daxue chubanshe.

Lunheng jiaoshi 論衡校釋. 1990. By Wang Chong 王充 (27–100). Annotated by Huang Hui 黃暉. Beijing: Zhonghua shuju.

Lunyu yizhu 論語譯注. 1992. Annotated by Yang Bojun 楊伯峻. Beijing: Zhonghua shuju.

Maoshi zhushu 毛詩注疏. Annotated by Mao Heng 毛亨, Zheng Xuan (127–200), and Kong Yingda (574–648). In *Chongkan Song ben Shisanjing zhushu fu jiaokan ji.*

Mengzi yizhu 孟子譯注. 1992. Annotated by Yang Bojun 楊伯峻. Beijing: Zhonghua shuju.

Mengzi ziyi shuzheng 孟子字義疏證. 1982. By Dai Zhen 戴震 (1724–1777). Beijing: Zhonghua shuju.

Murthy, Viren. 2000. "The Democratic Potential of Confucian *Minben* Thought." *Asian Philosophy* 10.1: 33–47.

Nikkilä, Pertti. 1982 and 1992. *Early Confucianism and Inherited Thought in the Light of Some Key Terms of the Confucian Analects.* 2 vols. Studia Orientalia 53 and 68. Helsinki: Finnish Oriental Society.

Niu Baotong 牛寶彤. 2016. *Tang Song ba dajia tonglun* 唐宋八大家通論. 2 vols. Lanzhou: Gansu jiaoyu chubanshe.

O'Neill, Timothy. 2010. "Harbinger of Sequestered Intent: Language Theory and the Author in Traditional Chinese Discourse." Ph.D. dissertation. The University of Washington.

———. 2013. "Xu Shen's Scholarly Agenda: A New Interpretation of the Postface of the *Shuowen jiezi.*" *Journal of the American Oriental Society* 133.3: 413–440.

Qi Peirong 齊佩瑢. 2015 (1962). *Xungu xue gailun* 訓詁學概論. Beijing: Shangwu yinshuguan.

Rodgers, Daniel T. 1988. "Keywords: A Reply." *Journal of the History of Ideas* 49.4: 669–676.

San jing xinyi jikao huiping 三經新義輯考匯評. 2011. By Wang Anshi 王安石 (1021–1086). Compiled by Cheng Yuanmin 程元敏. Shanghai: Huadong shifan daxue chubanshe.

Shuowen guangyi 説文廣義. 1988. By Wang Fuzhi 王夫之 (1619–1692). Edited by *Chuanshan quanshu* bianji weiyuan hui 船山全書編輯委員會. In *Chuanshan quanshu* 船山全書, vol. 9. Changsha: Yuelu shushe.

Shuowen jiezi zhu 説文解字注. 1981. By Xu Shen 許慎 (ca. mid 1st century to early 2nd century). Annotated by Duan Yucai 段玉裁 (1735–1815). Shanghai: Shanghai guji chubanshe.

Shuowen tongxun dingsheng 說文通訓定聲. 1983. By Zhu Junsheng 朱駿聲 (1788–1858). Wuhan: Guji shudian.

Skinner, Quentin. 1969. "Meaning and Understanding in the History of Ideas." *History and Theory* 8.1: 3–53.

Tang Junyi 唐君毅 (1909–1978). 1986. *Zhongguo zhexue yuanlun* 中國哲學原論. Taipei: Xuesheng shuju.

Thesaurus Linguae Sericae. http://tls.uni-hd.de/home_en.lasso

Ting shi 桯史. 1981. By Yue Ke 岳珂 (1183–1243). Edited by Wu Qiming 吳企明. Beijing: Zhonghua shuju.

Vogelsang, Kai. 2012. "Conceptual History: A Short Introduction." *Oriens Extremus* 51: 9–24.

Wang Anshi quanji 王安石全集. 1999. By Wang Anshi 王安石 (1021–1086). Edited by Qin Ke 秦克 and Gong Jun 龔軍. Shanghai: Shanghai guji chubanshe.

Wang Anshi "Zishuo" ji 王安石《字説》輯. 2005. Compiled by Zhang Zongxiang 張宗祥 (1882–1965). Edited by Cao Jinyan 曹錦炎. Fuzhou: Fujian renmin chubanshe.

Wang Guowei 王國維 (1877–1927). 2003. *Guantang jilin wai er zhong* 觀堂集林外二種. Edited by Peng Lin 彭林. Shijiazhuang: Hebei jiaoyu chubanshe.

Wenxin diaolong zhu 文心雕龍註. 1986 (1960). By Liu Xie 劉勰 (ca. 469–532). Annotated by Fan Wenlan 范文瀾. Hong Kong: Shangwu yinshuguan.

Williams Raymond. 1985. *Keywords: A Vocabulary of Culture and Society*. New York: Oxford University Press.

Xiao Gongquan 蕭公權 (Hsiao Kung-chuan, 1897–1981). 1983. *Zhongguo zhengzhi sixiang shi* 中國政治思想史. 2 vols. Taipei: Zhongguo wenhua daxue.

Xu Fuguan 徐復觀 (1904–1982). 1989. *Liang Han sixiang shi* 兩漢思想史. 3 vols. Taipei: Xuesheng shuju.

———. 1994. *Zhongguo renxing lun shi* 中國人性論史. Taipei: Xuesheng shuju.

Xu Keqian. 2006. "Early Confucian Principles: The Potential Theoretic Foundation of Democracy in Modern China." *Asian Philosophy* 16.2: 135–148.

Xunzi jijie 荀子集解. 1992. Annotated by Wang Xianqian 王先謙 (1842–1917). Edited by Shen Xiaohuan 沈嘯寰 and Wang Xingxian 王星賢. Beijing: Zhonghua shuju.

Yanjing shi ji 揅經室集. 1993. By Ruan Yuan 阮元 (1764–1849). Edited by Deng Jingyuan 鄧經元. Beijing: Zhonghua shuju.

Yanzi chunqiu jishi 晏子春秋集釋. 1962. Edited and annotated by Wu Zeyu 吳則虞 (1913–1977). Beijing: Zhonghua shuju.

Yu Ying-shih (Yu Yingshi) 余英時. 1976. *Lun Dai Zhen yu Zhang Xuecheng: Qingdai zhongqi xueshu sixiang shi yanjiu* 論戴震與章學誠：清代中期學術思想史研究. Hong Kong: Longmen shudian.

Zhang Dainian 張岱年 (1909–2004). 2005. "Lun gudai zhexue de fanchou tixi" 論古代哲學的範疇體系. In *Zhongguo guannian shi* 中國觀念史, edited by Zhang Dainian and Yuan Shuya 苑淑婭, 3–15. Zhengzhou: Zhongzhou guji chubanshe.

Zhang Qianfan. 2010. "Humanity or Benevolence? The Interpretation of Confucian *ren* and Its Modern Implications." In *Taking Confucian Ethics Seriously: Contemporary Theories and Applications*, edited by Kam-por Yu et al. Albany: State University of New York Press, 53–72.

Zhang Yu 張煜. 2012. *Xinxing yu shi chan: bei Song wenren yu fojiao lungao* 心性與詩禪：北宋文人與佛教論稿. Shanghai: Huadong shifan daxue chubanshe.

Zheng Jixiong (Cheng Kat Hung) 鄭吉雄. 2008a. *Dai Dongyuan jingdian quanshi de sixiangshi tansuo* 戴東原經典詮釋的思想史探索. Taipei: Guoli Taiwan daxue chuban zhongxin.

———. 2008b. "Lun Qing ru jingdian quanshi de tuozhan yu xianzhi" 論清儒經典詮釋的拓展與限制. *Shandong daxue xuebao* 山東大學學報 1: 28–41.

———. 2009. *Guannian zi jiedu yu sixiang shi tansuo* 觀念字解讀與思想史探索. Taipei: Xuesheng shuju.

Zhong Shaohua 鍾少華. 2012. *Zhongwen gainian shi lun* 中文概念史論. Beijing: Zhongguo guoji guangbo chubanshe.

Zhongyong zhangju 中庸章句. In *Dianjiao Sishu zhangju jizhu.*

Zhouyi zhushu 周易注疏. With commentaries by Wang Bi 王弼 (226–249) and Han Kangbo 韓康伯 (332–380). In *Chongkan Song ben Shisan jing zhushu fu jiaokan ji.*

Zhuangzi jinzhu jinyi 莊子今注今譯. 1994. Annotated by Chen Guying 陳鼓應. Beijing: Zhonghua shuju.

Zhuzi yulei 朱子語類. 1986. Compiled by Li Jingde 黎靖德 (fl. 1260). Edited by Wang Xingxian 王星賢. Beijing: Zhonghua shuju.

Zuo Tradition / Zuozhuan: Commentary on the "Spring and Autumn Annals." 2016. Translated and introduced by Stephen Durrant, Wai-yee Li, David Schaberg. 3 vols. Seattle: University of Washington Press.

Zuozhuan. See *Chunqiu Zuozhuan zhu.*

The Making of Keywords

1

How to Name or Not to Name: That Is the Question in Early Chinese Philosophy*

Carine Defoort

An Academic Mutilation

The *Zhuangzi* 莊子 often portrays people who are crippled and nevertheless full of potency. One of them, Shushan Wuzhi 叔山無趾 ("Shushan Toeless"), wants to study with Confucius and is initially turned down because of the deformation of his foot due to a punishment for an earlier crime. Confucius berates him for not having taken good care of himself. But in a later conversation with Lao Dan 老聃, Shushan Toeless concludes that Confucius is actually more mutilated (*xing* 刑), namely by his reputation and success, and that there is little hope for him.[1] The point of this paper is that scholars are all mentally crippled, like Confucius, but that there is no cause for despair. There is nothing wrong with the fact that our

---

*   An earlier version of this paper was presented at the Chinese University of Hong Kong, at the conference on "Pre-Qin Thinkers: Philosophical Thoughts and Debates" (December 2016), University of Texas, Dallas (March 2017), and "The International Academic Conference for Paradigm and Values of Chinese Philosophy within a Global Context" hosted by the Society for Asian and Comparative Philosophy, Beijing (June 2017). I thank the organizers, Nicolas Standaert, Roger Ames, Yuri Pines and Wai-yee Li for their comments.

1   *Zhuangzi* 5: 14/13–15 ("De chong fu" 德充符). All my references to transmitted masters-texts are from Lau (1993–2002), sometimes followed by more conventional references for the *Lunyu* and *Mencius*. I sometimes refer to an existing translation ("see also") without necessarily strictly following it.

way of thinking is shaped or formed (*xing* 刑)[2] so that it both restricts our view and yet allows us to see things. The search for pure facts, untainted by interpretive shaping, is no more than a hermeneutic tool, an alluring fantasy guiding the reader's efforts. Rather than getting rid of the concepts or frames that we impose on the material, one can try to describe and analyze them. This paper presents and evaluates three mental "mutilations" that I incurred from an interpretive obsession that steered some of my research.

It all began with my obsessive fascination for one remarkable habit of early Chinese masters: their repetitive insistence on what they—or we, or one (should)—call something. In classical Chinese the subject of the sentence—who does the calling—is often not explicitly stated, nor is the distinction between description and prescription always clear. Since specifications in terms of naming or calling fail to attract much philosophical attention, they often remain unnoticed or even untranslated. When Mencius states, e.g.: "As for someone who steals goodness, call him a 'thief'; and someone who cripples rightness, call him a 'crippler'; and someone who steals and cripples, call him a 'solitary person'" 賊仁者謂之賊，賊義者謂之殘, 殘賊之人謂之一夫,[3] D. C. Lau consistently replaces "call him" with "is." His translation goes as follows: "A man who mutilates benevolence is a mutilator, while one who cripples rightness is a crippler. He who is both a mutilator and crippler, is an 'outcast'."[4] The fact that English translations abound with the verb "to be" is not necessarily condemnable. But the resulting philosophical insistence on searching for the *essence* of the notions of "king" or "thief" before using them in argumentation is biased.[5]

---

2   Note that the character *xing* 刑 frequently serves as a loan character for *xing* 型 (model, pattern) and *xing* 形 (shape, form).

3   *Mengzi* 2.8: 11/15 (*Mencius* 1B8).

4   Lau 1984: 68.

5   Reflection on the influence on the verb "to be" on Western philosophy was initiated by Graham 1959.

I believe that competing definitions of keywords are of crucial importance in the early master-texts, more than the supposed essence that some Western philosophers postulate on a higher or deeper level. I suspect that the recurrent formulations in terms of "calling" (*wei* 謂) are only the tip of an iceberg in the importance attributed to naming, calling, specifying, or defining. To name or not to name—and, more importantly, *how* to name—that is the question.[6] In order to formulate what I consider the nature and importance of the stress on naming in early Chinese texts, this paper focuses more on the early masters' *use* of language than their *views* on it.

I start out with some concrete examples of powerful naming in relation to obedience (part 1). Then we move to three methodological tools for analyzing them: the doctrine of "correct naming" (*zheng ming* 正名) from Chinese philosophy (part 2), the notion of *paradiastole* from the Western rhetorical tradition (part 3), and the idea of "persuasive definitions" from analytical philosophy (part 4). Methodologies for analyzing the power of language in these texts—including, as I hope to demonstrate below, the *zheng ming* approach—are inevitably somewhat anachronistic and foreign. This constitutes both their strength and their weakness. On the one hand, they can provide novel tools for exploring some characteristics of this insistence on how a term is to be defined or how a situation ought to be called. At the same time, they inadvertently risk misconstruing the original argument. The core material for this paper consists of sources that are generally dated in the Warring States (453–221 BCE) and the Han (206/202 BCE–220 CE) periods.

---

6   Even though there was no clear equivalent notion of "being" in early Chinese texts, there was some overlap between "naming" and "being" since 謂 and 為 (to be, become, function as, be considered) were often used interchangeably. Moreover, before the Qin and Han dynasties, 謂 was usually written as 胃 (stomach), perhaps carrying associations with "digesting." See http://humanum.arts.cuhk.edu.hk/Lexis/lexi-mf/search.php?word=%E8%AC%82.

1. What Do You Call Obedient?

Imagine a smoking father of twins instructing his thirteen-year-old daughters to fetch him a pack of cigarettes. Neither of the two wants to do this because they are concerned with his health. When they come home without cigarettes, their father scolds them for not being obedient. Despite their shared concern and attitude, the twins' responses differ. One daughter declares that for the sake of her father's own good, she prefers to disobey him: in her mind the value of health trumps that of mere obedience. Her twin sister, however, holds on to the value of obedience, insisting that real obedience may go against instructions that harm her father's health. While neither of the two does what their father asked, their argumentative strategies differ: the former daughter appears recalcitrant, explicitly challenging the value of obedience by appealing to a higher good; the latter seems more respectful in basically cherishing the familiar duty of obedience and only redefining it. Without insisting on an essential difference between these two strategies, nor on a strict division between East and West, the basic argument of this paper is that the latter approach is somewhat more Chinese.

Let us take a look at two values corresponding to obedience in early Chinese texts: loyalty 忠 (*zhong*) in the political context and filial devotion 孝 (*xiao*) in the family. As to the former, the *Xunzi* 荀子 states, "Benefiting the ruler while contradicting his orders, I call this 'loyalty'" 逆命而利君謂之忠.[7] Zisi 子思 tells Lord Mu of Lu 穆公 that "one who constantly points out his ruler's flaws can be called a loyal minister" 恆稱其君之惡者可謂忠臣矣.[8] And the *Mozi* 墨子 claims, "If superiors commit mistakes, await the moment to correct them; if you have a good idea, discuss it with your superiors and not with the others. [...] This is what I call a loyal minister" 上有過則微之以諫, 己有善則訪之上而無敢以告 [⋯⋯] 此翟之所謂忠臣

---

7   *Xunzi* 13: 63/28 ("Chen dao" 臣道).
8   *Lu Mugong wen Zisi* 魯穆公問子思 manuscript, see Cook 2012: 425–426.

者也.[9] Like the latter daughter, neither Xunzi, nor Zisi, nor Mozi argue here against the value of loyalty. They specify their understanding of the term in a variety of ways that allow for contestation and independent judgment. Explicit rejections of *zhong* are rare in the early corpus, even in the case of stupid, cruel, or irresponsible rulers.[10]

As for *xiao*, the *Lunyu* 論語 quotes Confucius as saying, "If for three years, one makes no changes to one's father's ways, one can be called 'filial'" 三年無改於父之道, 可謂孝矣.[11] In another context, he is quoted as stating, "When bean soup and drinking water make [the parents] totally happy, this is what is called 'filial'" 啜菽飲水盡其歡，斯之謂孝.[12] And Zengzi 曾子 declares: "What the superior person considers 'filial' is to instruct one's parents in the Way, by anticipating their intentions and carrying out their aims" 君子之所謂孝者，先意承志，諭父母於道.[13] What is important at this point is not what exactly is said in these statements, but their form (a definition of terms) and the variety of their content. As in the case of *zhong*, these three statements on *xiao* only constitute a very minor selection of all the proposed interpretations of the term. And the definitions of *zhong* and *xiao* together only constitute a minor sample of all attempts to redefine or specify terms in the early texts, with the more famous ones being "regicide" (*shi* 弒), "chaos" (*luan* 亂) and "ritual" (*li* 禮). This is probably the case for many keywords discussed in this volume.[14]

The specification of terms as *zhong* and *xiao* happens most explicitly—but not always, nor exclusively—when it is stated that something "may be called loyalty/filial devotion" 可謂忠/孝(矣), or

---

9   *Mozi* 49: 113/1–4 ("Lu wen" 魯問).

10   For a provocative challenge of *zhong* in general, see e.g. Shenzi 慎子 (or Shen Dao 慎到): *Shenzi* 4: 4/2 ("Zhi zhong" 知忠); see also Harris 2016: 43.

11   *Lunyu* 1.11: 2/4 (*Lunyu* 4.20).

12   *Liji* 4: 26/13–14 ("Tanggong xia" 檀弓下).

13   *Da Dai liji* 52: 29/23–24 ("Zengzi da xiao" 曾子大孝).

14   For the changing meanings of *zhong* (loyalty), see Chapter 6 (by Liu), of *xiao* (filiality), see Chapter 7 (by Epstein), and of the slogan *fu guo* (enrich the state), see Chapter 4 (by Graziani).

specifying "what one calls loyalty/filial devotion" 所謂忠/孝, or stating that "this is what one calls loyalty/filial devotion" 此之/是謂忠/孝. Disciples' questions about loyalty/filial devotion 問忠/孝 also lead to the master's interpretation of the term. Even when one is said to "consider something loyalty/filial devotion" 以×為忠/孝 or that something "is (not) loyalty/filial devotion (非) 忠/孝也, I believe that we are often witnessing the same defining activity, despite the occurrence of the verb "to be" in the translation. Conversely, the use of verbs for naming and defining, such as *wei*, does not always indicate a strong statement about the meaning of a term or the nature of a situation.

Before moving to the three specific methodologies, let me specify what this paper does not do. First of all, it is not my intention to clarify what *zhong* and *xiao* really meant for early masters. My interest in the variety of specifications would thwart this very attempt. Nor do I aim at reconstructing the history or distribution of the terms and their interpretation, a task that previous scholars have undertaken.[15] Nor is it, finally, my intention to find the most appropriate translation for every instance of *zhong* and *xiao* that we encounter. I realize that neither "loyal(ty)" nor "filial (devotion)" are perfect translations in every context, but for the current purpose this is an advantage. Both expressions—"loyal(ty)" and "filial (devotion)"—ought to remain vague containers that are filled and emptied whenever they served a new purpose. My concern is how the handling of these containers worked.

2. *Zheng Ming:* A Chinese Doctrine

The earliest tool to interpret the masters' naming acts that I considered was the so-called doctrine of "rectification of names" or "correct use of names" 正名 (*zheng ming*), which is generally attributed to Confucius and Confucianism. Since the 20th century, this doctrine has been increasingly

---

15   For *zhong*, see Sato 2010; for *xiao*, see Chan and Tan 2004.

highlighted in studies of Chinese philosophy, and has been more or less explicitly associated with the use of terminology in early texts, beginning with Confucius' alleged praise and blame techniques in recording cases of regicide in the *Chunqiu* 春秋 (Spring and Autumn annals). This is how, according to Hu Shi 胡適 (1891–1962), "Confucius sought to embody" his ideal of rectified names.[16] I wondered whether the notion of *zheng ming* could be used to clarify the masters' insistence on how things ought to be named or how terms should be defined. I soon discovered, however, that this expectation relies more on Hu Shi's philosophical inventiveness than on the early master-texts.

Hu Shi studied at Columbia University with John Dewey (1859–1952) and graduated with a dissertation (1917), later published as *The Development of the Logical Method in Ancient China* (1922). It was first reworked into Chinese as *Zhongguo zhexue shi dagang* 中國哲學史大綱 (Outline of Chinese philosophy, 1919). This philosophical output of the young Hu Shi has been extremely influential in and beyond the field of Chinese philosophy.[17] Hu claimed to present a totally novel interpretation of early Chinese thought that was nevertheless authentically Chinese. He identified its typically Chinese aspect with the masters' views on language. When forty years later this book was republished under the title *Zhongguo gudai zhexue shi* 中國古代哲學史 (History of ancient Chinese philosophy, 1958), Hu kept insisting that all masters were interested in *ming* and Confucius more specifically in *zheng ming*. He still considered this focus on naming the core of his innovating approach and expressed regret about the fact "that later authors of histories of Chinese philosophy had seldom been able to thoroughly understand this methodology."[18]

---

16   Hu Shih 1922 (Zheng Dahua 2003, vol. 35: 392–399).

17   Only two years after its publication, the Chinese version had gone through seven editions and had a circulation of 16,000 copies. Hu Shih 1922 (Zheng Dahua 2003, vol. 35: 301).

18   Hu Shi 1958 (Zheng Dahua 2003, vol. 5: 536, 535).

Indeed, no previous scholar had given *zheng ming* such prestige and attention.[19] Hu's views initially also met with resistance in Chinese academia by scholars who considered them superficial, un-Chinese, and westernized.[20] Hence, the current almost unanimous focus on *zheng ming* in the interpretation of Confucius' thought—and by extension of Confucianism and Chinese philosophy—hardly existed before Hu Shi. The extant pre-Han sources moreover suggest that no early master wrote about *zheng ming* in that particular way, namely as a consistent and important, typically Confucian philosophy of language. But today, a scholarly contribution on Confucius that does not highlight his *zheng ming* doctrine has become a refreshing exception.[21] I believe that this view was largely initiated by Hu Shi, who combined an insistence on the importance of Confucius' *zheng ming* statement with a consistent philosophical interpretation.

My contention focuses on the supposed importance of *zheng ming* for Confucius and most pre-Han masters. The remarkable inflation of 20th-century academic debates concerning the translations and interpretations of the notion of *zheng ming* rely on the shared assumption of its importance. This is what I call into question here.[22] In order to question the ground on which different interpretations compete, I distinguish four common steps that contribute to the *zheng ming* hype: first comes one foundational passage from the *Lunyu* singled out as being extremely important (2.1), then

---

19   Hu Shi was however influenced by scholars such as Zhang Taiyan 章太炎 (1869–1936), Liu Shipei 劉師培 (1884–1919), and Yan Fu 嚴復 (1853–1921), who mostly noted *zheng ming* in their search for logic in early Chinese texts. See e.g. Kurtz 2011: 284–336. In relation to *zheng ming*, he was even more influenced by Kang Youwei, as I argue in a forthcoming paper.

20   See Sang Bing 2003: 32–34, 44–53.

21   Other critical voices of the dominance of *zheng ming* in the study of Confucius are Waley 1938: 21–22, Creel 1974: 112–119, and Van Norden 2007: 146–172.

22   In terms of the methodology adopted from C. L. Stevenson (see part 4 of this paper), we could divide the current *zheng ming* hype into two parts: emotively, it is heralded as extremely important; descriptively, its meaning is subjected to lively discussion. As Stevenson pointed out, the latter assumes the former.

a set of other *Lunyu* statements is added as illustration of the importance of names (2.2), which is followed by an uncontested core interpretation (2.3), and finally supported is by reference material from other early sources (2.4). Even though the young Hu Shi largely shaped this common ground, it is not my intention to criticize him for doing this. While I appreciate the originality of this interpretive construction, I find the constant repetition and quasi-canonical status of this view today problematic.

2.1 Singling out One *Lunyu* Passage

For Hu Shi, the development of the logical method in ancient China began with Confucius, in whose philosophy *zheng ming* deserved a central status. Since Confucius saw "'rectification of names' as the heart of the problem of social and political reformation," Hu insisted that it "is the problem which we must constantly bear in mind in studying the logic of Confucius."[23] As the expression *zheng ming* occurs in only one *Lunyu* passage, he began with a detailed analysis of this dialogue between Confucius and Zilu about the best way to assist the ruler of Wei. One possible translation of the dialogue goes as follows:

> 子路曰：「衛君待子而為政，子將奚先？」子曰：「必也正名乎！」子路曰：「有是哉，子之迂也。奚其正？」子曰：「野哉由也！君子於其所不知，蓋闕如也。名不正，則言不順；言不順，則事不成；事不成，則禮樂不興；禮樂不興，則刑罰不中；刑罰不中，則民無所錯手足。故君子名之必可言也，言之必可行也。君子於其言，無所苟而已矣。」

> Zilu said: "If the Lord of Wei left the administration of his state to you, what would you put first?" The master said: "If something has to be put first, it is the correctness of names." Zilu said: "Is that so? What a roundabout way you take! Why bring correctness in at all?" The master said: "You, how boorish you are. Where a gentleman is ignorant, one would expect

---

23   Hu Shih 1922 (Zheng Dahua 2003, vol. 35: 255, 360–361).

him not to offer any opinion. When names are not correct, instructions/speech will not be followed; when instructions are not followed, affairs will not culminate in success; when affairs do not culminate in success, rites and music will not flourish; when rites and music do not flourish, punishments will not fit the crimes; when punishments do not fit the crimes, the common people will not know where to put hand and foot. Thus when the gentleman names something/someone, the name is sure to be usable in instructions, and when he instructs it/him this is sure to be practicable. A gentleman is anything but casual where instruction/speech is concerned." [24]

Scholars of early Confucianism or Chinese philosophy of language usually start with this dialogue.[25] Sometimes *zheng ming* is explicitly declared very important, as "a functional concept throughout the *Analects*,"[26] or a "doctrine [that] underlies all the features of Confucian political theory that make it unique."[27] It is also often treated in a separate section under the heading "Rectifying names," "Rectification of Names," "The Ordering of Names," or "The Correct Use of Names."[28] Even the mere fact that scholars choose to mention or discuss this dialogue attests to the importance attributed to it. There is a wealth of other topics in the *Lunyu* that hardly ever make it into a book on Confucius or Chinese philosophy, although they—unlike *zheng ming*—occur much more often than just once in the Master's conversations.

In this single dialogue, Confucius indeed insists on the importance of *zheng ming*, but no master in the Warring States seems to have noticed it:

---

24 *Lunyu* 13.3: 33/27–34/3.

25 To mention only some, see Fung 1973, vol. 1: 59; Schwartz 1985: 91; Graham 1989: 25; Hansen 1992: 66; Makeham 1994: xv; Ren 1983: vol. 1: 68–71; Nivison 1999: 757; Katz-Goehr 2009: 36–42; Martinich 2014: 379–381. The most remarkable book in this respect is Gassmann 1988, a monograph dedicated to the study of *zheng ming* in the *Spring and Autumn Annals*, although the pre-Han sources themselves almost never associate praise and blame with *zheng ming*.

26 Hsiao 1980: 98, n. 43.

27 Hansen 1992: 66.

28 See, respectively, Hansen 1992: 65–71; Nivison 1999: 757–758; Hall and Ames 1987: 268–275; and Defoort 1997: 168–174.

as far as we know, no transmitted or excavated source admired, quoted, or explicitly referred to this dialogue. Even *Xunzi's* "Zheng ming" chapter contains no reference whatsoever to Confucius, or to this or any other *Lunyu* passage. Some scholars might see this lacuna as support for a relatively late date of this dialogue.[29] But perhaps it merely attests to the lack of importance attributed in those days to a dialogue that now seems to be glaring us in the face.[30]

2.2 An Extra Set of *Lunyu* Statements

Hu Shi realized that one dialogue is not enough to support a totally novel reading of Confucius and Chinese culture. "This somewhat brief summary cannot be fully understood without collateral illustrations which I now propose to supply."[31] He then went on to provide what any interpretation needs in order to stand, namely textual evidence. He first quoted the cryptic statement about a "*gu* not being a *gu*" 觚不觚,[32] then moved on to the paranomastic definition of governing (*zheng*) in terms of correcting (*zheng*) 政者正也,[33] and ended up with the ruler ruling, the servant serving, the father acting as father, and the son as son 君君臣臣父父子子.[34]

Rather than joining the reflection on the translation and meaning of these lines, I only want to point at the large consensus in current scholarly statements about Confucius' philosophy of language quoting at least these

---

29   For discussion of the dating of this dialogue, see e.g. Waley 1938: 21–22 and Makeham 1994: 163–165.

30   Belief in the "authenticity" (or early date) of the dialogue tends to correlate positively with the importance attributed to *zheng ming*. Hu Shi, for instance, was very critical toward the "tremendous burden of tradition" in dating matters, but he fully "accepted only one date without question—that of Confucius." See Hu Shih 1922 (Zheng Dahua 2003, vol. 35: 298, 300).

31   Hu Shih 1922 (Zheng Dahua 2003, vol. 35: 355).

32   *Lunyu* 6.25: 14/5.

33   *Lunyu* 12.17: 32/18.

34   *Lunyu* 12.11: 32/3–4. Hu Shih 1922 (Zheng Dahua 2003, vol. 35: 355–358).

three statements.[35] This textual cluster has become part of the standard portrayal of Confucius' supposed *zheng ming* doctrine, along with the Zilu dialogue. Were it not for Hu Shi's influential interpretation, I wonder how much scholarly attention Confucius' enigmatic statement concerning a *gu* vessel would have received and how often it would have been connected with the act of naming.

2.3 Setting up the Interpretation

In the *Lunyu* dialogue with Zilu, the master proposes *zheng ming* as an effective political tool and supports this with a rather puzzling and often discussed chain of arguments. Is Confucius stating here that merely by rectifying names or terms one can fundamentally correct people's actions and save society from turmoil? Or is he indirectly inviting people to live up to their social labels? All the ink that has been spilled on these questions relies on the assumption that the master is expressing his important philosophy of language in this unique dialogue.[36] While bypassing its detailed interpretation, I only want to indicate two characteristics of Hu Shi's interpretation that have been largely accepted: his insistence on the systematic nature of Confucius' views and its inherent Chineseness.

Philosophy departments constituted the institutional context in which Hu Shi's ideas took shape and further thrived. This may have contributed to the supposedly systematic nature attributed to Confucius' view on names. This characteristic is strengthened by the recurring expression "*zheng ming-ism*" 正名主義 in Hu Shi's work. The suffix *zhuyi* (-ism) indicates the theoretical, coherent and philosophical nature of the idea in the eyes of Hu Shi and some of his contemporaries. Liang Qichao 梁啟超 (1873–1929), for

---

35   Further elaborations usually add *Lunyu* 12.11, 16.14, 6.24, and sometimes also *Lunyu* 3.1 and *Lunyu* 3.2. Makeham 1994: 39–44 discusses five "examples of *zheng ming*" in the *Lunyu*: 12.11, 16.14, 3.1, 3.2, and 6.24 [= 6.25 above].

36   See e.g. Defoort 1997: 168–174; Hansen 1992: 65–71; Makeham 1994: 35–50, 163–165; Van Norden 2007: 82–96; Loy 2014: 146–152.

instance, in his late work on Confucius (1921), had the honesty to admit that he was puzzled by the *Lunyu* 13.3 dialogue with Zilu. But reading Hu Shi's interpretation seems to have inspired his understanding of Confucius' "*zheng ming*-ism."[37] And Feng Youlan 馮友蘭 (1895–1990), who agreed with Hu Shi on this point, may have been a major channel of this view, since his work was more influential in the academia than Hu Shi's. The focus on philosophy of language in analytical philosophy has further launched this dialogue to unprecedented heights.[38]

The second general characteristic of Hu Shi's *zheng ming* interpretation is the insistence on its inherently Chinese nature. "This notion must appear to an Occidental reader to be rather fanciful and untenable. But it is an idea which has had tremendous influence upon Chinese thought, and especially upon the development of historical sciences in China."[39] Such claims originate from a confrontation with other cultures and are inevitably somewhat infected by them. Without China's contact with the West and Hu's training in the U.S., he probably would not have discovered this inherently Chinese notion. The same holds for Feng Youlan. I agree with Van Norden that he "is one of the most Western-centric readers of Chinese thought" and that due to his influence, along with "the centrality of the philosophy of language in twentieth-century Western philosophical thought, it is tempting for us to see *Analects* 13.3 as having a centrality in Kongzi's thought that it may not merit."[40] The proclaimed indigenous nature of the *zheng ming* theory nevertheless helps to explain its great success in contemporary China and in the West.

---

37   For his puzzlement, see Liang Qichao 1921 (1996): 21. For his reference to Hu Shi's work, see Liang Qichao 1921 (1996): 23.

38   Feng Youlan 1931 (1984): 59–61.

39   Hu Shih 1922 (Zheng Dahua 2003, vol. 35: 391–392).

40   Van Norden 2007: 93.

2.4 Reference Material on *Zheng Ming* in Other Early Sources

The last step in Hu Shi's enhancement of Confucius' doctrine was to trace its influence on other masters. Explicit references to *zheng ming*—or *ming zheng* 名正, *ming bu zheng* 名不正, *zheng qi ming* 正其名—in the early sources are scarce, but Hu Shi added other textual support, as he did in the *Lunyu*. His selection contained Mencius' statement about Confucius' evaluative role in the *Chunqiu* 春秋, the thirty-six records of regicide in the *Chunqiu*, the "Zheng ming" chapter of *Xunzi* 荀子, and *Shizi* 尸子, *Yinwenzi* 尹文子, *Hanfeizi* 韓非子, and *Guanzi* 管子. He also stressed the connection with the *Yijing* 易經 and Later Mohism. In his eyes, they were all inspired by the same concern with language: "the doctrine of the rectification of names as the central problem of Confucianism."[41]

In current scholarship, the core of *zheng ming* evidence, aside from the *Lunyu* passages, tends to be more restricted and somewhat fixed. Usually included are: *Xunzi*'s "Zheng ming" chapter, some sayings attributed to Shen Buhai 申不害,[42] one occurrence of *ming zheng* in *Hanfeizi*,[43] further leading to the "shapes/performance and names/titles" (*xing ming* 刑/形名) policy, and finally to Han speculations in terms of "names versus substance" (*ming shi* 名實). Usually left out, despite their reference to *zheng ming*, are two consecutive *Lüshi chunqiu* 呂氏春秋 (Sire Lü's Spring and Autumn annals) chapters,[44] two *Shizi* chapters,[45]

---

41 Hu Shih 1922 (Zheng Dahua 2003, vol. 35: 388).

42 For statements about "names" (*ming*) or "instructions" (*yan* 言) being "rectified," see *Shenzi* 申子 1: 2/10. See also Creel 1974: 354 no. 5. For fragments that are not in the ICS concordances (Lau Dim-Cheuk 1993–2002), see Creel 1974: 349 no. 1.6, 351 no. 1.8, and 353 no. 4.

43 *Hanfeizi* 8: 10/29 ("Yang quan" 揚權).

44 *Lüshi chunqiu* 16.8: 97/22–98/24 ("Zheng ming" 正名) and 17.1: 99/1–1,000/8 ("Shen fen" 審分).

45 *Shizi* 1.5: 4/25–5/26 ("Fen" 分) and 1.6: 6/1–7/12 ("Fameng" 發蒙).

five *Guanzi* chapters,[46] two *Chunqiu fanlu* 春秋繁露 (The Luxuriant dew of the Spring and Autumn annals) chapters,[47] and some fragments from the *Liji* 禮記 (Records of ritual),[48] *Heguanzi* 鶡冠子,[49] *Xinshu* 新書 (New writings),[50] and *Guliang zhuan* 穀梁傳 (Guliang's commentary on the Spring and Autumn annals).[51]

Some of these omissions may be inspired by the relatively late date of the sources. They actually attest to an increasing interest in naming toward the Han dynasty, when the earliest explicit reference was also made to the dialogue between Confucius and Zilu in *Lunyu* 13.3.[52] Another reason might be their lack of philosophical stress on and consistency in *zheng ming* statements. Many sources do not express either explicit agreement or disagreement on the meaning of *zheng ming*. The expression seems to be simply used in various

---

46   *Guanzi* 31: 84/21–22 ("Jun chen xia" 君臣下), which is possibly the earliest recorded implicit awareness of the *Lunyu* 13.3 dialogue, since it connects the *zheng ming* policy with making others obedient (*shun* 順). See also Rickett 1985: 423. There is perhaps even a far echo of the *junjun chenchen* saying in the cryptic statement higher up (31: 83/30–31) that "if the four corrections are not correct and the five officials do not function as officials, it is said to be chaos" (四正不正，五官不官曰亂). See also Rickett 1985: 420. Rickett (1985: 412) dates this chapter in the middle of the third century BCE. For other occurrences of *zheng ming* in this source, see also *Guanzi* 36: 97/14–19 ("Xinshu shang" 心術上), 38/ 99/22–23 ("Bo xin" 白心), 43: 109/10 ("Zheng" 正), 78: 176/27–28 ("Kui du" 揆度).

47   *Chunqiu fanlu* 35: 44/19–47/5 ("Shen cha minghao" 深察名號) and 36: 47/7–28 ("Shi xing" 實性).

48   *Liji* 24: 123/16 ("Ji fa" 祭法).

49   *Heguanzi* 8: 8/25 ("Duo wan" 度萬).

50   *Xinshu* 7: 48/8 ("Xian xing" 先醒).

51   *Guliang zhuan,* Duke Yin 隱公 7.2: 5/24, about barbarian names not being correct.

52   Explicit attention to *Lunyu* 13.3, sometimes combined with *Lunyu* 12.11, seems to begin around the Han dynasty. See e.g. *Shiji* 23: 1159 ("Li shu" 禮書), *Shiji* 47: 1933–34 ("Kongzi shijia" 孔子世家), *Shiji* 130: 3308 ("Taishigong zixu" 太史公自序); *Hanshu* 99 xia: 4160 ("Wang Mang zhuan xia" 王莽傳下); *Xinxu*, 5: 28/24 ("Za shi" 雜事 5), and *Han Shi waizhuan* 5: 41/19. *Guliang zhuan* also shows some awareness of Confucius' statement on *zheng ming*, saying that "a gentleman […] is anything but casual" 君子 [……] 無所苟而已矣. *Guliang zhuan* Xi 16.2: 46/11–14). It occurs in a comment on a *Chunqiu* record about six fish-hawks flying backwards past the capital of Song in 644 B.C. Legge (1994: 171) considers these reflections nonsensical. Nylan (2001: 258) dates this source "possibly in the first century BC."

contexts and with different meanings, all vaguely related to language and power. This diversity is representative of pre-Han reflections on the topic.[53] *Zheng ming* may have covered a nexus of interrelated issues.

Let us return to the original question of whether the notion of *zheng ming* could be useful to explain the masters' insistence on how one names something or defines a term. It is an interesting hypothesis, as Hu Shi has shown. We cannot rule out the possibility that Confucius treated language in a manner that he—perhaps after some intellectual maturation—ended up calling *zheng ming*, unfortunately only once in a rather cryptic statement that remained unnoticed in pre-Han literature. Makeham is convinced that "[I]t is nonetheless true that there are many passages in the *Analects* that deal with the correction of names even though they do not employ the specific term *zheng ming*."[54] While Hui Chieh Loy is more cautious in his claim that Confucius may have applied his own theory of *zheng ming*, nobody has thus far convincingly proven that the Master actually did this in the *Lunyu* or any other source.[55] In Warring States sources, *zheng ming* was neither very important nor particularly consistent. It was not associated with Confucius.

The earliest explicit connection of *zheng ming* with calling *(wei)* is probably in *Lüshi chunqiu* "Zheng ming." It connects the ruler's act of *zheng ming* with how he calls *(wei* 謂) the situation around him and with how ministers try to influence him by naming *(wei)*.[56] This is only

---

53 Even within one source, such as the *Guanzi*, the various statements on *zheng ming*—discussing the use of titles, measuring devices, a quietist type of policy, and punishments—do not indicate any awareness of agreement or disagreement on the topic.

54 Makeham 1994: 164. Van Norden (2007: 91–93) calls the phenomenon that a notion may be implicitly present before being made explicit "semantic assent" (inspired by V. W. O. Quine).

55 Loy 2014: 146–152. For counterarguments, see Van Norden 2007: 82–96.

56 *Lüshi chunqiu* 16.8: 98/1–3 ("Zheng ming" 正名). "The problem is that those he calls 'worthy' turn out to be inadequate, those he calls 'good' turn out to be wicked, and what he calls 'acceptable' turns out to be perverse." 其患在乎所謂賢、從不肖也，所為善、而從邪辟，所謂可、從悖逆也. See also Riegel and Knoblock 2000: 401. In the example that follows (16.8: 98/8–24) Yinwen 尹文 shows how King Min of Qi's 齊湣王 (r. 301–284 BCE) way of naming personnel candidates was contradictory and inconsistent, which caused the defeat of his state and harm to his person.

a small step removed from associating masters arguing in terms of *wei* with the *zheng ming* policy. Hence, the *zheng ming* doctrine might be fruitfully deployed to interpret early Chinese masters' insistence on naming and specifying. But the textual evidence thus far is very meager. Hence, despite its indigenous roots and its current popularity, I do not consider it particularly apt to analyze the master's insistence on how to call something.

3. *Paradialstole*: A Rhetorical Trick

The second methodological tool that I used to reflect on the Chinese masters' recurrent insistence on how things were (or should be) called was *paradiastole* (Greek: παραδιαστολή).[57] This rhetorical device dates from Greek antiquity and became particularly controversial in the 17th century, as documented by Quentin Skinner. While the original Greek term has only been preserved in Roman texts, Aristotle (384–322 BCE) may have used the device in his *Art of Rhetoric* when suggesting that a choleric or angry person may be called "frank" or "open," an arrogant person "magnificent" and "dignified," a foolhardy person "courageous," and a recklessly extravagant one "liberal."[58] Quintilian (c. 35–c. 100 CE), the author of *Institutio Oratoria,* a masterpiece on Western rhetoric, was the first to elaborate on it.[59] Paradiastolic speech was sometimes seen as a matter of offering a re-description of an action, and sometimes as proposing a new meaning for a term related to virtues and vices.[60] The orator's aim was to challenge and replace the audience's original evaluation of a given action or situation, to augment or extenuate its moral significance, and thus to enlist the audience for his cause.

---

57   Defoort 1997: 136–144, 166–167, 196–197.

58   Freese 1967: 97–99.

59   Skinner 1994: 273–275.

60   Skinner 1991: 11.

Throughout Western history, from antiquity to modernity, this rhetorical device has generally been considered a form of deceit, a trick with words, a euphemism, flattery, verbal magic, fatal imposture, an opposition to truth, a subversion of speech, a satanic transformation, etc.[61] A few decades ago, I thought that a positive notion of *paradiastole* would be attractive in the interpretation of early Chinese masters. First, it places the author in a political context, fully acknowledging his or her intention to convince rulers or competing advisers of his or her views, and thereby to influence policies or emend social reality. It moreover focuses on politically important or evaluative keywords, such as "regicide," "king," "chaos," "theft," "loyalty," or "filial devotion," and not on supposedly neutral words such as "horse" and "ox" (as do the Later Mohists), nor "tree" and "snow" (as Western philosophers tend to do when discussing epistemological issues). And finally, the masters' insistence on how to call something is clearly not a deceitful trick, at least not in their eyes.

The notion of *paradiastole* has not been picked up in the study of early Chinese texts. This might be due to a deep difference underlying the apparent similarities listed above. The mainstream view in the West sees reality as what exists on a physical or a metaphysical level. Humans must then try to discover and adequately represent it in thoughts or in language. This view had consequences for a device as *paradiastole*: when an essentially choleric person is merely called "frank," a real vice is falsely made to appear like a virtue through the use of a rhetorical trick. Skinner describes how paradiastolic speech met with vehement, unmixed hostility. Its critics insisted on morality being part of nature, on the "intrinsic essence" of things, or on the inviolable existence of simple facts.[62]

This dominant view can be associated with a basic metaphor that opposes reality to appearance: since the default frame is the correspondence between the (tangible or abstract) things on the one hand, and language or

---

61   Skinner 1991: 4–43.

62   Skinner 1991: 29, 40–43.

thought expected to transparently mirror them on the other, epistemological reflection conveniently starts out with such neutral realities as snow or trees. For less tangible items as theft or loyalty, one has to refer to a higher, invisible, or metaphysical realm that ideally can also be objectively known and expressed in language. If that is not possible, they remain elusive items in a mystical and unspeakable world. Even Thomas Hobbes (1588–1679), who argued that names were to be determined by the fiat of an Arbitrator— thus being arbitrary but not capricious—considered *paradiastole* a problem, a threat, and an obstacle to his ideal of a true science of vice and virtue.[63]

This admittedly very rough outline of a worldview in which *paradiastole* could hardly thrive can be opposed to an equally simplified sketch of the early Chinese framework. Of course, the masters knew that there existed a reality made of more or less tangible things. Some masters even cared very much about its correct representation in one way or another. But most of them worried about having influence, which they knew occurred on a level where matters were not totally fixed by merely being reality. Such important notions as theft, loyalty, king, or regicide were at least to some extent determined by how those in power understood them. As one master put it, "This is how a true king installs names: with names being settled, he has discrimination of entities; with the Way proceeding, his intention is carried through; he then prudently leads his people and unifies them by these measures." 王者之制名：名定而實辨，道行而志通，則慎率民而一焉。[64]

Discussion among Chinese masters therefore tended to focus on how to influence this naming act. The paradigmatic case concerns re-definitions of crucial terms surrounding the pejorative label of "regicide" for violent dynastic founding acts.[65] This focus on naming might invite criticism of Western or modern scholars insisting that the Chinese master should first indicate what a "king" essentially is before misleading the audience with

---

63   Skinner 1991: 55–56.
64   *Xunzi* 22: 108/4 ("Zheng ming" 正名).
65   See Defoort 2000; Van Auken 2014.

rhetorical tricks. This criticism, I believe, reflects the interpreter's bias in favor of mirroring a given reality. In early masters-texts, however, the specification of terms is often the core of the argument, variously relying on the personal or institutional authority of the speaker, or on implicitly shared views, the terms' embeddedness in one's overall behavior, their consistency and constancy, their easy applicability, reliability and effect, or sometimes their correspondence with a mundane or higher order reality.

This variety of arguments supporting the naming acts is not our concern here, but what deserves our attention is the alternative dominant metaphor of cutting the un-cut, or distinguishing the not-yet-distinguished by means of names. Instead of referring to a transcendent realm of existing realities, many Chinese masters exert themselves in carefully carving out similar but importantly different terms. For instance, Xunzi's daring definition of loyalty quoted above is accompanied by three other definitions of neighboring terms: "benefiting the ruler while following his orders, I call it docile" 從命而利君謂之順, "harming the ruler by following his orders, I call it flattery" 從命而不利君謂之諂, and "harming the ruler while negating his orders, I call it usurpation" 逆命而不利君謂之篡.[66] If anything is deemed mysteriously unnamable in this implicit Chinese metaphor, it is not predominantly a fixed essence located in a transcendent realm, but rather an amorphous sphere preceding the inherently arbitrary act of naming. It is the dark, formless, but potent core from which everything emerges, an evolution in which language actively takes part. The notion of *paradiastole* is too embedded in a dual worldview to defend such a positive notion of the naming act.

4. Persuasive Definitions: An Analytic Tool

The third and last methodological tool that I encountered in my attempts to tackle the masters' insistence on how to call things was the notion of

---

66   *Xunzi* 13: 63/28–29 ("Chen dao").

"persuasive definitions" presented by C. L. Stevenson (1908–1979), an American analytic philosopher, student of Ludwig Wittgenstein, and office mate of Donald Munro at the University of Michigan.[67] Stevenson differentiated between two types of argumentation, starting out from a simple distinction between the descriptive and the emotive meaning of a term.[68] The former is a term's emotively neutral content or description, the latter its emotive force. His hypothetical example was the term "cultured," descriptively meaning "widely read and acquainted with the arts" and emotively inciting admiration and support within a specific society. A member of that society who wants to receive praise but lacks training in reading or the arts might argue that true culture amounts to imaginative sensitivity, which can also be cultivated through music and movies. This person might even support his claim by referring to the "essence" of culture. His argumentative success—and consequently his reception of praise for knowing music and movies rather than books and the more conventional arts—would thrive on the combination of two things in that society: the sustained positive emotive meaning of the term "cultured" combined with this new descriptive meaning. Alternatively, in the case of a strong negative emotive meaning, the derogatory term would lead to blame instead of praise.

This form of argumentation is what Stevenson called "persuasive definition," whenever one opponent "gives a new descriptive meaning to a familiar word without substantially changing its emotive meaning," with the conscious or unconscious purpose of changing the direction of people's interests, habits, choices, behavior, or acts.[69] In debates arguing in terms of persuasive definitions, a strong emotive meaning tends to go well together with a vague or flexible description. Conversely, arguments that critically question established values often combine a weak (or weakened)

---

67 See the interview by Cheung Chan-fai 2008: 10; personal communication with Donald Munro (email of May 29, 2016).

68 Stevenson 1938: 331 speaks of "conceptual" and "emotive" meaning. Stevenson 1972: 206–226 replaces "conceptual" by "descriptive."

69 Stevenson 1938: 331.

emotive meaning with a relatively undisputed descriptive content. Despite Stevenson's own appreciation of persuasion, his analysis of the mechanism is colored by a cultural context that was hostile toward rhetoric. He therefore had to search the Western corpus for persuasive definitions "masked in the guise of logical analysis" or seeming "to have the detachment of a purely scientific economics." Western authors beginning with Plato concealed their persuasive intent and the change in descriptive meaning so that it would escape the attention of the readers, and "did not remind them that they were being influenced."[70]

In early Chinese debates, however, defining is not a peripheral trick but a central claim, the core of the argument. Support for a definition can vary from authority to efficiency, consistency, and even reality. But this is beyond our concern here. Returning to the strategies of the thirteen-year-old twins of a smoking father, we could state that within a traditional family, the descriptive meaning of obedience is to follow one's parents' instructions; since the emotive meaning is positive, calling a child "obedient" amounts to praise and encouragement. One type of disagreement, and according to Stevenson, the most visible and challenging one, is to reject the shared or assumed emotive meaning of the term, as did the first twin daughter. The second daughter, however, went for a "persuasive definition," which Stevenson considered the more unobtrusive challenge, one that respects the emotive meaning of the term while trying to change its descriptive meaning.

In early Chinese texts, not following the instructions of one's ruler or parent could thus be defended in two opposite ways. In a context with relatively mild or mixed feelings about "loyalty" (*zhong*) or "filial devotion" (*xiao*), one could argue that in some cases discarding these values in the face of higher principles is the acceptable or even heroic option. One thereby challenges the positive emotive meaning of the terms without further specifying what one means by them. But in a community that attributes

---

70   Stevenson, 1938: 338, 344, 333.

a strong emotive—in this case positive—meaning to these terms, as was the case in early China, only a small minority went for this option. The alternative way to defend one's challenge to an unreasonable father or abusive ruler was to use a persuasive definition: change the descriptive meaning of the term and retain its emotive force.

Stevenson insisted that persuasive definitions should be definitions of terms and not attributions of a laudatory or pejorative epithet to an item in reality.[71] This distinction between re-defining a term on the one hand and persuasively naming reality on the other was not clearly made, either for *paradiastole* or in early Chinese claims about naming. What follows is a threefold elaboration on the use that we can nevertheless make of Stevenson's insights when analyzing the masters' positive and unhidden insistence on naming: the importance of emotive meaning, the specification of a descriptive meaning, and the force of dissuasion in the naming act.

4.1 A Strong Emotive Meaning

For the act of naming or defining to work effectively, it is crucial that the keywords have a strong or rich emotive meaning, whether positive (e.g. loyalty, filial devotion) or negative (e.g. regicide, chaos). Specification of emotively neutral words (e.g. tree, snow, ox, horse) fails to "move" others. This e-motive meaning can be triggered by the dynamic, emotional, normative, evaluative and directive use of terms.[72] Since it constitutes the force that touches the audience's feelings, attitudes, or habits, and that makes them decide, evaluate, act, judge, or guide, I sometimes speak of emotive "force" rather than just "meaning." In Stevenson's hypothetical example, only when "culture" is consistently used with awe by those who lack it and with self-satisfaction by those who have it, when it has become unnatural to employ

---

71 Stevenson 1938: 336. Due to the fact that Stevenson's examples of persuasive definitions—all in Western texts—are subtle and hidden, I do not always find this distinction very clear.

72 The "emotive" meaning puts people into "motion" but is not necessarily "emotional."

the term in any but a laudatory tone, is it "suitable to awaken in the audience a favourable attitude" and only then will it "redirect people's admiration."[73] Nobody would bother to redefine "culture" were it not for its positive aura. Claims about what a name means are therefore often accompanied by an expression of respect for or even insistence on its shared evaluation.

This emotive aspect of redefined terms tallies well with other aspects of the early masters' arguments that could be further explored. First, it resonates with the emerging expression in late Warring States texts of a worldview in which everything—including names—can energetically put things into motion. Secondly, it fits well with the occasionally proud insistence on the community where something is called as it is. Think, for example, of Confucius stating that the act of denouncing one's thieving father is not called "straight" (zhi 直) in his village. This occurred in the following dialogue:

> 葉公語孔子曰「吾黨有直躬者，其父攘羊而子證之。」孔子曰「吾黨之直者異於是。父為子隱，子為父隱。直在其中矣。」
>
> The Governor of She said to Confucius: "In our village there is a man nicknamed 'Straight Body.' When his father stole a sheep, he denounced him." Confucius answered: "Straightness in our village is quite different from this. Fathers cover up for their sons, and sons cover up for their fathers. Therein lies straightness."[74]

It contains no claim to universality as would be expected when naming is supposed to neutrally reflect reality. Confucius' naming act in the sheep-stealing case, thirdly, shows how terms can gain and lose emotive force, as did "straight." In this dialogue its appreciation by both collocutors is assumed, but in general the term zhi 直 is not often explicitly singled out for redefinition in early Chinese texts. Terms can thus be asleep or awakened as their description becomes a topic of debate and their emotive

---

73 Stevenson 1938: 331–332.
74 *Lunyu* 35/22–23 (*Lunyu* 13.18).

meaning is enhanced. Finally and most importantly, as a result of all this, the shared appreciation of a certain value does not at all indicate agreement on the topic. In an intellectual context where persuasive definitions thrive, this appreciation is little more than the basis for disagreement. Rather than explicitly rejecting the opponent's values—what Westerners tend to do according to Stevenson—disagreement focuses on how one understands or defines shared values. The agreement on the emotive meaning is the necessary ground for disagreement within a certain community. It is the façade behind which the real discussion takes place.[75]

4.2 A Weak Descriptive Content

Along with the sustainment or increase of a term's emotive meaning comes the desire to change its descriptive meaning. If you can convince the Ministry of Culture that real culture importantly includes an imaginative sensitivity for movies and music, some of the government funding might flow in your direction. Or if one wants funding and appreciation for non-Western thought, one should get it in the descriptive meaning of the emotively powerful term "philosophy."[76] The current descriptive meaning of a term has to be vague enough to open up for new content and thus channel the emotive force into novel directions. Much like rituals or laws, important terms are channels of such energy. If you do not plan to deplete them of energy and discard them—which would be the more challenging option—you have to convincingly introduce new content into the channel. New specifications are possible as long as the term's description is not fixed

---

75   The same mechanism is at work, I believe, in a wide variety of other cases: the shared appreciation of an ode, a text, a model, a law, an ideology, or a person. Appeal to Confucius or Confucianism, for instance, only superficially indicates agreement and sets the scene for challenging, novel thoughts. See e.g. Makeham 2008: 4–17; Hunter 2017: 12–20.

76   The alternative approach would be to diminish the emotive meaning of "philosophy" and propose for various types of non-Western thought another, emotively strong term that also attracts funding. See Defoort 2001: 404–405.

by political, juridical or other authority. In Western arguments, the new definition often claims some sort of undeniable reality, stating what "real" or "true" culture "essentially" is.[77]

In Chinese texts, however, if arguments for naming or defining are provided, they vary widely from all sorts of authority, to efficiency, consistency, reality, etc. What matters for the proposed definition is that the new content can be shown to be importantly analogous to the existing content—like a close neighbor—and hence to be deserving of the same treatment or leading to the same result. Adding new content to a powerful keyword is therefore a condensed form of analogical reasoning. If, for example, you were moved to fund art because it is culture, and if I convince you that movies are also culture, you should consider funding them too. As for a ruler's willingness to reward a minister's loyalty, if Zisi can add "giving criticism" to the meaning of *zhong*, he would deserve a similar treatment. Even the Later Mohists, whose interest in oxen and horses I have compared with Western philosophers' preferred use of neutral terms, nevertheless share their compatriots' interest in discriminating and categorizing so as to, ultimately, guide people's behavior and rulers' policies.[78]

A second difference with Stevenson's notion of "persuasive definitions" is that the new content is not always hidden or subtle, or necessarily "within the boundaries of its customary vagueness."[79] The claim that true culture amounts to an imaginative sensitivity for drinking and sleeping would be very innovative and therefore unconvincing in a funding application. In early Chinese arguments, however, the central position of naming and defining seems to have created a wide variety in the portions that could be emended in the customary description. Zisi's specification of a "loyal minister," e.g. as "one who constantly points out his ruler's mistakes," was

---

77   Stevenson 1938: 334. For a similar mechanism in the defense of terms against the threat of *paradiastole*, see Skinner 1991: 40–43.
78   See e.g. Fraser 2016: 22–24, 49–61.
79   Stevenson 1972: 210.

not particularly subtle but rather meant to challenge Lord Mu of Lu. What contributed to the challenge was the novelty of the description and its divergence from the generally shared descriptive meaning.

A novel definition is not necessarily offensive. In a dialogue recorded in the *Zuozhuan* between the marquis of Jin and his minister, Ru Qi 女齊 (d. circa 535 BCE), the latter disputed his ruler's description of the visiting duke of Lu as "knowledgeable about rituals" (*zhi li* 知禮) merely for mastering all the ceremonial details of interstate visits. Ru Qi therefore redefined the term "ritual" (*li* 禮) as "that by which one maintains his state, carries out administrative commands, and does not lose his people" 禮所以守其國, 行其政令, 無失其民者也. The marquis' response is not recorded, but the narrative concludes with the "gentleman saying that Shu Hou [Ru Qi] showed by these remarks that he understood ritual" 君子謂叔侯於是乎知禮.[80] Returning to the different specifications of loyalty quoted as examples at the outset of this paper, we can see how they add to the variety of considerations channeled into the proposed definitions: While Zisi defiantly insisted on his moral independence, the *Xunzi* considered the receiver of benefit as a crucial factor, and the *Mozi* took into account one's capacity to accept blame and to divert praise to the ruler. Other definitions of the same term in the corpus at large explicate who one is loyal to, what this virtue amounts to, or how one shows it.

Finally, a particular case of changing descriptive meaning emerges when two originally neighboring terms seem to compete for descriptive space, as with loyalty to one's ruler (*zhong*) and filial devotion to one's parents (*xiao*). Considering their possible conflict in the Chinese tradition, it is interesting to see how at the beginning of the imperial era the latter gained immense emotive standing while being descriptively stretched to the point of absorbing the former. Zengzi is quoted in the *Liji* as stating that "being disloyal in serving one's ruler is not filial devotion" 事君不忠，非

---

80   *Zuozhuan* Zhao 5.3 (*Zuozhuan* 332/5–11). For an analysis of this meaning of "*li*," see Pines 2002: 99–104.

孝也[81] and the *Xiaojing* states that "when [officers] serve their ruler with filial devotion, they are loyal" 以孝事君則忠.[82] As Tan Sor-hoon points out, "filial devotion became so important that it encompassed various other virtues," which eventually led to such a descriptive flexibility that the father-son relation could lose its priority. "One could thereby justify neglecting one's family to some extent, even overlooking certain mourning rites while serving the ruler."[83]

4.3 Dissuasive Step

A third and last useful characteristic of "persuasive definitions" for the analysis of early Chinese texts is the notion of dissuasion, the opposite of persuasion. If dissuasion is part of the argument, it often occurs as a step preceding or following the persuasive alternative. It is the explicit emptying of the term so as to provide it with novel content. This happened, for example, when Ru Qi presented his view of ritual to the marquis of Jin. He insisted that a polite reception and departure gifts did not deserve the label "ritual" (*li*). "That is ceremony (*yi*) and should not be called ritual" 是儀也。不可謂禮.[84] Not only did he empty the term *li* of its more customary content, he also moved the old stuff into another, emotively less powerful linguistic container (*yi*), clearly not something that the marquis should be impressed by. Below follow two variations of the possible power of dissuasion in early master-texts.

The first variation is when a description is being denied without the immediate or complete provision of an alternative. This can happen in negations, as when Confucius in the *Lunyu* answers his disciple's question about filial devotion. The master complains about what his contemporaries call *xiao*: "As for filial devotion nowadays, it refers to the ability to feed. Even dogs and horses all get to be fed" 今之孝者是謂能養。至於犬馬

---

81 *Liji* 25: 127/21 ("Jiyi" 祭義) and *Lüshi chunqiu* 14.1: 69/24 ("Xiaoxing" 孝行)

82 *Xiaojing* 5: 1/29 ("Shizhang" 士章). See also Chapter 7 of this volume.

83 Tan 2002: 180.

84 *Zuozhuan*, Zhao 5.3: 332/7.

皆能有養. He continues with a rhetorical question that somewhat refills the term: "If not for respect, then how to distinguish [the different types of behavior]?" 不敬，何以別乎?[85] This initial dissuasive step followed by a rhetorical question gives the statement a special psychological force: it invites the audience to think along with the master and actively join him in not only rejecting a particular description but also spelling out a more appropriate one. The linguistic channel of *xiao* is emptied of content but still so full of emotive force that it asks to be refilled. The answer to the next disciple leaves even more space for such a mental contribution: "Having [an appropriate] expression is difficult. When there is a task to be fulfilled, have the young take up its burden; when there is wine and food to be enjoyed, let the older generation have them: Would we ever consider this to constitute filial devotion?" 色難。有事，弟子服其勞；有酒食，先生饌：曾是以為孝乎?[86] The rhetorical question suggests that for the young to work and allow the old to enjoy is not the most felicitous or complete content of filial devotion. The implied negation turns Confucius' answer into an invitation to think about it, with the "expression" 色 at the outset of his answer functioning as a hint as to the term's more appropriate descriptive meaning. One further step in emptying a keyword would be to deny its content without providing any alternative hint at all. The emotive force can then no longer be channeled in one specific direction. In this metaphor the unnamable would not be a reality residing in a transcendent realm, but rather a formless mass of undivided, brimming energy. During instants of not naming, refraining from cutting, and remaining in the uncut, one would experience the fullness of unshaped energy.

A second and yet stronger trick to grab the audience's attention is to have perplexing statements in which the dissuasive act plays an important role, as when Mencius explains to the king why he is no real king (or why the "royal" person does not "reign") 王之不王 or when he

---

85   *Lunyu* 3/11–12 (*Lunyu* 2.7).
86   *Lunyu* 3/14–15 (*Lunyu* 2.8).

condemns the "ritual that is no ritual" 非禮之禮 or the sense of "duty that is no duty" 非義之義.[87] More than Confucius' rhetorical questions, such a perplexing negative statement produces a tension between a commonly known descriptive meaning and a newly suggested one. Since the two identical characters clearly stand for related terms with opposite emotive meanings, the audience is challenged by the cryptic statement to discover the other descriptive meanings attached to them. The same happens with perplexing expressions such as "great benefit does not benefit" 大利不利,[88] "the benefit that does not benefit" 不利之利,[89] or "not consider benefit beneficial" 不以利為利.[90] The identical use of the character for *li* 利 causes some momentary puzzlement and forces one to actively work one's way through its new content and value. By insisting on what benefit is not, the expression stimulates the audience to think along. Only then will one discover and consequently remove the type of benefit that is not really beneficial.

Conclusion

Looking back at much of my own previous research, I notice how crippled it is, like Shushan Toeless and Confucius in the *Zhuangzi* story at the outset of this paper. My reading of early texts has been driven over and again by an obsession, namely the insistence in early master-texts on naming and redefining. I presented the three tools that have shaped my approach—*zheng ming, paradiastole,* and persuasive definitions—in the chronological order of my academic journey. While they are all three inevitably foreign to the original material (the first one most delusively so), they can also be useful and enlightening. Having discovered the notion of persuasive definitions, I stopped

---

87   *Mencius* 1.7: 4/31, 5/4–5 (*Mencius* 1A7) and *Mencius* 8.6: 41/15 (*Mencius* 4B6).

88   *Liu Tao* 2/1: 12/3 ("Fa qi" 發啟).

89   *Lüshi chunqiu* 22.1: 143/30 ("Shen xing" 慎行).

90   *Liji* 43.2: 166/22–24 ("Da xue" 大學). For more details on these expressions, see Defoort 2008.

searching for novel tools, but increasingly reflected on its possible adaptation and application to Chinese texts. It can be employed to pay attention to a large variety of keywords in China: their shared emotive value, their amazing descriptive flexibility, and the power of dissuasion when they are emptied of content and not immediately refilled. The notion of persuasive definitions moreover accords well with a worldview full of brimming energy going in and out of linguistic containers, inviting renegotiations of their form, and thus moving people into novel directions. Attention to the fluctuating power of keywords in Chinese texts, as well as the variety of competing meanings that they harbor, would take us a long way in reinterpreting early Chinese thought.

Bibliography

Chan, Alan and Sor-hoon Tan, eds. 2004. *Filial Piety in Chinese Thought and History*. London: RoutledgeCurzon.

Cheung Chan-fai. 2008. "Professor Donald Munro on the State of Chinese Philosophy: Experiences with Tang Junyi and His Legacy." *APA Newsletter on Asian and Asian-American Philosophers and Philosophies* 8.1: 9–11.

Cook, Scott. 2012. *The Bamboo Texts of Guodian: A Study and Complete Translation*. Vols. 1–2. Ithaca, NY: Cornell East Asia Series.

Creel, Herrlee, G. 1974. *Shen Pu-hai: A Chinese Political Philosopher of the Fourth Century B.C.,* Chicago: University of Chicago Press.

Defoort, Carine. 1997. *The Pheasant Cap Master (Heguanzi): A Rhetorical Reading*. Albany, NY: State University of New York Press.

———. 2000. "Can Words Produce Order? Regicide in the Confucian Tradition." *Cultural Dynamics* 12.1: 85–109.

———. 2001. "Is There Such a Thing as Chinese Philosophy? Arguments of an Implicit Debate." *Philosophy East and West* 51.3: 393–413.

———. 2008. "The Profit that does not Profit: Paradoxes with *li* in Early Chinese Texts." *Asia Major* (Third Series) 21.1: 153–181.

———. Unpublished. "Confucius and the 'Rectification of Names': Hu Shi and the Emergence of a Modern Hype."

Feng Youlan 馮友蘭. 1984 [1931]. *Zhongguo zhexue shi* 中國哲學史, vol. 1. Beijing: Zhonghua shuju.

Fraser, Chris. 2016. *The Philosophy of the* Mòzǐ. New York: Columbia University Press.

Freese, John Henry. 1967 [1926]. *Aristotle with an English Translation. The "Art" of Rhetoric.* London: William Heinemann Ltd.

Fung, Yu-lan (Feng Youlan). 1973 [1937]. *A History of Chinese Philosophy*, 2 vols. Translated by Derk Bodde. Princeton: Princeton University Press.

Gassmann, Robert. 1988. *Cheng Ming. Richtigstellung der Beziechnungen.* Bern and New York: Peter Lang.

Graham, Angus C. 1959. "Being in Western Philosophy Compared with *Shih/fei* and *Yu/wu* in Chinese Philosophy." *Asia Major* (Second Series) 7: 79–112.

———. 1989. *Disputers of the Tao: Philosophical Argument in Ancient China.* La Salle, IL: Open Court.

Hall, David and Roger Ames. 1987. *Thinking Through Confucius.* Albany NY: State University of New York Press.

Hansen, Chad. 1992. *A Daoist Theory of Chinese Thought. A Philosophical Interpretation.* Oxford: Oxford University Press.

Hanshu 漢書. 1962. By Ban Gu 班固 (32–92) et al. Annotated by Yan Shigu 顏師古 (581–645). Beijing: Zhonghua shuju.

Harris, Eirik Lang. 2016. *The Shenzi Fragments. A Philosophical Analysis and Translation.* New York: Columbia University Press.

Hsiao Kung-chuan. 1980 [1979]. *A History of Chinese Political Thought.* Translated by Frederick Mote. Taipei: Caves Books.

Hu, Shih (Hu Shi). 1922. *The Development of the Logical Method in Ancient China.* Reprinted in Zheng Dahua 2003, vol. 35: 298–606.

Hu Shi 胡適. 1919. *Zhongguo zhexueshi dagang* 中國哲學史大綱, later called *Zhongguo gudai zhexueshi* 中國古代哲學史. Reprinted in Zheng Dahua 2003, vol. 5: 193–534.

———. 1958. "Preface to Taiwanese edition" *of Zhongguo gudai zhexueshi* 中國古代哲學史. Reprinted in Zheng Dahua 2003, vol. 5: 535–541.

Hunter, Michael. 2017. *Confucius Beyond the Analects.* Leiden: Brill.

Lau, Dim-Cheuk. 1984 [1970]. *Mencius.* London: Penguin Books.

———. *1993–2002. ICS Ancient Chinese Texts Concordance Series.* Hong Kong: Commercial Press.

Legge, James. 1994 [1872]. *The Chinese Classics. With a Translation, Critical and Exegetical Notes, Prolegomena, and Copious Indexes.* vol. 5, *The Ch'un Ts'ew with the Tso Chuen,* Taipei: SMC Publishing Inc.

Liang Qichao 梁啟超. 1996 [1921]. "Kongzi" 孔子. In *Yinbingshi heji* 飲冰室合集, vol. 8, collection 36: 1–64. Beijing: Zhonghua shuju.

Loy, Hui Chieh. 2014. "Language and Ethics in the *Analects.*" In *Dao Companion to the* Analects, edited by Amy Olberding, 137–158. Dordrecht: Springer.

Katz-Goehr, Amira. 2009. "On Being 'Straight' *zhi* 直: Analects 13.18." In *At Home in Many Worlds. Reading, Writing and Translating from Chinese and Jewish Cultures. Essays in Honour of Irene Eber,* edited by Raoul Findeisen et al., *35–53.* Wiesbaden: Harrassowitz Verlag.

Knoblock, John and Jeffrey Riegel. 2000. *The Annals of Lü Buwei.* Stanford: Stanford University Press.

Kurtz, Joachim. 2011. *The Discovery of Chinese Logic.* Leiden: Brill.

Makeham, John. 1994. *Name and Actuality in Early Chinese Thought.* Albany: State University of New York Press.

Makeham, John. 2008. *Lost Soul. "Confucianism" in Contemporary Chinese Academic Discourse.* Cambridge, MA: Harvard University Asia Center.

Martinich, Aloysius. 2014. "Political Theory and Linguistic Criteria in Han Feizi's Philosophy." *Dao. A Journal of Comparative Philosophy* 13.3: 379–393.

Nivison, David S. 1999. "The Classical Philosophical Writings." In *The Cambridge History of Ancient China,* edited by Michael Loewe and Edward L. Shaughnessy, 745–812. Cambridge: Cambridge University Press.

Nylan, Michael. 2001. *The Five Confucian Classics.* New Haven: Yale University Press.

Pines, Yuri. 2002. *Foundations of Confucian Thought. Intellectual Life in the Chunqiu Period 722–453 B.C.E.* Honolulu: University of Hawai'i Press.

Ren Jiyu 任繼愈. 1983. *Zhongguo zhexue fazhanshi* 中國哲學發展史, 4 vols. Beijing: Renmin chubanshe.

Rickett, W. Allyn. 1985. *Guanzi: Political, Economic, and Philosophical Essays from Early China,* vol. 1. Princeton: Princeton University Press.

Sang Bing 桑兵. 2003. "Heng kan cheng ling ce cheng feng: xueshu shicha yu Hu Shi de xueshu diwei" 橫看成嶺側成峰: 學術視差與胡适的學術地位. *Lishi yanjiu* 歷史研究 5: 35–42.

Sato, Masayuki 佐藤將之. 2010. *Gudai Zhongguo de "zhong" lun yanjiu* 古代中國的 "忠"論研究. Taibei: Taida chuban zhongxin.

Schwartz, Benjamin. 1985. *The World of Thought in Ancient China.* Cambridge MA: Harvard University Press.

Shiji 史記. 1997. By Sima Qian 司馬遷 (ca. 145–90 BCE) et al. Annotated by Zhang Shoujie 張守節 (7th c.), Sima Zhen 司馬貞 (679–732), and Pei Yin 裴駰 (5th c.). Beijing: Zhonghua shuju.

Skinner, Quentin. 1991. "Thomas Hobbes: Rhetoric and the Construction of Morality." *Proceedings of the British Academy* 76: 1–61.

———. 1994. "Moral Ambiguity and the Renaissance Art of Eloquence." *Essays in Criticism. A Quarterly Journal of Literary Criticism* 44.4: 267–292.

Stevenson, Charles L. 1938. *"Persuasive Definitions" Mind* 47: 331–350.

———. 1972 [1944]. *Ethics and Language.* New Haven: Yale University Press.

Tan, Sor-hoon. 2002. "Between Family and State: Relational Tensions in Confucian Ethics." In *Mencius. Contexts and Interpretations,* edited by Alan K. L. Chan, 169–188. Honolulu: University of Hawai'i Press.

Van Auken, Ann Newell. 2014. "Killings and Assassination in the *Spring and Autumn* as Records of Judgment." *Asia Major* (Third Series) 27.1: 1–31.

Van Norden, Bryan. 2007. *Virtue Ethics and Consequentialism in Early Chinese Philosophy.* Cambridge: Cambridge University Press.

Waley, Arthur. 1938. *The Analects of Confucius.* New York: Vintage Books.

Zheng Dahua 鄭大華 (ed.). 2003. *Hu Shi quanji* 胡適全集. Hefei: Anhui jiaoyu chubanshe.

2

Chinese *he* 和 in Many Keys, Harmonized in Europe

Joachim Gentz

Introduction

China, in particular pre-modern China, is often associated with the notion of "harmony." The harmonic equilibrium between *yin* and *yang*, the harmonic flow of *qi* (vital *pneuma*), the harmonic balance of forces in *fengshui*, the *dao* as principle of natural harmony, the harmony of body and mind in Chinese medicine and of humans and the cosmos in Chinese philosophy—these are "facts" we all are familiar with from esoteric and wellness discourses.

The three traditional teachings (*sanjiao* 三教) of China—Confucianism, Daoism, and Buddhism—are associated with harmony as they all seem to aim at states of balanced equilibria. Their relationship is perceived as syncretistic and harmonious, and the absence of religious wars seems to prove this assumption and leads to further claims about the peacefulness and tolerance of Chinese religions in general.[1]

---

1   For a critical discussion see Gentz 2011 and 2013.

Confucianism in particular is perceived as a philosophy of social harmony.[2] In 2005 even the Communist Party of China (CPC) started to propagate the ideal of a "harmonious society" (*hexie shehui* 和諧社會), not as the result of a successfully accomplished class struggle but as a particular feature of the Chinese approach to a socialist market economy;[3] it even complements scientism.[4] Since around 2007 this ideal has been widely criticized by Chinese intellectuals as a euphemism for party censorship and has been mocked by netizens in diverse forums, including uses of the famous river crab homophone (*hexie* 河蟹) and the verbalization of the noun *hexie* as "to harmonize" or "having been harmonized" (*bei hexie le* 被和諧了, referring to intellectual suppression).[5]

China is commonly classified as a "culture of consensus" as opposed to a Western "culture of debate."[6] In the German Wikipedia entry for Chinese culture ("Chinesische Kultur"), *harmony* is listed as the second of nine essential traits of Chinese culture. This entry is so representative of a wide consensus on Chinese culture that it has not been changed in the otherwise highly volatile Wikipedia over the last thirteen and a half

---

2   See a recent book-length attempt by Li Chenyang (2014b) who in a related article goes so far as to claim that "*he* 和 (harmony, harmonization) is the most cherished ideal in Chinese culture, and more specifically, in Confucianism" (2014a: 379). When discussing pre-Confucian political culture, Perelomov (1993: 33–38) also takes *he* as the singularly important component of Chinese culture. He even identifies *he* as a special code (=keyword) that is peculiar to Chinese ethnicity (p. 33). His interest in *he* however lies in the validation of the right to dissent and criticize when he discusses the famous prime minister of Qi, Yan Ying 晏嬰 (ca. 578–500 BCE).

3   For a critical discussion, see Roetz 2009.

4   Oldstone-Moore 2015: 52–58.

5   Norden and Richaud 2014; Norden 2016.

6   Using Japan as an example, Ruth Benedict, seventy years ago, coined the rather controversial distinction between Asiatic "cultures of shame" in which norms are more determined from the outside and individuals therefore strive for harmony with the exterior world, and Western "cultures of guilt" in which norms are stronger and intrinsically self-determined within the individual. See Benedict 1946.

years.[7] Harmony in Chinese culture is linked to such diverse areas as religion and cosmology, politics, morality, human relations and behavior in this Wikipedia entry. Roger Ames, probably inspired by the ongoing discourse, uses *he* 和 also as a central philosophical term denoting a Chinese *creatio in situ* as opposed to the Western *creatio ex nihilo*.[8]

Harmony discourses always become animated in times of chaos and discord. The early "Masters Literature"[9] disputes manifold ways of how best to achieve peace and order in a situation of constant warfare and disorder during the Warring States (453–221 BCE) period. But the "Disputers of the Tao"[10] were not merely concerned with the right ways of achieving order. Concrete visions of peace, harmony and proper order also differed greatly among these thinkers, even among thinkers belonging to the same tradition. Their visions differed both in terms of the particular aspects that were emphasized and regarding the ranking of concepts and terms in their respective normative vocabulary.[11] Reconstructions of "the Confucian concept of harmony"[12] or "the Confucian philosophy of harmony"[13] are thus not very convincing.

In the following discussion, I will argue in the first section that there is no consistent and unified idea or terminology of harmony in early Chinese texts. Instead we find discussions about various aspects of harmony that

---

7   The nine traits are: Groupthink and discrimination between insiders and outsiders (Gruppendenken und Insider-Outsider-Diskriminierung), *Harmony* (*Harmonie*), Face (Gesicht), Indirectness (Indirektheit), Collectivity (Kollektivität), Awareness of hierarchy (Hierarchiebewusstsein), Ritualization (Ritualisierung), This-worldliness (Diesseitigkeit), and Sinocentrism (Sinozentrismus). http://de.wikipedia.org/wiki/Chinesische_Kultur (created 17 Sept 2006). These nine points are pretty much congruent with the twelve points discussed in the twelve chapters of Part II of "The Ways of Thinking of the Chinese," formulated by Nakamura Hajime in his famous and controversial *The Ways of Thinking of Eastern People*, which he had already drafted in the mid-1940s. Harmony, however, does not play a central role in Nakamura's work. In Chapter 12 he only uses this term to refer to what we would call religious syncretism (Nakamura 1960: 284–297).

8   Ames 2005.

9   Denecke 2011.

10 Graham 1989.

11 The latter is discussed by Roetz 2015: 315.

12 Yu 2015.

13 Li Chenyang 2014b.

make use of a broad range of terms, each with multiple meanings within different contexts. Current Western and Chinese discussions about harmony in China follow in most cases three fallacious assumptions: a) that harmony is a central and consistent concept in Chinese philosophy and culture;[14] b) that because the character *he* 和 is the most representative term used for harmony in early Chinese texts, it should be regarded as a conceptual term; and c) that the Western term "harmony" is a good translation for *he* and can be used in most contexts to translate it adequately. *He* 和 will therefore also be the keyword that I will analyze most closely.

In the second section I will try to reconstruct when, how and why—despite the absence of a consistent keyword for harmony in the Chinese tradition—the Western term "harmony" came to be used to cover all these various aspects of harmony and to epitomize Chinese culture as a whole.

1. "Harmony" in Early Chinese Texts

1.1 The Term *he* 和 in Early Chinese Texts

Historically, some of the terms denoting certain aspects of harmony belong to the earliest layer of Chinese language that we are able to reconstruct. The character *he* 和 has not been found in oracle bone inscriptions.[15] Its variant forms

---

14 Chan (2011) offers a slightly different approach, concluding his article with the statement: "It is true that harmony occupies a privileged place in Confucian philosophy and Chinese culture at large, but it should not be assumed that it has been uniformly understood" (2011: 62). He thus agrees with most scholars on the importance of harmony as a central idea in Chinese culture, but is critical about its consistency. In his introduction (Chan 2011: 37) he writes, "The ideal of harmony is often singled out as central to Chinese philosophy and distinctive of the East Asian value system as a whole [...] However, it is difficult to pinpoint the meaning of harmony in Chinese thought, for it remains very much a diffused concept, embedded in not one but a host of concepts." Some contributions (by Ziporyn and others) to the workshop on "Conceptions of Harmony in Chinese Thought" held at Nanyang Technological University in 2018 also emphasized the diversity of harmony models in China.

15 Guo Qi (2000: 451, 453) claims that it appears as a composite of 口 and 禾 in oracle bone inscriptions, but he provides no evidence. Scholars who follow his claim only refer to this publication (e.g. Li Chenyang 2014a: 379).

he 龢 and *yue* 龠 do occur but, like the term *xie* 燮, are used as designations for specific kinds of sacrifices so cannot be regarded as early forms of the term. However, *xie* 協 and *xie* 劦 are both used in the meaning of "together," "common," or "common efforts"/"combined forces," and related words such as *he* 合, *tong* 同, and *hui* 會 (all meaning "together"), and *ning* 寧 and *an* 安 (both meaning "safe/peaceful/quiet") are also seen in oracle bone inscriptions.[16]

He 和 and its variant form *he* 龢 are found in bronze inscriptions dated around the 9th century BCE,[17] mainly on bronze chimes where they designate the harmonizing quality of the chimes[18] and were also used to refer to the harmonization of the *min* 民 (populations) and their governance.[19] *He* 盉 is another related character seen in bronze inscriptions and denotes the combining of ingredients to make soup.[20] All three characters were used interchangeably and refer in general to the composition of different things to create a product that is pleasant to the senses when the things are well composed (different sounds create pleasant music, different ingredients create pleasant taste).[21] *He* thus describes the threefold structure of a) a

---

16   Xu Zhongshu 1988: 106, 113–114, 199, 284, 504, 573, 577, 802, 848, 1479, 1480.

17   Scholars have different views on which of the two characters is the original written representation of the word "harmony." See the discussion by Guo Qi (2000: 453–454), who follows Wang Li's *Tangyuan cidian* (also in his choice of examples in the article), but whose own explanation based on an assumption about the development of human culture and thought (human voice is earlier than musical instruments) is not very convincing.

18   Falkenhausen 1993: 124.

19   Falkenhausen 1993: 1–4 and Li Chenyang 2014b: 24. See the identical formulation "*he yu zheng*" 龢于政 in both the Shi Qiang-*pan* 史牆盤 and the Shi Xun-*gui* 師訇簋 (Cook and Goldin 2016: 98, 113). Two passages in *Zuozhuan* and *Guoyu* compare political with musical harmony indicating an assumption that musical harmony is the original concept: 八年之中，九合諸侯，如樂之和，無所不諧 (*Zuo zhuan*, Xiang 11.5b, p. 993) and 夫政象樂，樂從和，和從平 (*Guoyu* "Zhouyu xia" 30, *juan* 3.6).

20   Yu 2015: 18; Li Chenyang 2014b: 24–25.

21   Guo Qi (2000: 452) argues that the earliest layer of meaning of the term is "humans or animals uttering sounds that mutually follow upon each other, in other words, responding to each other" 人或動物互相跟著發聲. Chan (2011: 37–38) and Li Chenyang 2014a follow his interpretation. It is also the definition that Xu Shen 許慎 gives in his *Shuowen jiezi* 說文解字 as 和, 相應也 (Duan Yucai 1988: 57) which, Guo Qi believes, catches the basic meaning of the term (2000: 451).

unit of a composite whole that consists of b) individual constituents that c) relate to one another in a specific way (that pleases the human senses).[22]

An analysis of the concrete use of the term *he* in later early Chinese texts from the 5th to the 3rd centuries BCE can provide a basis for a systematic classification of the different perspectives on this threefold structure and on further sub-specifications within these perspectives.

The earliest sources in which this concept is reflected upon more theoretically are a speech attributed to Yan Ying 晏嬰 in *Zuozhuan* 左傳[23] and another speech by Shi Bo 史伯 in the Zheng section ("Zhengyu" 鄭語) of the *Guoyu* 國語.[24] Although the passages have been translated in almost all texts that discuss the concept of *he*, they are so central to an understanding of the early political implications of the term that they need to be quoted here again.[25] I shall start with *Zuozhuan*:

---

22 Chan (2011) distinguishes two forms of harmony by differentiating between musical and culinary harmony, arguing that musical harmony always follows a hierarchical order while culinary harmony blends different ingredients to form a harmonious flavor. While I find it useful to make this distinction and can see the political implications here, I do not find it convincing to ascribe these two modes of creating harmony to music and cooking respectively.

23 *Chunqiu Zuozhuan zhu*, Zhao 20.8: 1419–1420. The same discussion in a slightly different and shorter form can also be found in the *Yanzi chunqiu* 1.18: 66 ("Jian shang" 諫上).

24 *Guoyu* 16.1: 470–473.

25 The two passages are quoted in Feng Youlan's *History of Chinese Philosophy* 中國哲學史 from 1931 (Bodde transl. 1952: 34–36) and also in Zhang Dainian's discussion on the concept of *he* 和 in his article on some particularities of Chinese philosophy in 1957 (in another article on some basic philosophical categories in Chinese philosophy from the same year, *he* 和 is not mentioned; see Zhang Dainian 1998a and 1998b). They are also quoted in Zhang's later *Key Concepts and Categories of Classical Chinese Philosophy* 中國古典哲學概念範疇要論 as first examples for the key concept "harmony" (Chapter 37: "*He* 和, *Taihe* 太和"; Harmony, Ultimate Harmony). See Zhang Dainian 1989: 127–130; and 2002: 270–276. They play a central role in Guo Qi's interpretation (2000: 463–464) and are also quoted and translated in Roetz 2009: 15–16, Yu 2015: 16–17; Li Chenyang 2014b: 25–26 and other scholarly discussions on *he*. The contrast between *he* and *tong* is also well known from the famous saying in *Lunyu* 論語 13.23: "The master said: The gentleman aims at harmony but not at uniformity, the petty man seeks uniformity but not harmony" 子曰：「君子和而不同，小人同而不和」.

齊侯至自田，晏子侍于遄臺，子猶馳而造焉。公曰：「唯據與我和夫！」晏子對曰：「據亦同也，焉得為和？」公曰：「和與同異乎？」對曰：「異。和如羹焉，水、火、醯、醢、鹽、梅，以烹魚肉，燀之以薪，宰夫和之，齊之以味，濟其不及，以泄其過。君子食之，以平其心。君臣亦然。君所謂可而有否焉，臣獻其否以成其可；君所謂否而有可焉，臣獻其可以去其否，是以政平而不干，民無爭心。故《詩》曰：『亦有和羹，既戒既平。鬷嘏無言，時靡有爭。』先王之濟五味、和五聲也，以平其心，成其政也。聲亦如味，一氣，二體，三類，四物，五聲，六律，七音，八風，九歌，以相成也；清濁、小大、短長、疾徐、哀樂、剛柔、遲速、高下，出入、周疏，以相濟也。君子聽之，以平其心。心平，德和。故《詩》曰：『德音不瑕』。今據不然。君所謂可，據亦曰可；君所謂否，據亦曰否。若以水濟水，誰能食之？若琴瑟之專壹，誰能聽之？同之不可也如是。」

When the Prince of Qi returned from the hunt, Yan Ying waited upon him at the Chuan Terrace. Liangqiu Ju galloped his horses to join them there. The lord said, "Liangqiu Ju alone is in harmony with us!" Yan Ying replied, "Ju is just conforming (*tong* 同). How can he be said to be in harmony?" The lord said, "Are harmony and conformity different?" Yan Ying replied, "They are different. Harmony is like a stew. Water, fire, jerky, mincemeat, salt, and plum vinegar are used to cook fish and meat. These are cooked over firewood. The master chef harmonizes them, evening them out (*qi* 齊) with seasonings, compensating (*ji* 濟) for what is lacking, and diminishing (*xie* 洩) what is too strong. The noble man eats it and thereby calms his heart.

With a ruler and subject it is the same. When there is something wrong in what the ruler considers right, the subject sets forth the wrong in order to perfect the right. When there is something right about what the ruler considers wrong, the subject sets forth the right in order to eliminate the wrong. In this way the administration is calm and does not violate standards, and the people will have no heart for contending with one another. Thus it says in the *Odes*, 'There is a well harmonized stew. We are careful and calm. We advance silently; there is no contention.'

The former kings' seasoning (*ji* 濟) of the five flavors and harmonizing of the five tones were for the calming of hearts and the perfecting of government.

Sounds are just like flavors. The single breath, the two forms, the three genres, the four materials, the five tones, the six pitches, the seven notes, the eight airs, the nine songs—these are used to complete one another (*xiang cheng* 相成*)*. The clear and the muddy, the piano and the forte, the short and the long, the presto and the adagio, the somber and the joyous, the hard and the soft, the delayed and the immediate, the high and the low, the going out and the coming in, the united and the separate—these are used to complement one another *(xiang ji* 相濟*)*. The noble man listens to it and thus calms his heart. When the heart is calm, the virtue is in harmony. Thus, as it says in the Odes, 'The sound of his virtue is unblemished.'

Now Liangqiu Ju is not like this. Whatever you, the ruler, consider right, Lingqiu Ju also calls right. Whatever you consider wrong, Ju also calls it unacceptable. If [in a soup] water just complements (*ji* 濟) water, who can eat it? If zithers and dulcimers hold to a single sound *(zhuan yi* 專壹*)*, who can listen to it? This is how conformity does not work."[26]

One of the central explanative terms for *he* 和 in this passage is *ji* 濟, which is often translated as "complementing," and has the connotations of aiding, benefitting and relieving, thus provides a further semantic dimension to the description of the relationship between the constituents of the composite whole as a harmonious unit. In this relationship, constituents add something to each other and thereby improve, strengthen, complete and accomplish the unit to achieve a perfected harmonious whole. In terms of the threefold structure described by *he,* the focus of the discussion in this text thus lies on the difference in the kinds of relationship between the constituents in units, with a *he* quality on the one hand and units with a *tong* quality on the other. In *he*-units the relationship between the individual constituents is one of difference and diversity. In *tong*-units, by contrast, it is a relationship of identity and uniformity.

---

26   Translation based on Durrant, Li and Schaberg 2016: 1585–1587, with some amendments.

The *Guoyu* passage discusses the same contrast between *he* and *tong* and similarly puts emphasis on the different relationships between the constituents in *he*-units (which is based on the balance of different constituents 以他平他) and in *tong*-units (in which identical constituents supplement each other 以同裨同). In its conclusion, it even goes a step further than *Zuozhuan* by claiming that any growth and development depends on the blending of different things (*he* 和) and that, by contrast, conformity (*tong* 同) necessarily leads to exhaustion and decline:

公曰：「周其弊乎？」對曰：「殆於必弊者也。《泰誓》曰：『民之所欲，天必從之。』今王棄高明昭顯，而好讒慝暗昧；惡角犀豐盈，而近頑童窮固。去和而取同。夫和實生物，同則不繼。以他平他謂之和，故能豐長而物歸之；若以同裨同，盡乃棄矣。故先王以土與金木水火雜，以成百物。是以和五味以調口，剛四支以衛體，和六律以聰耳，正七體以役心，平八索以成人，建九紀以立純德，合十數以訓百體。出千品，具萬方，計億事，材兆物，收經入，行姟極。故王者居九 之田，收經入以食兆民，周訓而能用之，和樂如一。夫如是，和之至也。於是乎先王聘后於異姓，求財於有方，擇臣取諫工而講以多物，務和同也。聲一無聽，物一無文，味一無果，物一不講。王將棄是類也而與剸同，天奪之明。欲無弊，得乎？」

The lord said: "Is Zhou possibly going to decline?" Shi Bo replied: "It is almost at a stage where it will necessarily decline. 'The Great Harangue' [chapter of the *Book of Documents*][27] says: 'What the people desire, Heaven will certainly follow.' Now the king [You of Zhou, 周幽王, r. 781–771 BCE] neglects the great, bright, clear, and illustrious [people] and prefers the slanderous, wicked, dim and ignorant; he detests the upright and talented and draws close to the stupid and stubborn. He abandons harmony and chooses conformity (*tong* 同). Yet in truth it is harmony that generates all things, whereas conformity does not lead any further. To

---

27 While this quote can be found in 'The Great Harangue' ("Tai shi" 泰誓) chapter of the transmitted edition of the *Book of Documents*, we do not know which version of the text Shi Bo is referring to.

balance something with something different is called harmony. Because this allows for abundance and growth, all kinds of things turn back to it. If, however, something is supplemented by the same thing, then it will be exhausted and hence discarded. Therefore, the former kings combined earth with metal, wood, water and fire in order to accomplish the hundred kinds of things. For this reason they harmonized the five tastes in order to perfectly suit the senses of the palate, they strengthened the four limbs in order to guard the body, they harmonized the six pitch-pipes in order to attune the ear, they rectified the seven sense organs in order to serve the heart, they balanced the eight body parts in order to complete the human form, they set up the nine organs in order to establish pure virtue, they arranged the ten ranks in order to organize the hundred institutional bodies. They produced the thousand kinds of things, completed the ten thousand methods, calculated the hundred thousand matters, used the hundred million kinds of things, received the billion sources of income and carried all this out to control the infinite. Thus the kings dwelling on the lands of the nine regions received the billion sources of income in order to feed the hundreds of millions of people, and after they were all instructed they could be made useful so that there was harmony and happiness as if they were one. A situation like this is actually the ultimate harmony. That thereupon the former kings married queens from different clans, sought resources from other regions, when selecting ministers chose those skilled in remonstrations and conducted discussions about many different kinds of things this was all for the sake of exerting themselves to harmonize the individual uniformities. When there is only one sound, there is nothing to listen to; when there is only one kind of thing, there is no pattern; when there is only one taste, there is no effect; when there is only one kind of thing, it is not discussed. If the king is about to give up this kind [of harmony] and permits only narrow uniformity, then Heaven deprives him of clarity. Can the wish that there shall be no decline, then be accomplished?"

In both passages, the terms *he* 和 and *tong* 同 are set up as contrasting terms, with *he* being the ideal of combining heterogeneous things and encouraging dissenting opinions and remonstrance to create a perfectly fruitful order that has the potential to thrive, and *tong* in contrast being dull, consensual, subservient or even sycophantic, without musicality and flavor and leading to decline.[28] Both texts connect *he* to the positive effect of balancing (*ping* 平). Both texts connect the balanced composition of sounds and soup ingredients to balanced politics. *Zuozhuan* quotes the "Lie zu" 烈祖 Ode (Mao 320) of the *Shijing* 詩經, which also praises the right balance of the "harmonious" sacrificial soup.[29] *Zuozhuan* further connects the effect of the harmonious products to the balance of the ruler's mind (*xin* 心), which is thus regarded as belonging to the same category of organs to which ears, mouth and eyes belong, organs that are sensitive to the harmony of balanced compositions.

The *Tang chu yu Tangqiu* 湯處於湯丘 ("Tang was dwelling at Tang Mound") manuscript from the Tsinghua (Qinghua) University collection follows the same basic assumption. Yet, it not only connects *he* to the positive effect of balancing (*ping* 平) like *Zuozhuan* and *Guoyu* above, but further adds the positive transformative effects exerted on the body by perfectly composed ("harmonious") dishes. It then continues to extend the positive transformative effect of harmonization to the body politic as well, using *he* as a verb (*he min* 和民) in a discussion that focuses on the effect a perfectly composed government exerted on the populations. In this introductory passage, the text plays with two meanings of the term *he*: the skill of creating a perfect

---

28　Note that *tong* does not always have this connotation in other texts from the Confucian canon. See, for example, the following passage from the "Hongfan" 洪範 chapter of the *Shangshu* 尚書 in which it denotes the lucky case of different independent institutions sharing the same view on a matter without subservience: 汝則有大疑，謀及乃心，謀及卿士，謀及庶人，謀及卜筮。汝則從，龜從，筮從，卿士從，庶民從，是之謂大同。身其康彊，子孫其逢，吉。 "When you have doubts about any great matter, consult with your own mind; consult with your high ministers and officers; consult with the common people; consult the tortoise-shell and divining stalks. If you, the shell, the stalks, the ministers and officers, and the common people, all agree about a course, this is what is called a great concord (*tong*), and the result will be the welfare of your person and good fortune to your descendants." Legge 1991 (1865): 337. Note that "great concord" (or "great uniformity," *da tong* 大同) became the epitome of Confucian utopia since the Han period (for *locus classicus*, see *Liji* 332 ["Li yun" 禮運]).

29　亦有和羹、既戒既平。("Shang Sacrificial Odes" 商頌). The idea of a simple and unseasoned sacrificial soup (大羹不致) that does not need any condiments is equally prevalent in the *Zuozhuan* (Huan 2) with parallels (大羹不和) in the *Liji* (in chapters "Li qi" 禮器, "Jiao te sheng" 郊特牲, and "Yue ji" 樂記), *Huainanzi*, *Lüshi Chunqiu* and *Shiji*.

composition on the one hand, and the effect of this perfect composition to transform something else on the other. All these are expressed in a textual composition that produces musical harmony by using a meter and (slant) rhyming as if it were a song:

湯處於湯丘，
取妻於有莘。
有莘媵以小臣。小臣善為食烹之和，有莘之女食之，絕芳旨以粹，
身體痊平，*breŋ
九竅發明，*mraŋ
以道心嗌，*q[i]k
舒快以恒。*[g]ˤəŋ[30]
湯亦食之，曰：允！此可以和民乎？
小臣答曰：可。[31]

When Tang was dwelling at Tang's Mound, he took a wife from the clan of Youshen. The Youshen bride was accompanied by the domestic servant (Yi Yin). The domestic servant was good at perfect compositions in his cooking and whenever the woman of Youshen ate them, she had a strong fragrance that was delicate and pure, her body became stable and balanced, her nine orifices gleamed, it led her mind to serenity and made her leisurely cheerfulness firm. Tang also ate it and said: "Ah! Can this [method also] be used to harmonize the populances?" The domestic servant said: "It can."

The opening passage of the *Zhong yong* 中庸 (Doctrine of the mean), famous for its conceptualization of *he* and the main source for associating *he* with *zhong* 中 (centeredness),[32] further connects the concept of harmony

---

30 Reconstructions according to Baxter and Sagart 2014, slant rhymes with the third of four elements typically not rhyming. For other reconstructions of this sentence with different graphs and punctuations, see Wang Jinfeng 2016: 66.

31 Li Xueqin 2015: 61–62, 135.

32 The term is therefore also taken up as a part of the compound keyword *zhonghe* 中和 in Chen Chun's 陳淳 (1159–1223) work on Neo-Confucian keywords, the *Beixi ziyi* 北溪字義 (Beixi on the meanings of words). Following this introductory passage, the text of the *Zhong yong* entirely focuses on the term *zhong* 中 (and *yong* 庸), the term *he* plays no further conceptual role in it.

to a state of emotions that reflect the state of unaroused inner centeredness in their aroused form when they meet the perfect measures of the *dao*. As *he* denotes the relationships of distinct constituents, it cannot describe a state of unaroused inner centeredness in which things are not yet distinct. The striking claim of this text is thus that it defines *he* as a relationship of distinct constituents that is equivalent to their unified centered state "as if" they were still one:

喜怒哀樂之未發，　　謂之中；
發而皆中節，　　　　謂之和；
　　　　　　　　　　中也者，天下之大本也；
　　　　　　　　　　和也者，天下之達道也。
致中和，天地位焉，萬物育焉。

The state when joy, anger, sorrow and happiness are not yet aroused is called centered. When they are aroused and all find their center in perfect measures, this is called harmonious (*he*). The centered is the root of All under Heaven, the harmonious is what has achieved the right path (*dao*) in All under Heaven. When the centered and harmonious have been achieved, then Heaven and Earth are in perfect position therein and all things flourish therein.[33]

He in this context refers to the commonality of the constituents that unites them in a harmonious composite whole. The perfect ritual and moral measures (*jie* 節) provide the new centering structure for a newly aroused diversified reality. Like the introductory passage of the *Tang chu yu Tangqiu* discussed above, this opening passage of the *Zhong yong* plays with two meanings of a term, in this case *zhong* 中, which refers to the center or centeredness of unaroused emotions in the first instance and to the centering effect of the perfect measures when emotions are aroused in the second. *He* is conceived as the result of this centering effect.

33　*Liji xunzuan* 31: 772 ("Zhong yong").

The *Xunzi* 荀子, possibly composed a few decades later than the *Zhong yong* and the *Tang chu yu Tangqiu*, takes a further step by addressing two new questions related to the anthropological conditions that enable humans to create harmony. First, the *Xunzi*, like *Zuozhuan* and *Guoyu*, assumes that harmony in the cosmos is obtained by constant change and transformations triggered by antagonistic forces. But it goes a step further by entering into an epistemological discussion and denying that the formless mechanisms of cosmic harmony can be understood by humans:

> 列星隨旋，日月遞炤，四時代御，陰陽大化，風雨博施，萬物各得其和以生，各得其養以成。不見其事，而見其功，夫是之謂神。皆知其所以成，莫知其無形，夫是之謂天功。唯聖人為不求知天。

> When the arrayed stars follow each other in their circular movements, sun and moon shine successively, the four seasons preside in periods, *yin* and *yang* undergo their great transformations, and winds and rains disseminate widely, then the ten thousand kinds of things each obtain their harmonious place in order to come into being and they each obtain their nourishment in order to be completed. [In this process there is something] of which one does not see its workings but only sees its accomplishments: this is called the divine, [and there is something] of which everyone knows how it achieves completion but nobody knows its formless state: this is called the accomplishment of heaven. Only sages do not seek to understand heaven.[34]

The *Xunzi* does not talk about a harmony of heaven here, harmony relates always to the individual kinds of relationships between the constituents within the greater order. Each of these harmonies is different and the *Xunzi* repeatedly emphasizes that the complexity of this harmony cannot be grasped:

> 萬物為道一偏，一物為萬物一偏。愚者為一物一偏，而自以為知道。無知也。

---

34   *Xunzi* 17: 309 ("Tian lun" 天論).

The ten thousand kinds of things are but one facet of the *dao* and one kind of thing is just one facet of the ten thousand things. The foolish ones consider only one facet of one kind of things and think that they know the *dao*. This is ignorance.[35]

Second, like *Zuozhuan* and *Guoyu*, the *Xunzi* argues that differentiation (of the constituents of the composite whole) is a pre-condition for a proper order. Harmony in turn is the positive quality of such a diversified and yet unified order. The *Xunzi*, however, goes beyond *Zuozhuan* and *Guoyu* by addressing this question: What is the human condition that enables humans to create harmony? If they are not able to understand the principles of cosmic harmony, as pointed out in the examples above, how are they able to produce harmony in the socio-political realm? The *Xunzi*'s response is that it is a unique human sense of proper order (*yi* 義) that allows humans to differentiate (*fen* 分) and enables them to form social groups (*qun* 群). This is how they achieve a harmonious diversity.

> 水火有氣而無生,草木有生而無知,禽獸有知而無義,人有氣、有生、有知,亦且有義,故最為天下貴也。力不若牛,走不若馬,而牛馬為用,何也?曰:人能群,彼不能群也。人何以能群?曰:分。分何以能行?曰:義。故義以分則和,和則一,一則多力,多力則彊,彊則勝物;故宮室可得而居也。故序四時,裁萬物,兼利天下,無它故焉,得之分義也。〔……〕君者,善群也。群道當,則萬物皆得其宜,六畜皆得其長,群生皆得其命。故養長時,則六畜育;殺生時,則草木殖;政令時,則百姓一,賢良服。

> Water and fire have *qi* but no life, plants have life but no cognition, animals have cognition but no sense of proper order. Humans have *qi*, life, cognition and a sense of proper order. Therefore, they are the most precious in the world. They are not as strong as oxen and not as fast as horses, and yet oxen and horses serve them. Why? I argue: humans are able to organize themselves in groups, those others don't. So how are humans

---

35   *Xunzi* 17: 319 ("Tian lun" 天論).

able to organize themselves in groups? I argue: by differentiation. So how can differentiation be implemented? I argue: by a sense of proper order. And so, when differentiation is based on a sense of proper order, harmony is achieved. Harmony in turn leads to unity, unity leads to greater strength, greater strength leads to power and with power one controls all kinds of things, and that is how one can live in palaces and houses. Hence that one can arrange things according to the four seasons, regulate the ten thousand kinds of things, and in every respect benefit all under heaven is just due to this one reason: it has been achieved by a differentiating sense of proper order. [...] The ruler is the one who is good at organizing humans in groups. If the method of forming humans in groups is properly executed, then the ten thousand kinds of things will all obtain what is appropriate for them, the six domestic animals will all obtain their growth, and the grouped living beings will all obtain their full life spans.[36]

Although the *Xunzi* makes frequent use of the term *he* (in contrast to the *Mengzi* 孟子, where this term appears only three times),[37] it is mostly used as a component term in combination with, or as a parallel to, other terms and rarely carries its own conceptual weight.[38] In this passage, however, it has its own conceptual value as a particular quality of a group of humans (as opposed to groups of plants or animals) that forms a unity on the basis of diversification. Harmony denotes a situation where diversity is ordered in a way that each different thing has its appropriate place in relation to the others according to the human sense of proper order, which allows and demands hierarchically structured diversification. Xunzi's notion of *he* thus conceptualizes a unity that is not based on an intrinsic original centeredness of diverse non-related components, as in the *Zhong yong* above, but on a sense of proper order that creates hierarchically related differentiations.

---

36 *Xunzi* 9: 163 ("Wang zhi" 王制).

37 See Chan 2011 for a most interesting attempt at explaining *Mengzi*'s critical attitude towards *he*.

38 For the differentiation between conceptual terms that are used as single and independent terms that carry their own semantic weight and "component terms" that mostly occur in combination with other terms, see Gentz, forthcoming.

Xunzi thus introduces a sense of proper order (*yi* 義) as a new human basis for the realization of *he* 和 in the human realm in a theory that takes a hierarchical order of the constituents of the composite whole as the highest form of equability *(ping* 平) and thus continues to correlate *he* and *ping*. in his very own way.[39] Roetz shows quite convincingly how Xunzi's idea of achieving "harmony" (*he* 和) by means of *yi* 義 (which Roetz translates as "justice") is peculiar to this one thinker and can only be adequately explained within his own philosophical system of thought.[40] Harmony in the *Xunzi* becomes part of its philosophy on the human condition.

The basic structure denoted by the term *he* is still present in this usage; it implies a composite whole that is perfect and can be appreciated by humans when its constituents are arranged according to particular principles of composition. In the *Xunzi*'s case, the composite whole is human society, the constituents are the members of society with different capabilities, and the relationship between these constituents, the principle of composition, is the diversification of humans according to a sagely sense of proper order.

In the *Zhuangzi* 莊子 the composite whole is mostly the unity of Heaven, and the constituents are often *yin* and *yang* in the cosmological realm. In the human realm it is mostly differences created by one-sided views, often based on what the *Zhuangzi* regards as random analytical and linguistic categorical differentiations, so much so that the constituents appear in many cases as artificial constructs. The principle of composition is the insight of the sage into the actual unity behind those supposed oppositions and their relative co-dependence and complementarity:

> 物固有所然，物固有所可。無物不然，無物不可。故為是舉莛與楹，厲與西施，恢恑憰怪，道通為一。其分也，成也；其成也，毀也。凡物無成與毀，復通為一。唯達者知通為一，為是不用而寓諸庸。庸也者，用也；用也者，通也；通也者，得也。適得而幾矣。因是已。已而不知其然，謂之道。勞神明為一，而不知其同也，謂

---

39   See also Roetz 2015: 320–321.

40   Roetz 2015.

之朝三。何謂朝三？曰狙公賦芧，曰：「朝三而莫四。」眾狙皆怒。曰：「然則朝四而莫三。」眾狙皆悅。名實未虧，而喜怒為用，亦因是也。是以聖人和之以是非，而休乎天鈞，是之謂兩行。

All kinds of things certainly have what makes them what they are and certainly have what allows them to be in a certain way. No kind of thing is not what it is and no kind of thing is not in a certain way. In this respect choosing a haulm or a beam, a loathsome person or someone as beautiful as Xi Shi, things that are vast, crooked, fiddled or strange—from the perspective of the *dao* they are all connected as one. Their dividedness *(fen* 分*)* is their formation; their formation is their demise. In general, things have no formation and demise; they turn to their connection as one. Only those with insight know how to connect them as one. In doing so they do not make use of them but go with their [intrinsic] applications. [Intrinsic] applications lead to making [adequate] use of something; making [adequate] use of something leads to connecting it [as one], and connecting it [as one] leads to attaining [unity]. Properly attaining [unity] leads to becoming subtle. And following this [approach] leads to ceasing [to be "so"]. When one ceases [to be "so"] and yet does not know about it, this is called the *dao*. But to trouble oneself with creating a unity without understanding how things are the same is called "Three in the morning." What does "Three in the morning" mean? It is said that there once was a monkey keeper who was feeding chestnuts to his monkeys and said to them: "You'll get three in the morning and four in the evening." Thereupon all the monkeys were furious. So he said, "Alright then, you'll get four in the morning and three in the evening," whereupon all the monkeys were delighted. The relation of name and reality had not been impaired while furiousness and delight were made [adequate] use of—this is also following this [same approach]. For this reason, the sages settle *(he* 和*)* this with affirmation and negation while resting in heavenly balance. This is called twofold acting.[41]

---

41   *Zhuangzi* 2: 15–16 ("Qiwu lun" 齊物論).

Like the *Xunzi*, the *Zhuangzi* in this passage assumes that a harmonious unity is inseparable from diversification (*fen* 分), and yet the *Zhuangzi* regards diversification just as an artificial means to deal with things in the world according to circumstances—they are not features of the things themselves, as things belong together in one unity. Harmony is created by sages by using affirmation and negation, thus artificially dividing them in order to regulate them appropriately is something only sages understand. In all these respects the *Zhuangzi* seems to be quite close to the *Xunzi*. But the two texts clearly differ when it comes to human nature. According to the *Zhuangzi*, true harmony emerges from a human nature that is not misled by the one-sided domination of a dividing mind but that is balanced between insight and placidity, which should mutually nourish each other.

> 古之治道者，以恬養知；知[42]生而無以知為也，謂之以知養恬。知與恬交相養，而和理出其性。夫德，和也；道，理也。德無不容，仁也；道無不理，義也；義明而物親，忠[43]也。

> Those in antiquity who practiced the *dao* nourished their insight by means of placidity. Insight came into being but nothing was done just by means of insight—this is called using insight to nourish placidity. Thus insight and placidity mutually nourished each other, and harmony and patterned order came forth from their natures. As a matter of fact, true virtue provides harmony and the *dao* provides patterned order. When true virtue embraces everything, then there is true benevolence; when the *dao* patterns everything, then there is true righteousness. If true righteousness is bright and all kinds of things get close, there is true loyalty.[44]

The chapter "Shan xing" 繕性 cited above offers a counter-narrative to the typical Confucian narrative of how the sage kings of antiquity established

---

42 Some editions do not have this character: the CHANT series or Qian Mu's 莊子纂箋 for example. But the character is there in Wang Xianqian's edition that I follow here, it is also in Guo Qingfan's *Zhuangzi jishi* 莊子集釋.

43 Some editions have 中 here instead of 忠. I follow Wang Xianqian's edition.

44 *Zhuangzi* 16:135 ("Shan xing" 繕性).

culture and virtues out of a disordered original state of humanity. According to the *Zhuangzi,* harmony was achieved not by virtues based on insight alone (this is rather how, according to the *Zhuangzi*'s narrative, it was destroyed by the Confucian heroes) but by a balance of insight and placidity which are given here as the two main constitutive components of a perfect practice of the *dao* with all its true virtues, of which true righteousness is but one, which leads to harmony and patterned order as expressions of human's true nature. The harmonious relationship of these two constituents is that of mutual nourishment.

Looking at the texts discussed above, we thus find the term *he* used to describe the productive tension of diverse constituents that enrich and drive

- the dynamics of a balanced composite whole;
- the effect of a perfectly composed whole;
- the commonality of non-related different constituents rooted in a common original center;
- the hierarchical relationship between separated constituents in a composite whole ordered according to the human sense of righteousness,
- or the ineffable harmony of a whole that humans' distorted analytical minds obsessively divide into constituents of a composite whole. These constituents are inseparable and permanently create and nourish each other.

If we look at the way the term *he* 和 is used in other, slightly later, Warring States and Han texts in which it appears more frequently, such as in the *Guanzi* 管子, *Lüshi chunqiu* 呂氏春秋, *Huainanzi* 淮南子, and *Chunqiu fanlu* 春秋繁露 (Luxuriant dew of the *Spring and Autumn Annals*), we find that it continues to describe, in most cases, this threefold relationship between the composite whole, its constituents and their respective relationships or principles of composition that we found described in different ways in the texts discussed above. And as in those texts, it refers to different aspects of this complex nexus with further distinctions.

In order to address and classify the manifold aspects and connotations of *he* in this broader range of early texts, the next section will focus on the different terms used in early texts to cover the semantic field of harmony and the ways they are related to *he* in lexicographical definitions and binominal constructions.

1.2 Terms of Harmony

The early glossary *Erya* 爾雅 (Approaching correct meanings) and dictionary *Shuowen jiezi* 說文解字 (Explanation of simple graphs and analysis of composite characters) support the impression that a broad repertoire of more or less specific terms belong to the semantic field of "harmony" and that *he* 和 is the most generic term under which the others are subsumed.[45]

---

45 The *Erya* uses *he* 和 in several instances as a definiens, with the central entry in the "Shi gu" 釋
   詁 chapter: 諧，輯，協，和也，關關，噰噰，音聲和也，愲，爕，和也。 (*Erya* 1: 31; see
   also 3: 131, 7: 194–196, 8: 198). The term *tiao* 調 does not appear in the *Erya*.
        In the *Shuowen jiezi*, *he* 和 appears in seven cases as a direct gloss (誠、調、韻、爕、
   曆、怡、溆, all are glossed 和也) and in thirteen cases as a crucial part of the definition (鮨：
   樂和鮨也 *xie*: music being harmonious; 誾：和說而諍也 *yin*: gently admonishing someone;
   講：和解也 *jiang*: calmly explaining; 糂：以米和羹也 *san*: using rice to season a soup; 糟：
   糜和也 *tan*: seasoned gruel; 腼：面和也 *mian*: a harmonious facial expression; 駤：馬和也
   xie: a well-adjusted horse; 垸：以黍和灰而鬢也 *huan*: to use lacquer and mix [*he*] it with ash
   to coat something; 䁖：和田也 *rou*: to fertilize [*he*] fields; 協：同心之和 *xie*: the harmony of
   like-mindedness; 勰：同思之和 *xie*: the harmony of minds thinking alike; 協：眾之同和也
   xie: the multitude being together in harmony; 輯：車和輯也 *ji*: carriages gathering together).
        The relation of *tiao* 調 to *he* 和 is noticeable in the *Shuowen* not only because it is directly glossed
   with *he* (調：和也), but because it is used in turn to define the two earlier variants of *he*: 鮨：調也
   and 盉：調味也. *Tong* 同 and *he* 合, both terms related to the semantic field of "harmony," are also
   terms which are used more often than other characters to define words belonging to their semantic
   fields in the *Shuowen jiezi* (共：同也。昆：同也。捆：同也。劦：同力也。協：同心之和。
   勰：同思之和。協：眾之同和也。會：合也。同：合會也。佮：合也。緣：合也), but
   they are not used as frequently as *he* 和. *Xie* 諧, a term rarely used on its own, almost always appearing
   only as a component in a compound, also used as the most common modern Chinese expression for
   harmony as a compound with *he* (*hexie* 和諧), is only used twice in the *Shuowen jiezi*—in a mutual
   explanation with *he* 詥 (諧：詥也。詥：諧也).

He 和 is frequently used as an element in compounds. These compounds give us some insight into possible connotations that are associated with the term. The following terms (in the footnotes below) are some of the compounds in which we find *he* in early texts applied to the realms of humans, affairs, objects or more abstract concepts;[46] in word classes of verbs, adverbs, adjectives, and nouns; connoting semantic fields of concord and accord,[47] unity,[48] equality, equilibrium and balance,[49] peace, calmness, tranquility, firmness and stability,[50] togetherness,[51] beauty, smoothness and grace,[52] and so forth. *He* 和 is most often combined with *tiao* 調 (perfectly balanced), but it is also often associated with *an* 安 (peaceful, tranquil, secure), *shi* 適 (appropriate and suitable, as in "harmony emerges from appropriateness" 和出於適),[53] *dang* 當 (equal, appropriate, adequate, as in "harmony is born from adequacy" 和生於當),[54] *shi* 時 (timing) and so forth. No other character from the broader semantic field of "harmony" is used in early Chinese texts in so many compounds as the character *he*.

The semantic fields in which the above *he*-compounds appear denote in most cases the relationships between the constituents of the composite whole: "concord and accord" describes an effective working relationship in regard to an operative mode; "unity" describes their relative difference within the whole; "peace, calmness, tranquility, firmness and stability" describes the effect of their relationships on the whole; "togetherness"

---

46 Guo Qi (2000: 455–462) provides a very helpful discussion of the meanings of 和 in these different realms, but his conclusion simplifies his findings by boiling it down to the basic meaning of *hexie* 和諧, which is analytically a little dissatisfying.

47 和合，合和，調和，和調，和協，協和，和順，和洽，和龤，雍和。

48 和同，同和，和通。

49 中和，和平，平和，均和。

50 和平，平和，和安，安和，和靜，和寧，固和。

51 和應，和親，和輯。

52 美和，滑和，惠和，雍和。

53 *Lüshi chunqiu* 5.2: 255 ("Da yue" 大樂).

54 *Guiguzi* 12: 189 ("Fu yan" 符言).

describes the principle that holds them together; "beauty, smoothness and grace" describes the aesthetic effect of their composition. Compounds of *he* thus do not in general refer to harmony as a whole or the individual elements; rather, they specify the second of the threefold aspects, namely the different aspects of the relationships between the constituents of harmony.

In order to get a sense of the interchangeability of terms that can denote different (or identical) aspects of harmony in early texts, I have looked at an example that allows us to see the terms in a comparative light, namely the ways the perfect relationship between *yin* 陰 and *yang* 陽 (which I assume to be conceived as harmonious) are expressed in six early Chinese texts that reflect on this relationship: the *Zhuangzi, Lüshi chunqiu, Huainanzi, Chunqiu fanlu, Hanshi waizhuan* 韓詩外傳 (External commentary on the Han version of the *Odes)* and *Baihu tong* 白虎通 (Comprehensive debates in the White Tiger Pavilion).[55] If we take the different terms that are used in these texts to designate the perfect relationship between *yin* and *yang*, we arrive at a repertoire in which *he* 和 figures quite prominently. It occurs in nine of the thirty-five terms and expressions that I found.[56]

---

55 Since the list of text passages is too long and disrupts the reading flow I have deleted it from this publication. An author's version with the examples included is available from the following websites: https://www.pure.ed.ac.uk/admin/workspace/personal/family/researchoutput/, https://www.researchgate.net/profile/Joachim_Gentz/contributions, or https://idcore.academia.edu/JoachimGentz.

56 和 (in harmony), 調 (in balance), 調和 (in balanced harmony), 和調 (in harmonious balance), 成和 (completing harmony), 和靜 (harmoniously tranquil), 相照 (illuminating each other)、相蓋 (surpassing each other)、相治 (regulating each other), 調適相似 (in appropriate balance and resembling each other), 適 (properly suited), 宜 (fitted), 變 (in change), 化 (in transformation), 變化 (in change and transformation), 次 (in proper sequence), 相錯 (united in an interlocked mode), 錯行 (acting by turns), 錯合 (united in an interlocked mode), 錯氛 (in interlocked perfusion), 交 (in intercourse), 合和 (in united harmony), 和合 (harmoniously united), 合 (united), 合別 (uniting and separating), 同氣相動 (moving each other with their congenial *qi*), 和平 (harmoniously balanced), 平 (balanced), 相接 (connecting to each other), 交接 (mutually connected), 嘔 (belching out), 無為 (not acting), 會 (meeting), 往來 (coming and going together), 中和 (in centred harmony).

The semantic field defined by these terms and expressions can partly be divided into the same basic aspects of harmony that we also found in our analysis of *he* 和-compounds above: concord and accord,[57] unity,[58] equality, equilibrium and balance,[59] peace, calmness, tranquility, firmness and stability,[60] togetherness (categories of mutual complement might also belong to this). The aspect of beauty, smoothness, and grace is missing, probably because *yin* and *yang* are regarded as abstract concepts and not as concrete objects.

The other part of the semantic field is specific to the *yin-yang* relation, the harmony of which is conceived as being derived from a permanent mutual transformation of opposites: mutual complement,[61] process of constant movement, change and transformation,[62] process of production and creation.[63]

In this part of the semantic field, the character *he* plays almost no role, probably because *he* is used to describe harmonious states, not harmonious processes. We rarely find *he* used to describe harmonious changes and the harmonious succession of the five phases (*wuxing* 五行) or of the four seasons (*sishi* 四時) either.[64]

1.3 The Semantic Field of Terms for Harmony

The repertoire above refers to different aspects of *yin yang*, which could all be subsumed under the broad term "harmony." Our systematic analysis of

---

57 和，調適相似，適，宜。
58 合和，和合，合，合別，同氣相動。
59 中和，調，調和，和調，和平，平。
60 和靜，和平，平。
61 成和，相照、相蓋、相治，相錯，錯行，錯合，錯氣，交，交接，相接。
62 變，化，變化，次，合別，同氣相動，會，往來。
63 嘔，無為。
64 The expression *sishi he* 四時和 occurs a few times in the early literature, but nowhere do we find the formulation *wuxing he* 五行和. Expressions like *hehua* 和化 or *hebian* 和變 (harmonious change or transformation) only occur once in a very late Warring States text (chapter "Jie Lao" 解老 of the *Han Feizi* 韓非子) and a few times in Han dynasty texts.

different usages of *he* 和 (and comparable terms denoting "harmony") in a handful of early texts has already revealed the range of possible meanings behind this/these term/s. Looking at more textual examples, an analysis of which would go beyond the scope of this chapter, I have classified my findings systematically into nine different basic perspectives on the threefold structure of the composite whole, its constituents and their mutual relationships or principles of composition, each of which include further sub-specifications. The meaning of the term "proper" that I use in this list is determined by the types of ideal order envisioned in different texts.[65]

1. The content of the composite whole:
   a) cosmic, b) social, c) political, d) sensual (food, music, beauty), e) bodily health, f) emotions, g) ritual, h) text, i) weather/harvest.

2. The structure and principles of the order of the composite whole:
   a) timeliness (sequential order), b) proper place (spatial order), c) proper relationship between the constituents, d) proper cultivation of each constituent.

3. Individual constituents:
   a) cosmic (Heaven and Earth 天地, sun and moon 日月, stars 星, wind and rain 風雨, cold and warm 寒暑, hard and soft 剛柔, four seasons 四時, *yin* and *yang* 陰陽, five phases 五行, *qi* 氣), b) divine (all numinous beings 百神), c) social (superiors and inferiors 上下, fathers and sons 父子, rulers and ministers 君臣, young and old 長幼, people 民, the hundred clans 百姓, five relationships 五教, three branches of kin 三族, family 家, marital relationships 夫婦), d) spatial (inner and outer 外内, distant and near 遠近), e) political (All under Heaven 天下, state 邦, capital 國, governance 政, numerous

---

65 Chan (2011: 43) points out two different kinds of such orders that in his view operate on a different logic and lead to different conceptions of harmony, one that is based on categories of classifications which follow a hierarchical order which he associates with, and in my view unnecessarily reduces to, musical harmony. The other one, which he associates with (and reduces to) cooking, is an order of elements of equal status. However, my analysis seems to prompt the conclusion that there are more models of harmonious order than just these two and they are not connected to particular metaphorical discourses.

officers 庶官, lords 諸侯, three armies 三軍, orders 令), f) personal (heart 心, oneself 身), g) sensual (five colors五色, five sounds 五音, five tones 五聲, five tastes 五味, music 樂, soup 羹), h) bodily and psychological (blood and physical energies 血氣, meridians 經, muscles and blood vessels 筋脈, five viscera 五藏, emotions 情, joy and anger 喜怒, aspirations 志, heart-mind 心), i) things (all kind of things 萬物).

4. The relation of the constituents within the composite whole:
a) each constituent has its proper time/place, b) each constituent is separated from the other, c) each constituent has a place/function according to its capability/talent/social status/social role/office, d) each constituent has its proper spatial/timely ruling domains/phases (according to *yin yang, wuxing* and other orders), e) there is an equilibrium between all constituents (*ping* 平, *zhong* 中), f) the constituents provide a repertoire from which they are chosen by deliberating the circumstances.

5. The way the constituents came to be at their proper time/place:
a) following the ritual order of sage kings, b) following the order of the ruler, c) by conviction and agreement, d) by human virtues (such as a sense of righteousness), e) by the order of the law, f) by themselves.

6. The way the constituents match:
a) corresponding to each other, b) complementing each other, c) supporting/nourishing/benefitting each other, d) in exchange with each other, e) operating separately, f) cooperating with each other, g) agreeing with each other, h) being peaceful and free of conflict, i) united in an effort towards a common goal, j) providing independent and equally important options.

7. The way constituents are made to fit the composition:
a) tuning the constituents, b) bringing them to an agreement, c) weighing them against circumstances.

8. The effect of the composite whole:
a) peace, b) balance of cosmic forces, c) political unity, d) political/military strength, e) wealth/good harvests, f) social order, g) blessing/luck/success, h) health/longevity.

9. The quality of the composite whole:
   a) unity, b) balance, c) order.

All these various aspects may be covered by the term "harmony/harmonic/
harmonize," yet we miss exactly these systematic differences if we cover all
of them indiscriminately by using this one term only (as most of us do
and most translations in the last decades have done),[66] which has led to
providing identical (*tong*) translations instead of appropriate (*he*) ones.

The use of terms in early Chinese texts does not lend itself easily to
systematic analyses and the locating of keywords with a fixed meaning.[67]
Although the contexts often make it very clear which systematic meaning
is intended when a particular term is used, as we have demonstrated in
our text analyses in 1.1 above, the terminology in most texts does not
consistently follow the systematic differentiations of the thoughts expressed
throughout the text. Rather, it often follows literary principles of symmetry,
parallelism, opposition and variation. This has an important impact on any
analysis of Chinese keyword terms. It is precisely because order, peace and
harmony were central concerns of early Chinese thinkers that numerous
terms were used to denote various aspects of these concepts. But because
these terms were not applied consistently, they have never gained the
status of systematic or ideological keywords. Many of these terms, and in
particular *he* 和, were emphasized as central philosophical terms in later
texts and were often highlighted as pivotal concepts that describe the
highest achievements and values of specific philosophical discourses, in

---

66 Both the translation of the *Huainanzi* by Major, Queen, Meyer and Roth (2010) as well as
the translation of the *Lüshi chunqiu* by Knoblock and Riegel (2000), for example, consistently
translate the character *he* 和 as "harmony/harmonic/harmonize." The manifold nuances of that
character that we still find adequately reflected in early sinological translations have been fully
subjugated to the hegemonic harmony discourse.

67 I am grateful to Li Wai-yee for having pointed out to me the important fact that "one can have
a rich semantic field without 'systematic analyses'—i.e., one can 'locate keywords' even if they
have many variant meanings—indeed, variations may be the precondition for the making of
a keyword."

particular in the Neo-Confucian traditions.[68] And yet, in Chinese meta-reflexive self-reflections up to the 20th century, none of these terms ever arrived at the same conceptual level as other keyword terms such as *li* 禮 (ritual), *qi* 氣, *dao* 道, *xiao* 孝 (filial piety), or *zhong* 中 (center/middle/mean) that have been used to define Chinese cultural identity. There is not even a classical text focusing solely on *he* (a *Hejing* 和經, for example), or any early Chinese essay that I am aware of.

It is all the more surprising to find "harmony" in so many Western and Eastern accounts of Chinese (and other Eastern) cultures from the early 20th century onward as one of the key conceptual terms used to define the nature, character, spirit, and essence of Chinese culture, as pointed out in the introduction to this volume. In the following part, I will therefore discuss why the use of the term *he* 和 changed in the 20th century and how and when "harmony" became one of the most central and popular concepts in many analyses of Chinese culture, philosophy, religion and society.

2. Chinese Harmony in the 20th Century

2.1 China and Japan

Let us first turn to China and Japan. In China, the concept of "harmony" does not play a strong discursive role during the late 19th and early 20th centuries, when discussions on Chinese culture or the Chinese character were intense. If we look at this from the perspective of Chinese philosophical discourse, for example, we can observe that it does not play the role of an analytical term in the early histories of philosophy by Hu Shi

---

68   The term *he* 和 is not used once in the Buddhist sutras that are most central to Chinese culture, like the *Heart Sūtra* (*Prajñāpāramitāhṛdaya*/般若波羅蜜多心經) and the *Diamond Sūtra* (*Vajracchedikā Prajñāpāramitā Sūtra*/金剛般若波羅蜜多經). It occurs fifteen times in the 69,384 characters long *Lotus Sūtra* (*Saddharma Puṇḍarīka Sūtra*/ 妙法蓮華經), a negligible percentage of .02% of the text.

胡適 (1919) and Feng Youlan 馮友蘭 (1931). That it is nowhere discussed in the first Chinese history of Chinese philosophy *(Zhongguo zhexue shi* 中國哲學史) published by Xie Wuliang 謝无量 (1884–1964) in 1916, shows that it did not play any role in the Japanese discourse about Chinese philosophy either, as Xie's history is copied from Takase Takejirō's 高瀨武次郎 (1868–1950) *Shina tetsugakushi* 支那哲學史 from 1910, in which the term is also not discussed.[69] In Uno Tetsuto's 宇野哲人 (1875–1974) even more famous *Shina tetsugakushi kōwa* 支那哲學史講話 from 1914, it also does not play a prominent role. Instead, Xie Wuliang emphasizes the importance of the concept of the center (*zhong* 中), which according to him was discovered during the times of Yao and Shun, as the highest ethical norm.[70]

In Japan, the term *wa* 和 plays a much more significant role as a cultural keyword.[71] It has been used as a self-designation for Japan and the Japanese since it replaced the earlier homophonous graphic pejorative transcription *wa* 倭 meaning "dwarf" or "submissive people" and was assigned a special place as the most important of seventeen moral guidelines defined in the *Nihon shoki* 日本書紀 (*Nihongi* 日本紀) in 720 CE,[72] a guideline that has played a crucial role in Japanese philosophy, ethics, religion and politics since. It therefore seems unlikely that the concept of "harmony" was taken

---

69   On the history of Chinese histories of philosophy, see Gentz 2012.

70   Xie Wuliang 1916: 15. As with most of his contents, Xie copied this from Takase's history in which Takase writes that the concept of the center was invented by the sage kings Yao 堯 and Shun 舜. Takase in turn took this from Zhou Rudeng 周汝登 (1547–1629), who in his *Shengxue zongzhuan* 聖學宗傳 (1605) claimed that the sage king Yao had discovered (*jie* 揭) the character *zhong* and that with this the true transmission of the Way (*daotong* 道統) had begun (蠡測曰: 帝堯首揭中字。斯道統之真宗所自啟也, Zhou Rudeng 1989: 49). See Gentz (2012) for a more detailed analysis.

71   See Wierzbicka 1997: 248–254.

72   Triplett 2006: 179. The first article says: "Harmony is to be valued, and an avoidance of wanton opposition to be honoured. All men are influenced by class-feelings, and there are few who are intelligent. Hence there are some who disobey their lords and fathers, or who maintain feuds with the neighbouring villages. But when those above are harmonious and those below are friendly, and there is concord in the discussion of business, right views of things spontaneously gain acceptance. Then what is there which cannot be accomplished!" See *Nihongi*, vol. 2: 128–133.

over from Japan in early 20th century Chinese discourses on the Chinese national character.

2.2 European "Harmony" and the Orient

That harmony is a concept essential to Chinese culture is a view that, it seems, became firmly established in Europe and the United States only in the late 1920s and 1930s. Neither in the earlier missionary reports on China nor in the detailed and thorough analyses of China provided by the enlightenment philosophers does the concept of harmony play any significant role. Prior to the late 1920s, it was used here and there in literature on China, especially in translations of Chinese texts (mostly used to translate the character *he* 和), and sometimes it was mentioned in combination with the term center (*zhong* 中), reflecting the importance that this term had in the opening passage of the *Zhong yong* 中庸. But it was never used in a general or meta-reflexive way as a systematic and analytical term. It never formed a part of the many essentialist statements about China in the 18th or 19th centuries. Chinese terms that nowadays are consistently translated as "harmony/harmonious" were translated into various European terms in these early works, which described matters in a much more critical and differentiated manner.[73] Even Leibniz (1646–1716) used the term "harmony" in his extensive discussions on Chinese culture and philosophy only when he subsumed something Chinese under his own concept of "pre-established harmony" (*prästabilierte Harmonie*). In the works of Herder (1744–1803), Hegel (1770–1831), and Schelling

---

73 Terms and expressions such as "concord," "accord," "balance," "combinations," "compounds," "evenly balanced," "just," "impartial," "equitable," "state of equilibrium," "regularly arranged order," "united/unitary/unity," "monism," "junction," and "inseparableness," are used by these authors (in German: "Einklang," "Übereinstimmung," "Vereinigung," "Verschmelzen," "Anpassung," "Zusammenwirken," "Willfährigkeit," "Ganzsicht," "Angleichung," "Gleichklang," "Ausgeglichenheit," "Verbundenheit/Verbundensein," "parallel," "konform," "Organismus," "Gleichung," "Ineinander," "Einbettung," "gleicher Pulsschlag," "Nachahmung," "Einheit," "Einheitlichkeit," "Entsprechung," and, sometimes, "Harmonie").

(1775–1854), the notion of "harmony" is absent in their discussions on China. In missionary literature, such as DuBose's *Dragon, Image, and Demon* (1886),[74] Edkins' *Religion in China* (1877), Martin's *The Chinese, their Education, Philosophy, and Letters* (1880), Smith's famous *Chinese Characteristics* (1890), or Gorst's *China* (1899), the term is absent as well.[75] In his China-friendly *Letters from John Chinaman* (1901), Dickinson does not use it either.[76]

In the early sinological literature, the term also plays no role. It is not prominent in Brandt's *Die chinesische Philosophie und der Staats-Confucianismus* (1898) where it occurs only in two passages of his *Zhong yong* 中庸 translations,[77] Carus' elaborate analyses of Chinese cosmology (1902 [orig. 1896] and 1907),[78] Parker's *China and Religion* (1905),[79] Giles' *China and the Chinese* (1902) or his *Civilization of China* (1911), and Soothill's *The Three Religions of China* (1913).[80] Even De Groot makes almost no use of it in his book on *Universismus* in 1918,[81] a book that is full of descriptions of Chinese concepts of concord and the interplay of cosmic forces.

Not the study of Chinese culture, it seems, but two developments independent from it (and from each other) have led to the momentous circumstances under which the notion of "harmony" came to be associated with China in the late 1920s. On the one hand, it was the career of this

---

74   He uses the term "harmonious" twice (pp. 62, 91).

75   John Ross (1852–1915), a missionary from the United Free Church of Scotland, is an exception. In his *Original Religion of China* (1909) he uses the term "harmony" seventeen times on 344 pages (pp. 47, 86, 101, 137, 166, 171, 172, 184, 213, 222, 237, 254, 285, 286, 287, 304, 305), mostly in his translations of Chinese texts, but not once the adjective "harmonious."

76   The term only appears once in the whole book to describe the inability of Westerners to be in harmony with themselves. Dickinson 1920 (1901): 20.

77   Brandt 1898: 18, 25–26.

78   Carus 1902 (1896) and 1907.

79   Soothill 1913: 16, 23, 25, 286, and 291.

80   Not a single occurrence.

81   I found only four instances of the terms "harmonisch/e" in his text translations on pp. 34, 131, 314, 375, and not a single occurrence of the term "Harmonie." His student Erich Schmitt uses the term "Harmonie" several times in his 42-page PhD thesis, "Daoist Monasteries in the Light of Universism" (1916), but again without any analytical weight (pp. 9, 25, 27, 32, 33, 34).

notion in the parlance of European languages where the terms "harmony/ Harmonie/harmonie" advanced to become downright vogue expressions in the late 19th and early 20th centuries after an initial blossoming in Hermetic and Mesmeric circles; on the other hand, an increasingly broad Western interest in Asian philosophies and religions that had arisen in the late 19th century also contributed to this association.

During the 17th century, "harmony" was a central official term in confessional politics' regulations of theological quarrels relating to orthodoxy and heterodoxy in Brandenburg-Prussia. Because one of the major issues of these quarrels was the repudiation of Spiritistic and Pietistic movements by academic theologians,[82] it is all the more striking that the term "harmony" was prominently used by exactly these "deviant" movements around the end of the 18th and beginning of the 19th century in Europe. The notion gained an important impetus in the late 18th century through the new movement of Mesmerism which, after Franz Mesmer's (1734–1815) establishment of the *Société de l'Harmonie Universelle* in 1784, founded about thirty more Mesmerian "Harmonious Societies" in and beyond France,[83] all of which disappeared at one sweep with the onslaught of the French Revolution in 1789.[84] The term "harmony" had been established as a term bridging scientific mathematical principles, musical proportions, and theories of physical vibration and human perception in Jean-Philippe Rameau's (1683–1764) treatises on harmony,[85] in which he established harmony as a natural principle that equally guided the scientific, musical, physiological and psychological realms, a principle that fascinated the French *encyclopédistes* and must have appeared inspiring and

---

82 Taatz-Jacobi 2014: 243–244.

83 Among these, the "Harmonious Society" founded by Marquis de Pységur in Strasbourg in 1784, as well as those in Lyon and Ostend, were the most important. Further *Sociétés* were founded in Bordeaux, St. Etienne and Santo Domingo, and further lodges were founded in Germany (Karlsruhe, Heilbronn, Bremen, Berlin) and in Switzerland. Peter 2005 (plagiarized in Schmötzer 2015: 151).

84 Ellenberger 1970: 73.

85 *Traité de l'harmonie réduite à ses principes naturels* (Paris, 1722); *Nouveau système de musique théorique* (Paris, 1726); *Génération harmonique* (Paris, 1737); *Démonstration du principe de l'harmonie* (Paris, 1750).

highly attractive for Franz Mesmer as well.[86] Although the term "harmony" neither appears in the Bible (neither in the King James Version nor in other European translations that I am aware of) nor was it used in writings by Jakob Böhme (1575–1624) or by other authors that greatly influenced Pietism, it started at the beginning of the 19th century to appear frequently in self-designations of radical Pietistic movements. It was used in the name of the "Harmonists," founded by Johann Georg Rapp (1757–1847), who established settlements called "Harmony" and "New Harmony" in Pennsylvania in 1805,[87] and also in the name of a community called the "Schwaikheimerian Harmony of the Children of God" (*Schwaikheimer Harmonie der Kinder Gottes*), founded by Georg Friedrich Fuchs (1752–1821) in 1812, a community that emigrated to Russia between 1816 and 1819. At the same time, it was also used by theologians to defend Christianity. In these contexts, harmony served as an apologetic term that indicated a possible marriage between theology and a philosophy based on reason.[88] The term "harmony" was also frequently used by social utopians like Charles Fourier (1772–1837) or Wilhelm Christian Weitling (1808–1871).[89] Also, starting from the late 18th century, "Harmony Societies" were founded in German cities.[90] In contrast to the Mesmerist lodges, Pietistic movements, theological apologetics or socialist utopians, these were exclusive cultural associations of the upper middle class, which besides art, entertainment and reading also carried out philanthropic activities, reflecting a global trend.[91] Harmony, it seems, became a central conceptual

---

86   Charrak 2001. The appeal of defining natural laws of harmony prevails still in the works of Chambers (1844), Donders (1848), and Goldschmidt (1901).

87   Rapp adapted the name "Harmony" before Charles Fourier published his treatise on universal harmony ("Harmonie universelle") in 1803. Miles 2008: 180.

88   Seiler 1802; Gebhard 1817.

89   Fourier 1803 (fully quoted in Beecher 1986: 104–105) and 1808, Weitling 1842.

90   Leipzig 1776, Magdeburg 1783, Hamburg 1789, Mannheim 1803, Warendorf 1810, Würzburg 1812, Hamm 1816, Bochum 1817, Paderborn 1820, Iserlohn 1858 (founded 1802 "following the example of other cities" [*nach dem Beyspiele anderer Städte*], 1858 renamed).

91   In Quebec the *Harmonic Society/Société harmonique de Québec* was founded in 1819 as the first of several music societies that all shared the same name and besides the promotion of music and art also carried out philanthropic activities.

term in diverse Western discourses that attempted to establish new approaches promising to heal a rupture between faith, reason, and emotions that started to loom precariously in 18th-century Europe and America.

It was probably in the context of Mesmerism that the term "harmony" was for the first time associated with Asia. Joseph Ennemoser (1787–1854) wrote in 1819 that the people in the Orient (*im Morgenlande*) lived in sacred harmony with nature (*in heiliger Harmonie mit der Natur*).[92] However, during the 19th century, the strong interest in Asia by Mesmerists such as Ennemoser and Karl Joseph Hieronymus Windischmann (1775–1839), and later propagators of an "Oriental Renaissance" like Edgar Quinet (1803–1875),[93] was not yet systematically connected with the term "harmony."[94] Mesmerists, like most European intellectuals of that time, adopted cultural theories claiming that climatic influences caused cultural differences. According to those theories, warm climates generated passive, non-martial, acquiescent people and encouraged ecstatic, somnambulist states.[95] It is in the context of these theories, which over the course of the 19th century gained distinctly racist traits, that the first shaping of the idea that Asian religions are non-aggressive and peaceable can be traced.

Mesmerism and its concept of harmony were strongly received in Occultist, Spiritistic and Theosophic circles in the second half of the 19th century.[96] Added to that was the revival of Pythagorean concepts of harmony and more scientifically grounded approaches to define harmony.[97] This multi-faceted reinvigoration of the term "harmony" had a great influence on intellectual life and art production in Europe. Harmony is an

---

92 Ennemoser 1819: 185, also quoted in Baier 2009: 210. I am indebted to Maren Sziede for this reference.

93 Quinet 1857 (1842): 51–65, especially 54–56.

94 Baier 2009: 231–243.

95 Zotz 2000: 58–59; Baier 2009: 232.

96 Baier 2009: 277.

97 Keil 2012: 133–172. See also the works of Chambers (1844), Donders (1848) and Goldschmidt (written in 1893, published in 1901).

important theme in the titles of the impressionist paintings of Monet (1899) and Matisse (1908) as well as in their thoughts about art (Matisse, *Notes d'un Peintre*, 1908);[98] Cézanne, van Gogh, Gauguin, Delacroix and other Romantic artists, writers (Carlyle, Baudelaire) and thinkers used the word also as a central conceptual term in their theories of art; it was a key element in Symbolist aesthetic theory.[99] Harmony was also at the center of musical developments between 1908 and 1911 when, under the influence of Occultist and Theosophical writings, Schönberg (1874–1951) started to compose atonal and dissonant music against the traditional harmonic rules.[100] With Tagore (1861–1941) and Gurdjieff (1866/1877?[101]–1949) and his students, the term was further developed in intellectual circles and increasingly gained momentum. In the 1920s and 1930s the term "harmony" appeared in all areas of life almost as a vogue expression. Paintings of Kandinsky (1924), Devaux (1925) and Klee (1927, 1936) included "harmony" in their titles; Mondrian developed this term in the 1920s as a central utopian concept in his neoplasticism. The term can also be found in titles of films, especially those that were produced during the mid 1910s[102] and the early 1930s.[103] This was also reflected in academic research. In 1926, Hans Kayser published his

---

98   Matisse also often uses the term "accord." Flam 1995: 26.

99   Maurer 1985: 348–483, 350; Maurer 1998: 21–30.

100   Keil 2012: 186–197.

101   The exact year of Gurdjieff's birth is not known. Webb 1980: 25–26 gives a number of different years of birth (1872, 1873, 1874, 1877, 1886).

102   *Canned Harmony* (1912), *The Great Harmony* (1913), *Harmony and Discord* (1913), *Discord and Harmony* (1914), *Strangled Harmony* (1915), *Harmony in A Flat* (1916), *Life's Harmony* (1916), *Flat Harmony* (1917), *Hustle and Harmony* (1917).

103   *Red Hot Harmony* (1928), *Harmony Heaven* (1929), *The Harmony Boys* (1929), *Close Harmony* (1929), *Peace and Harmony* (1930), *A Feast of Harmony* (1930), *Harmony at Home* (1930), *Honeymoon Harmony* (1930), *Harmony Row* (1933), *Too Much Harmony* (1933), *Harlem Harmony* (1934), *Harmony Lane* (1935), *Key to Harmony* (1935), *Stolen Harmony* (1935), *Strangled Harmony* (1935), *Two Hearts in Harmony* (1935), *Harmony Parade* (1936), *Scenes in Harmony* (1936), *Hands in Harmony* (1936), etc. An equally striking accumulation occurs only in 2009: *A Perfect Harmony* (2009), *American Harmony* (2009), *Ballad of Broken Angels: Harmony* (2009), *DisHarmonyMatch.com* (2009), *Driving Mad Harmony* (2009), *Harmony and Me* (2009), *Harmony Town* (2009).

Morphologische Fragmente einer allgemeinen Harmonik as the first part of his new foundational research on harmonics. In the context of the 1920s, the term "harmony" also became a central building block in an increasingly positive discourse on China.

After a century of critical disenchantment,[104] Asian philosophies and religions gained a new positive meaning during the late 19th century in Mesmerist, Occultist, Theosophical and philosophical circles and through this reception also gained a wider, more positive resonance and generated broader interest in the West at the beginning of the 20th century. Following the great systematic translation enterprises of Max Müller (1823–1900), James Legge (1815–1897), Richard Wilhelm (1873–1930) and others, a new wave of reception of Chinese philosophy and religion can be detected in small intellectual and Lebensreform ("life-reform") circles in Europe. It was between the two world wars, however, that a massive orientation towards Asian religions and philosophies occurred, especially among young middle class intellectuals.[105] The cause of this new orientation was an alienation of many Europeans from European culture after the devastating destructions of the First World War (and in Germany the excessive inflation until 1923), all of which cast doubt on the model of Western culture as a whole. A cultural pessimism developed as a consequence of this, and European culture was criticized as aggressive, materialistic, and lacking in human and spiritual values. Asia in contrast appeared as a peace loving, spiritual culture and provided an important conceptual antipole for cultural critics such as Oswald Spengler (1880–1936) or Rudolf Christoph Eucken (1846–1926).[106]

---

104   Osterhammel 1998.

105   "Für eine kurze Zeit nach dem Ende des Ersten Weltkriegs hatten auf Asien zurückgreifende Lehren, die während der wilhelminischen Zeit nur eine beschränkte geistige Oberschicht und einige lebensreformerische Zirkel erreicht hatten, das Ohr der größeren Gruppen der Intelligenz, besonders unter der bürgerlichen Jugend(bewegung). Eine ‚neue Religiosität' entstand." Linse 1991: 335–336, quoted in Grasmück 2004: 26.

106   Eucken/Chang 1922; Lee 2003: 554–557.

The reception of Daoism in Germany tripled in these years; translations of the *Daode jing* 道德經 alone escalated from eleven in 1918 to thirty-two in 1927.[107] However, Asian religions and philosophies need to be regarded as only one facet of a rich spectrum of alternative religiosity that blossomed wildly, especially in the 1920s.[108] Like so many other trends that had existed already before the First World War in marginal and eccentric forms, Chinese philosophy and religion now moved into a more central position.[109]

It seems that a combination of two factors—the general dissemination of the term "harmony" on the one hand and the widened active interest in Asian philosophies and religions on the other—caused the term "harmony" in the 1930s to suddenly play a more significant role in the description and analysis of China.

Krause makes almost no use of the term "Harmonie" in his *Ju-Tao-Fo: die religiösen und philosophischen Systeme Ostasiens,* published in 1924 (the terms *zhonghe* or *he* are not listed in his index volume). In Hackmann's *Chinesische Philosophie,* Forke's *Gedankenwelt des chinesischen Kulturkreises* as well as in his *Geschichte der chinesischen Philosophie,* all three published in 1927, the term is only used occasionally in a descriptive manner, never as a systematic term.[110] Although Hackmann refers to Ernst Cassirer's concept of "mythical thinking"[111] (the second volume of Cassirer's *Philosophie der symbolischen Formen: Das mythische Denken* had just been published in

---

107 Grasmück 2004: 26, 47–50, 59–60, 123.

108 See the numerous examples in Linse 1983.

109 Makropoulos 1991.

110 See Hackmann 1927, pp. 26, 34, 61, 106, 204–205. In the discussions on mystical and natural philosophy as well as the chapter on *yin* and *yang* in his *Gedankenkreis,* Forke does not use the words "Harmonie/harmonisch" once. I have found "harmonische" only once, translating 和 (p. 89), it is not part of his own parlance. He also hardly uses the word in his *Geschichte* (pp. 35, 324), again mainly in translations of 和, which he translates variously as "Eintracht" (p. 57), "Vereinigung" (p. 267), "harmonisch" (pp. 293 [same passage as p. 89 in his *Gedankenkreis*], 318, 546) or "Harmonie" (pp. 152, 326, 340, 344).

111 Hackmann 1927: 35.

1925), and Cassirer had since 1902 been strongly attracted by Leibniz's concept of a "pre-established harmony" (*prästabilierte Harmonie)* to philosophically secure the unity of a universe and a consciousness that Cassirer considered to be split into manifold forms, the term does not play any role in Hackmann's writings on China.[112] Wolfram Eberhard also refers to Cassirer in his 1933 work on the cosmological speculation in China during the Han.[113] He does not, however, use the term "harmony" very often in this work;[114] the term plays a much more central role in his draft of the astronomical world view in ancient China from 1936.[115]

The first work in which I found a frequent systematic use of the term "harmony" to describe Chinese philosophy and religion is Herrlee Glessner Creel's (1905–1994) *Sinism* published in 1929. The term is equally central in Marcel Granet's (1884–1940) *La pensée chinoise* from 1934. This new usage of "harmony" as an analytical meta-reflexive term continued in later publications on China and was fully in vogue in 1950s discourses on China. Derk Bodde (1909–2003) discussed "harmony" as an independent philosophical topic in an essay on "Harmony and Conflict in Chinese Philosophy" from 1953;[116] Thomé H. Fang (Fang Dongmei 方東美, 1899–1977) defined Chinese mentality as a "cultivated sense of comprehensive harmony" in his *The Chinese View of Life: The Philosophy of Comprehensive Harmony in 1957*;[117] Gustav Mensching (1901–1978) classified the special

---

112　See Cassirer 1902, esp. pp. 398–399; see also the analysis in Moynahan 2014 (chap. 4, pp. 85–120), as well as Kajon 1988: 257.

113　Eberhard 1970: 12–13.

114　Eberhard 1970: 13, 14.

115　Eberhard 1970: 245.

116　In the middle of this essay (p. 54) he writes: "By now it should be evident that basic among Chinese thought patterns is the desire to merge seemingly conflicting elements into a unified harmony."

117　Fang 1957: ii: "Chinese mentality is best characterized by what I call the cultivated sense of comprehensive harmony;" and: "For several thousands of years, we Chinese have been thinking of these vital problems in terms of comprehensive harmony which permeates anything and everything" (Fang 1957: 18).

spirit (*Sondergeist*) of Chinese religions in his general classification of religions of 1959 as their orientation towards "cosmic harmony"; and in 1963 Helmuth von Glasenapp (1891–1963), in his discussion of "Chinesischer Universismus," which he regarded as one of the five world religions, constantly used the term "Harmonie," a term that De Groot, who invented the concept of Chinese universism in 1912, had not used at all.[118] The concept of "harmony" had thus been started to be fully established outside the China field as a wide spread normative and analytical term expressing quintessential features of Chinese philosophy and culture by the 1950s.

Conclusion

"Harmony", one of the central keywords used to explain Chinese culture, is a rather recent keyword that up until ninety years ago had never been used to denote the general character of Chinese culture. The word *he* 和 plays an important role in a number of early Chinese texts such as the *Shangshu*, the *Zhuangzi*, the *Guanzi*, the *Xunzi*, the *Huainanzi*, or the *Lüshi chunqiu*, but it is almost absent or plays a minor role in other central texts such as the *Lunyu* 論語, *Mengzi*, *Laozi* 老子, *Xiaojing* 孝經, *Gongyang zhuan* 公羊傳 and *Guliang zhuan* 穀梁傳 (Gongyang and Guliang commentaries on the *Spring and Autumn Annals*), *Heguanzi* 鶡冠子, *Shangjun shu* 商君書 (Book of Lord Shang), *Han Feizi* 韓非子, early military texts, *Chunqiu fanlu* with the exception of chapters 74 and 76), and *Liezi* 列子, and it does not appear in the *Gongsunlongzi* 公孫龍子. In most other texts, and even in great parts of the texts in parts of which it plays an important role, it is mainly used descriptively or as a component term in combination with, or

---

118   *Religion in China. Universism: A Key to the Study of Taoism and Confucianism* (1912). Two years earlier, in *The Religion of the Chinese* (1910), De Groot used the concept of "Universalistic Animism" instead of "Universism." In these lectures he uses the formulation "in harmony with" (the Tao, the classics, the world of the gods, the order of the universe) five times (pp. 62, 105, 107, 150, 169), but he does not refer to "harmony" as a Chinese concept.

as a parallel to, other terms and rarely carries its own conceptual weight. It never developed into an analytical or ideological key term, probably because too many terms occupied the same semantic field of harmony and were not consistently applied to denote identical meanings in the great variety of aspectual meanings that were discussed in all their differentiated nuances in relation to the complex issues of harmony, peace, proportion, balance, unity, accord etc. in pre-modern China.

The prominent Western use of the term "harmony" in the 20th century to epitomize Chinese culture seems not to have been grounded in Chinese texts in the first place. Nor was it taken over into the Western discourse from late 19th or early 20th century Chinese or Japanese self-reflexive discourses about Asia or China. Rather, it developed within an inner-European discourse as a general notion of anything that promised the healing of a disjointed reality. In the light of a "transcendental homelessness," it designated everything that allowed an insight into some new intact reality beyond the growing (and after WWI considered as absolute) contingency of cultural and moral values in Europe.[119] The expanding notion of "harmony" encountered Chinese philosophies and religions in the late 1920s, just in the very moment when these were so widely received that they were perceived as a possible new intellectual and spiritual home of a new Europe and could thus be conceived as part of the new European visions of harmony. This new image of China in turn started to shape the Chinese understanding of their own pre-modern terms for "harmony" and had a great influence on Chinese discussions about the character of their own broken national culture, perhaps for the very same reasons that the term became increasingly prominent in late Warring States and early Han China as a response to a broken world.

---

119   Makropoulos 1991.

Bibliography

Ames, Roger T. 2005. "Collaterality in Early Chinese Cosmology: An Argument for Confucian Harmony (*he* 和) as *Creatio In Situ*." *Taiwan Journal of East Asian Studies* 2.1: 43–70.

Baier, Karl. 2009. *Meditation und Moderne: Zur Genese eines Kernbereichs moderner Spiritualität in der Wechselwirkung zwischen Westeuropa, Nordamerika und Asien*. Vol. 1. Würzburg: Königshausen & Neumann.

Beecher, Jonathan. 1986. *Charles Fourier: The Visionary and His World*. Berkeley: University of California Press.

Beixi ziyi 北溪字義. 1983. By Chen Chun 陳淳 (1159–1223). Edited by Xiong Guozhen 熊國楨 and Guo Liushui 高流水. Beijing: Zhonghua shuju. See translation by Chan.

Benedict, Ruth. 1946. *Chrysantheme und Schwert. Formen der japanischen Kultur*. Frankfurt a.M.: Suhrkamp.

Bodde, Derk. 1953. "Harmony and Conflict in Chinese Philosophy." In *Studies in Chinese Thought*, edited by A. Wright, 19–80. Chicago: University of Chicago Press.

Brandt, Max von. 1898. *Die chinesische Philosophie und der Staats-Confucianismus*. Stuttgart: Strecker and Moser.

Carus, Paul. 1902. *Chinese Philosophy: An Exposition of the Main Characteristic Features of Chinese Thought*. Chicago: Open Court; London: Kegan, Trench, Trübner.

———. 1907. *Chinese Thought: An Exposition of the Main Characteristic Features of the Chinese World-Conception*. Chicago: Open Court; London: Kegan, Trench, Trübner.

Cassirer, Ernst. 1902. *Leibniz' System in seinen wissenschaftlichen Grundlagen*. Marburg: N.G. Elwert.

Chambers, Robert. 1844. *Vestiges of the Natural History of Creation*. London: Churchill.

Chan, K. L. Alan. 2011. "Harmony as a Contested Metaphor and Conceptions of Rightness *(Yi)* in Early Confucian Ethics." In *How Should One Live? Comparing Ethics in Ancient China and Greco-Roman Antiquity*, edited by R. A. H. King and D. Schilling, 37–62. Berlin: De Gruyter.

Chan, Wing-tsit, ed. and trans. 1986. *Neo-Confucian Terms Explained (The Pei-hsi tzu-i) by Ch'en Ch'un 1159–1223*. New York: Columbia University Press.

Charrak, André. 2001. *Raison et perception. Fonder l'harmonie au XVIIIe siècle*. Paris, Vrin-Mathesis.

Chunqiu Zuozhuan zhu 春秋左傳注. 1990. Annotated by Yang Bojun 楊伯峻. Rev. ed. Beijing: Zhonghua shuju.

Cook, Constance A. and Paul R. Goldin, eds. 2016. *A Source Book of Ancient Chinese Bronze Inscriptions*. Berkeley, CA: The Society for Study of Early China.

Creel, Herrlee Glessner. 1929. *Sinism. A Study of the Evolution of the Chinese World-View*. Chicago/Illinois: Open Court.

De Groot, J. J. M. 1910. *The Religion of the Chinese*. New York: The Macmillan Company.

————. 1912. *Religion in China. Universism: A Key to the Study of Taoism and Confucianism*, New York and London: G. P. Putnam's Sons, The Knickerbocker Press.

————. 1918. *Universismus. Die Grundlage der Religion und Ethik, des Staatswesens und der Wissenschaften Chinas*. Berlin: Reimer.

Denecke, Wiebke. 2011. *The Dynamics of Masters Literature Early Chinese Thought from Confucius to Han Feizi*. Cambridge, MA: Harvard University Press.

Dickinson, G. Lowes. 1920 (1901). *Letters from John Chinaman*. London: Dent.

Donders, Franciscus Cornelis. 1848. *De Harmonie van het Dierlijke Leven. De Openbaring van Wetten*. Utrecht: C van der Post.

Duan Yucai 段玉裁. 1988. *Shuowen jiezi zhu* 說文解字注. Shanghai: Shanghai guji chubanshe.

DuBose, Hampden C. 1886. *The Dragon, Image, and Demon; or, The Three Religions of China: Confucianism, Buddhism, and Taoism. Giving an Account of the Mythology, Idolatry, and Demonolatry of the Chinese*. London, S. W. Partridge and Co.

Eberhard, Wolfram. 1970. *Sternkunde und Weltbild im alten China: Gesammelte Aufsätze*. Taipei: Chinese Materials and Research Aids Service Center.

Edkins, Joseph. 1877. *Religion in China. Containing A Brief Account of the Three Religions of the Chinese, with Observations on the Prospectus of Christian Conversion Amongst that People*. London: Trübner.

Ellenberger, Henri F. 1970. *The Discovery of the Unconscious: The History and Evolution of Dynamic Psychiatry*. New York: Basic Books.

Ennemoser, Joseph. 1819. *Der Magnetismus nach der allseitigen Beziehung seines Wesens, seiner Erscheinungen, Anwendung und Enträtselung: in einer geschichtlichen Entwicklung von allen Zeiten und bei allen Völkern wissenschaftlich dargestellt*. Leipzig: Brockhaus.

Erya jinzhu 爾雅今注. 1989. Annotated by Xu Chaohua 徐朝華. Tianjin: Nankai daxue chubanshe.

Eucken, Rudolf/Chang, Carsun. 1922. *Das Lebensproblem in China und Europa*. Leipzig: Quelle und Meyer.

Fang, Thomé H. (Fang Dongmei 方東美). 1957. *The Chinese View of Life: The Philosophy of Comprehensive Harmony*. Hong Kong: Union Press.

Falkenhausen, Lothar von. 1993. *Suspended Music: Chime-Bells in the Culture of Bronze Age China*. Berkeley: University of California Press.

Feng Youlan 馮友蘭. 1931. *Zhongguo zhexue shi* 中國哲學史. Shanghai: Shen Chou.

Flam, Jack D. 1995. *Matisse on Art*. Berkeley: University of California Press.

Forke, Alfred. 1927. *Die Gedankenwelt des chinesischen Kulturkreises*. München: Oldenbourg.

———. 1927. *Geschichte der alten chinesischen Philosophie*. Hamburg: Friederichsen.

Fourier, Charles. 1803. "Harmonie universelle," *Bulletin de Lyon* 15: 83–84.

———. 1808. *Théorie des quatre mouvements et des destinées générales*. Lyon (Leipzig): Rusand.

Fung Yu-lan (Feng Youlan) 1952. *A History of Chinese Philosophy*. Translated by Derk Bodde. Princeton: Princeton University Press.

Gebhard, Martin Anton. 1817. *Harmonie. Erklärung dieser Idee in drey Büchern und Anwendung derselben auf den Menschen in allen Beziehungen*. Munich: Falter.

Gentz, Joachim. 2011. "Rational Choice and the Chinese Discourse on the Unity of the Three Religions (*sanjiao heyi* 三教合一)." *Religion* 41.4: 535–546.

———. 2012. "Es bleibt alles in der Familie: Eine Geschichte von Reisen in Philosophischen Kreisen." In *Reisen im Zwischenraum – zur Interkulturalität von Kulturwissenschaft. Festschrift für Helmolt Vittinghoff*, edited by F. Ehmcke and M. Müller, 55–88. Würzburg: Ergon-Verlag.

———. 2013. "Religious Diversity in Three Teaching Discourses." In *Religious Diversity in Chinese Thought*, edited by Joachim Gentz and Perry Schmidt-Leukel, 123–139. New York: Palgrave Macmillan.

———. Forthcoming. "A Trustworthy Companion: Xin 信 as Component Term in Early Chinese Texts." In *From Trustworthiness to Secular Beliefs – Changing Concepts of xin 信 from Traditional to Modern Chinese*, edited by Christian Meyer and Philip Clart.

Giles, Herbert A. 1902. *China and the Chinese*. New York: Columbia University Press.

———. 1911. *The Civilization of China*. New York: H. Holt.

Glasenapp, Helmuth von. 1963. *Die fünf Weltreligionen: Hinduismus, Buddhismus, Chinesischer Universismus, Christentum, Islam*. Munich: Hugendubel.

Goldschmidt, Victor. 1901. *Über Harmonie und Complication*. Berlin: Julius Springer.

Gorst, Harold E. 1899. *China*. London: Sands & Co.

Graham, Angus Charles. 1989. *Disputers of the Tao: Philosophical Argument in Ancient China*. La Salle, Illinois: Open Court.

Granet, Marcel. 1934. *La pensée chinoise*. Paris: Albin Michel.

Grasmück, Oliver. 2004. *Geschichte und Aktualität der Daoismusrezeption im deutschsprachigen Raum*. Münster: LIT.

Guo Qi 郭齊. 2000. "Zhongguo lishi shang zhexue fanchou 'he' de xingcheng" 中國歷史上哲學範疇「和」的形成." *Zhongguo wenzhe yanjiu jikan* 中國文哲研究集刊 16: 451–486.

Guoyu jijie 國語集解. 2002. Compiled by Xu Yuangao 徐元誥. Beijing: Zhonghua shuju.

Guiguzi jijiao jizhu 鬼谷子集校集注. 2012. Edited and annotated by Xu Fuhong 許富宏. Beijing: Zhonghua shuju.

Hackmann, Heinrich. 1927. *Chinesische Philosophie*. Munich: Ernst Reinhardt.

Hu Shi 胡適 (1891–1962). 1919. *Zhongguo zhexue shi dagang (juan shang)* 中國哲學史大綱. 卷上. Shanghai: Shangwu yinshuguan.

Kajon, Irne. 1988. "Das Problem der Einheit des Bewußtseins im Denken Ernst Cassirers." In *Über Ernst Cassirers Philosophie der symbolischen Formen*, edited by H. J. Braun, H. Holzhey, and E. W. Orth, 249–273. Frankfurt: Suhrkamp.

Kayser, Hans, Orpheus. 1926. *Morphologische Fragmente einer allgemeinen Harmonik*. Berlin: Kiepenheuer.

Keil, Werner. 2012. *Dissonanz und Harmonie in Romantik und Moderne*. Munich: Fink.

Knoblock, John and Jeffrey K. Riegel, eds. and trans. 2000. *The Annals of Lü Buwei*. Stanford: Stanford University Press.

Krause, F. E. A. 1924. *Ju-Tao-Fo. Die religiösen und philosophischen Systeme Ostasiens*. Munich: Ernst Reinhardt.

Lee, Eun-Jeung. 2003. *"Anti-Europa"—Die Geschichte der Rezeption des Konfuzianismus und der konfuzianischen Gesellschaft seit der frühen Aufklärung*. Münster: LIT Verlag.

Legge, James. 1991 (1865). "The Shoo King or the Book of Historical Documents." In *The Chinese Classics*, vol 2. Taipei: Southern Materials Center Publishing Inc., vol. 1–4.

Li Chenyang. 2014a. "Confucian Harmony: A Philosophical Analysis." In *Dao Companion to Classical Confucian Philosophy*, edited by V. Shen. London/NY: Springer.

———. 2014b. *The Confucian Philosophy of Harmony*. London/NY: Routledge.

Li Xueqin 李學勤 (ed.). 2015. *Qinghua daxue cang zhanguo zhujian 5* 清華大學藏戰國竹簡 (伍). Beijing: Zhongxi shuju.

Liji xunzuan 禮記訓纂. 1996. Annotated by Zhu Bin 朱彬 (1753–1824). Beijing: Zhonghua shuju.

Linse, Ulrich. 1983. *Barfüßige Propheten: Erlöser der zwanziger Jahre*. Berlin: Siedler.

———. 1991. "Asien als Alternative? Die Alternativkultur der Weimarer Zeit: Reform des Lebens durch Rückwendung zur asiatischen Religiosität." In *Religionswissenschaft und Kulturkritik. Beiträge zur Konferenz, The History of Religions and Critique* of Culture in the Days of Gerardus van de Leeuw (1890–1950), edited by Hans Kippenberg and Brigitte Luchesi, 325–364. Marburg: Diagonal.

Lunyu yizhu 論語譯注. 1992. Annotated by Yang Bojun 楊伯峻. Beijing: Zhonghua shuju.

Lüshi chunqiu jiaoshi 呂氏春秋校釋. 2002. Annotated by Chen Qiyou 陳奇猷. Shanghai: Shanghai guji chubanshe.

Major, John S., Sarah A. Queen, Andrew Seth Meyer, and Harold D. Roth, eds. and transl. 2010. *The Huainanzi*. New York: Columbia University Press.

Makropoulos, Michael. 1991. "Tendenzen der zwanziger Jahre. Zum Diskurs der Klassischen Moderne in Deutschland." *Deutsche Zeitschrift für Philosophie* 39: 675–687.

Martin, W.A.P. 1880. *The Chinese. Their Education, Philosophy, and Letters*. London: Trübner & Co.

Maurer, Naomi Esther Margolis. 1985. "The Pursuit of Spiritual Knowledge: The Philosophical Meaning and Origins of Symbolist Theory and its Expression in the Thought and Art of Odilon Redon, Vincent Van Gogh, and Paul Gauguin." PhD dissertation. Chicago, Illinois.

———. 1998. *The Pursuit of Spiritual Wisdom: The Thought and Art of Vincent Van Gogh and Paul Gauguin*. Madison, N.J.: Fairleigh Dickinson University Press.

Mensching, Gustav. 1959. *Die Religion—Erscheinungsformen, Strukturtypen und Lebensgesetze*. Stuttgart: Schwab.

Miles, Malcolm. 2008. *Urban Utopias: The Built and Social Architectures of Alternative Settlements*. New York: Routledge.

Moynahan, Gregory B. 2014. *Ernst Cassirer and the Critical Science of Germany, 1899–1919*. London: Anthem.

Nakamura Hajime. 1960. *Ways of Thinking of Eastern Peoples: India, China, Tibet, Japan*. Tokyo: Printing Bureau, Japanese Government.

Nihongi, Chronicles of Japan from the Earliest Times to A.D. 697. 1896. Translated by William George Aston. London: Keagan and Co.

Nordin, Astrid and Lisa Richaud. 2014. "Subverting Official Language and Discourse in China? Type River Crab for Harmony." *China Information* 28.1: 47–67.

Nordin, Astrid H. M. 2016. *China's International Relations and Harmonious World: Time, Space and Multiplicity in World Politics*. London: Routledge.

Oldstone-Moore, Jennifer. 2015. "Scientism and Modern Confucianism." In *The Sage Returns: Confucian Revival in Contemporary China*, edited by K. J. Hammond and Jeffrey L. Richey, 39–64. Albany: SUNY Press.

Osterhammel, Jürgen. 1998. *Die Entzauberung Asiens. Europa und die asiatischen Reiche im 18. Jahrhundert*. Munich: Beck.

Parker, Edward Harper. 1905. *China and Religion*. New York: E .P. Dutton.

Perelomov, Leonard S. 1993. *Konfutsij: Zhizn', Ucheniie, Sud'ba*. Moscow: Nauka.

Peter, Burkhard. 2005. "Mesmer." In *Personenlexikon der Psychotherapie*, edited by G. Stumm et al., 325–327. New York: Springer.

———. 2015. "Biographie von Franz A. Mesmer, Dr.phil. et med." Available at http://www.burkhard-peter.de/index.php?id=9&lang=en (last access 26.1.2020).

Quinet, Edgar. 1857 (1842). *Le génie des religions*, reprinted in *Oeuvres complètes de Edgar Quinet*, edited by E. Quinet, 9–411. Paris: Pagnerre.

Roetz, Heiner. 2009. "China und die 'Harmonische Gesellschaft': Die Welt als Garten." *DCG Mitteilungsblatt* 51: 10–17. https://www.uni-trier.de/fileadmin/fb2/SIN/Symposien/DVCS_2012_Abstracts.pdf.

———. "Xunzi's Vision of Society: Harmony by Justice." In *Governance for Harmony in Asia and Beyond*, edited by Julia Tao et al., 315–328. London/NY: Routledge.

Ross, John. 1909. *The Original Religion of China*. New York: Eaton & Mains; Cincinnati: Jennings & Graham; Edinburgh & London: Oliphant, Anderson & Ferrier.

Schmötzer, Werner. 2015. *Heilmagnetismus—Homöopathie und die §§ 286-290 des Organon: Eine naturheilkundliche-anthroposophische Betrachtung*. Berlin: Pro Business.

Schmitt, Erich. 1916. *Taoistische Klöster im Lichte des Universismus*. Berlin: Reichsdruckerei.

Seiler, Georg Friedrich. 1802. *Das Zeitalter der Harmonie, der Vernunft und der biblischen Religion. Eine Apologie des Christentums gegen Thomas Paine und seines Gleichen in Deutschland*. Leipzig: Crusius.

Smith, Arthur Henderson. 1890. *Chinese Characteristics*. Shanghai: North China Herald Office.

Soffel, Christian. 2014. "Harmonie als Grundlage des Konfuzianismus? Eine kritische Spurensuche im *Lunyu* und in anderen frühen Texten." In *Harmonie und Konflikt in China*, edited by Christian Soffel and Tilman Schalmey, 47–58. Wiesbaden: Harrassowitz.

Soothill, William Edward. 1913. *The Three Religions of China; Lectures Delivered at Oxford*. London, New York: Hodder and Stoughton.

Taatz-Jacobi, Marianne. 2014. *Erwünschte Harmonie. Die Gründung der Friedrichs-Universität Halle als Instrument brandenburg-preußischer Konfessionspolitik – Motive, Verfahren, Mythos (1680–1713)*. Berlin: de Gruyter.

Takase Takejirō 高瀬武次郎 (1868–1950). 1910. *Shina tetsugakushi* 支那哲學史. Tōkyō: Bunseidō Shoten.

Triplett, Katja. 2006. "The Discourse on *wa* or Harmony in Contemporary Japanese Religions and Society." In *Religious Harmony: Problems, Practice, and Education*, ed. by Michael Pye et al., 179–188. Berlin/NY: Walter de Gruyter.

Uno Tetsuto 宇野哲人 (1875–1974). 1914. *Shina tetsugakushi kōwa* 支那哲學史講話. Tōkyō: Daidōkan Shoten.

Wang Jinfeng 王進鋒. 2016. "Qinghua jian (wu) sanpian jishi" 清華簡（伍）三篇集釋. Unpublished compilation for the conference "Human, Nature, Morality, and Fate in the Tsinghua University Bamboo Manuscripts" 清華大學藏戰國竹簡國際學術研討會, Erlangen, May 9–13.

Wang Li 王力. 1987. *Tongyuan zidian* 同源字典. Beijing: Shangwu yinshuguan.

Webb, James. 1980. *The Harmonious Circle: The Lives and Work of G. I. Gurdjieff, P. D. Ouspensky, and Their Followers.* London: Thames and Hudson.

Weitling, Wilhelm. 1842. *Garantien der Harmonie und Freiheit.* Vivis: Im Verlage des Verfassers.

Wierzbicka, Anna. 1997. *Understanding Cultures through Their Key Words: English, Russian, Polish, German, and Japanese.* Oxford: Oxford University Press.

Wu Yi 吳怡. 1986. *Chinese Philosophical Terms* (中國哲學術語). Lanham/NY/London: University Press of America.

Xie Wuliang 謝无量. 1916. *Zhongguo zhexue shi* 中國哲學史. Shanghai: Zhonghua shuju.

Xu Zhongshu 徐中舒 (ed.). 1988. *Jiaguwen zidian* 甲骨文字典. Chengdu: Sichuan cishu chubanshe.

Xunzi jijie 荀子集解. 1992. Annotated by Wang Xianqian 王先謙. Edited by Shen Xiaohuan 沈嘯寰 and Wang Xingxian 王星賢. Beijing: Zhonghua shuju.

Yanzi chunqiu jishi 晏子春秋集釋. 1962. Edited and annotated by Wu Zeyu 吳則虞. Beijing: Zhonghua shuju.

Yu, Kam Por. 2015. "The Confucian Conception of Harmony." In *Governance for Harmony in Asia and Beyond*, edited by Julia Tao et al., 15–36. London/NY: Routledge.

Zhang Dainian 張岱年. 1982 (1936) *Zhongguo zhexue dagang: Zhongguo zhexue wenti shi* 中國哲學大綱：中國哲學問題史. Beijing: Zhongguo shehui kexue chubanshe.

———. 1998a (1957). "Zhongguo gudai zhexue zhong ruogan jiben gainian de qiyuan yu yanbian" 中國古代哲學中若干基本概念的起源與演變. *Dangdai xuezhe zixuan wenku (Zhang Dainian juan)* 當代學者自選文庫（張岱年卷）, Hefei: Anhui jiaoyu chubanshe, 57–87.

———. 1998b (1957). "Zhongguo gudian zhexue de jige tedian" 中國古典哲學的幾個特點." *Dangdai xuezhe zixuan wenku (Zhang Dainian juan)* 當代學者自選文庫（張岱年卷）, Hefei: Anhui jiaoyu chubanshe, 88–109.

———. 1989. *Zhongguo gudian zhexue gainian fanchou yaolun* 中國古典哲學概念範疇要論. Beijing: Academy of Social Sciences.

———. 2002. *Key Concepts in Chinese Philosophy. Translated by Edmund Ryden.* New Haven: Yale University Press.

Zhou Rudeng 周汝登 (1547–1629). 1989 (1605). *Shengxue zongzhuan* 聖學宗傳. In *Kongzi wenhua daquan* 孔子文化大全. Jinan: Shandong youyi shushe.

Zhuangzi jijie 莊子集解. *1987*. Annotated by Wang Xianqian 王先謙. Beijing: Zhonghua shuju.

Zotz, Volker. 2000. *Auf den glückseligen Inseln: Buddhismus in der deutschen Kultur*. Berlin: Theseus.

Zuo Tradition/Zuozhuan 左傳. *Commentary on the "Spring and Autumn Annals"*. 2016. Translated by Stephen Durrant, Wai-yee Li and David Schaberg. Seattle: University of Washington Press.

Zuozhuan. See *Chunqiu Zuozhuan zhu*.

3

From "Scribe" to "History": The Keyword *shi* 史

Stephen Durrant

Throughout Chinese history, writings about the past have carried great cultural importance and have become a source of immense pride. The learned scholar Qian Mu 錢穆 (1895–1990), in an essay entitled *Zhongguo shixue zhi jingshen* 中國史學之精神 (The spirit of Chinese historiography), claims, "The interest of Chinese in history is more intense (*nonghou* 濃厚) than that of the people of any other country."[1] While Qian Mu's assertion might be warranted, the single written Chinese character most readily identified with "history," 史 *shi*, has a complex history itself, which those who make comparative claims should keep firmly in mind. The Greek word ἱστορία, from which the English word "history" derives, refers to a type of forensic or fact-based inquiry. It is an activity that seeks to discover what actually happened. How to go about finding the truth becomes a question at the heart of ἱστορία.[2] *Shi*, by way of contrast, names an official government position which we typically, but somewhat perilously, translate

---

1   Qian Mu 2003a: 27. All translations are my own unless otherwise indicated.

2   Hence the concern about "truth" found in both Herodotus and Thucydides. For a good discussion of this issue, see Baragwanath and Bakker 2012: 1–58. The emphasis upon truth in Greek historiography does not necessarily imply that early Greek historical writing was more accurate than that of China. One can indeed make the opposite argument; see, for example, Du Weiyun 1988.

as "scribe." Eventually, *shi* comes to mean "that which scribes write down," and at a certain moment in time describes a broad category of texts we might as well, leaving reservations aside, simply label "historical writing" or, with proper caution, just "history."[3] Our major focus in what follows will be this last stage as it is reflected in the "Jingji zhi" 經籍志 ("Treatise on classics and other texts"), hereafter generally referred to as "the bibliographic treatise" or "the treatise") of *Suishu* 隋書 (History of the Sui dynasty), a vast catalogue of texts that took shape in the seventh-century CE. But before turning attention to that particular catalogue, some general background is required.

1. From "Scribes" to What They Write

The body of scholarship on the derivation, meaning, and usage of the character *shi* 史 in early Chinese texts continues to grow, as does concern about whether we should persist in translating *shi* as "scribe."[4] By way of summary, several conclusions from this scholarship are germane to the topic under discussion here.

First, the written character *shi* 史, all agree, originally depicted a hand holding something: a bamboo strip, an archival document, tallies for an archery contest, and so forth.[5] Whatever the thing in the hand might actually

---

3   Caution because "history," at least in English, is not just a type of writing but also "the study of past events" and "the total accumulation of past events" (*The Concise Oxford Dictionary* 1995, p. 643). *Shi* has neither of these latter two meanings in the early period, but refers exclusively either to an office or to a particular type of written document associated with that office. On this issue, see the instructive comments of Harbsmeier 1997: 60–66.

4   See Xu Fuguan 1989, vol. 3: 217–230; Xu Zhaochang 2006; Vogelsang 2003/04: 1–9 and 2007: 17–91; Schaberg 2013; and, most recently, Selbitscka (forthcoming). While I have found these works particularly stimulating, they are only a few of many significant scholarly works on this topic.

5   For some opinions on this subject see *Shuowen jiezi gulin* 3:1262–64; Wang Guowei 2003: 129–130; Li Zongtong 1991: 1–5.

be, the explanation of the character by the influential early lexicographer Xu Shen 許慎 (ca. 58–ca. 147 CE) remains critical. *Shi* 史, he believes, depicts a hand that sets things right: "It means someone who records affairs. It comes from a hand holding the character *zhong* 中. Zhong means correct." 記 事者也。从又持中,中正也.[6] While it is unlikely that the character could have originally depicted something as abstract as the principle of moral or factual rectification, Xu Shen presumably reflects the way it was analyzed in his time. His explanation, it would seem, links the character very much to a scribal tradition of producing accurate records. Characters, of course, write words, and Wolfgang Behr places the word *shi* ("scribe") in a cluster of other words with the meanings "to employ, send" (*shi* 使), "a clerk, official" (*li* 吏), "to carry out assignments" (*shi* 使), "a gentleman-official" (*shi* 士), "to record" (*ji* 記/紀) and even "to cut jade, mark, draw a line" (*li* 理).[7] The meanings of this word family point to both the official nature of *shi* activity and also to the *shi* duty to make marks or records.

Second, the functions in early China of the office of scribes and its derivatives (*taishi* 太史 "grand scribe," *neishi* 內史 "court scribe," *waishi* 外史 "scribe of external affairs," etc.) vary and are by no means limited to tasks we might immediately associate with the English word "scribe." Xu Fuguan 徐復觀 (1903–1982) argues that scholars who have studied this issue "neglected the original duties of *shi*, which were of the same nature as those of the invocator (*zhu* 祝) and basically concerned serving spirits—that is, they were involved with the pursuit of religious activities." Even with those instances when *shi* were involved in making a record, Xu says, "It was in all cases connected to religion."[8] Kai Vogelsang's careful examination of the earliest functions of *shi* uncovers no evidence in the oracle bones, bronze inscriptions or earliest Chinese texts that such officials were historians or

---

6   *Shuowen jiezi gulin* 3: 1262.
7   Behr 2005: 13–17.
8   Xu Fuguan 1989, vol. 3: 220. For an exceedingly rich article on the "cultic origins" of early Chinese historiography and the persistence of a religious component even in the work of Sima Qian, see Pines 2009.

even primarily scribes. He further notes that in the entire *Chunqiu* 春秋 (*Spring and Autumn Annals,* hereafter, *Annals*), supposedly compiled by Lu-state *shi,* the word *shi* never appears. Vogelsang believes that the "historical turn" may have come from involvement of *shi* officials in prophecy and astronomy, which induced them to use the past as a way of predicting the future.[9]

Third, while the word *shi* is not found in *Annals,* it does appear more than seventy times in the late 4th-century BCE *Zuozhuan* 左傳, China's first extensive narrative history. This text affords the opportunity to scrutinize in some detail exactly how *shi* functioned in the Spring and Autumn and Warring States periods. David Schaberg has done just that and concludes, "Most common by far of the duties of the *shi* who appear in *Zuozhuan* narratives are the duties relating to sacrifices, especially to nature spirits or in response to natural disasters," thus conceding, very much like Xu Fuguan and Vogelsang, that *shi* have largely religious or ritual responsibilities in the *Zuozhuan.*[10] However, Schaberg goes on to note: "The official duties of the *shi* revolved around the use of texts, written or unwritten, under special circumstances."[11] Armin Selbitschka's impressive examination of the offices and duties of *shi* in excavated texts reaches conclusions that largely dovetail with those of Schaberg: "It is preferable to understand the late pre-imperial and early imperial *shĭ* as a person in official employ who was trained in writing, but who was required to be familiar with divinatory, occult practices, arithmetic procedures and some medicine." Elsewhere, he notes that training as a *shi* had as its purpose "to secure a job in public administration, which in turn, led to the production of written documents."[12]

Fourth, the mistaken conclusion that *shi* always means simply "scribe" and the false notion that this "scribe" is already a historian in the

---

9   Vogelsang 2003/04: 9.
10   Schaberg 2013: 27.
11   Schaberg 2013. Several passages in *Zuozhuan* center very directly on the textual duties of *shi*: Lord Xiang 25.2, Xuan 2.3, Xiang 14.6, Xiang 29.11, Zhao 1.9, Zhao 2.1, among others.
12   Selbischka 2018.

narrow sense of the word has led to a sort of backward thinking that goes something like this: As far back as the character *shi* 史 appears, even in the early inscriptional texts, China has had active historians. Moreover, such thinking asserts, since *shi* are government officials, history has been an official concern in China virtually since the beginning, a pervasive notion not just in China but also among some of the most revered Western sinologists, as Vogelsang has shown.[13] Sima Qian 司馬遷 (ca. 145–ca. 88 BCE), indisputably a historian, has played no small role in establishing this manner of thinking. His "Self-Narration" (*Zi xu* 自序) in Chapter 130 of *Shiji* 史記 begins with the claim that "the Sima family has for generations managed the Zhou scribal writings" 司馬氏典周史, thus creating the impression that his own work and that of his father continues a longstanding, official, family task, which he elsewhere pushes all the way back to legendary times. Sima Qian quotes his dying father making the claim, "Our ancestors were grand scribes for the Zhou house ... will it end with me?" 余先周室之太史也 ⋯⋯ 絕於予乎？[14]

In summary, a *shi* in this early period is far from being a simple scribe, who records events and copies records. Nevertheless, certain famous episodes in *Zuozhuan*, as well as passages in Sima Qian's "Self-Narration," and Xu Shen's explanation of the written character *shi* 史, along with other passages in early Chinese texts,[15] do encourage later scholars to focus on the scribal dimension of the *shi*'s responsibility. Such a focus, along with

---

13   Vogelsang (2007: 17–21).

14   *Shiji* 130: 3285.

15   One famous example is in *Lunyu* (*Analects*) (15:26), wherein Confucius may be criticizing *shi* for not exercising sufficient care in what they record: 子曰，吾猶及史之闕文也, which Waley (1938: 198) translates as, "The Master said, 'I can still remember the days when a scribe left blank spaces,'" an understanding that was followed, among others, by Brooks and Brooks (1998: 133): "The Master said, 'I still go back to when scribes left blanks.'" D. C. Lau's translation (Lau 1979: 135), however, would not automatically make this a comment about how a scribe made records: "The Master said, 'I am old enough to have seen scribes who lacked refinement.'" Some view *shi* 史 here as referring not to the office "scribe" but to "scribal writings" (see, for example, *Lunyu yizhu* 15.26: 165). As I suggest in this essay, such a reading of *shi* may be anachronistic.

later developments in the keyword *shi*, has had, as just noted above, a deep influence upon how the rise of historical writing in China has often been portrayed.

During the Six Dynasties period and culminating in the early Tang (618–907) *Suishu* bibliographic treatise, *shi* undergoes something of a transformation and emerges as the name of one division in a four-fold scheme of bibliographical classification, the so-called *sibu* 四部 "four divisions" system.[16] As such, *shi* stands alongside *jing* 經 "classics," *zi* 子 "master's texts," and *ji* 集 "collections" and should be understood as "scribal texts" or, somewhat more loosely, "historical texts." This marks a significant break with the bibliographic treatise, "Yiwen zhi 藝文志" (Treatise on arts and writings), found several hundred years earlier in *Hanshu* 漢書 (History of the [Former] Han dynasty), which classifies works we would normally consider as historical texts in a section entitled "*Chunqiu*" 春秋 (Annals).[17]

Lu Yaodong 逯耀東 (1933–2006) argues that the classification of historical works in *Hanshu* is symptomatic of a larger issue: "The historiography of the period of the Han is completely subordinate to classical study (*jingxue* 經學). It is not an independent subject."[18] While no independent conception of historical writing may yet have existed, *Annals* had gained great prestige for possessing what Lu calls "the very highest principles of Chinese historiography."[19] Once we understand the dominance that *Annals* exercised over attempts to record the past, we understand why

---

16   The *sibu* system derives from earlier bibliographies such as Xun Xu's 荀勖 (?–289 CE) *Xinbo* 新簿. See Lu Yaodong 2000: 65–67.

17   *Hanshu* 30.1715. That is to say, such texts as *Guoyu* 國語 (Discourses of the states), *Zhanguo ce* 戰國策 (Stratagems of the Warring States) and Sima Qian's *Shiji*, labeled at that time the *Taishi gong shu* 太史公書 (Writings of the Lord Grand Scribe), are all listed in the "Yiwen zhi" category headed by the classic *Chunqiu*. For more on *shi* in early bibliographic categories, see Durrant 2017; Dudbridge 2017; Li Wai-yee 2017.

18   Lu Yaodong 2000: 30. Thus, in Liu Xin's 劉歆 (50 BCE–23 CE) *Qilue* 七略 (Seven summaries), an earlier bibliography upon which Ban Gu has largely relied, there is no such category as a "history section."

19   Lu Yaodong 2000: 32.

Sima Qian goes to such lengths to assert a strong connection between that text and his own work, even though he clearly knows that such an assertion is presumptuous and carries dangerous political implications.[20]

Lu Yaodong proceeds to trace the gradual emancipation of historical studies from classics studies and its emergence in the Wei-Jin period as an independent and productive field of intellectual endeavor. One can see evidence of this new status in the appearance of the term *jing shi* 經史 to designate two parallel bodies of texts. To give only one example, the following passage appears in *Sanguo zhi* 三國志 (Record of the Three Kingdoms):

默知其不博，乃遠游荊州，從司馬德操、宋仲子等受古學。皆通諸經史，又專精於左氏春秋。

[Yin] Mo knew his learning was not broad, so he traveled a great distance to Jingzhou and received instruction in ancient learning from such men as Sima Decao (Sima Hui 司馬徽) and Song Zhongzi (Song Zhong 宋衷). In all cases, he mastered the various classics (*jing*) and histories (*shi*), and also became particularly adept at the *Annals of Mr. Zuo.*[21]

At about the same time, the term *sanshi* 三史 "three histories" begins to appear, further evidence that the problematic term *shi* had come to mean something like "historical texts." We know, also, that several decades earlier, most likely in the years of the Eastern Han emperors Huan (146–168) and Ling (168–189), Sima Qian's historical text, previously called *Taishi gong*

---

20 The presumption, which he both asserts and denies, is that he is a new Confucius and that his text deserves to be put alongside what in his time was believed to be Confucius's great masterpiece. The danger is that such a work as the *Annals* should appear as a corrective to political decline, "when on high there is no enlightened ruler" 上無明君, to quote the words of Sima Qian's interlocutor Hu Sui 壺遂. Thus, comparing his own historical work to the *Annals* could be interpreted as an attack on his prickly ruler Emperor Wu 漢武帝 (r. 141–87 BCE). That Sima Qian is aware of this danger is clear from his response to Hu Sui (*Shiji* 130: 3299–3300).

21 *Sanguo zhi* 42.1026. *Zuozhuan* presumably derives from this *Annals of Mr. Zuo*, a name that appears throughout the Han period and, as here, into the Six Dynasties. On this issue, and the question of Zuo Qiuming 左丘明, see Durrant, Li, and Schaberg 2016: XX–XXI.

shu 太史公書 (Book of the Lord Grand Scribe), *Taishi gong ji* 太史公記 (Records of the Lord Grand Scribe), or simply *Taishi gong* 太史公 (The Lord Grand Scribe), came to be known under the title *Shiji* 史記.[22] In this post-Han cultural context it is quite right to translate the latter title as "records of history" or more colloquially, "historical records," whereas Nienhauser appropriately translates the earlier name as "records of the Grand Scribe."

The critical link between *shi* as designation of an official, and *shi* as a type of text might be the binome *shiji* 史記, a term first encountered in the *Lüshi chunqiu* 呂氏春秋 (Sire Lü's Spring and Autumn annals):

子夏之晉，過衛，有讀史記者曰：「晉師三豕涉河。」子夏曰：「非也，是己亥也。夫『己』與『三』相近，『豕』與『亥』相似。」至於晉而問之，則曰「晉師己亥涉河」也。

When Zixia was on his way to Jin and passing through Wei, someone who had read the scribal records quoted them as follows: "The Jin troops and three pigs crossed the [Yellow] River." Zixia said, "That's wrong. This is *jihai*. The character *ji* closely resembles *san,* 'three,' and *shi* 'pig' closely resembles *hai*." When they arrived in Jin, they inquired about this and discovered the records said, "The Jin troops, on the *jihai* day, crossed the [Yellow] River.[23]

This very late Warring States text refers to scribal records, and the form of the particular record encountered above, apparently drawn from Jin official documents, resembles closely what we see in Lu scribal records found in *Annals*. [24] The term *shiji* ("scribal records") appears relatively frequently in Sima Qian's history. We are told therein, for example, that "the senior scribe of Zhou, Boyang 伯楊, read the scribal records and announced

---

22   On this, see the detailed study of Zhang Dake et al. 2005: 45–54.

23   *Lüshi chunqiu* 22.6: 1527 ("Cha zhuan" 察傳).

24   Elsewhere, Mencius refers to Jin scribal records similar to the Lu *Annals* under the name "*Cheng*" 乘 (*Mengzi* 8.21: 177).

'Zhou will be destroyed'" 周太史伯陽讀史記曰周亡矣,[25] that Confucius "relied on the scribal records to fashion *Annals*" 因史記而作春秋,[26] and that the First Qin Emperor's destruction of "the scribal records of the lords was particularly extensive" 諸侯史記尤甚.[27] Perhaps through the mediation of this two-character phrase, the single character *shi* as "scribe" comes to mean "what scribes wrote" or "historical records."

2. What Is This New Thing Called "History"?

It was noted above that *shi* as a category of written works first emerges during the Six Dynasties period, a process that leads to the official bibliographic treatise found in the *Suishu*. In the next section, we will look more closely at the treatise and the way it configures the category *shi*. But first, we turn briefly to three works that precede the *Suishu* treatise and establish a foundation both for the way subsequent generations have thought about the emergence of historical writing in China and also for what we might call "critical historiography": Ban Biao's 班彪 (3–54 CE) "General Remarks" 略論, his son Ban Gu's 班固 (32–92) comments summarizing the *Chunqiu* category of the *Hanshu* bibliographic treatise, and a chapter entitled "History and Traditions" 史傳 found in Liu Xie's 劉勰 (ca. 465–522) monumental *Wenxin diaolong* 文心雕龍 (Literary mind and carvings of dragons).[28]

Ban Biao's "General Remarks," preserved in Fan Ye's 范曄 (398–445) *Hou Hanshu* 後漢書 (History of the Latter Han dynasty), was part of his effort to continue Sima Qian's historical work.[29] One can divide its content

---

25 *Shiji* 1: 147.

26 *Shiji* 14: 509, 47: 1943, 121: 3115.

27 *Shiji* 15: 686.

28 This sequence of vital texts in the rise of Chinese historiography is suggested in Qu Lindong 1999: 21.

29 *Hou Hanshu* 40A: 1325–1329. For a full translation of the essay, see Clark 2008: 198–201.

into two parts: first, a short genealogy of historical writing; and second, a summary and evaluation of Sima Qian's history. Such a structure implies that Sima Qian's work, however problematic Ban Biao may regard it, is a culmination of all historical writing that precedes him and a challenge to all that would follow. His genealogy of historical writing begins with the "three dynasties" 三代—Xia, Shang, and Zhou—during which there was "an office of scribes, generation after generation, to manage the records" 世有史官以司典籍. After the decline of the Zhou, each state had scribes and maintained state records, Ban Biao says, quoting a well-known *Mencius* passage as proof of this.[30] Surprisingly, Ban's essay says nothing of Confucius' role in editing *Annals* but mentions in rather swift succession *Zuoshi zhuan* 左氏傳 (Tradition of Mr. Zuo), its supposed companion volume *Guoyu* 國語 (Discourses of the states), *Shiben* 世本 (Origins of the generations), *Zhangguo ce* 戰國策 (Stratagems of the Warring States), and Lu Jia's 陸賈 (235?–155? BCE) *Chu Han chunqiu* 楚漢春秋 (Annals of Chu and Han) and subsequently says that Sima Qian's work relied heavily upon these earlier texts.

From Ban Biao's vantage point, writing at the beginning of the Eastern Han period, the tradition more or less begins with the office of the scribe and leads directly to the work of the "director grand scribe Sima Qian" 太史令司馬遷. Even though he evaluates much of Sima Qian's work rather negatively, he does concede that Sima Qian shows "the talent of a good scribe" 良史之才. His concerns about Sima Qian's history, which we need not discuss in any detail here, focus largely on the latter's supposed failure to adhere to classical principles, alleged mistakes and inconsistencies in the organization of his work, and stylistic infelicities such as needless repetition.[31]

Ban Gu's short essay at the conclusion of the "*Chunqiu*" division of his bibliographic essay, presumably drawn in large measure from his predecessors Liu Xiang 劉向 (79–8 BCE) and Liu Xin 劉歆 (46 BCE–23

---

30   *Mengzi yizhu* 8.21: 177.

31   For further comments on this, see Durrant 2015: 217–241.

CE), also asserts the high antiquity of the office of scribes but elaborates on his father's account in words that later scholars will regularly repeat:

君舉必書，所以慎言行，昭法式也。左史記言，右史記事，事為春秋，言為尚書，帝王靡不同之。

When the ruler acted, it was required to make a record[32] as a means to assure caution in words and deeds and to illuminate laws and rules. A scribe of the left recorded words; a scribe of the right recorded deeds.[33] Deeds became *Annals* and words became *Shu* (hereafter, *Documents*). All emperors and kings complied with this.[34]

This passage elaborates the workings of the office of the scribes, drawing in part on *Liji* 禮記 (Records of the rites, see below), and connects it to two great classics, *Annals* and *Documents*. Ban Gu then gives prominence to Confucius but immediately links the Sage to Zuo Qiuming: "Because Lu was the domain of the Zhou Duke, and its ritual and cultural patterns were complete in all their specifics, and its scribal officers kept to their rules, [Confucius] joined with Zuo Qiuming in viewing its scribal records" 以魯周公之國，禮文備物，史官有法，故與左丘明觀其史記。[35] The result of this event is both Confucius's poignant work *Annals* and the subsequent *Zuozhuan*, in which Zuo Qiuming provides correct explanations of the *Annals* based upon what he saw and learned along with Confucius. The remainder of Ban Gu's essay speaks of *Gongyang*, *Guliang* and other texts

---

32   As will be noted further below, the four characters *jun ju bi shu* 君舉必書, translated here as "When the ruler acted, it was required to make a record," are drawn directly from *Zuozhuan* (Lord Zhuang 23.1: 226). However, the two contexts are quite different. In *Zuozhuan*, the statement refers specifically to the need to make a record of the Lord of Lu's travels as a part of maintaining proper ritual order (see Durrant, Li and Schaberg, 2016: 199). The passage above uses the statement as a general justification for recording the actions and the words of ruling lords.

33   *Liji* 禮記 also notes these two types of scribes but reverses their duties, claiming that the scribe of the right recorded words and the scribe of the left actions (see *Liji jijie* XXIX.13: 778 ["Yu zao" 玉藻]).

34   *Hanshu* 30: 1715.

35   The translation of this portion of the essay and what follows is that of Durrant, Li and Schaberg, 2016: XLIII–XLIV. The translation just above from the same essay is mine.

that derive directly from *Annals* and/or the *Zuozhuan*, as well as *Zhanguo ce, Chu Han chunqiu,* and Sima Qian's history under the name the *Taishi gong* 太史公.

Neither Ban Biao nor Ban Gu discuss general principles of historical writing beyond offering a critique of Sima Qian, nor do they engage with issues of historical accuracy. They are writing, as it happens, on the other end of the Eurasian land mass and within a hundred years or so of Cicero's (104–43 BCE) famous statement: "In history the standard by which everything is judged is the truth, while in poetry it is generally the pleasure one gives."[36] In regard to this issue of "the truth," to which we shall return below, and on several other questions, Liu Xie goes well beyond his predecessors. First of all, to include a chapter on history in a text like *Wenxin diaolong* is evidence that after historical writings finally separated from the canonical classics, it remained within the purview of literary studies.[37] Moreover, unlike Ban Biao, whose essay is entitled only "General Remarks," Liu Xie uses the word *shi* in his title, pairing it with *zhuan* 傳. As is the case with so many of the binominal chapter titles in Liu's *Wenxin diaolong*, this title probably points toward two different but interrelated facets of this particular form of writing. Since what begins the chapter is a brief discussion of the rise of the scribal office, which repeats much of what we have seen in Ban Biao and Ban Gu, we might suppose that *shi*, as used in Liu's title, refers specifically to the type of writing undertaken by scribes—thus, "scribal writing." Adding to what has probably become a standard narrative of the rise of scribal writing, Liu says:

---

36 *Laws* 1.5. This is not meant to imply that early Chinese scribes and historians were unconcerned about accuracy. Nothing could be further from the truth (see, for example, the famous case of the scribes of Qi, who sacrificed their lives to preserve an accurate record in *Zuozhuan* [Lord Xiang 25 and also Durrant 2005]). What we do not have in the early Chinese tradition, however, is much explicit discussion of the principle of "truth" or "accuracy" in historical writing.

37 Lu Yaodong 2000: 47–52. For Liu Xie's chapter, see *Wenxin diaolong* 4.16: 559–620. I should add that Liu also devotes a chapter to "classics" and that the larger category to which they belong, the subject of Liu's book, is not "literary studies" as we understand it but *wen*, a broad category referring to any "refined" written text that is part of the cultural legacy.

《曲禮》曰：「史載筆。」史者，使也。執筆左右，使之記也。古者左史記事者，右史記言者。言經則《尚書》，事經則《春秋》也。

The "Quli" says, "A scribe carries along a writing brush." One who is a scribe is employed in service. Being on the ruler's left or right and holding a writing brush, they are deployed to make records. Anciently, the scribe on the left recorded events, and the scribe on the right recorded words. The classic of words is *Documents*; the classic of events is *Annals*.[38]

Liu also notes, as Ban Biao before him, that after the decline of Zhou power, each state had its own scribes, but he then emphasizes Confucius's role in fashioning the Lu state records into *Annals* and imparting to that text a particularly profound but elusive meaning. Thus, Liu sets the stage for the appearance of the second genre, *zhuan*, in his title: "[Zuo] Qiuming, being of the same time [as Confucius], truly grasped [the meaning of] the subtle words" (丘明同時，實得微).[39] Continuing on with yet another paronomastic definition, Liu adds, "[Qiuming] created the *zhuan* (傳) form. *Zhuan* means to pass along (*zhuan* 轉). Having received the essential meaning of the classic from what is being passed along, one presents it to posterity" 創為傳體。傳者，轉也；轉受經旨，以授於後.[40]

From what follows in his account of the development of historical writing, the reader gains the impression that *shi* is largely equated in Liu's mind with *ji*, the type of annalistic records that state scribes supposedly wrote. Consequently, he is pointing forward with his chapter title and his explanations of genre towards Liu Zhiji's 劉知幾 (661–721 CE) famous distinction between the two major forms of historical writing: the *jiti* 紀體 "annals form" and the *jizhuanti* 紀傳體 "annals-traditions form." However, ji (annals) is not paired with *zhuan* (traditions) in Liu Xie's title because he has stated already that such non-annalistic texts as *Shu* are the products of scribes, specifically scribes of the left who make records of words, and he does not wish to exclude works of this type from his survey.

---

38   *Wenxin diaolong* 4.16: 560.

39   *Wenxin diaolong* 4.16: 569.

40   Ibid.

Liu Xie's survey of the early rise and tradition of historical writing, much like Ban Biao's before him, reaches a high point with Sima Qian's *Shiji*. Rather than dwelling on Sima Qian's deficiencies, he references Ban Biao's essay, and then passes on to Ban Gu, whom he praises for adhering to the teachings of the sage and for his outstanding literary style, thus aligning himself very much on Ban's side of the emerging Ban-Ma controversy.[41] Liu then continues with an account of Wei-Jin historiography. However, in the last section of his chapter, he engages in an innovative discussion of several principles and problems of historical writing. This portion of the chapter represents a major step forward in Chinese "critical historiography" and leads 200 years later to Liu Zhiji's imposing work *Shitong* 史通 (A comprehensive study of historical writing), the first book-length work of critical historiography to appear anywhere in the world.[42] Liu Xie's discussion might be boiled down to the three items noted below.

First, a scribe, according to Liu, must engage in careful examination of all available textual evidence. His work is text-intensive:

是以在漢之初，史職為盛。郡國文計，先集太史之府，欲其詳悉於體國也。

Therefore, in the beginning years of the Han, the official duties of the scribe flourished. The writings and registers of the commandaries and kingdoms were first collected in the archives of the Grand Scribe with the desire that he would become thoroughly familiar with understanding the state.[43]

41   During the Six Dynasties period and thereafter, scholars frequently debated the relative strengths and weaknesses of Sima Qian's and Ban Gu's histories. This debate is sometimes referred to as the "Ban-Ma controversy."

42   Lucian of Samosata (125–180 CE) produces a relatively brief piece on the methodology of historical writing, and much later, roughly at the time *Suishu* is taking form in China, Isidore of Sevilla (560–636) wrote some reflections on historiography in his *Etymologies*, but these are hardly comparable in scope and size to Liu Zhiji's work.

43   *Wenxin diaolong* 4.16: 602.

Sima Qian might have been a traveler, as certain passages in *Shiji* attest, but his history largely results from compiling earlier written sources, a significant point considered in more detail below.[44]

Second, a historical work should cover a carefully determined period of time, seek to be an effective synopsis (*zonghui* 總會), show a wise selection and balance (*quanpei* 銓配), and find a middle ground between being cryptic and being redundant. The period of time covered must be carefully selected, for "when the era is far off, falsehoods multiply" 代遠多偽, but "when it is contemporary, the distortions multiply" 時同多詭. Thus, both ancient history and contemporary history have their characteristic pitfalls with the result that "only a disinterested mind will do" 唯素心乎![45]

Third, as the above point indicates, to produce an accurate and reliable account of the past is the goal of historical writing. It is critical to stress this aspect of Liu Xie's chapter precisely because there is less meta-discussion of the problem of truthfulness in historical writing in early China than in early Greece.[46] The early Chinese concern about the proper form and literary presentation of history, which can be found from Ban Gu's criticisms of Sima Qian down to Liu Zhiji, overwhelms consideration of how a historian

---

44 On this Sima Qian contrasts significantly with the fathers of Greek historiography, who relied largely either on eyewitnesses or those who could expound on earlier times. Herodotus, it seems, was largely dependent upon informants as he travelled, but his preference for the "eye" over the "ear" is well-known (see Hartog 1988: 260–309). Thucydides is of course narrating events that are largely contemporary and in which he participated. Breisach (1994: 68) says of Tacitus: "What he reported on he knew from his own experience and from the work of earlier historians. Like other ancient historians, he did not routinely frequent depositories of records." One can imagine Sima Qian sitting among roll after roll of bamboo strips upon which were written earlier records and documents. One can hardly imagine the earliest Western historians working in such a fashion.

45 *Wenxin diaolong* 4.16: 612.

46 See Durrant 2005. If we are to look for critical historiography in early China, we might best seek it out, as Pines suggests (2005: 219–222), in late Warring States philosophical writings.

gets at the truth.[47] Liu Xie, however, argues explicitly that accuracy is the goal: "One writes [history] relying upon the factual" 按實而書, "one prizes reliable history" 貴信史也,[48] etc. But, as we shall see, the expanding boundaries of "history," at least as we witness them approximately two centuries later, somewhat becloud Liu Xie's insistence upon "factuality" and "reliability" as hallmarks of historical writing.

3. The Boundaries of "History" in the *Suishu* "Jingji zhi"

In discussing the implications of the development of the four-division system of cataloguing, Lu Yaodong places particular emphasis upon *Suishu* "Jingji zhi" and notes that the division on historical writing in this famous treatise "not only analyzes the course of the development of historical studies during the Wei-Jin period but also summarizes its results."[49] As such, it stands both as a conclusion to what went before and as a foundation for much that follows.

The ten treatises now found in the *Suishu,* which includes the bibliographic treatise under consideration here, were not written as part of that work. Denis Twitchett explains, "These were originally conceived of and written as a separate book, *Wudai shi zhi* 五代史志 'The Treatises for the histories of the Five Dynasties.' Completed in 656, this work was independent of *Suishu,* which had been completed twenty years before in 636...."[50] As such, the division of historical writings included in the

---

47 Qian Mu (2003b: 136–137) voices a similar issue in his criticism of Liu Zhiji. While he notes that *Wenxin diaolong* and *Shitong* occupy a similar position with regard to literature and history, respectively, he ranks the former much higher than the latter and goes on to decry the fact that Liu Zhiji is only concerned with historical writing, narrowly speaking, and not with larger issues of historical understanding. This criticism, while true enough in some sense, overlooks the fact that the *shi* 史 Liu Zhiji was studying was "historical writing" and not "history," a subtle but critical difference.

48 *Wenxin diaolong* 4.16: 609.

49 Lu Yaodong 2000: 71.

50 Twitchett 1992: 81.

bibliographical treatise and subsequently incorporated into *Suishu* preceded Liu Zhiji's *Shitong* by approximately fifty years.

In terms of the total number of chapters listed in the works catalogued, the division of historical writings is far larger than any of the other three divisions. The size announced within that division is 817 works in 13,264 chapters. However, a careful counting of the actual works listed in the earliest extant edition of *Suishu* yields 802 works in 13,218 chapters. Whatever the precise numbers may originally have been, it reflects an impressive increase in historical writing during the 500 years since the *Hanshu*. In fact the *total* number of works catalogued in the entire *Hanshu* "Yiwen zhi" is more than 200 fewer than in the *Suishu* division of historical writings *alone*. This means that the period from the end of the Han until the first decades of the Tang, however understudied it may be in Western sinology, is absolutely critical to the study of early Chinese historiography.[51]

The large number of works noted above leads to the key question under consideration here: how is the category *shi* configured and understood in this seminal treatise? The one-word answer would be "broadly," and a two-word answer "very broadly." Certainly any attempt to sort into a mere four categories the complex, burgeoning world of texts produced in the centuries just before the compilation of "Jingji zhi" will require those categories to be very broad indeed and to possess somewhat murky boundaries.

Within the division of historical writings in the *Suishu*, bibliographic treatises are thirteen lists of texts, each with an accompanying explanation.[52] In order, these are labeled as follows: "standard histories" (*zhengshi* 正史), "ancient histories" (*gushi* 古史), "miscellaneous histories" (*zashi* 雜史), "histories of overlords" (*bashi* 霸史), "diaries of activity and repose" (*qijuzhu* 起居注), "chapters on old events" (*gushi pian* 古事篇), "chapters on duties and offices" (*zhiguan pian* 職官篇), "chapters of

---

51   A point emphasized in Crowell 2006.
52   *Suishu* 33: 953–996.

notes on ceremony" (*yizhu pian* 儀注篇), "chapters on punishments and laws" (*xingfa pian* 刑法篇), "miscellaneous biographies" (*zazhuan* 雜傳), "records of geography" (*dili zhi ji* 地理之記), "chapters on genealogical lineages" (*puxi pian* 譜系篇), and "chapters of catalogues" (*bulu pian* 簿錄篇). In terms of the number of works included, miscellaneous biographies is by far the largest section, with 217 books listed. However, these are mostly small books and total only 1,286 chapters or approximately six chapters on average per book. The largest section in terms of the total size of works included is the standard histories, which lists only 67 books but nonetheless contains over 3,000 chapters. On the other end of the spectrum, the two smallest sections—chapters on old events and chapters of catalogues—list twenty-five books with 404 chapters and thirty books with 214 chapters, respectively.

One way of dividing the thirteen sections is to draw a distinction between those we might consider historical writing, narrowly speaking, and those that present raw historical material. The first category would include the first four sections: standard histories, ancient histories, miscellaneous histories, and histories of overlords. Each of these, and only these, have the word *shi* "historical writings" as part of the name by which they are designated. One might then put chapters on old events and miscellaneous biographies in this category as well, but the remaining sections, chapters on penal law, records of geography, etc. include the type of raw material from which history might be constructed. As noted above, each of the thirteen lists of books includes a paragraph or two summarizing the content of that section, and a general summary of all thirteen sections is found at the end of the entire division of historical writings. Through these small essays we begin to see more clearly just how *shi* at that time was conceptualized.

A certain narrative wends its way through these essays. It begins with the notion that from the earliest times there existed an office of scribes (*shiguan* 史官) composed of extraordinary men with "broad learning and powerful discernment" 博文強識, who supervised numerous subordinates. Consequently, "of earlier words and former actions, there were none they did not know about" 前言往行，無不識.[53] In several of the essays, this golden era is associated with the description of the bureaucracy found in *Zhouguan* 周官 (Offices of the Zhou, otherwise known as *Zhouli* 周禮 [Rituals of the Zhou]). In fact, many of the tasks implicit in the composition of the types of records listed in the thirteen sections, as we shall see in several cases, supposedly derive from one or another part of this idealized ancient bureaucracy. At a certain point in time—never precisely dated but apparently during the Warring States period—the office of scribes was "discarded and discontinued" 放絕. This decline concluded when the notorious Qin ruler "destroyed the statutes of the former kings" 滅先王之典 so that the "system that had been handed down no longer existed" 遺制莫存.[54]

This narrative goes on to praise the Han as a time when elements of the older, pre-Qin system were restored and preserved. It singles out such early Han figures as Xiao He 蕭何 and Shusun Tong 叔孫通 for their contributions to this cause.[55] Perhaps the most critical moment in this resurgence comes when Emperor Wu "for the first time established a lord grand scribe and commanded Sima Tan to act in this position" 始置太史公，命司馬談為之.[56] The new office, grand scribe, a variant of a supposedly older scheme, became a collection point for all sorts of records. Afterwards, the Han "rather conformed to the old precedent" 頗循其舊, and Ban Gu is singled out as someone who "followed this" 因之.[57] But from the Wei and Jin dynasties on down, the restored tradition was increasingly neglected and eventually genuine scholars were ignored, so that "groups of men occupying positions but doing nothing glanced about in scorn from high pavilions, while scholars of well-founded words, waved their writing

---

53   *Suishu* 33: 992.
54   *Suishu* 33: 956.
55   *Suishu* 33: 967, 972, 974.
56   *Suishu* 33: 956.
57   *Suishu* 33: 992.

brushes from humble thatched huts down below" 尸素之儔，盱衡延閣之上，立言之士，揮翰蓬茨之下.[58]

The period from the end of the Han down through the Sui might have witnessed unprecedented textual production, but a frequent refrain in the division of historical writings underlines how much was lost or scattered during these politically tumultuous times. As a result, the task of those compiling the bibliography is to seek out and preserve whatever textual remnants of the past they can find. The essay at the end of the chapter on punishments and laws strikes a chord that resonates as well throughout other essays: "The Han code has been lost for a long time, and the old precedents and judgments also for the most part are in disarray or lost. Now we make a record of what is extant and can be examined and compile it as chapters on punishments and laws" 漢律久亡，故事駁議，又多零失。今錄其見存可觀者，編為刑法篇.[59] Briefly, then, the story told in the division essays is one of a bureaucratic system characterized by thoroughness and efficiency (the early Zhou) gradually falling into decline (the Warring States) and then being entirely destroyed (Qin), followed by an act of salvage and restoration (Han) and then gradual decline once again (Six Dynasties), requiring finally the act of restoration that stands before us as the *Suishu* treatise itself.

Two important and interrelated themes recur throughout these essays, both highly relevant to how *shi* was understood at that time: first, imperial power, through its officials, plays the central role in compiling and preserving historical records; second, the main task of historical labor is to collect and excerpt records, largely *administrative* records, for preservation, contending time and time again with forces of neglect, dispersion, and destruction.

As noted above, the office of scribes as described in *Zhouguan* is given particular emphasis in the history of historical writing found in the "Jingji zhi." The compilation of standard histories, as we would expect, is connected to such offices:

---

58   Ibid.
59   *Suishu* 33: 974.

古者天子諸侯，必有國史，以紀言行，後世多務，其道彌繁。夏殷已上，左史記言，右史記事，周則太史、小史、內史、外史、御史，分掌其事，而諸侯之國，亦置史官。

In ancient times the Son of Heaven and the lords were certain to have state scribes to make note of words and actions. In later generations, the duties of the state scribes increased, and their way of operating became more complex. From the Xia and Yin periods on, scribes of the left recorded words and scribes of the right recorded deeds. In the Zhou grand scribes, lesser scribes, court scribes, scribes of external activities and administrative scribes divided and managed these duties, and the states of the lords also established bureaus of scribes.[60]

The essays may not connect the compilation of ancient histories as directly to the office of scribes as the compilation of standard histories, but this lesser form, if we may regard it as such, still owes its origin to two events with strong links to officialdom. The first of these is the Han emperor Xian's 漢獻帝 (r. 189–220) famous opinion that "the text of Ban Gu's *Hanshu* is verbose and difficult to consult" 以班固漢書文繁難省, which induces him to order Xun Yue 荀悅 (148–209) to simplify *Hanshu* and reduce it to a strict chronological form resembling *Annals* and *Zuozhuan*. The second is the discovery in 280 CE from the Ji Tomb of "a scribal record of the state of Wei" 魏國之史記也, what we now call *Zhushu jinian* 竹書紀年 (The bamboo annals), from which scholars can "understand that *Annals* is the standard method for ancient scribal records and that those who compiled accounts largely followed the *Annals* form" 以為春秋則古史記之正法，有所著述，多依春秋之體. Accordingly, the section on ancient histories lists *Zhushu jinian* and Xun Yue's *Hanji* 漢紀 (Han annals) among its thirty-four exemplars, the first linked to a government tradition of scribal record keeping and the second to an imperial order.[61]

---

60   *Suishu* 33: 956.

61   *Suishu* 33: 959. For an excellent study of the *Zhushu jinian*, see Shaughnessy 2006: 131–255.

Most other forms of historical writing, as defined in the essays, also provided a direct or indirect link to officialdom, especially those containing raw documentation from which history is built up. The diaries of activity and repose are traced back to a *Zuozhuan* comment, "When the ruler acts, it must be recorded" 君舉必書, and are further connected to a purported tradition of "women scribes" 女史 who worked inside the palace.[62] Records of old events derive from a tradition of bureaucrats presenting various official documents and "storing them in official archives" 藏于官府,[63] a practice also attested, the treatise reminds us, in *Zuozhuan*.[64] Chapters on duties and offices originate in a practice of writing names and duties on bamboo strips of official appointments. For notes on ceremonies, the government-appointed grand scribe has the responsibility "to take charge of documents and categorize them so as to bring harmony to official business" 太史執書以協事之類是也.[65]

In several instances the link to officialdom is admittedly tenuous, and such cases deserve special attention precisely because they reveal the somewhat blurry edges of the historical writing. The two most obvious cases are the miscellaneous histories and miscellaneous biographies sections, each marked by that portentous word *za* 雜 alerting us to something not entirely homogenous, something neither fish nor fowl. The rise of miscellaneous histories is connected in the treatise to an early Han attempt to salvage something after "the Qin disposed of ancient script texts and records were scattered and lost" 秦撥去古文，篇籍遺散. As part of this salvage operation, the materials now found in *Zhanguo ce* were collected and Lu Jia produced his *Chu Han chunqiu*. Other works followed but all the works listed as miscellaneous histories are somewhat marginalized when the essay concludes as follows: "In matching appropriate words very closely to actual

---

62   *Suishu* 33: 966. Cf. n. 32 above.

63   *Suishu* 33: 976.

64   *Zuozhuan* Ding 1.1: 1524. These repositories are also called "covenant archives" (*mengfu* 盟府) in Zuozhuan. Cf. notes 70 and 72.

65   *Suishu* 33: 696.

events, they in all cases do not resemble *Chunqiu, Shiji,* and *Hanshu,* but have been produced rashly and are not a proper standard for historical records" 其屬辭比事，皆不與春秋、史記、漢書相似，蓋率爾而作，非史策之正也.[66] Since the works in this section derive largely from non-official sources, the content is suspect: "Moreover they contain tales from back alleys and are fantastic and absurd. No one can discern whether they are true or false" 又有委巷之說，迁怪妄誕，真虛莫測.[67] The only justification offered for preserving such things is that "they, for the most part, are all the affairs of emperors and kings" 然其大抵皆帝王之事. Thus, such historiography, presented without any reference to the office of scribes or any other government entity, is a product of political breakdown, a sort of aberrant and unreliable form. Nevertheless, miscellaneous histories can be broadly perused "in order to extract their essential information" 以酌其要;[68] redeemable because it concerns persons of political significance, especially, as the essay itself says, "emperors and kings."

Miscellaneous biographies are still more problematic. First of all, as already noted, this is by far the largest section of the *shi* division with a surprisingly large number of works (217) included, mostly works deriving

---

66   The phrase "matching appropriate words very closely to actual events" (*zhu ci bi shi* 屬辭比事) appears earlier in *Liji* and is a skill described there as "that which *Annals* teaches" 春秋教也 (*Liji jijie* XLVII.26: 1254 ("Jing jie" 經解).

67   The *Suishu* "Jingji zhi," like the earlier *Hanshu* "Yiwen zhi," also has a separate bibliographic category for "common tales" (*xiaoshuo* 小說) and both texts identify such tales with "talk on streets and discussions in alleys" (*jietan xiangyu* 街談巷語, see *Hanshu* 30: 1745 and *Suishu* 34: 1012, the latter writing *jieshuo* 街說 rather than *jietan* 街談). In both cases, such tales are said to derive not from scribal offices, but from a special government office entitled, somewhat derogatorily, "the office of minor matters" (稗官). The question of which texts containing such tales find their way into the "miscellaneous histories" or "miscellaneous biographies" sections of "Jingji zhi" and which are categorized under "common tales" is an issue for further study; one might take as a starting point Lu Yaodong 2000: 221–252. Assuredly the history/fiction axis in early China is quite different from that in other traditions. However, this has not prevented traditional Chinese critics from disapproving of the rather broad conception of "history" in the Six Dynasties period and reflected in "Jingji zhi" (on this, see examples in Lu Yaodong 2000: 221–222).

68   *Suishu* 33: 962.

from the late Han through the Six Dynasties period. The sheer size of this division fully justifies the claim that "the separate biography" (*biezhuan* 別傳), which takes the individual historical figure as a basic unit, was the major new historiographical form to appear during the process of transformation in historiography that occurred in the Wei-Jin period."[69] Some believe this proliferation of biographical writing results from the weakening of Confucianism during the Wei-Jin period and the increased emphasis upon the individual.[70] Second, listed in this section are such works as *Liexian zhuan* 列仙傳 (Biographies of immortals), *Shenxian zhuan* 神仙傳 (Biographies of transcendents and immortals), Gan Bao's 干寶 *Soushen ji* 搜神記 (In search of the supernatural) and other works that today we would hardly classify as history. Quite unlike the case with miscellaneous histories, significant effort is spent in the treatise to link this section to official activity.

The essay describing the miscellaneous biographies begins: "The ancient office of scribes found it necessary to broaden what it recorded and was not merely concerned with the actions of the ruler. According to *Zhouguan*, the scribes of external activities managed the memoranda of the four quarters, and so it was the scribal records of the lords that consolidated and included them" 古之史官，必廣其所記，非獨人君之舉。周官，外史掌四方之志，則諸侯史記，兼而有之. Indeed, *Zuozhuan* is quoted as establishing a precedent for preserving accounts of important individuals: "Guo Zhong and Guo Shu are to the right of Wang Ji and were King Wen's court ministers. Their merit was achieved in the king's household and is preserved in the covenant archives" 虢仲、虢叔，王季之穆，勳在王室，藏於盟府.[71] Information on individuals was abundant—the result, we are told, of a very thorough bureaucratic apparatus and one devoted to the appointment of worthy persons for office:

---

69 Lu Yaodong 2000: 7. This form is "separate" in that it is not attached to a standard history and thus circulates "separately."
70 Lu Yaodong 2000: 2–6.
71 *Zuozhuan* Xi 5.8: 308, as translated in Durrant, Li, and Schaberg 2016: 277.

周官，司寇凡大盟約，涖其盟書，登于天府。太史、內史、司會，六官皆受其貳而藏之。是則王者誅賞，具錄其事，昭告神明，百官史臣，皆藏其書。故自公卿諸侯，至于羣士，善惡之迹，畢集史職。而又閭胥之政，凡聚眾庶，書其敬敏任卹者，族師每月書其孝悌睦媚有學者，黨正歲書其德行道藝者，而入之於鄉大夫。鄉大夫三年大比，考其德行道藝，舉其賢者能者，而獻其書。王再拜受之，登于天府，內史貳之。是以窮居側陋之士，言行必達，皆有史傳。

According to *Zhouguan*, the supervisor of criminal justice, in all cases of important covenants or agreements, oversees the covenant documents and registers them in the royal archive. The grand scribe, court scribe, supervisor of meetings, and the six offices all receive copies and file them away. So it is that when kings punish or reward, they make a complete record of the circumstances and announce them to the bright spirits. The scribal ministers of the various bureaus in all cases file away these documents. Consequently, from dukes, high ministers, and lords on down to the men-of-service, traces of good and evil are exhaustively gathered together as a scribal duty. And, moreover, whenever the administration of village leaders assembles the people, it makes a record of those who are respectful, quick-witted, responsible, and compassionate; the lineage preceptors each month wrote down those who were filial, fraternal, lived in harmony with family and in-laws, or were learned. The chief of the unit of five hundred households each year wrote down those who behaved with virtue and displayed principle and skill and presented them to the district high officials. Every three years, the district high officials held a great competition. They would examine their character, deeds, principles, and skills and recommend the worthy and capable and present documentation concerning them. The king bowed twice as he received these documents and registered them in the royal archive. The court scribe made a second copy. So it was that gentlemen of shabby dwellings and meager status were sure to be known and all had a scribal biography.[72]

---

72 *Suishu* 33: 981–982.

As a result of this highly organized statewide effort, information about countless individuals could supposedly be located in official government files. Almost no one's deeds, good or evil, could escape the far-seeing eye of well-organized administration.[73]

This elaborate structure supposedly collapsed as the office of scribes declined. The resuscitation of a system upon which biography could be based is quite interestingly associated with the Han practice whereby officials at the local level regularly submitted "account books" 計書.[74] As a result, the essay says, "Acts of good or of evil were in every case completely collected" 善惡之事，靡不畢集. We are immediately informed that both Sima Qian and Ban Gu relied upon these sources for the completion of the biographies in their respective histories. As praiseworthy as these two great Han historians might have been, they overlooked many individuals, so the essay says, whose lives passed in obscurity. Liu Xiang is singled out for having produced biographies of just such overlooked persons. Still, these works receive a decidedly mixed review: "In all cases, such biographies relied upon his intentions being lofty, but they were hastily produced and are not found in the standard histories" 皆因其志尚，率爾而作，不在正史. As in the case of miscellaneous histories, the essay acknowledges that miscellaneous biographies contain much that is spurious or fantastic, but then such questionable material is justified because "if we delve into their origins, they are most likely also the minor concerns of the office of the scribes" 推其本源，蓋亦史官之末事也.[75]

---

73 Despite my belief that the system presented here is somewhat idealized, assuredly *Zuozhuan,* if it can be believed, portrays a world in which official records were abundant. Whenever a lord travels "it must be recorded" (Zhuang 23.1: 226) and when he returns, "merits are recorded on bamboo strips" (Huan 2.7: 91), when one is appointed to service "one's name is written on a bamboo slip" (Xi 23.4: 403), the covenants of previous Zhou kings are "stored away in the covenant archives" 盟府 (Xi 26.3: 440), bad behavior means one's goes down "in infamy in the records of the princes" (Wen 15.2: 609), and so forth. For more on the extensive tradition of record-keeping that seems to have existed in Spring and Autumn and Warring States China, see Durrant, Li, and Schaberg 2016: XXXIX–XLII.

74 On this practice, see Loewe 2004: 44 and particularly footnote 11.

75 *Suishu* 33: 982.

The treatise emphasizes the official nature of almost all *shi* texts, repeatedly linking the history of this form of writing to the establishment, fall, and transformation of government bureaucracy. This stands in stark contrast to the apparent fact that most important texts of early Chinese historiography were by no means official works. Hans van Ess refers in his recent study of *Shiji* and *Hanshu* to the dominance in the early Chinese tradition of historical works "not founded on a state office of scribes, but in projects of private historiography."[76] Du Weiyun 杜維運 (1928–2012) stresses the same point in the following words:

> The pre-Tang period is a time when private individuals wrote history. *Chunqiu* was brought to completion by Confucius writing as a single private individual. *Shiji* is the words of the single family of Sima Qian. *Hanshu* was completed by Ban Biao, Ban Gu, and Ban Zhao and is an account compiled by persons in a private capacity. *Sanguo zhi*, *Hou Hanshu*, *Songshu*, and *Nan Qishu* all are private compilations . . . Therefore, prior to the Tang, writing history was a private occupation.[77]

However significant the role individual initiative played in early Chinese historiography, the treatise consistently tries to shade its message to imply a salient connection between early masterworks of historical writing and the central government. Indeed, each of the projects Du mentions, even if undertaken individually, was based on the work of anonymous *shi* officials who prepared the raw materials. This is true even in the cases of the two towering Han historians Sima Qian and Ban Gu. The treatise says that Sima Tan was the first to occupy the position of lord grand scribe and that his office was the collection point for records from throughout the realm. This centralized document repository allowed such historians as "Sima Qian and Ban Gu to compile and complete them" 司馬遷、班固，撰而

---

76 Van Ess 2014: 1:2.

77 Du Weiyun 2007, vol. 2: 195.

成之.[78] In the case of Ban Gu's *Hanshu*, the treatise further emphasizes that Emperor Ming commanded Ban Gu to complete the work begun by his father Ban Biao, thus implying that *Hanshu* is at least to some degree the result of an imperial order. Moreover, such works are somewhat belatedly listed as standard histories and therefore by implication find their ultimate source in the tradition of the office of scribes.

The second theme running through the treatise is closely related to the first: historical texts are largely presented as products of compilation or excerption. If Confucius really did consider himself someone who "transmits and does not create" 述而不作[79] and if Sima Qian was sincere in characterizing himself with the same formula,[80] then the entire historiographical tradition is one based largely upon transmission and continuity rather than creative genius. Such an emphasis is entirely congruent with what Esther Klein has said about the tendency among Huan Tan 桓譚 (43 BCE–28 CE), Wang Chong 王充 (27–100), and other early readers to regard *Shiji* as much more a compilation than a work of "creation."[81] We might be tempted to brush this aside by simply arguing that the history of the past is by nature a compilation, a genre based entirely on earlier documentation. While this may be true, we still laud the creativity of historians. For example, a long tradition persists in China of viewing Sima Qian's work to be a creative response to personal suffering, a theme that we might trace to his "Letter to Ren An" and the "Postface" to *Shiji*.[82]

---

78 *Suishu* 33: 981. Elsewhere the treatise gives Sima Tan particular prominence. He first occupied the new office, collected numerous texts, and, according to this account, Sima Tan, not Sima Qian, "relied upon *Mr. Zuo* (a text, as noted earlier, often identified with *Zuozhuan*), *Guoyu*, *Shiben*, *Zhanguo ce* and *Chu Han chunqiu*, and joined them together with events that occurred later to form the words of a single family" 談乃據左氏、國語、世本、 戰國策、楚漢春秋，接其後事，成一家之言 (*Suishu* 33: 956). Sima Qian is credited with completing a work that was very well along—at least so it seems from the treatise—when his father passed away in 110 BCE.

79 *Lunyu yizhu* 7.1: 65.

80 *Shiji* 130: 3300.

81 Klein 2011: 192ff.

82 Much is said about this particular issue in Durrant, Li, Nylan and van Ess 2016.

The work of collection and compilation that lies at the heart of early historiography as presented in the treatise is a labor that attempts to counter powerful forces of destruction and loss. Some of these, such as the Qin book burning or the frequent political upheavals of the Six Dynasties period, are cataclysmic, but others simply come through the erosion time exacts in an era when many documents were fragile and limited in circulation. The treatise particularly underscores the easy loss of raw historical documents. Diaries of activity and repose, for example, were supposedly maintained as early as Emperor Wu of the Han and "were apparently kept in the inner palace and were the responsibility of women scribes. Nevertheless, they have all vanished and can no longer be known" 似在宮中，為女史之職。然皆零落，不可復知.[83] Describing chapters on duties and offices, we are informed that "from the Song and Qi on down, such books increasingly proliferated, but chapters and sections, standing alone or conjoined, were easily lost or scattered" 宋、齊已後，其書益繁，而篇卷零疊，易為亡散.[84] Sometimes loss occurs from a simple failure to comprehend the significance of documents. One of the saddest and most famous cases is the loss of documents discovered from the tomb of King Xiang of Wei in 280 CE: "Those who uncovered the tomb did not consider them significant and [the documents] were often scattered and fell into disarray" 發冢者不以為意，往往散亂.[85]

The treatise itself is an attempt, as the conclusions of so many of the essays remind us, to preserve a record of what remains of an ever-threatened collection. The irony, of course, is that the very creation of a centralized bureaucratic apparatus to collect and store documents means that such a collection becomes particularly vulnerable to political upheaval and change. The forces of collection and dispersion portrayed over and over again throughout the "Treatise" will continue to operate in China for many centuries to come.

---

83 *Suishu* 33: 966.
84 *Suishu* 33: 969.
85 *Suishu* 33: 959. On the issue of the scattering and later editing of these texts, see Shaughnessy 2006.

The *shi* division of the treatise is only one manifestation of an increasingly rich Chinese tradition of historiography. Within a few decades of its completion, as we have already noted, Liu Zhiji published his *Shitong*. Among this monumental work's rich but sometimes frustrating offerings is a chapter entitled "The Establishment of the Office of Scribes" 史官建置. Here, the official activity of the office of scribes is so critical as to be the final bulwark against personal annihilation: "If only the office of scribes does not break off and the writings on bamboo and silk persist indefinitely, then a person may die and become part of empty obscurity, but it is as if his deeds were present, shining forth like the stars and the Milky Way" 苟史官不絕，竹帛長存，則其人已亡，杳成空寂，而其事如在，皎同星漢.[86] By the time Liu Zhiji, who once worked in the Tang dynasty Bureau of History, wrote these lines, the Tang government had constructed a significant bureaucratic apparatus for the collection and production of official history. While this "had by no means yet reached a final form such as was to be achieved under later dynasties,"[87] the interests of that new bureau, and the persistent belief that it had roots even in remote antiquity, continue to shape Chinese historiography well into the future.

4. So, What Is *shi*?

Shi is first and foremost the name of an office. Eventually it comes to mean that which this office, in its various bureaucratic incarnations, produces. The problem is that the conception of *shi* changes over time and leads to a layering effect, with later conceptions projected into the past and reshaping what had happened before. This is to say little more than that the keyword *shi* has its own history, so that any unified translation of this term can be misleading depending on the period in question. It is clear from *Zuozhuan*

---

86   *Shitong tongshi* II: 303.
87   Twitchett 1992: 30.

that *shi* did on occasion make written notice of events, of which *Chunqiu* is an exemplar. But to think that was their only responsibility, or perhaps even their chief responsibility, is clearly an error. The translation "scribe" is reductive, but any other translation seems equally so. While little evidence exists outside of the problematic *Zhouguan* that the bureaucratic structure in which scribes worked was a highly elaborate one, it is surely possible that it was more so than early records indicate. All this changed during the early Han period. The establishment of a lord grand scribe, the office Sima Tan held, was less motivated by the desire to reverse a wholesale destruction of records during the Qin than by the administrative problem of running a far-flung empire. We know that the Han was awash in records, of which the famous account of documents mentioned above were probably only one small part. The treatise projects this elaborate structure into the distant past, with *Zhouguan* and occasionally *Zuozhuan* citations as its authority, and thereby creates the impression of a kind of depth and stability to the tradition of scribes that probably never existed. But the description of the duties of the *shi* bureaucracy in the treatise depicts it more as a place for the collection of raw documents than the production of new histories. We might be more accurate, then, to translate Sima Tan's position, *taishi gong*, as lord grand archivist.[88] Even his great historical project is presented as more of a natural extension of his work in the archives than as an act of creative historiography.

The whole issue becomes even more complicated when *shi* comes to be used as the name of a type of writing originally generated by those who occupied the *shi* office. Unlike the word "history," *shi* is not founded in a particular type of investigation but in a record deriving from a certain official activity. As this category of writing necessarily expands under the demands of a four-fold cataloging system, the texts listed as *shi* must be linked in some way to a scribal tradition, however tenuous that linkage might be, and

---

88   For this translation, see Durrant, Li, Nylan, Van Ess 2016: 18–21. The implication of the treatise is that the primary duty of this office was to manage documents and records, not necessarily produce new ones.

projected into the distant past with reference to ancient bureaucratic practices that may in fact have never existed, at least not in the way they are described. In the process, historical writing is robbed of its history and depicted as a timeless government duty that only changes as the state waxes and wanes. Such a conception downplays individual initiative: *Zuozhuan* is seen as a natural extension of the official scribal writing embodied by *Chunqiu*, *Shiji* becomes little more than the completion of an official duty of compilation, *Hanshu* the result of an emperor's command, and even works of considerable creative energy like Ge Hong's *Shenxian zhuan* or Gan Bao's *Soushen ji* are reduced to a reworked remnant of official scribal activity. The richness of a great and complex tradition is diminished to government bureaucratic activity. The "Jingji zhi" assuredly does provide us with an invaluable glimpse both at the variety and wealth of the early Chinese textual tradition, and at the same time it demonstrates how this rich tradition was flattened into a broad conception of governmental power and bureaucracy.

Bibliography

Baragwanath, Emily and Mathieu de Bakker. 2012. *Myth, Truth and Narrative in Herodotus*. Oxford: Oxford University Press.

Behr, Wolfgang. 2005. "Language Change in Premodern China: Notes on Its Perception and Impact on the Idea of a 'Constant Way.'" In *Historical Truth, Historical Criticism, and Ideology: Chinese Historiography and Historical Culture from a New Comparative Perspective*, ed. Helwig Schmidt-Glintzer, Jörn Rüsen, and Achim Mittag, 13–51. Leiden: Brill.

Breisach, Ernst. 1994. *Historiography: Ancient, Medieval & Modern*. Chicago and London: University of Chicago Press.

Brooks, Bruce and Taeko Brooks. 1998. *The Original Analects: Sayings of Confucius and His Successors*. New York: Columbia University Press.

Chunqiu Zuozhuan zhu 春秋左傳注. 1990. Edited and annotated by Yang Bojun 楊伯峻. Rev. ed. Beijing: Zhonghua shuju.

Clark, Anthony. 2008. *Ban Gu's History of Early China*. Amherst, New York: Cambria Press.

Confucius, The Analects. 1979. Translated by Lau, Dim-Cheuk. London: Penguin Books.

Crowell, William G. 2006. "Review of On-cho Ng and Q. Edward Wang. Mirroring the Past: The Writing and Use of History in Imperial China." *Early Medieval China* 12: 183–204.

Du Weiyun 杜維運. 1988. *Zhong xi gudai shixue bijiao* 中西古代史學比較. Taipei: Dongda.

———. 2007. *Zhongguo shixue shi* 中國史學史, 3 vols. Taipei: Sanmin.

Dudbridge, Glen. "Libraries, Book Catalogues, Lost Writings." *The Oxford History of Classical Chinese Literature*. Edited by Wiebke Denecke, Wai-yee Li, and Xiaofei Tian, 147–161. New York: Oxford University Press.

Durrant, Stephen. 2005. "Truth Claims in *Shiji*." *Historical Truth, Historical Criticism, Historical Ideology: Chinese Historiography and Historical Culture from a New Comparative Perspective*. Edited by Helwig Schmidt-Glintzer, Achim Mittag, and Jorn Rosen, 93–114. Leiden: Brill.

———. 2015. "Ban Biao, Ban Gu, Their Five *Shiji* Sources, and the *Chu Han chunqiu*." *Views from Withn, Views from Beyond: Approaches to the* Shiji *as an Early Work of Historiography*. Edited by Hans van Ess, Olga Lomová, and Dorothee Schaab-Hanke, 217–241. Wiesbaden: Harrassowitz.

———. 2017. "Histories (*shi* 史)." In *The Oxford History of Classical Chinese Literature*, edited by Wiebke Denecke, Wai-yee Li, and Xiaofei Tian, 184–200. New York: Oxford University Press.

Durrant, Stephen, Michael Nylan, Wai-yee Li, and Hans van Ess. 2016. *The Letter to Ren An and Sima Qian's Legacy*. Seattle: University of Washington Press.

Hanshu 漢書. 1962. By Ban Gu 班固 (32–92), et al. Annotated by Yan Shigu 顏師古 (581–645). Beijing: Zhonghua shuju.

Hartog, François. 1988. *The Mirror of Herodotus*. Translated by Janet Lloyd. Berkeley, Los Angeles, and London: University of California Press.

Hou Hanshu 後漢書. 1965. By Fan Ye 范曄 (398–445). With commentaries by Li Shan 李善 (630–689) et al. Beijing: Zhonghua shuju.

Klein, Esther Sunkyung. 2011. "The History of a Historian: Perspectives on the Authorial Role of Sima Qian." Ph.D. dissertation. Princeton University.

Li Wai-yee. 2017. "Traditional Genre Spectrum: Editor's Introduction." In *The Oxford History of Classical Chinese Literature*, edited by Wiebke Denecke, Wai-yee Li, and Xiaofei Tian, 163–169. New York: Oxford University Press.

Li Zongtong 李宗侗. 1991. *Zhongguo shixue shi* 中國史學史. Taipei: Wenhua daxue.

Liji jijie 禮記集解. 1995. Compiled by Sun Xidan 孫希旦 (1736–1784). Edited by Shen Xiaohuan 沈嘯寰 and Wang Xingxian 王星賢. Beijing: Zhonghua shuju.

Liu Zhiji (661–721). 2014. Chaussende, Damien, transl. 2014. *Traité de l'historien parfait by Liu Zhiji*. Translated by Damien Chaussende. Paris: Les belles lettres.

Loewe, Michael. 2004. *The Men Who Governed Han China*. Leiden and Boston: Brill.

Lu Yaodong 逯耀東. 2000. *Wei Jin shixue de sixiang yu shehui jichu* 魏晉史學的思想與社會基礎. Taipei: Dongda.

Lunyu yizhu 論語譯注. 1992. Annotated by Yang Bojun 楊伯峻. Beijing: Zhonghua shuju.

Lüshi chunqiu jiaoshi 呂氏春秋校釋. 2002. Annotated by Chen Qiyou 陳奇猷. Shanghai: Shanghai guji.

Mengzi yizhu 孟子譯注. 1992. Annotated by Yang Bojun 楊伯峻. Beijing: Zhonghua shuju.

Pines, Yuri. 2005. "Speeches and the Question of Authenticity in Ancient Chinese Historical Records." In *Historical Truth, Historical Criticism, and Ideology: Chinese Historiography and Historical Culture from a New Comparative Perspective*, edited by Helwig Schmidt-Glintzer, Jörn Rüsen, and Achim Mittag, 197–226. Leiden: Brill.

———. 2009. "Chinese History Writing: Between the Sacred and the Secular." In *Early Chinese Religion: Part One: Shang through Han (1250 BC–220 AD)*, edited by John Lagerwey and Marc Kalinowski, 315–340. Leiden: Brill.

Qian Mu 錢穆. 2003a. *Zhongguo shixue fawei* 中國史學發微. Taipei: Dongda.

———. 2003b. *Zhongguo shixue mingzhu* 中國史學名著. Taipei: Sanmin.

Qu Lindong 瞿林東. 1999. *Zhongguo shixueshi gang* 中國史學史綱. Beijing: Xinhua.

Schaberg, David. 2013. "Functionary Speech: On the Work of *Shi* 使 and *Shi* 史." In *Facing the Monarch: Modes of Advice in the Early Chinese Court,* edited by Garret P.S. Olberding, 19–41. Cambridge, MA: Harvard University Asia Center.

Selbitschka, Armin. 2018. "'I Write Therefore I Am': Scribes, Literacy, and Identity in Early China." *Harvard Journal of Asiatic Studies* 78.2: 413–478.

Shaughnessy, Edward L. 2006. *Rewriting Early Chinese Texts*. Albany: State University of New York Press.

Shiji 史記. 1959. By Sima Qian 司馬遷 (ca. 145–ca.88 BCE) et al. Annotated by Pei Yin 裴駰 (5th c.), Sima Zhen 司馬貞 (679–732), and Zhang Shoujie 張守節 (7th c.). Beijing: Zhonghua shuju.

Shitong tongshi 史通通釋. 1988. By Liu Zhiji 劉知幾 (661–721). Annotated by Pu Qilong 浦起龍 (1679–1762). Shanghai: Shanghai shudian.

Shuowen jiezi gulin 説文解字詁林. 1928. By Xu Shen 許慎 (ca. 58–149) et al. Edited by Ding Fubao 丁福保 (1874–1952). Shanghai: Yixue shuju.

Sima Qian (ca. 145–ca. 88 BCE). 1994–2008. *The Grand Scribe's Records*. 6 vols. Translated by William H. Nienhauser Jr., et al. Bloomington: Indiana University Press.

Suishu 隋書. 1979. By Wei Zheng 魏徵 (580–643) et al. 3 vols. Beijing: Zhonghua shuju.

The Analects of Confucius. 1938. Translated by Arthur Waley (1889–1966). New York: The Macmillan Company.

The Concise Oxford Dictionary. 1995. Oxford: Clarendon Press.

Twitchett, Denis. 1992. *The Writing of Official History under the T'ang*. Cambridge: Cambridge University Press.

Van Ess, Hans. 2014. *Politik und Geschichtsschreibung in alten China: Pan-ma i-t'ung* 班馬異同. Wiesbaden: Harrassowitz.

Vogelsang, Kai. 2003–2004. "The Scribes Genealogy." *Oriens Extremus* 44: 1–9.

———. 2007. *Geschichte als Problem: Entstehung, Formen und Funktionen von Geschichtsschreibung im Alten China*. Wiesbaden: Harrassowitz.

Wang Guowei 王國維 (1877–1927). 2003. *Guantang jilin (wai er zhong)* 觀堂集林（外二種）. Edited by Peng Lin 彭林. Shijiazhuang: Hebei jiaoyu chubanshe.

Wenxin diaolong yizheng 文心雕龍義證. 1989. By Liu Xie 劉勰 (ca. 469–532). Annotated by Zhan Ying 詹鍈. Shanghai: Shanghai guji.

Xu Fuguan 徐復觀. 1989. *Liang Han sixiang shi* 兩漢思想史. 3 vols. Taipei: Xuesheng.

Xu Zhaochang 許兆昌. 2006. *Xian Qin shiguan de zhidu yu wenhua* 先秦史官的制度與文化. Heilongjiang renmin chubanshe.

Zhang Dake 張大可 et. al. 2005. *Shiji wenxian yu bianzuan xue yanjiu* 史記文獻與編纂學研究. Beijing: Huawen.

Zuo Tradition/Zuozhuan 左傳: *Commentary on Spring and Autumn Annals*. 2016. Translated by Stephen Durrant, Wai-yee Li, and David Schaberg. Seattle and London: University of Washington Press.

Zuozhuan. See *Chunqiu Zuozhuan zhu*.

Socio-political Keywords

4

What's in a Slogan? The Political Rationale and the Economic Debates behind "Enrich the State" (*fuguo* 富國) in Early China

Romain Graziani

The reason being, in this case, that the government had recently been telling farmers to grow as much corn as possible. "Food is a munition of war," they were told, "and the farm should be treated as a munitions factory." And so, where once there had been green, now there was gold.

Jonathan Coe, *The Rain before It Falls*[1]

Introduction

In contrast to the progress of material culture, the evolution of words challenges the ability of historians to detect rich layers of meanings that tend to merge into each other when seen from a distance. In certain historical moments of deep changes, language and terminology are not immediately adapted or updated to reflect current usage or new social circumstances. Certain words or notions survive the intuitions or the institutions from which they originally stemmed. Boundaries are blurred by the natural evolution of words and new pragmatic adjustments. In short, whereas history of material culture deals among others with dating and description

---

1   Coe 2009: 50–51.

of tools (plow, swords, carts), intellectual history may envision keywords or core notions in a society as tools whose shapes can remain unaltered for some time but whose functions, users and locations are subject to constant changes. And yet, thorny and vexed as it may prove, this exercise in cognitive archeology is a critical task for historians who study ideas, values and representations.

In the following pages, I shall focus on a slogan that splices together one of the most appealing keywords of the Warring States period (453–221 BCE), *fuguo* 富國 ("enrich the state"), and its frequent corollary *qiangbing* 強兵 ("strengthen the army"). The key-phrase *fuguo* in Chinese political culture has a long, winding and complex history that illustrates the idea that keywords command an attitude of hermeneutic wariness. Indeed, the term *guo* 國 is, so to speak, fraught, or blessed, with a semantic ambivalence that makes the slogan teeter between two goals, the state and the country, or in other terms the government or the people.[2] *Fuguo* can signify two contradictory programs: 1) make the *country* rich by protecting the interest of the people against usury and private speculation; 2) enrich the *state*, and thus the government by taking out what people have stockpiled—their food, grains or their cash reserves.

Starting from this semantic ambivalence that gives rise to two distinct economic agendas, I shall address the following questions: what kind of individuals should be primarily enriched: the commoners, the elite, or the ruler, and who should be prevented from becoming rich? How should the *guo* be enriched concretely: with grain or gold, with manpower or new lands? And by which methods? I will examine in the following pages the

---

2 One should note here in passing the polysemy of the *min* 民, which we translate here as "people." During the Warring States period, the logic of contrast (determined by categories) seems to have determined the exact meaning of *min* in each occurrence: humans as opposed to the spirits, the ruled in distinction with the ruler, or the commoners in contrast with the elite. The semantic spectrum of *min* is explained in Pines (2009: 190). Pines (2009: 262n13) further mentions Qiu Xigui's suggestion that when deities or Heaven are invoked or mentioned, *min* may well refer to all human beings, ruler and ruled alike.

major policies that were devised and sometimes implemented: taxations, cuts in expenses, exploitation of natural resources, agricultural production, state monopolies and financial speculation.

I shall try to show that the slogan *fuguo* was originally part of a narrative on the legitimation of a strong centralized state; it voiced the urge to implement certain economic policies that are sometimes at odds with one another. The recurrence of the slogan across Chinese history may well have given the ruling elite the sense of a common language, a continuous mission and a set of common goals. It belongs to a cluster of political keywords and formula that set a framework within which crucial debates on the nature of the state could take place.

It is hard to know when and by whom exactly the phrase *fuguo* (and sometimes its corollary *qiangbing*) were first coined and promoted. Their earliest extant traces are in the *Shangjunshu* 商君書 (hereafter, *Book of Lord Shang*), though the policies encapsulated in this term surely predate the compilation of the book.[3] At the time, it must have come off as an offensive formula when deciphered in the light of the ruler's moral mission as sanctified in earlier textual traditions. And yet, this slogan blazed a trail for other thinkers and statesmen over the course of the fourth and third centuries BCE. It pinpoints the reformist spirit of the day and encompasses the entire Chinese world of the Warring States period, especially Qin, Wei (where it is associated with Li Kui 李悝 [d. ca. 400 BCE]), and Qi.

I shall start by analyzing the sociopolitical background of this slogan, explain its economic implications and account for its consequences for the social organization of the state. In doing so, I shall refer to elements of a broader debate among four major texts of the Warring States period, *Mozi* 墨子, *Xunzi* 荀子, the *Book of Lord Shang*, and *Guanzi* 管子, in which we

---

3   故治國者，其專力也，以富國強兵也。 "Hence he who rules the state well consolidates force to attain a rich state and a strong army" (*Shangjunshu* III.8: 60 ["Yi yan" 壹言]; Transl. Pines 2017: 8.2). For the recurrence of this formula in association with Qin statesmen, see *Zhanguo ce* 3.13: 117 ("Qin ce 秦策" 1); *Shiji* 74: 2343; for its association with Han Fei 韓非 (d. 233 BCE), see *Yantielun* X.55: 567.

can retrace economic and political debates revolving around the notion of *fuguo* (and partly of *qiangbing*). The semantic ambivalence of the key term *guo* and the various possible ways of defining wealth foster the debate about the best way to manage human communities and ensure prosperity.

1. New Trends in Warring States Times

The political, economical, and military history of the Warring States period has been extensively studied by Yang Kuan 楊寬 and Mark Edward Lewis, among others.[4] In what follows I shall therefore give only a brief overview of the context that directly underlies the political slogan under consideration. Of primary importance for our discussion are decisive innovations in the art of smelting and casting iron from ca. 5th century BCE. These entailed momentous consequences for agricultural production, warfare methods and commercial activities. Tools and weapons became more rapidly produced, and much more diverse and enduring.[5] Their widespread dissemination improved agricultural productivity and prompted the rapid clearing of wastelands for cultivation. During the Warring States period, we can observe a general trend toward a rational management of agriculture in states such as Qi, Wei and Qin. Advances in hydro-agricultural methods and modes of plowing led in turn to new forms of taxation and innovative ways of levying funds. The basis of economic development lay in the maximization of agricultural production and the optimal exploitation of salt, iron, other resources, and soil, which entailed an exploitative attitude towards nature.

The increasing efficacy in the management of agriculture was spurred by the proliferation of massive armies, which necessitated huge supplies of

---

4   Yang Kuan 2003; Lewis 1990 and 1999.

5   For instance, traditional weapons (such as lance 矛 and halberd 戈) were henceforth produced
     in greater quantities and forged in the newly strengthened iron, in parallel with the extension
     of armament (such as iron armors, helmets, crossbows, grappling-lances 鉤鉅 and spears with
     hooks 戟). See Yang Kuan 2003: 303–309.

food. If a "strong army" was an imperative, it became inextricably tied to the obligation of "enriching the state." The symbiosis of the two slogans fostered the economic debates of the period.

Progresses in industry and in the production of agricultural goods also buttressed the market economy. The most remarkable phenomenon over the course of these three centuries (roughly 500–200 BCE) is obviously the development of commerce and industry, which exerted a critical influence on several statesmen and political reformists. These favorable conditions for commerce could account for the rise of merchants, some of whom were able to build gigantic fortunes and gain unprecedented prominence. Their newly gained positions, as we shall see below, compelled thinkers and statesmen to ask who should be allowed to get rich, on what grounds, and which merits preferably should be rewarded.

In the wake of these new departures, profit-maximizing attitudes towards the natural world gradually emerged by the end of the Spring and Autumn period (Chunqiu 春秋, 770–453 BCE), and transformed traditional methods to manage territories. This economic dynamism also expands on the scale of time: the computing skills and the ready availability of arithmetic operations enabled astute merchants and profit-oriented ministers to make financial plans and even to speculate on future profits.[6] This economic turn reshaped discourses on human agency among a certain elite. Territories could now be viewed as a huge pool of material resources, and each profession was evaluated according to its usefulness and output.

The large-scale economic ideas that merchants put into practice for their private interests or for the benefit of the state were permitted not only by new tools but also by significant improvements in abstract reasoning and in calculus operations, which facilitated control over the material world by numbers and figures, and enabled complex operations such as anticipation

---

6   See below in the section devoted to the *Guanzi*.

of recipes or the prediction of supplies and demands.[7] This cognitive progress pertains to three domains: 1) tax policy, 2) the administration of natural resources and 3) labor organization.

After this all too brief outline of the historical background in which the slogan *fuguo* appears, we can now turn to the major texts that promote and discuss the idea of "enriching the people." I will first examine a trend of thought that overlaps with doxographic categories in order to set forth a historical continuity between Mohist and Confucian texts, which all favor the interpretation of *guo* for the benefit of "the people."

2. Society against the State?
Enrichment of the Country in the *Mozi*

The Mohist school gives a moral translation of the political principle of "enriching the country" in two striking formulas: "seek the interest of the whole world" 求天下之利 and "get rid of what causes harm to the world" 除天下之害.[8] These formulas are both an explanation of what should be done and a prohibition of what is usually undertaken for the sake of the state. The *Mozi* assumes that the rulers and the high officials in charge of the state "all want to have a rich country, a big population and an orderly use of punishments and administration" 今者王公大人為政於國家者，皆欲國家之富，人民之眾，刑政之治.[9] Yet, the enrichment of the state is not viewed as a process of predatory accumulation. It is above all a question of self-restriction. Mohists try to drive home the idea that time, skills, and strength have necessarily objective limits. Therefore, a high level of material and cultural refinement is seen as a yardstick to measure the widespread

---

7   See Chemla and Ma 2015. A good illustration of these progresses of abstract reasoning in economic policies is provided by *Guanzi* XIII.72 ("Hai wang" 海王, transl. Rickett 1998: 373–374).

8   See the beginning of chapter "Fei yue shang" 非樂上 ("Against Music, 1") (*Mozi* VIII.32: 379).

9   *Mozi* II.8: 66 ("Shang xian shang" 尚賢上).

level of poverty in the country. The Mohist interpretation of the key formula "enrich the country" drives a wedge between the people and the state, since the latter, as it appears, contains the very seeds of the ruin of the former. Accordingly, a sage ruler should endeavor to enrich its people—partly by self-imposed cuts on expenses. This core idea stems from the early stratum of Mohist chapters, written between the 5th and 4th centuries.[10]

> 聖人為政一國，一國可倍也；大之為政天下，天下可倍也。其倍之非外取地也，因其國家，去其無用之費，足以倍之。

> When a sage rules over the state, the wealth of the whole state can be doubled. When he rules over the whole world, its wealth will be doubled. This increase is not due to the seizing of lands abroad: simply relying on countrymen, and cutting unnecessary expenditures, suffices to bring about this increase.[11]

One of the keys to the enrichment of the state lies in the increase of a young and healthy population. Rather than endeavoring to attract people from other states, the *Mozi* sketches out the pioneering idea of a new birth policy (purportedly inspired by the ancient kings):[12]

> 昔者聖王為法曰：「丈夫年二十，毋敢不處家。女子年十五，毋敢不事人。」此聖王之法也。

> In ancient times, the sage kings said: "No man of twenty would dare to be without a family; no girl of fifteen should dare to not serve a man." Such is the model of the ancient kings.[13]

---

10   For useful references on the datation of the *Mozi*, see Wu Yujiang 1994: 1025–1055. Different views are summarized in Defoort and Standaert 2013.

11   *Mozi* VI.20: 147 ("Jie yong 節用 shang").

12   Historically, this policy can be ascribed to King Goujian of Yue: see *Guoyu jijie* 20: 635 ("Yue yu shang" 越語上) on marriages and 20: 636 on government measures in support of women giving birth.

13   *Mozi* VI.20: 147 ("Jie yong shang").

Three main sources of extravagance and wastefulness are identified and repeatedly denounced: 1) elaborate music and rituals, 2) lavish funerary customs, and 3) aggressive large-scale warfare.[14]

Enriching the state is above all a question of preventing the constant depletion of wealth, people and energy for the sake of fulfilling desires that stand outside the strict sphere of natural needs. The elite who splashes out on luxurious goods and delicacies is urged to resorb the economic conflict between their spending habits and the needs of the multitude. Obviously, neither architectural patrimony of urban centers nor the personal treasure of the ruler (collection of pearls and jades, rare fauna, etc.) are elements to be taken into account in the wealth of a state.[15]

2.1 The Fair Fruit of Frugality

The ambiguity embedded in the term *guo* enables the slogan *fuguo* 富國 to win apparent consensus. The author of the chapter "Geng zhu" 耕柱 asks very rhetorically if the treasures of the past are really liable to enrich the state/the people (*guojia* 國家) and associates this term in the same passage to the expressions "benefit the people" (*li min* 利民) and "benefit men" (*li ren* 利人).[16] The author of "Ci guo" 辭過 ("Dismissing excess"), a later chapter of *Mozi* which sums up earlier doctrinal elements, suggests that the sages of the past were primarily concerned by the lot of commoners. The enrichment of the population found a partial solution in the reduction of daily habits to bare necessities, even for the ruler, instead of promoting a program of economic development based on the optimal exploitation of natural resources and manpower. The authors make their point quite clearly:

---

14 The *Zuozhuan* 左傳 hold these activities as the main business of the elite: 國之大事，在祀與戎: "The great affairs of the state consist in sacrifices and wars" (*Chunqiu Zuozhuan zhu*, Cheng 13: 861)

15 *Mozi* VI.20: 147 ("Jie yong shang").

16 *Mozi* XI.46: 658 ("Geng zhu").

故其用財節，其自養儉，民富國治。

They were frugal in spending resources and simple in their diet, so that the people were rich and the country was well ordered.[17]

Here "the people" (*min* 民) refers to the population of the country as opposed to the ruler and his entourage wastefully lavishing themselves with extravagant dishes. Sage rulers are even portrayed in many a passage as determined to live like humble commoners, as if the more frugally they live, the richer the country becomes.

逮至其厚，黍稷不二，羹胾不重，飯於土塯，啜於土〔形〕〔鉶〕，〔斗〕〔勺〕以酌。

Even when [Yao] was at his most lavish, he took only one portion of millet, and chose between stew and minced meat so as not to have both. He ate out of an earthen vessel,[18] drank out of an earthen cauldron (*xing*), and poured his wine out of a ladle.[19]

The sage rulers' ascetic way of life is an indicator of the health and wealth of the country. They lead the way in bringing the constant squandering of resources and the bleeding of people to a halt. This self-imposed frugality must set an example in rectifying other common detrimental practices, such as music, funerals and wars.

---

17 *Mozi* I.6: 47 ("Ci guo").

18 The meaning and relevance of the character *liu* 塯 here remain puzzling. Many commentators unable to explain this term, which does not appear in the *Shuowen jiezi* 說文解字, offer emendations based on similar passages in *Shiji*, or later in the *Taiping yulan* 太平預覽. The character *liu* could be replaced by *gui* 簋, which figures in similar passages in the chapter "Shi guo" 十過 from the *Han Feizi* and in another passage from the "Basic Annals of the First Emperor" in the *Shiji* 史記.

19 *Mozi* VI.21: 255 ("Jie yong zhong"). Observations of this ilk might have inspired Han Fei's sarcastically commiserate comment on Yao's and Yu's lifestyles, living in a shack, poorly clothed and toiling as slaves (*Han Feizi* XIX.49: 676 ["Wu du" 五蠹]).

2.2 Funerals as Economic Necrosis

The very gist of the chapter "Restraint in Funerals" ("Jie zang xia" 節葬下), directed against elaborate mortuary ceremonies and extended mourning (厚葬久喪) is, to put it pithily: "Stop killing yourself by toiling for the dead." All that goes underneath the earth is pure waste, even if one seeks the favors of the spirits.

The author of this "manifesto for the living" of sorts goes so far as to prescribe scrimping and saving when it comes to adorning the dead and choosing their coffins: no more inner and outer coffins, no more elaborately embroidered shrouds, hill-high funerary mounds or subterranean galleries; no more graves filled with carts, horses, gold, jade, pearls, fine weapons, furniture or rare hides, let alone the scores (and in some cases, hundreds) of people forced to accompany a lord or a royal person in the tomb 眾者數百，寡者數十.[20] Against this mortal lavishness, the chapter prescribes a funerary program of economic austerity. One of the core tenets of this program is the reduction of materials dedicated to the care of dead bodies (aptly expressed in the chapter "Restraint in consumption," "Jie yong zhong" 節用中, with parallels in the chapter "Jie zang xia").

These restrictions on the practice of burial are just a thrust in the Mohists' massive onslaught on the economy of death. The chapter "Restraint in Funerals" further denounces the inconsiderate splurge of energy and time dictated by ritual considerations, which cannot but impoverish the country and debilitate its people. Many a mourner secluded in a hut is obliged by filial ethics to appear famished, gaunt and ailing. These injuries to the body prescribed in the Ru 儒 schools, as discussed for

---

20   *Mozi* VI.25: 264 ("Jie zang xia"). The Qin tomb 1 in Nanzhihui 南指揮, which is part of a giant
      necropolis for the Qin ruling lineage in Fengxiang (Shaanxi) is an apposite confirmation of what
      the *Mozi* denounces. This tomb, deemed to have been that of Lord Jing 秦景公 (r. 576–537
      BCE), exemplifies the exorbitant sumptuary privileges of nobility with its huge proportions
      (300 meters long and twenty-four meters deep), its precious carpentry work, and above all the
      presence of 166 human victims (Falkenhausen 1999: 486).

instance in the *Lunyu* 論語 (*Analects*) or the *Liji* 禮記 (*Records of rites*), lead to the illnesses and the death of many.[21]

The consequences of these funerary ethics are much more pervasive. What with the living accompanying the dead in the tomb, the mourners' severely weakened conditions and the prohibition on sexual intercourse (which postpones child-bearing), not only does the population diminish dangerously, but society at large experiences frightful ordeals. The length of the mourning period, from one to three years,[22] means that officials cannot attend to their supervising tasks, artisans cannot build, and peasants cannot plant and cultivate in a timely fashion.

The author of the chapter under consideration then speculates on the outcomes of the crippling of administrative and economic activities: the shortage of food and supplies weakens far more persons than mourners alone. This widespread predicament generates hostility and immoral conducts in families, who fall prey to hate, despair and disorder. No doubt other states will seize this opportunity to attack a country in which the devotion of resources to the dead has reduced the living population and decimated the army. Hence the radical conclusive stance:

以此求富，此譬猶禁耕而求穫也。

This way of seeking wealth amounts to seeking a harvest while prohibiting tilling.[23]

2.3 Pomp and Circumstances: The Discordant Effects of Music on Society

The famously iconoclastic essay "Against Music" ("Fei yue" 非樂) musters a range of forceful (and less forceful) reasons to reject one of the central

---

21   See for instance *Lunyu* 17.21: 188; *Mengzi* 5.2: 114, 9.4: 215, 9.5: 219, 9.6: 221–222; 13.46: 322; *Liji* "Tan gong 檀弓 shang" *passim*.

22   Three years in the Chinese way of counting, which is closer to two years and one or two months.

23   *Mozi* VI.25: 264 ("Jie zang xia").

institutions of the early Chinese ritual dispensation. The core problem is that politically endorsed and ritually-based performances of music encapsulate all the perverted and egoistic interpretations of wealth. Music commands the production of rare and richly crafted instruments for the satisfaction of the happy few at the expense of the common people.

> 將必厚措斂乎萬民，以為大鍾、鳴鼓、琴瑟、竽笙之聲。
>
> In order to produce music out of big bronze bells, resounding drums, zithers and flutes, it is necessary to levy heavy taxes on the people. [24]

These pleasurable activities, being performed in a sophisticated ceremonial setting, require the ostentatious display of finely embroidered silk clothes and fine dishes. "To deprive the people of the resources for food and clothing on account of these is something that benevolent persons would not do" 以此虧奪民衣食之財，仁者弗為也.[25]

A less compelling argument states that the very performance on musical instruments such as heavy bronze cast bells requires the strength and skill of people in their prime, precisely the kind of people who should be busy tilling and farming, or weaving and spinning. Music is therefore condemned as an institution that implies the economic spoliation of the common people,[26] as a social function detrimental to the general productivity of laborers, and as a public undertaking that runs afoul of the common good (of what benefits the people, *liren* 利人).

The *Mozi* envisages what would become of the state in which everybody would grow fond of music, from the ruler down to the peasants. It would unmistakably keep officials and commoners from working while attending musical performances. The sovereign would shirk off his duties, gentlemen would not exert their minds, and peasants would neglect the

---

24 *Mozi* VIII.32: 380 ("Fei yue shang").

25 Ibid.

26 Note here that the strength of this argument rests on the idea that a significant number of people are enrolled in musical activities, and that they are not stipended in any way for their tasks.

very material basis of human sustenance.[27] The author of the chapter goes as far as predicting the ruin of the country filled with music amateurs: with no one left to collect taxes, "the states granaries and warehouses would not be filled" 倉廩府庫不實![28]

2.4 The Mohist Crusade against War

The last and most compelling attack on the squandering of human and material resources is focused on wars that are not undertaken for a strictly defensive purpose. Chapter 18 of the *Mozi* contends that the wealth of a state does not consist in the extent of its territory or number of cities it possesses but lies in its population and the number of people who can dwell in these cities and cultivate the land. Yet, rulers fail to understand the importance of assessing the ratio between spatial expansion and demographic density. Those brimming with hubris wind up with empty cities, unmanned fortresses and a scarcity of farmers, just because wars have caused too many damages and too many victims among soldiers and civilians.[29] In the third version of chapter "Against wars of aggression" ("Fei gong 非攻 xia") the author recalls that the costs of warfare are borne by the populace and deplete general wealth. In time of war, peasants do not have the time to plow their fields and likewise women can no longer weave or sow. We find in this chapter a forceful description of the atrocities of war rarely found in early Chinese texts:

> 入其國家邊境,芟刈其禾稼,斬其樹木,墮其城郭,以湮其溝池,攘殺其牲牷,燔潰其祖廟,勁殺其萬民,覆其老弱。

---

27   *Mozi* VIII.32: 382 ("Fei yue shang").

28   Ibid.

29   See also *Mozi* VI.20: 148 ("Jie yong shang"), which enumerates the catastrophic consequences of long wars (from several months to a whole year) on the population: the number of people inevitably decreases and the birthrate goes down, whereas the number of poor and ill increases. When eating and drinking are not [supplied] in a timely way, it generates illnesses, diseases, and death 飲食不時,作疾病死者.

As soon as soldiers cross the borders and enter another state, they cut down its crops and fell the trees; they bring down the walls and ramparts of the city and fill up the ditches and ponds; they capture and kill the sacrificial animals and set fire to the ancestral temples; they brutally murder the people and exterminate the old and the weak.[30]

The moral and religious reasons for condemning aggressive warfare lie beyond the ambit of this chapter. Suffice it to say that the economic consequences of a violent conquest are equally disastrous for both the loser and the winner, and that the prize of victory does not exactly enrich the country.

夫殺人之為利人也，博（薄）矣。又計其費，此為害生之本，竭天下百姓之財用，不可勝數也，則此下不中人之利矣。

The benefit one gets from killing someone, surely, is meager. And furthermore, when one calculates the expense [one goes through], this is the basic cause of harming life. The depletion of the people's resources is innumerable, from which we should conclude that [aggressive wars] are not in the best interest of the people.[31]

The originality of the Mohist position is that, in contradistinction to what is advanced in the *Book of Lord Shang* or the *Guanzi* (discussed below), it conceives of the increase of wealth not so much along the lines of a heightened rhythm of production but in terms of spending habits: the issue is not earning more, but spending less. Wealth increases not through material accumulation, territorial expansion or production, but with the demand addressed to the elite to find contentment with little in terms of clothing, furniture, food, or entertainment.[32] It is the willfulness

---

30   *Mozi* V.19: 218 ("Fei gong xia").

31   *Mozi* V.19: 219 ("Fei gong xia"). I follow the corrections suggested by Yu Yue 俞樾 (1821–1907) and Sun Yirang 孫詒讓 (1848–1908).

32   Economic austerity will stay in a very marginal position on the political agenda of other Warring States thinkers. Xunzi will partly resume it (see below in the text), and the *Guanzi* will allude to it as a source of improvement for the state, but not enough to ensure its survival (See *Guanzi* XXIV.81: 552, section VI).

to satisfy one's greed and permanent appetite for prestige that ruins the country and destroys the population. Luxury precludes the possibility of a general welfare. Part of the appeal of the Mohist position, in spite of its austere style and pedestrian prose, is its consistency of spirit when fighting mass immiseration and gross inequities. "The sage rulers would abstain from doing anything that causes additional expenditures without bringing any benefit to the common people" 諸加費不加民利者，聖王弗為.[33] In sum, hardly anything should separate a ruler's way of life from a poor peasant's in terms of material possessions and daily habits. Such is one of the remarkable results of fair and efficient measures to enrich the country. Mozi's rationale is that a prosperous country is one in which the distance is lessened between superiors and inferiors, precisely the opposite of a state which allows the constant creation of material wealth. A wealthy country means a healthy population, not an opulent lifestyle for the ruling class.

3. The People vs. the State: Xunzi Gingerly Treading on Mohist Ground

If Confucius only professed his disdain when asked to discuss techniques and trades,[34] by the 4th century BCE, ritualists had to reconsider this contemptuous attitude towards profit and menial work. Mencius (Mengzi 孟子, 4th century BCE) dedicates a significant portion of his reflection to questions of agrarian economy and makes propositions about peasants' livelihood, though the extant eponymous text never mentions the phrase

---

33   See *Mozi* IV.21: 256 ("Jie yong zhong").
34   See for example *Lunyu* 13.4 about husbandry and gardening.

fuguo 富國.[35] In keeping with Mencius, Xunzi asks how much land should be allotted to a family of peasants if the state wants to give them a chance to get rich.[36] In the long run, we clearly see Confucian-oriented thinkers integrating in their political and moral reflections concerns for allotment, production, taxation and distribution of wealth.

Social tensions generated by the lack of balance between the ever-expanding desire to possess and the ever-worsening scarcity of resources are all the more likely to aggravate, as people cannot live apart and the human population keeps growing. They must help each other lest they should be impoverished and eventually perish.[37] Starting from these anthropological tenets, Xunzi follows, particularly in the chapter not fortuitously titled "Enrich the State" ("Fu guo" 富國), two consistent strands: 1) the economic development of the state based on the enrichment of people, and 2) an institutional solution to the problem of disorder with the creation of hierarchies and social divisions, which moderate one's consumption according to one's merits and rank. Divisions created by rituals ensure order, which in turn secures the enrichment of the state.[38]

In the chapter "The King's Regulations" ("Wang zhi" 王制), *Xunzi* defines four conflicting ways of pursuing the enrichment of the state, listed in a moral decrescendo:

---

35 For instance, he estimates the space to be allotted to farmers (*Mengzi* 10.2: 235). He reminds the ruler of Wei about the importance of not interfering with the busy seasons in the fields and mentions the necessity of certain prohibitions about fishing and cutting wood so that all the people can be properly fed, and discusses the planting of mulberries, the breeding season and the benefits of education through village schools (*Mengzi* 1.3: 5; 1.5: 10; 1.7: 17). The text mentions the need to make regular and timely inspections in order to help people when the time has come to sow or to harvest (*Mengzi* 2.4: 33). Elsewhere we find a discussion on the taxation of land (*Mengzi* 2.5: 36), on tax exemptions (*Mengzi* 3.5: 77), and on land allocation (*Mengzi* 5.3: 118 and 5.3: 21).

36 The answer being a hundred *mu* 畝, see chap.19. Note that this was considered a standard plot of land in the second half of the Warring States period. See, e.g., *Book of Lord Shang* 6.2.

37 See for instance *Xunzi* XIII.19: 346 ("Li lun" 禮論).

38 See for instance *Xunzi* VI.10: 177–183 ("Fu guo"); V.9: 152 ("Wang zhi").

故王者富民，霸者富士，僅存之國富大夫，亡國富筐篋，實府庫。筐篋已富，府庫已實，而百姓貧：夫是之謂上溢而下漏。入不可以守，出不可以戰。

The true king enriches the people. The hegemon enriches gentlemen (*shi*). The state that barely survives enriches the nobles. The state that perishes enriches its coffers and fills up its treasuries. When the coffers are rich and the treasuries are full, but the common people are destitute, this is called "overflowing at the top but leaking at the bottom." At home, one cannot protect oneself, and abroad one cannot wage war.[39]

The overall enrichment of the state is necessarily a bottom-up process: the more directly you seek wealth at the top, the more you undermine the foundations of the state. But if the ruler starts to implement his policy of enrichment from the grassroots of the country, he will also benefit the superiors. In other words, a ruler and his elite should not seek wealth directly for themselves: their affluence and prosperity should be regarded as the expected outcome of a policy that primarily favors the welfare of the multitude. We can clearly detect here a continuity with the Mohist position, siding with the multitude and cautioning the elite about the lethal dangers of rulers filling up their coffers at the expense of the people. In the chapter "Enrich the state," this continuity is particularly evident in the appropriation of the Mohist theme of self-discipline and moderation (*jie* 節):

足國之道：節用裕民，而善臧其餘。節用以禮，裕民以政。

A state reaches sufficiency when it imposes moderation in consumption and enriches the people, and excels in storing up the surpluses. Moderation in consumption is attained through ritual; enrichment of the people is attained through governance.[40]

---

39 *Xunzi jijie* V.9: 153–154 ("Wang zhi"), transl. Hutton 2014: 71. Note that where Hutton translates shi 士 as "gentry," I substitute the word "gentleman." "Gentry" may suggest a social status and land ownership that most *shi* did not enjoy.

40 *Xunzi* VI.10: 177 ("Fu guo").

The lesson is that if a ruler harms his people by favoring his own enrichment, the hate and hostility he will unmistakably arouse in the population will deter soldiers from bravely fighting for him. Here the selfish interpretation of *fu guo* leads directly to the weakening of the army. "And that is how those who aim at strengthening themselves end up being weakened" 是彊者之所以反弱也.[41] Such is the paradox of the typical self-defeating attitude of greedy rulers. "He who holds to strength and greatness, does not work at gaining strength" 知彊大者不務彊也.[42] We have here the paradox of virtue in the fashion of the *Laozi* 老子: you should not seek something directly for yourself, you have to let it come as the virtuous effect of a broader policy that is not directly focused on self-interest.

What does this policy concretely imply? Taxes should be kept low in rural areas, and taxes on commercial activities and taxes paid at customs should not be disproportionate; *corvée* and public mandatory work (including military conscription) should be kept to a minimum 罕興力役—at any rate they should not interfere with agricultural cycles.[43] A rich state thus requires as necessary conditions the moderation of taxation,[44] the frugality of expenditures, the mustering of all the available workforce in the country, the storing up of surpluses, and the motivation of farmers who are supposed or expected to enjoy their labor in the fields. Up to a certain point, the *Xunzi* endeavors to show there is no antagonism but on the contrary a continuity between the enrichment of the common people and the enrichment of the state.

裕民則民富，民富則田肥以易，田肥以易則出實百倍。

---

41   In *Xunzi* V.9: 155 ("Wang zhi").

42   Ibid.

43   *Wu duo nong shi* 無奪農時. See *Xunzi* VI.10 : 179 ("Fu guo") and VII.11: 229 ("Wang ba" 王霸).

44   "(The true king) only takes one-tenth of the produce from the fields. The mountain passes and markets are overseen but no fees are collected. The exploitation of mountain forests and dammed marshes is not taxed, but is prohibited in certain seasons." (*Xunzi* V.9: 160, transl. Hutton 2014: 74).

For when one enriches the people, then the people will be wealthy. When the people are wealthy, then the fields will be fertile and well maintained. When the fields are fertile and well maintained, then their yield will be a hundred times greater.[45]

And further:

下貧則上貧，下富則上富。

If people are poor, so shall the ruler. If people are rich, so shall the ruler.[46]

3.1 Luxury as a Key Marker of Social Hierarchies: Veering Off from the Mohist Course?

In spite of this economic concern for the commoners' lot, the *Xunzi* unambiguously holds it for the general good that clearly marked degrees of difference should be maintained between superiors and inferiors (i.e., between educated gentlemen and basic laborers).[47] Hence the usefulness of producing decorative objects and sophisticated insignia, to the extent that such objects can be used as key markers of social (and moral) hierarchy:

故為之雕琢、刻鏤、黼黻文章，使足以辨貴賤而已。

Thus (the former kings) created carving and inlay, insignias and patterns. They let them suffice for distinguishing noble and lowly, and that is all.[48]

---

45   *Xunzi* VI.10: 177 ("Fu guo"). Transl. Hutton 2014: 84 (modified).

46   *Xunzi* VI.10: 194 ("Fu guo").

47   The radically different views held in the *Mozi* and the *Xunzi* concerning the production of fine objects and the expenses they imply ultimately hinge on the value each vest in ritual. While the *Mozi* refuses to consider ritual as a crucial institution securing order and social harmony through visible hierarchical divisions, the *Xunzi* time and again emphasizes the impossibility for a society to function without the set of prescripions and prohibitions stipulated by ritual. From the *Xunzi*'s perspective; the sumptuary gradations associated with *li* are not an unfair exploitation of economic activity for the benefit of the happy few, but a basic necessity for the proper functioning of the whole society. On this aspect of the economic of ritual, see Pines 2000, passim.

48   *Xunzi* VI.10: 180 ("Wang ba"). Transl. Hutton 2014: 86.

Finest goods adorn good men[49] and precious objects mark the ranks of precious subjects,[50] thereby contributing to the aesthetic manifestation of an orderly society. In spite of an appeal to moderation in expenses and consumption habits, the *Xunzi* does not press the elite to proceed to drastic cuts in its food, clothes or funerary customs with the same vehemence found in the *Mozi*:

喪祭械用皆有等宜。聲、則非雅聲者舉廢。

In funerals and sacrifices, the implements all accord with rank and proper position. As for music, everything that is not proper must be discarded.[51]

The argument advanced for the wellbeing of peasants is also valid with merchants, for whom taxes should be light or even suppressed.[52] If Xunzi allows leeway for commercial activities,[53] he feels the concern energetically voiced by Shang Yang a century before, for whom the main problem with artisans and merchants is their number more than their trade itself.

工商眾則國貧，無制數度量則國貧。

A country with plenty of artisans and merchants is poor. And the country remains poor as long as their number is not properly assessed and regulated.[54]

---

49 See *Xunzi* V.9: 162 ("Wang zhi").

50 When it comes to the use (of objects and goods) above, they serve to embellish sages and worthy men, while below they serve to feed the people and see to their happy contentment (致其用，上 以飾賢良，下以養百姓而安樂之; *Xunzi* V.9: 162 ["Wang zhi"]).

51 *Xunzi* V.9: 159 ("Wang zhi"). Clothing too must follow these social regulations, which prescribe a splendid appearance when it comes to rulers and high dignitaries (ibid.) Transl. Hutton 2014: 73.

52 Here the fiscal propositions of "Wang zhi" composed in Qi, a state known to favor merchants, slightly vary from that of "Fu guo" composed in the state of Zhao. On these nuances see Liang Tao 2016: 50.

53 See also the end of chapter "Wang ba" which describes an orderly and powerful state in which farmers, merchants, craftsmen, officers, and grand ministers all do their work properly. Merchants are described as doing their work in an earnest and honest fashion, without deceiving anybody.

54 *Xunzi* VI.10: 194 ("Fu guo"). This passage just precedes the lines quoted above, marking the continuity between the condition of the people and that of the state.

In spite of their moralizing undertones, the measures prescribed in the book are far from being disinterested, since the *Xunzi* shows a clear awareness of the advantages for the government, in terms of income and revenue, of having a prosperous population. A savvy calculation underpins the noble concern for the people. The ruler who knows how to keep expenditures low and how to enrich the people will necessarily gain a reputation for being good and fair (*ren* 仁 and *yi* 義) and his riches will supposedly accumulate, rivaling the heights of hills and mountains. Xunzi's calculated generosity with the people is wittily expressed in the paradox of benefits induced by a "non-profit policy":

> 不利而利之，不如利而後利之之利也⋯⋯利而後利之，不如利而不利者之利也。

> To profit from the people without profiting them is not as profitable as first profiting the people and then profiting from them. ... To profit the people first and then profit from them is not as profitable as profiting the people and not profiting from them.[55]

Seen from this perspective, the all-purpose slogan "enrich the state" may give the impression that everyone in the state may gain benefit and protection from the policy it commands; and yet, its logic may hide a darker truth of constraints and violence against the people it is supposed to preserve and enrich. It is, as we shall see now, the pioneering merit of the *Book of Lord Shang* to exploit the semantic ambiguity lying at the core of the slogan in the opposite direction. If Shang Yang makes the economic development of the country his priority, he wants it all for the benefit of the state against the people.

---

55   *Xunzi* VI.10: 192 ("Fu guo"). Transl. Hutton 2014: 93 (translation modified).

4. *Fuguo qiangbing* 富國強兵 in the *Book of Lord Shang*

There is no doubt that in the 4th century BCE, the political slogan *fuguo* associated with *qiangbing* could be perceived as a fierce onslaught on the old ritualist dispensation, and had a whiff of scandal about it. If Confucian-oriented thinkers could prudently assume that the general wealth of the people benefits the state, neither the *Book of Lord Shang* nor most chapters of the *Guanzi* seem to have seen things from this angle. In the view of their authors, people cannot become rich without prejudicing the interest of the state. We can observe in both books the political rhetoric that emphasizes the antagonism between the interest of the state and that of its countrymen, or between rulers and subjects.[56] This antagonism is particularly emphasized in Shang Yang's offensive, binary and simplistic way of describing situations: When you elevate subjects, you degrade the state. When you degrade subjects, you elevate the state.[57]

> 民弱國強，民強國弱，故有道之國，務在弱民。
>
> The state is strong when people are weak. When people are strong, the state is weak. Therefore, a state that follows the right path strives to weaken its people.[58]

The *Book of Lord Shang* combines this analysis with a reflection on the optimal conditions for the economic development of the country. In Shang Yang's view, the two main priorities of the state are agriculture and warfare,

---

56 From a historical point of view, however, some states did endeavor to help the poorest and the most needy in getting the right tools. Some states provided technical assistance to the peasantry by starting off agricultural clearing, large-scale irrigation and hydraulic works or construction of dikes.

57 See in particular *Book of Lord Shang*, Chapter 4, "Getting Rid of the Powerful" ("Qu qiang" 去彊) and the exegesis to this chapter in Chapter 20, "Weakening the People" ("Ruo min" 弱民).

58 *Shangjunshu zhuizhi* V.20: 121 ("Ruo min"). I follow here and throughout this paper Pines's (2017) emendation of the text.

suited for a population that should be composed primarily of peasant-soldiers. Soldiers and farmers are like the cogs and springs of the complex machinery of the state fueled by economic and military development. The ruler must impose a strict definition and division of social classes in order to avoid randomness when planning production, anticipating revenues, and supplying the needs of the army. Rewards and punishments enable the ruler to rein in farmers, merchants, artisans, and idle talkers in order to maximize profit and streamline the process of material production and military mobilization.

To encourage the people to overcome the instinctual abhorrence of violent and dangerous activities such as warfare, they should be lured by the prospect of promotions, ranks of merit and accompanying economic benefits. The arch necessity of suppressing any alternative channel to social climbing, political promotion or economic gratification accounts for the repeated attacks on merchants, artisans, and scholars. Yuri Pines describes this political vision in the following terms: "By monopolizing the sources of social prestige and economic well-being, the ruler will create a situation in which a subject's selfish desires become attainable only through serving the state's goals."[59]

4.1 To Enrich the State, Impoverish the Rich and Suppress Independent Livelihood

Shang Yang, who hardly ever tarts up his brutal conceptions with moral considerations, repeatedly voices his concern that the people have to be debased to reinforce political authority and social stability. Not to the point of misery though, which would prove a self-destructive policy: he hammers home the message that the poor must be helped out of poverty and that rich people must relinquish their riches. But if a person becomes rich independently of the state's bestowal of ranks and privileges, he may

---

59   Pines 2016: 3–4.

therewith challenge the authority and the prestige of the state.[60] Should this occur, the state must act readily to strip these individuals of their sources of wealth:

> 故貧者益之以刑，則富；富者損之以賞，則貧。治國之舉，貴令貧者富，富者貧。

> Hence, when they [the people] are poor, increase their [wealth] by punishments, and they will become rich; when they are rich, diminish [their wealth] by rewards, and they will become poor. [To] raise up an ordered state, value causing the poor to become rich and the rich to become poor.[61]

Shang Yang cannot imagine for a second that wealthy subjects could benefit the state by the independent creation of wealth, by growing tax revenues or by balancing the scale of supply and demand.[62]

If Shang Yang is not the only author to inveigh against the making of big fortunes and the lavish lifestyle that comes along with it, he radicalizes the hostility against those who do not serve the state directly and who do not work in the fields or serve in the army, and fulminates against merchants who splurge on new luxury goods and treat themselves to a sumptuous way of life by dint of sheer speculation while avoiding real hard

---

60 See *Shangjunshu* I.3: 20 ("Nong zhan" 農戰).

61 *Shangjunshu* II.5: 39 ("Shuo min" 說民). Transl. Pines 2017, 5.6. "Diminishing wealth by rewards" apparently refers to the selling of ranks of merit to wealthy individuals (probably in exchange for grain). Symmetrically, the parallel clause "increase their wealth by punishment" would mean that penalizing idleness and lack of commitment to one's work has a beneficial outcome on people, who have no choice but to work for their own good.

62 Shang Yang, though one of the foremost figures of economic thought in pre-imperial China, remains at a very primitive stage of reasoning concerning the management and the creation of wealth. His faults and errors were roundly denounced during the Western Han dynasty, an era in which debates on the relationships between commerce and agriculture take a much more sophisticated form. "What unites these (Han) thinkers is that they recognize the problem when the agricultural base of society defaults and acknowledge that professional specialization and wealth creation through means other than agriculture had increasingly become the norm" (Sterckx, forthcoming).

work. Their lifestyle dwarfs the status of state-officials and might entice the latter into corruption.

In additions to this, the fortunes that merchants may gain quickly through deft maneuvers inevitably invite comparisons with the toilsome condition of peasants. If people know they can make easy gains by means of speculative rhetoric, they will flee the agricultural fields and eschew the battlefield. In the long run, if the ruler is unable to contain this hemorrhage of manpower, nobody would be left to put the hands to the plow or draw the sword.

Shang Yang's conception of agro-economic management is underlain by a profound ideal of autarky typical of primitive societies and by the belief that smothering commerce can only profit the country. By deciding to rely only on itself for what it uses and consumes, the state excludes the necessity of economic relationships with neighboring states.[63] Yuri Pines captures the problem of market and merchants very convincingly:

> Back then, Qin was still lagging behind most eastern states in its commercial development ... We may plausibly assume that during the time of formation of the *Book of Lord Shang* (primarily during Shang Yang's lifetime and within a generation or so after his death), commerce was still in its infancy in Qin and suppressing it could have appeared to the book's authors an easy task.[64]

The ideal state in which rulers can have everything they consume produced by the people is in fact a two-way proposition: conversely, the people must only consume what they produce. This may be one of the reasons for the proscription of luxury, which not only weakens and corrupts, but also

---

63   It should be noted here, as a specific instance of the gap between ideology and practice, that we are only characterizing the *Book of Lord Shang*'s simplistic vision, which does not accurately reflect Qin's actual policy over the course of the 3rd century BCE. Mercantile and agricultural economies are always intricate and complementary—otherwise there would not be any markets— and grain production requires merchants at different scales with different kinds of outreach.

64   Pines, forthcoming.

implies the massive importation of rare, refined and expensive products from other states, thus breaking the logic of a self-sufficient economy.

No wonder then that the *Book of Lord Shang* decrees several measures against merchants and traders[65] and prohibits the private trade of grain and of military supplies. As Pines states, "They should be squeezed of their profits, humiliated, and discriminated against to make their occupation exceedingly unattractive (2.5, 2.6, 2.10, 2.15, 2.17, 2.19)."[66] In order to reduce the number of merchants, the text prescribes a monopoly on natural resources and recommends heavy taxes on the price of meat and wine. Forced work must be imposed on merchants' households according to the number of people they support. The ruler must forbid the rental of carts to convey grain and must not allow filling them with private goods on the way back. Yet, these measures expressed in the *Book of Lord Shang* were in fact nowhere near as effective as they claimed to be, if they were ever implemented during the Warring States period. It might have been too difficult to impose on artisans and merchants the kind of control possible for farmers; unlike the latter, merchants kept moving from state to state and could have powerful protectors. The *Book of Lord Shang* thus places merchants at the lowest tier of his social construction along with public agents and officials (*guan* 官), who come off as a swarm of slovenly intermediaries, and repeatedly asserts that every subject who does not contribute to the objectives set by the watchword "enrich the state" should be forced back into useful labor or eliminated.

As for persuaders, scholars, experts, and gentlemen (*shi* 士), they are undesirable and useless riff-raff that should be suppressed, just as criticism should be weeded out in the state. Intelligence, eloquence, and shrewdness should never be rewarded.[67] Shang Yang hates indiscriminately all types of

---

65   See *Shangjunshu*, Chapter 2.

66   Pines 2017: 124, referring to Chapter 2 of the *Book of Lord Shang*.

67   See for instance *Shangjunshu* Chapter 3, "Nong zhan."

wanderers and idlers,[68] such as traveling advisors, masters of esoteric arts or interstate merchants: all are moving creatures (*you* 遊), uneasy cases for registration and census, unfettered by laws and regulations—they easily dodge taxes and their fortune is hard to determine.[69]

In sum, the slogan "enrich the state" implies a structural conflict between agricultural abundance and cultural elevation, while forcing to accept as the only source of social and economic gratification meritorious achievements in agriculture and warfare. People should be continually enrolled in an endless series of state-monitored campaigns between agricultural fields and battlefields.

4.2 Enrich the State with What? People or Goods, Grain or Gold?

4.2.1 Gain and Grain

Agriculture involves much more effort and time than any other activity. With respect to production or profit, what land can yield is rather weak in comparison with commercial operations. If the enrichment of the state was really a priority, why did the *Book of Lord Shang* direct the country's main effort towards agriculture? What was the rationale behind the authors' mottoes, watchwords, and slogans revolving around the idea of working the land?[70] Was it not conceivable to enrich the state and strengthen the army otherwise? Why rely exclusively on fixed-field production of grain in

---

68 Though Shang Yang was one himself, since he left his native state of Wei 衛 to seek a position and exert his talents, first in Wei 魏, then in Qin.

69 This idea is most powerfully enunciated in Chapter 6 (Pines 2017: 6.6–6.8).

70 See, for instance, Shang Yang's obsession in Chapter 2—one of the most ludicrously written chapters of the book—in which the author laboriously endeavors to promote the development and use of wild lands and expand agricultural areas. The catchphrase *cao bi ken yi* 草必墾矣 (wastelands will surely be cultivated), which is repeated about twenty times, can be construed as a specific rephrasing of the idea of enriching the state.

spite of all its well-known disadvantages? Perhaps a state the size of Qin could not control the production and the commercialization of goods. In this case, one can partially understand why the pursuit of wealth implies an exclusive focus on agriculture. One can nonetheless venture to set forth a few hypotheses about the *Book of Lord Shang*'s doctrinal insistence on agricultural production.

The first hypothesis is that agriculture is the activity best suited to concentrated production, fiscal planning and tax assessment. As opposed to other forms of culture, monocrop plantations (like millet in northern China) make harvests easy to appropriate, measure, tax, collect and transport. With the establishment of taxes paid in grain, peasants all belong to the homogenous class of taxpayers, and become anonymous units whose utility and merits are calculated on the basis of the revenues they generate for the state. The priority given to agriculture thus enables the state to create a legible, easily measured and fairly uniform landscape of taxable resources and to crowd on these lands a large population readily available for corvée and conscription.

Secondly, farmers lend themselves more easily to census and social control than other groups in the population partly because they lead a sedentary way of life. Moreover, the kind of drudgery associated with intensive agriculture (planting, threshing, harvesting, protecting the field against weeds, parasites and so forth) facilitates the surveillance of workers. Besides, farmers can be readily recruited into the army as infantry. And not only can they be mustered in times of war, but in times of peace they produce the foodstuffs the army needs. If agriculture is a compulsory occupation for most men in the country, war then logically remains the exclusive route to fame and fortune. Here lies seemingly the interdependence between the enrichment of the state and the strengthening of the army: the state can enrich itself and maintain a tight control over the country if and only if people find in war an occasion to get what cannot be obtained from any other activity or enterprise. Conversely, the military can only be strengthened if it is underwritten by a state economy based on a system of labor that can always lend itself to strict surveillance, in terms of human compliance and economic predictability. "Enrich the state, strengthen the army" means that the social type on which political authority relies can only be the peasant-soldier, whether farming or fighting—now busy feeding the army, now battling for the country.

Thirdly, though this is not explicitly stated in the *Book of Lord Shang*, it is not unreasonable to assume that the priority given to agriculture and war also enables the ruler to keep the people exhausted, uncouth, and uneducated (*pu* 樸), away from those who plan, scheme, and plot to become rich without toiling. For Shang Yang, men must be curbed into submission: plowing and tilling will take their full toll. The slogan "enrich the state, strengthen the army" entails a hidden necessity which no government today would put the way Shang Yang did, with his genuine cynicism: to make sure people stay unable to pursue activities that may jeopardize political authority.[71] In other words, the priority given to agriculture is not the best choice from an economic perspective, but it is surely the safest choice politically speaking.

4.2.2 To Enrich the Country, Populate the Land

The wealth of a nation lies not in the abundance of its product, nor in the number of rich subjects, but, as many voices in the *Guanzi* and the *Book of Lord Shang* seem to think—following the Mohist school—in its large population. What specifically distinguishes the *Book of Lord Shang* is that it builds an important part of its political thought on the assumption of a population increase, and takes into account the causes and the consequences of this increase for the construction of an orderly society.[72] In other words, a rich state is not a state in which people are rich, and a powerful state is not a state peopled by powerful individuals; a rich and

---

71　Note that the *Book of Lord Shang* is exceptional in its valorization of the people's simplicity (*pu* 樸), which among the received texts is paralleled only in the *Laozi* (Pines 2017: 91–92 and 263n36).

72　See *Shangjunshu* 7.1 (Pines's numeration).

powerful state is a state endowed with a large population of productive workers and valiant fighters.

Accordingly, in the *Book of Lord Shang*, the authors take into account the total number of activities (commerce, agriculture, industry, craftsmanship) in the country and assess their attractiveness. Now it appears that one of the main factors conducive to population increase is agricultural work, with the exploitation of new lands that keep bringing in people from other states.[73]

A wise ruler, concerned with political control and economic management, constantly tabulates human, animal and material resources.[74] Everything must be transparently converted into quantities, data easy to handle and readily available. As a means of reinforcing the state's control over the territory, the *Book of Lord Shang* even explains what should be the ideal composition of a thriving kingdom: 10% forests, 10% lakes and marshes, 10% rivers and valleys, 10% occupied by roads; mediocre fields must count for 20% and good lands for 40%. We have here one of the first attempts to develop in a systematic way the territorialization of economics in relation to the reordering of social classes.[75]

4.3 The Cyclic Accumulation and Destruction of Wealth

In the *Book of Lord Shang*, agriculture in its optimal cycle is associated with abundance and wealth (*fu* 富) but must inevitably revert to a cycle of need and frugality; the military is synonymous with force (*li* 力) but must endure destruction and death; only the ruler is characterized by an unfaltering power (*qiang* 彊). This adaptive balance ensures the ruler's grip on his people and the safety of his country. Shang Yang's hostility to the

---

73   See *Shangjunshu* Chapter 6, and more importantly Chapter 15.

74   See *Shangjunshu* 4.11 (Pines' numeration).

75   Naturally, this requisite cannot but be a horizon towards which the effective administration in Qin tried to draw closer and closer from the days of Shang Yang down to the end of the Qin dynasty at the end of the 3rd century BCE.

simple accumulation of wealth is visible everywhere throughout the book.[76] Thus, the ruler must know when he must build up and when he must destroy wealth and forces. All his riches (*fu*) and his armies' strength (*li*) should undergo a cycle of reinforcement and disposal, of accumulation and use (*tuan* 摶 and *yong* 用).

> 故能摶力而不能用者，必亂；能殺力而不能摶者，必亡。故明君知齊二者，其國強；不知齊二者，其國削。

> Hence, he who is able to consolidate force but is unable to use it will surely [bring about] turmoil; he who is able to spend force but is unable to consolidate it will surely perish. Hence, the clear-sighted ruler knows to adjust the two, and his state is powerful; he who does not know to adjust the two—his state will be dismembered. [77]

Power is a delicate and dynamic balance (*quan* 權) between misery and wealth. People who starve weaken the state because they have nothing to give, and people who have surfeit become idle, disobedient and accumulate wealth at the detriment of the state. In the ideal society hinted at in the *Book of Lord Shang*, no one must be able to dispose of one's own time and fortune. A clear-sighted ruler keeps his people on a tight leash, on the edge of hunger, always on the brink of poverty. Anyone who makes a fortune is held as a robber plundering the resources of the state.

In the chapter "Weakening the people" ("Ruomin" 弱民), the economic vulnerability of the people is consistently seen as the condition and the outcome of a powerful army or a wealthy state: the author envisions here a structural antagonism in terms of weights and balance. *Ruomin* lies necessarily in the semantic shadow of *fuguo*. What you add or subtract from one side of the scale can only diminish or increase the other. This arithmetic of power prevents a thinker like Shang Yang from imagining the possibility of a wealthy nation peopled with rich citizens. The antagonism

---

76   See for instance *Shangjunshu* III.8: 60 ("Yi yan"). Transl. Pines 2017: 8.2.

77   *Shangjunshu* III.8: 61 ("Yi yan"). Transl. Pines 2017: 8.2.

between the interests of the people and the needs of the state finds no point of convergence. A rich nation is not a nation of rich people.

Still, when the wars waged by the state prove long and difficult, the country lacks manpower, and the ratio between farmers and fields, people and land becomes a source of concern. When peasants drop the plow and take the spear, the reduction of wealth and the destruction of surpluses that could initially benefit political authority become detrimental. A latent conflict surfaces at this stage between the necessity to enrich the state and the reinforcement of the army.[78] The *Book of Lord Shang* offers a solution in a later (in terms of the date of its composition) chapter, "Attracting people" ("Lai min 來民"), which clearly evinces a sense of progress and adaptation, if we compare it with chapters 2 and 6 as Yuri Pines has shown.[79] The author advocates a policy of attracting laborers from abroad, with substantial perks (tax exemptions and no military duties for three generations). These new immigrants (hoped to total a million persons!) should be directed to the exploitation of mountains and marshes—exactly as is recommended in the *Guanzi* (see below)—and to farming.

Historically, the enrichment prescribed by Shang Yang was seen from a very narrow perspective: the optimal production of grain and fodder, which had to be absorbed, or partially taken over, by the military in order to prevent the accumulation of goods that could only weaken the authority of the ruler and the fighting spirit of the country. This form of agrarianism in early China was probably not driven by a strong belief in high returns and big profits for the state, but was rather instilled by fear in the face of the rapid and uncontrolled development of activities on which it had ever so

---

78   This conflict is the aggravated form of the interdependence between agriculture and the military. Or, more precisely, it reflects the self-binding nature of this interdependence: the author judiciously observes that the army at the disposal of the state cannot be numbered according to all the men it can muster but only to the number of people and horses to whom grain and fodder can be provided.

79   Pines 2017: 77–78 and Pines, forthcoming. For the chapter's dating, see Pines 2017: 37; Tong Weimin 2016.

little grip. The merit of agriculture is that it meets the immediate demands to feed the army and swell its ranks.

In a context of continuous wars and persistent threats of invasion, the slogan "enrich the state" did not trigger a real reflection on the production of wealth, but, tied to the need of a strong army, it drew Shang Yang and his followers to the obsessive concern with adjusting the mechanisms by which food and goods are generated according to the necessity of social control. It is no doubt from a military perspective, not from an economic one, that the ideal of enriching the state was equated with the radical promotion of agriculture and the hampering of commerce, private industry and free craftsmanship. The concrete content given to the first key formula (enrich the state) is the logical outcome of the second one (strengthen the army).

5. Tricks of the Trade: Statistics, Stratagems and Speculation in the *Guanzi*

The *Guanzi* sketches out a rich and complex conception of enrichment by playing on factors and situations that are not taken into account in the previous works we have examined. It seems to have taken stock of a strongly commercialized economy, along with the fact that Qi was one of the first states to make extensive use of coins. The ruler is urged to take the lead on the market by manipulating prices, by controlling supply and demand, by instituting monopolies, by setting up loan programs to help out laborers, by favoring foreign trade and territorial expansion, and finally by controlling currency and giving incentives to workers to motivate them. In other words, fiscal planning, savvy predictions of gain and loss, control of prices and hidden speculation are the avenues to a rich state.

The economic basis of a rich state, much wider than in the *Book of Lord Shang*, encompasses not only agricultural products, but more broadly the resources of forests, lakes, marshes, hydraulic constructions, supplies of water, silkworms, breeding, fruit, etc. The *Guanzi* does not reject secondary activities (*moye* 末業) as unprofitable or useless, but argues that efficient management of craftsmanship and private enterprise contribute to the wealth of the state, as encapsulated in this formulation: "[In former times] those who kept a record of all expenditures and tallied the results, paid attention to essential production, and regulated that which was nonessential, became prosperous (*fu*)" 計凡付終，務本飭末則富.[80] The *Guanzi* is referring here essentially to luxury goods, as distinguished from daily goods, and therefore stands in a clear-cut opposition to the harsh condemnation of luxury—for different reasons—in the *Mozi*, the *Book of Lord Shang*, and the *Han Feizi*.[81] A chapter like "Cheng ma" 乘馬 considers commerce and enterprise controlled by officials as an essential way to enrich the state, via a sustained effort of economic interventionism. Other passages in the *Guanzi* envisioned a human being, regardless of his age, as a consumer, or a mouth that needs salt; an able-bodied person was turned, so to speak, into a useful pair of arms which, when well-equipped and well managed, could grow wealth off the land.[82] As to families, they were seen as taxable households.

5.1 Lip-Service to Popular Welfare?

The antagonism between the wealth of the state and that of the people is moderated in the *Guanzi* in comparison to the repeated attacks we find in the *Book of Lord Shang*. The chapter "Ordering the State" ("Zhi guo" 治國)

80   *Guanzi jiaozhu* II.8: 139 ("You guan" 幼官); Transl. Rickett 2001: 173.

81   For the latter, see for instance the anecdotes about ivory chopsticks and the first sculpted lacquered bowls (*Han Feizi yizhu* XXII.24: 260 ["Shuo lin shang" 説林上]); see also the Mohist criticism of luxury in the first and third of "Jie yong" chapters. The *Guanzi* is highly critical of this trend towards frugality and moderation (see especially the chapter "Chi mi" [侈靡 "On Extravagance in Spending"]). Michael Loewe notes that, under the Western Han, "there may have been some attempt to promote trade by the consumption of luxurious products and articles of manufacture" (2007: 158).

82   Consumers of salt are seen in an abstract way in the *Guanzi* (chap. XXII.72: 1246–1247 and 1255–1256) as mouths (*kou* 口), and laborers who use iron tools are seen as arms (*bei* 臂).

argues that a good government first sets out to enrich the population, in order to make it more obedient.

凡治國之道，必先富民；民富則易治也，民貧則難治也。

It is ever so that the way to maintain a good order in a state is to be certain, first of all, to make its people prosperous. When the people are prosperous, they are easy to keep in order. When the people are poor, they are difficult to keep in order.[83]

It states further:

故治國常富，而亂國常貧；是以善為國者，必先富民，然後治之。

Therefore, a state that is well ordered is always prosperous, and a chaotic state is always poor. For this reason, those who are good at managing their states are certain, first of all, to make their people prosperous and afterward institute good order among them.[84]

When the whole country becomes rich, the state can enjoy a powerful army. Now a powerful army can obtain many decisive victories, which lead to the acquisition of extensive new territories. Chapter 78, "Calculations and Measures" ("Kui du" 揆度) states that when markets are not overly busy, then farms enjoy much more manpower, a situation which allows the prince to collect taxes from peasants without draining them dry.[85] Section VIII of the same chapter states that "if one is able to take from the rich to give to the poor, one may come to rule the empire."[86]

The late Warring States chapter "The Five Aids" ("Wu fu" 五輔), holding views akin to those in *Xunzi*, promotes a policy based on virtue and benevolence and focuses on the enrichment of the population (*guojia fu* 國家富). The author urges a series of social measures designed

---

83   *Guanzi* XV.48: 924. Transl. Rickett 1998: 176.
84   Ibid.
85   *Guanzi* XXIII.78: 1378. Transl. Rickett 1998: 435.
86   *Guanzi* XXIII.78: 1380. Transl. Rickett 1998: 436.

to secure the wellbeing of people and the circulation of wealth, and does not exclusively mention agricultural production. The state has a welfare responsibility in terms of credits and allocated funds. Among these measures we find the building of roads, the supply of lodgings, the clearing of sand pools, the construction of dams, the easing of taxes, the halt to exactions, the assistance to those stricken by poverty, etc.[87] Chapter 76, "The Best Methods for Ensuring Fiscal Control" ("Shan zhi shu" 山至數), also emphasizes the continuity between the welfare of the people and the wealth of the state:

> 君下令於百姓曰：民富君無與貧，民貧無與富。
>
> You should issue a policy directive to the hundred surnames stating, "If the people are rich, the prince cannot be poor; if the people are poor, the prince cannot be rich."[88]

But this statement may well be an ad hoc argument, aiming at preventing great officers and powerful families from enriching themselves at the expense of the state. The cause of the people serves the ambition to strip these wealthy families of their riches, as confirmed by the remainder of the chapter. Whereas other chapters of the *Guanzi* stress above all the practice of moderation and recommend keeping the people well fed and content in order to ensure their support to the ruler, the dominant voices in the economic chapters reveal their ambition to enrich the state at the expense of its subjects. The authors devise many stratagems to milk the population without any moral scruples.[89] Most of the time, when the welfare of the people is advocated, it is seen as a condition for optimal taxation and an

---

87 Chapter "Zhong kuang" 中匡 holds similar views in favor of the people.

88 *Guanzi* XXII.76: 1333. Transl. Rickett 1998: 413.

89 See *Guanzi* Chapter 73, in which some passages "seem totally devoted to providing the prince with advice on how to extract as much money as possible from the populace in order to satisfy his personal desires" (Rickett 1998: 377).

argument against the enrichment of merchants.[90] The overall guiding idea is to tap to the full people's strength 民力可盡也[91] and tax them as much as possible without stirring resentment or revolt, which would be a disaster in case of a military attack.

Many discussions between Guan Zhong 管仲 (d. 645 BCE) and his lord, Lord Huan 齊桓公 (r. 685–643 BCE), in their imaginary dialogues, especially in the economic chapters, are in keeping with what we have surveyed in the *Book of Lord Shang*. The state can only build up strength and wealth by resorting to an astute and systematic way of siphoning money off the people. I shall focus here primarily, though not exclusively, on the economic section of the *Guanzi*, the cluster of the fifteen "Light and Heavy" (*Qingzhong* 輕重) chapters[92] written between the Warring States and the early Han by several different anonymous hands, and which contains some of the most important ideas about political economics from the ancient world.

5.2 Princes, Prices and the Art of Speculation

The *Guanzi* contains the first economic reflections on interstate market forces[93] and recommends a high involvement of the state in economic matters, beyond the attempt to control price fluctuations. In order to enrich the state, the "Qingzhong" chapters prescribe the planning of fiscal management (*ce cheng ma* 策乘馬) and the profitable use of calculation

---

90 See for instance *Guanzi* XXIV.81 section XII: Lord Huan is advised by Guan Zhong on how to reduce the profits of merchants and traders and increase the profits of the peasants (*Guanzi* XXIV.81: 1465). See also XXIV.83 section XI: "I wish to weaken the people who are merchants and traders in order to benefit the people" (*Guanzi* XXIV.83: 1495).

91 *Guanzi* XXIV.81: 1451.

92 On the meanings of *qingzhong* 輕重, ranging from the weight of coins to economic policies, see Rickett 1998: 338–339.

93 See for instance *Guanzi* XXI.72: 1367–1368 ("Di shu" 地數); Rickett 1998: 428.

(*cheng ma* 乘馬 and *hui* 會) and statistics (*gui* 軌) along with various techniques (*shu* 數) regarding the exploitation of the population.[94]

One of these methods of enrichment is the establishment of grain reserves. A good government stocks up products that have become cheap owing to a surplus and sells off what has become dear owing to scarcity. Since the ruler can sell off when the price trend is upward, he can earn a profit ten times bigger, while he obtains the balance and the stability of foodstuffs on the market. For instance, the government supplies grain to the people in the spring when it is scarce, expensive, and urgently needed for food and seeding. When grain is cheap and plentiful during fall harvest, the people must repay in accordance with the adjusted monetary value of the original loan of grain. The government thus recovers several times the amount of grain initially loaned.[95]

國穀之分在上，國穀之重再十倍。…… 國穀之 ，一切什九。

When the amount of grain in state hands comes to exceed 50%, its value will increase twenty times (...) The official price of state grain will consistently produce a profit of 90%.[96]

5.3 Every Grain of Salt

The *Guanzi* develops pioneering views and technical arguments about taxation that rise above the simple question of deciding whether taxes should be light or heavy. The gist of the problem is to know how the state should proceed to milk a whole population without raising their anger.

94　The ruler exploits data and statistics, which he keeps secret, and uses them as weapons against the people to maintain its control of economy. See *Guanzi* XXII.74 ("Shan guo gui" 山國軌). In *Guanzi* XXII.75: 1304 ("Shan quan shu" 山權數) the ruler is advised to take advantage of years of poor harvests to increase the price of grain: "During bad years, it is easy to increase the price. One can become ten; ten can become a hundred" (Rickett 1998: 398).

95　See *Guanzi* XXII.73 ("Guo xu"), XXII.76 ("Shan zhi shu") and XXIII.78 ("Kui du").

96　*Guanzi* XXI.68: 1228 ("Chen cheng ma" 臣乘馬). Transl. Rickett 1998: 362–363.

Chapter 73, "The State's Store of Grain" ("Guo xu" 國蓄), prescribes a keen buy-and-sell policy in order to regulate prices on the market[97] and confidently argues that people can be manipulated and extorted for revenues, all for the exclusive benefit of the state.

> 民予則喜，奪則怒，民情皆然。先王知其然，故見予之形，不見奪之理。

> When the people have things given to them, they become happy, but when things are taken away, they become angry. Such is the nature of the people. Knowing this to be so, the former kings made a display of giving while concealing the nature of their taking away.[98]

The end of the chapter prescribes other daring measures to enrich the state at the expense of the people. For instance, when the government forces people to pay taxes on a very short notice, prices will go down, and the prince can accordingly reap a huge profit by exploiting the sudden fall of prices for properties and goods.[99]

In this economic program, people are reduced to an anonymous mass of consumers and taxpayers, the only concern of the government being the maximization of profits by increasing the base for levying taxes. One of the favored ways of enriching the government is taxing products of daily

---

[97] This form of heavy-handed economic interventionism may date back to Li Kui 李悝 in the state of Wei (i.e., ca. 400 BCE). Li Kui is said to have put into practice a price regulation policy, which he took as an easy way to fill the coffers of the state by speculating on fluctuations of supply and demand. He allegedly has shrewdly exploited the cycle of peaks and troughs in the demands for commodities (see *Hanshu* 漢書 24A: 1457–1458). Even if this account is correct, the state of Wei was never able to establish a reserve fund in order to implement the economic policy Li Kui advocated.

[98] *Guanzi* XXII.73: 1259. Transl. Rickett (1998): 378. See also the similar passage in XXIV.81: "Land rents and regular commercial taxes are things that naturally accrue to the prince; special levies and taxes are things that he must take by force" (transl. Rickett 1998: 471). See also chapter XXI.68, "Cheng ma," where Guan Zhong explains to Lord Huan how he should proceed: the government can artificially create shortages to drive up the price of the commodities they want to sell off. Guan Zhong further explains how to take advantage of price fluctuations and make handsome profits without arousing the population's resentment that might be incurred by special taxes.

[99] Last section of chapter "Guo xu" 國蓄 (*Guanzi* XXII.73: 1279).

consumption, hence the institution of monopolies on iron and salt. Chapter 72 offers specific estimations about the average consumption of salt and iron per man, woman and child in a household in a day and in a month.[100] The author prescribes, under the authority of Guan Zhong, who allegorically champions these new daring policies, a price increase for these items, and anticipates the revenues that can be sucked out of the total number of consumers in the state of Qi every day. While a new special tax would give rise to protest, even a small increase in the price of salt and iron suffices to generate huge incomes. And the people can do nothing about it.[101]

Without high taxes and special exactions on the people, the state cannot get rich and the army cannot become strong.[102] Chapter 73 also betrays Guan Zhong's obsessive worry about letting slip through his fingers any possible tax revenue. More generally, the "Qingzhong" chapters brim with astute stratagems and wily schemes to manipulate the local economy and interregional trade, and strip wealthy individuals of their capital. Mountains and seawaters are the first targets of the economic policy promoting the exploitation of natural resources. When composing his pioneering history of early China in his *Wenxian tongkao* 文獻通考 (Comprehensive investigations based on literary and documentary sources), Ma Duanlin 馬端臨 (1254–ca. 1324) expatiates on Guan Zhong's heavy insistence on predicating the survival of the state on the efficiency of its tax system.

> 至管夷吾相齊，負山海之利，始有鹽鐵之征。觀其論鹽，則雖少男、少女所食；論鐵，則雖一針、一刀所用，皆欲計之，苟碎甚矣。故其言曰：「利出一孔者，其國無敵；出二孔者，其兵平詘；出三孔者，不可以舉兵；出四孔者，其國必亡。」先王知其然，故塞人之養，隘其利途。故予之在君，奪之在君，貧之在君，富之在君。[103]

---

100   On the calculation of salt consumption in every household see also *Guanzi* XXIII.77: 1364 ("Di shu" 地數; Rickett 1998: 427).

101   See for instance *Guanzi* XXII.72: 1247 ("Hai wang" 海王).

102   See *Guanzi* XXII.76: 1322 ("Shan zhi shu" 山至數).

103   *Wenxian tongkao* XV.4A ("Zheng que kao er" 征権考二).

It is only when Guan Yiwu (Guan Zhong) became the Chancellor of Qi, which commands the advantageous resources of mountains and seas, that the state began to levy a tax on salt and iron. We can see when Guan Zhong discusses the issue of salt that he intends to take into account every modicum of salt consumed, even by young girls and boys; and when he discusses the issue of iron, he intends to calculate every fraction of iron one needs to make an object, be they as small as knives or needles. This is harsh and calculating in the extreme. That is why he said:[104] "If benefits come from a single source, the state will have no rival; if there are two different sources, then the army will hold back or come to a halt; if there are three sources, it will not be able to deploy its troops; and if there are four sources, the state will certainly perish." The kings of yore knew this, and that it why they restrained access to commodities and prevented the possibility of extra benefits. It is the prince who gives, it is the prince who takes, and it is the prince who makes people rich or poor.

5.4 The State's Tricks to Win the Market

As seen above, the objective of enriching the state implies a program of despoliation of people organized by tax laws, the optimal commercialization of natural resources and a high (and highly disguised!) taxation of production and work. Yet, in spite of boldly asseverated economic ideas, the *Guanzi* fails to formulate a consistent policy, and records divergent, if not opposite, views, sometimes disparaging, sometimes encouraging regarding the role of merchants. In the "Qingzhong" section, merchants are regularly attacked or condemned and the authors advocate a price policy in order to undermine rich traders and entrepreneurs. In other chapters such as "Xiao kuang" 小匡, merchants, by contrast, are seen as a fundamental social class

---

104   The following quotation is taken from *Guanzi* XXII.73 "Guoxu," dating from the late Warring States or the Western Han but evidently drawing on earlier materials (Rickett 1998: 377).

along with the "gentlemen" or educated "men of service" (*shi* 士).[105] In the chapter "On Maintaining Restraint" ("Jin cang" 禁藏), probably datable to late Warring States, the search of profit is described as a general proclivity of human nature and the endeavors of merchants should thus not be thwarted, but on the contrary skillfully exploited in order to increase the wealth of the state.[106]

Most of the time though, the policies and measures that are devised, advocated or advised by Guan Zhong confirm hostile dispositions against merchants, who are seen as vying with the government for fruitful commercial operations. The state appears here as a "super merchant and moneylender" who takes advantage of its political supremacy to eliminate competition[107] while powerful merchants are depicted, on the other hand, as aspiring rulers taking advantage of the people's distress.[108]

To sum up this survey of the *Guanzi*'s policies of enrichment, let us recall that the state is urged to absorb a maximum amount of gold, gain and grain from merchants, traders, moneylenders and peasants thanks to taxation, monopolies, statistics, speculations and stratagems. Rulers and ministers must impose measures and decrees that oblige the people to give away what little surplus or savings they may have, as if each grain of salt or rice they retained for themselves beyond their basic needs represented a loss

---

105   "Gentlemen, peasants, artisans, and merchants, these four types of people are the bedrock of the state" 士農工商四民者，國之石民者 (*Guanzi* VIII. 20: 400; Rickett 2001: 327).

106   "Indeed, it is the nature of men that whenever they see profit, they cannot help chasing after it, and whenever they see harm, they cannot help running away. When the merchant engages in trade and travels twice the ordinary distance in a day, uses the night to extend the day, and covers a thousand *li* without considering it too far, it is because profit lies ahead" 夫凡人之情，見利莫能勿就，見害莫能勿避。其商人通賈，倍道兼行，夜以續日，千里而不遠者，利在前也 (*Guanzi* XVII.53: 1015; Rickett 1998: 219–220).

107   For instance, Guan Zhong suggests to heighten bridges and lower the beds of waterways in order to impede their travels and stop them from taking advantage of the difference in price elsewhere (*Guanzi* XXIII.80: 1407 ["Qing zhong jia" 輕重甲]; Rickett 1998: 451).

108   See *Guanzi* XXIII.80: 1425–1426 ("Qing zhong jia"; Rickett 1998: 457–458), which mentions the competition between a ruler and a rich merchant as a situation where there are two princes or two kings within one country.

for the state. The only limit to these monopolistic methods of enrichment is the prudent consideration of the emotional reactions of commoners, who, in the economic interest of the state, should not be pressed too harshly, lest they resort to violence and hostility. At a certain point, the enrichment of the state against the country weakens the army and may even give rise to civil war (*nei zhan* 內戰).[109] These misgivings are the only factors likely to curb the state's omnivorous greed.

Conclusion

During the Warring States period, the idea dawned on many rulers and statesmen that the state should speculate on grain or fodder and engage in lucrative commercial activities. The practical business sense of merchants seasoned in negotiation techniques and experienced in the art of taking the lead in the market found a fruitful association with the technical skills of artisans and craftsmen who relied in their trade on units of measures and length, on numbers and calculus operations, and on a gamut of varied tools.

But with political thinkers in Qi and Qin, as evidenced in the *Guanzi* and the *Book of Lord Shang*, this trend partly backfired on the merchants themselves: the enrichment of the state around the 4th century BCE was propped up by a discourse more and more hostile to merchants, traders and free entrepreneurs. The fortunes they were able to build were seen as a challenge to the power and the wealth of the state. After having instilled in the state apparatus a profit-seeking disposition, they appeared as competitors and rivals who impoverished the state and weakened its authority.

The phrase *fuguo qiangbing* resurfaces regularly throughout Chinese imperial history. It fostered discussions and structured debates from the former Han up to the present day, especially in periods of intense political struggles or of looming threat from foreign powers (as in the Southern

---

109　*Guanzi* XXI.68: 1223 ("Chen cheng ma").

Song or the late Qing periods). According to texts and contexts, the slogan underwent slight lexical variations, the people (*min*) replacing, at times, the state (*guo*), at other times, the army (*bing*). It was reiterated in Japan during the Meiji era (1868–1912), reemployed by Chairman Mao several times, and is still listed today as the first of the Core Socialist Values adopted by the Communist Party of China at its 18th Congress (2012), as *fuqiang* 富強, a shortening of the original slogan pioneered in the *Book of Lord Shang*. The two sets of core oppositions (country versus state; people's wealth in keeping with or against the state's interest) may well be among the most enduring traits of Chinese political culture and continue to have polemical reverberations and nurture disagreement between the population and the political elite. China's rulers today inherit a rich repository of political paradigms dating from its pre-imperial past, on which they can draw at will to give a heightened sense of continuity by the circulation of these two-millennia old keywords.

Bibliography

Chemla, Karine and Ma Biao. 2015. "How Do the Earliest Known Mathematical Writings Highlight the State's Management of Grains in Early Imperial China?" *Archive for History of Exact Sciences* 69 (1): 1–53.

Chunqiu Zuozhuan zhu 春秋左傳注. 1981. Annotated by Yang Bojun 楊伯峻. Beijing: Zhonghua shuju.

Coe, Jonathan. 2008. *The Rain Before it Falls*. London: Penguin.

Defoort, Carine and Nicholas Standaert. 2013. "Introduction: Different Voices in the *Mozi*: Studies of an Evolving Text." In *The Mozi as an Evolving Text: Different Voices in Early Chinese Thought*, edited by Carine Defoort and Nicholas Standaert, 1–34. Leiden: Brill.

Falkenhausen, Lothar von. 1999. "The Waning of the Bronze Age: Material Culture and Social Developments, 770–481 B.C." In *Cambridge History of Ancient China, from the Origins of Civilization to 221 BC*, edited by Michael Loewe and Edward L. Shaughnessy, 450–544. Cambridge: Cambridge University Press.

Guanzi jiaozhu 管子校注. 2004. Compiled by Li Xiangfeng 黎翔鳳. Beijing: Zhonghua shuju.

Guoyu jijie 國語集解. 2002. Compiled by Xu Yuangao 徐元誥 (1876–1955). Beijing: Zhonghua shuju.

Hanshu 漢書. 1997. By Ban Gu 班固 (32–92) et al. Annotated by Yan Shigu 顏師古 (581–645). Beijing: Zhonghua shuju.

Han Feizi jijie 韓非子集解. 1998. Compiled by Wang Xianshen 王先慎 (1859–1922). Beijing: Zhonghua shuju.

Hutton, Eric L. 2014. *Xunzi: The Complete Text*. Princeton NJ: Princeton University Press.

Knoblock, John and Riegel, Jeffrey. 2013. *Mozi* 墨子: *A Study and Translation of the Ethical and Political Writings*. Berkeley: Institute of East Asian Studies, University of California.

Lewis, Mark Edward. 1990. *Sanctioned Violence in Early China*. Albany: State University of New York Press.

———. 1999. "Warring States: Political History." In *The Cambridge History of Ancient China: From the Origins of Civilization to 221 B.C.*, edited by Michael Loewe and Edward L. Shaughnessy, 587–650. Cambridge: Cambridge University Press.

Liang Tao 梁濤. 2016. "Xunzi renxing lun de lishixing fazhan: lun 'Fuguo', 'Rongru' de qingxing—zhixing shuo" 荀子人性論的歷史性發展——論「富國」、「榮辱」的情性——知性説. *Zhexue yanjiu* 哲学研究 11: 46–53.

Liji jijie 禮記集解. 1995. Compiled by Sun Xidan 孫希旦 (1736–1784). Edited by Shen Xiaohuan 沈嘯寰 and Wang Xingxian 王星賢. Beijing: Zhonghua shuju.

Liu Jiapeng 劉甲朋. 2010. *Zhongguo gudai liangshi chubei tiaojie zhidu sixiang yanjin* 中國古代糧食儲備調節制度思想演進. Beijing: Zhongguo jingji chubanshe.

Loewe, Michael. 2007. *The Government of the Qin and Han Empires 221 BCE–220 CE*. Indianapolis: Hackett.

Lunyu yizhu 論語譯注. 1992. Annotated by Yang Bojun 楊伯峻. Beijing: Zhonghua shuju.

Mengzi yizhu 孟子譯注. 1992. Annotated by Yang Bojun 楊伯峻. Beijing: Zhonghua shuju.

Mozi jiaozhu 墨子校注. 1994. Compiled and annotated by Wu Yujiang 吳毓江 (1898–1977). Beijing: Zhonghua shuju.

Pines, Yuri. 2009. *Envisioning Eternal Empire: Chinese Political Thought of the Warring States Era*. Honolulu: University of Hawai'i Press.

———. 2016. "Social Engineering in Early China: The Ideology of the *Shangjunshu* (*Book of Lord Shang*) Revisited." *Oriens Extremus* 55: 1–37.

———. 2017. *The Book of Lord Shang: Apologetics of State Power in Early China*. New York: Columbia University Press.

———. Forthcoming. "Agriculturalism and Beyond: Economic Thought of the *Book of Lord Shang*." In: *Between Command and Market: Economic Thought and Practice in Early China*, edited by Elisa Sabattini and Christian Schwermann. Leiden: Brill.

Rickett, Allyn W. 2001. *Guanzi. Political, Economic, and Philosophical Essays from Early China*. Volume I (rev. ed). Princeton: Princeton Library of Asian Translations.

———. 1998. *Guanzi: Political, Economic, and Philosophical Essays from Early China. A Study and Translation*. Volume II. Princeton: Princeton Library of Asian Tranlations.

Shangjunshu zhuizhi 商君書錐指. 2001. Edited by Jiang Lihong 蔣禮鴻 (1916–1995). Beijing: Zhonghua shuju.

Shiji 史記. 1997. By Sima Qian 司馬遷 (ca. 145–90 BCE) et al. Annotated by Zhang Shoujie 張守節 (7th c.), Sima Zhen 司馬貞 (679–732), and Pei Yin 裴駰 (5th c.). Beijing: Zhonghua shuju.

Sterckx, Roel. Forthcoming. "Agrarian and Mercantile Ideologies in Western Han," *Journal of the Economic and Social History of the Orient* 63.4 (2020).

Tong, Weimin. 2016. "On the Composition of the 'Attracting the People' Chapter of the *Book of Lord Shang*." *Contemporary Chinese Thought* 47.2: 138–151.

Wenxian tongkao 文獻通考. By Ma Duanlin 馬端臨 (1254–ca. 1324). In *Siku quanshu huiyao* 四庫全書薈要.

Wu Yujiang 吳毓江. 1994. "Mozi gepian zhenwei kao" 墨子各篇真偽考. *Mozi jiaozhu*.

Yantielun jiaozhu 鹽鐵論校注. 1996. Compiled by Huan Kuan 桓寬 (1st c. BCE). Annotated by Wang Liqi 王利器. Beijing: Zhonghua shuju.

Xunzi jijie 荀子集解. 1992. Annotated by Wang Xianqian 王先謙 (1842–1917). Edited by Shen Xiaohuan 沈嘯寰 and Wang Xingxian 王星賢. Beijing: Zhonghua shuju.

Yang Kuan 楊寬. 2003. *Zhanguo shi* 戰國史. Shanghai: Shanghai renmin chubanshe.

Zhanguo ce 戰國策. 1988. Compiled by Liu Xiang 劉向 (77–6 BCE), annotated by Fan Xiangyong 范祥雍, collated by Fan Bangjin 范邦瑾. Shanghai: Shanghai guji chubanshe.

5

"To Die for the Sanctity of the Name": Name (*ming* 名) as Prime Mover of Political Action in Early China*

Yuri Pines

In one of the most celebrated moments in *Sanguo yanyi* 三國演義 (Romance of the Three Kingdoms), Lord Guan 關公 (Guan Yu 關羽, d. 219), who faces inevitable defeat, refuses to submit to the state of Wu 吳, saying:

> 玉可碎而不可改其白，竹可焚而不可毀其節。身雖殞，名可垂於竹帛也。
>
> Jade can be smashed but its whiteness cannot be changed; bamboo can be burned, but its joints cannot be destroyed. Although my body will perish, my name will be handed down on bamboo and silk.[1]

This statement encapsulates the extraordinary importance of one's name (*ming* 名) in Chinese thought. Lord Guan's steadfast preservation of his integrity, his loyalty to the ruler-brother, Liu Bei 劉備 (161–223), and his readiness to face death rather than disgrace are all justified by the bottom line: his name will be handed down for generations. Needless to say, the

---

* This research was supported by the Israel Science Foundation (grant No. 240/15) and by the Michael William Lipson Chair in Chinese Studies. I am grateful to Paul R. Goldin and Li Wai-yee for their most helpful comments on earlier versions of this essay.

1 *Sanguo yanyi* 76: 991. Note that "bamboo joints" 節 is precisely the term used for personal integrity and steadfast commitment to one's moral principles.

novel itself, which narrates Lord Guan's heroic death, serves as the best testimony to his success. For well over one thousand years, Lord Guan has been one of the best-known names throughout China—both as a deity and as a remarkable human being.[2]

Self-sacrifice and heroic martyrdom are common throughout the world, past and present. Religion, ethics, or, more unusually, a secular ideology—all can prompt a human being to consider life as a light thing in comparison to higher goals. Jewish martyrdom is defined in Hebrew as "dying for the sanctity of the Name" (למות על קידוש השם), when the Name, of course, is that of God Almighty. In China one also dies (or acts in an extraordinary way against narrowly conceived selfish interests) out of commitment to a higher cause. Quite often the potential martyr declares that he is willing to die for the sake of his "name" (*ming* 名). This quest for "a name" is openly recognized, debated, and quite often endorsed, in a great variety of philosophical and literary works from the Warring States period (Zhanguo 戰國, 453–221 BCE) on. This discourse about the quest for a name, its legitimacy, and its social and political desirability is the focus of my study.

The word *ming* is one of the most multi-faceted terms in Chinese political, ethical, social, philosophical, and religious discourse. Even its most immediate literal meaning as an individual's appellation is imbued with social, political, and religious significance: one's name was a tabooed word for the person's inferiors and its usage was closely related to questions of social and political hierarchy.[3] The second semantic layer, the one on which my current study will focus, is that of repute, renown, fame. Closely related to this is the notion of *ming* as commemoration, which again will be discussed below. Third, and to a certain extent related to one's repute, was the meaning of *ming* as designation of one's social status, which also will be addressed below. The fourth semantic layer refers to *ming* as a

---

2   For the evolution of the cult of Lord Guan (first attested to under the Tang dynasty [618–907]), and for his literary commemoration (traceable back to the Song dynasty [960–1279]), see Duara 1988.

3   See details in Adamek 2016; Cao Feng 2017: 30–45.

terminus technicus in administrative and legal discourse.[4] Add to these the fifth, philosophical, meaning of *ming* as "a word" or "a term" (see Defoort, Chapter 1). This lengthy—and by no means exhaustive—list, as well as persistent interactions among distinct semantic layers of the term *ming*, suffice to demonstrate the difficulty—I would say even impossibility—of dealing with the term *ming* in a single study.[5]

Yet the goals of the present paper are relatively modest. Insofar as philosophical and, to a lesser extent, administrative aspects of *ming* have been explored in numerous studies, I shall not address them in what follows.[6] The focus of this study will be on the "name" as repute and its related meaning as one's social status. I shall survey the Warring States period debates about the desirability of the quest for *ming* and about its political and social implications. In the final two sections I shall explore how these debates are related to the usages of *ming* by the imperial literati and outline aspects of the imperial-period views of name-seeking. I hope that this study will add some new dimensions to our exploration of the interrelationships among ethics, politics, social practices, and religion in China, as well as among philosophical, historical, and literary texts.[7]

---

4 *Ming* may, for instance, refer to a "title" compared with "performance" (*xing* 形), as in *Han Feizi* 韓非子 (see Goldin 2013: 8–10; cf. Makeham 1990–1991), or to specific items of legal regulations, as in Chapter 26 ("Ding fen" 定分) of the *Shangjunshu* 商君書 (Book of Lord Shang); Pines 2017a: 243–248.

5 In a very recent insightful book, Cao Feng 曹峰 (2017) discusses *ming* in the context of political thought; yet his monograph and the present article almost do not overlap. This suffices to indicate the breadth of the applications of the term *ming* in Chinese intellectual discourse.

6 The single most prolific writer on various aspects of *ming* is John Makeham (see, e.g., Makeham 1990–1991, 1991, 1994). For explorations of the philosophical contents of *ming*, see also Möller 1997; Loy 2003; Geaney 2010; Solomon 2013; Tavor 2014.

7 The non-philosophical dimensions of *ming* were not adequately explored in the West (for major exceptions, see Makeham 1993 and parts of Makeham 1994). This situation is due to change after the publication of Mark E. Lewis's forthcoming monograph. Cao Feng lamented the distortions in the studies of *ming* imposed by the acceptance of a "foreign conceptual framework" (Cao Feng 2008: 225; cf. Cao Feng 2017: 20). In not a few Chinese studies, attempts were made to overcome this distortion; see, e.g., Gou Dongfeng 2013 and, most notably Cao Feng 2017.

1. Prelude: *Ming* in the Aristocratic Age

The term *ming* does not appear to have played a significant role in either political or ethical discourse prior to the Warring States period. It is all but absent from the Western Zhou period's (西周, ca. 1046–771 BCE) sections of *Shijing* 詩經 (Canon of poems) and *Shujing* 書經 (Canon of documents), while in bronze inscriptions it appears only as one's name or as a verb, "to name."[8] It is present, albeit indirectly, in another would-be canonical text, namely the *Chunqiu* 春秋 (Spring and Autumn annals, hereafter the *Annals*) of the state of Lu 魯. Without entering here into the controversies regarding the nature and the authorship of the *Annals* and its peculiar "rules of recording" (*shu fa* 書法), suffice it to say that certain records could be utilized to express "praise and blame" (*baobian* 褒貶) of historical personages. In particular, writing down a person's given name in certain contexts was a potent means of shaming through naming.[9]

The most celebrated story of naming a culprit as a means of censuring him is the condemnation of a Jin 晉 prime minister, Zhao Dun 趙盾. In 607 BCE, Zhao Dun orchestrated the assassination of his ruler, Lord Ling 晉靈公 (r. 620–607 BCE), while pretending to flee the state. The court scribe, Dong Hu 董狐, nevertheless recorded for the annals: "Zhao Dun murdered his ruler" 趙盾弒其君. Zhao protested, but Dong Hu explained

---

8   In a later interpretation of the inscriptions' contents, the Warring States period exegetes postulated: "An inscription comes from naming [oneself]. One names oneself to extol the perfection of one's ancestors, making it manifest for posterity" 銘者，自名也。自名以稱揚其先祖之美，而明著之後世者也。*Liji jijie* XLVII.25: 1250 ["Ji tong" 祭統]). Yet judging from the original setting of the inscriptions within the bronze vessels, they were primarily directed at the ancestors rather than to posterity (Falkenhausen 1993). Their relation to the later notion of individual commemoration deserves a separate study.

9   For my views of the *Annals*, see Pines 2009b: 316–323; for their rules of recording, see Van Auken 2007 (and see Van Auken 2016 for a broader study of the *Annals* and their commentaries). That naming a culprit in the *Annals* meant condemning his misdeeds is explicitly stated in *Zuozhuan* 左傳 (Xuan 4.2: 768). Even if this rule is merely a post-factum explanation, it seems to grasp accurately some of the recording patterns in the *Annals*. It should be noted though that naming in the *Annals* is not exclusively used for the purpose of condemnation; see more in Van Auken 2016.

that as Zhao neither left the state at the time of the murder nor punished the criminals thereafter, the legal responsibility was his. The veracity of the story and its underlying historiographic principles need not concern us here; what is important is that there is enough evidence to confirm that mentioning a person's name in the *Annals* in certain circumstances was a way of blaming him.[10]

When we turn to the major commentary of the *Annals* and our major source for the history of the Spring and Autumn period (Chunqiu 春秋, 770–453 BCE)—*Zuozhuan* 左傳—we can easily discern the statesmen's concern with their repute.[11] Being named in a negative context "on the bamboo tablets of the regional lords" (在諸侯之策; a referent to the annals that in all likelihood were produced in each of the major regional courts and not just in the state of Lu) was a major blow to one's reputation, a matter of grave concern.[12] By the same token, the appeal to the need to preserve one's "fine name" (*ling ming* 令名) was a potent argument in urging a leader to adopt a recommended policy course.[13] Whereas name-

---

10 *Zuozhuan*, Xuan 2.3: 662–663. Another equally celebrated case of naming a culprit in the *Annals* as a means to condemning him is the case of Cui Zhu 崔杼, who assassinated Lord Zhuang of Qi 齊莊公 (r. 553–548 BCE). Cui Zhu had no less than two scribes killed in order to prevent them from recording his guilt, but the scribes' persistence left him no option but to accept the damage to his name (*Zuozhuan*, Xiang 25.2: 1099). For other cases in which the *Annals'* naming of a ruler's murderer hints at a legally responsible person, who technically was not the killer, see Zhao Shengqun 2000: 251–257. For some cases in which the culprits succeeded in avoiding being named, see Pines 2009b: 329–330.

11 It is not my intention here to address anew the contentious issue about whether *Zuozhuan* reflects ideas of the aristocratic Spring and Autumn period or of the subsequent age of the Warring States; nor am I concerned with the precise nature of relations between *Zuozhuan* and the *Annals*. For different approaches, see Schaberg 2001; Pines 2002a and forthcoming; Li Wai-yee 2007, q.v. for further references.

12 See, e.g., *Zuozhuan*, Wen 15.2: 609; Xiang 20.7: 1055; and the discussion of these cases in Pines 2009b: 321–323. For an idea that the *Annals* represent the common tradition of the Zhou states, see Karapetiants 1988.

13 See, e.g., *Zuozhuan*, Xiang 24.2: 1089, Zhao 16.3: 1379. Interestingly, the binome "fine name" is relatively rare in pre-imperial texts; its usage is confined almost exclusively to *Zuozhuan* and a few sections of the parallel *Guoyu* 國語 (Discourses of the states).

seeking as such was censured as morally inappropriate for the "noble men" (*junzi* 君子), overall, the concern for one's reputation was considered fully legitimate.[14]

This said, when we compare the *Zuozhuan* narratives with the texts from the Warring States period, one may come to the conclusion that the quest for a name (fame, reputation) was not a significant factor in political and ethical life of the aristocratic age. Appeals to one's "fine name" recur from time to time, but never does the quest for a name stand alone as the major determinant of one's action. Even in terms of posthumous reputation, the word "name" does not appear as singularly important. In a major discussion of what it means "to die but not decay" (*si er bu xiu* 死 而不朽), recorded under the year 549 BCE, a Lu noble, Shusun Bao 叔 孫豹, explains to his Jin colleague that immortality does not imply mere preservation of the lineage's status, but something greater than that:

> 魯有先大夫曰臧文仲，既沒，其言立，其是之謂乎！豹聞之：「大上 有立德，其次有立功，其次有立言。」雖久不廢，此之謂不朽。若 夫保姓受氏，以守宗祊，世不絕祀，無國無之。祿之大者，不可謂 不朽。

> Lu had a former grandee Zang Wenzhong; he is dead already, but his words are still established: is that not what is meant ["to die but not decay"]? I, Bao, heard: "The best is to establish virtue; second to it is to establish merits; next is to establish words." If even as time elapses they do not fade away—this is what is called "not decaying." As for preserving one's clan and receiving a lineage [name] to guard the ancestral temple so that sacrifices do not fade for generations—this exists in every state. That, which is great among emolument, cannot be called "not decaying."[15]

In my view, the three ways of immortality outlined above may be related to the three levels of political success in aristocratic society. The first is

---

14   For criticism of name-seeking, see *Zuozhuan*, Xiang 26.11: 1123 and Xiang 27.4: 1129.

15   *Zuozhuan*, Xiang 24.1: 1087–1088. My translations from *Zuozhuan* borrow (and modify from time to time) Durrant, Li, and Schaberg 2016.

the major, epochal "establishment of virtue" (*li de* 立德), which perhaps hints at the meaning of *de* as the charismatic power of dynastic founders; this is a matter of success for the whole clan (*xing* 姓). The second level of "establishing merits" (*li gong* 立功) probably refers to the founding of an aristocratic lineage (*shi* 氏), the precondition for which was that the ancestor be meritorious enough to get an official position and a hereditary allotment, the *sine qua non* for the lineage's longevity. The third, and lowest level of "establishing words" (*li yan* 立言) refers to an individual's—rather than clan or lineage's—immortality. Here one would expect to find the word "name," should we speak of a Warring States period text. However, this term is absent, and this absence is not incidental.[16] Individual establishment of a "name" outside the lineage framework was not an option for a noble of the Spring and Autumn period. What a noble could "establish" were "words," i.e., making politically and morally important pronouncements that would be transmitted to posterity, as many exemplary speeches in *Zuozhuan* were. Yet to have the right to "establish words" one should be an aristocrat, a political insider. At least insofar as *Zuozhuan* is concerned, it never records lengthy ideologically important speeches of persons outside the hereditary power order. A name—in its Warring States period meaning, as an asset of political outsiders—is not mentioned in Shusun Bao's speech, nor elsewhere in *Zuozhuan*.

2. The Noble Man's Quest for a Name

Confucius (孔子, 551–479 BCE) is a watershed figure in China's intellectual history. Before his emergence, "establishing words"—i.e. bequeathing one's ideological legacy to posterity—appears to be a prerogative of hereditary

---

16   Actually, in some Chinese discussions of the role of a "name" in political discourse, this passage is routinely invoked as an example of name-seeking, without authors' paying attention to the absence of the term *ming*. See, e.g., Ruan Zhong 2003; Yang Jianqiang and Xiao Qunzhong 2015.

aristocrats. If any member of the lowest segment of nobility—the *shi* (士, "men-of-service") stratum—was intellectually active prior to Confucius, our sources remain silent about that. Confucius was the first speaker on behalf of the rising *shi*, and the first thinker to deal, even if cautiously, with the issue of the upward mobility of the *shi*. As is well known, one of his major breakthroughs was redefining the term *junzi* 君子 (the noble man) from a pedigree-based to a morality-based designation. A *shi* should aspire to become a *junzi*, which will make him into a legitimate member of the ruling elite.[17]

Unlike the aristocrats, whose employment was more or less ensured under the principle of hereditary office-holding, the *shi* had to prove their abilities in the ever escalating competition with nobles and with other *shi*. In this situation, one's renown was an important asset; conceivably, a famous *shi* would be more readily employed than his lesser-known peers. This explains the considerable interest in one's name that we encounter in the *Lunyu* 論語 (*Analects*). Thus, Confucius is quoted as saying: "The noble man is pained if by the end of his life his name is not mentioned" 君子疾沒世而名不稱焉. The Master speaks dismissively of those who failed to establish their renown by the age of forty or fifty. And he appears to be greatly annoyed by a remark that, despite his broad learning, his own name is not widely known.[18]

Confucius's quest for a name made some later thinkers, such as the Han man of letters Xu Gan 徐幹 (170–218), as well as some modern scholars, uneasy. Surely, the Master should have focused on "inner happiness" rather than on such a "dubious" thing as one's name.[19] I think these attempts to diminish the importance of a name for Confucius are not convincing. The Master did want to attain a fine reputation, just as he wanted to attain an official position; it is just that these goals were to remain subordinate to moral and ethical considerations. Confucius clarifies:

---

17   For the changing concept of *junzi* in the *Lunyu* vis-à-vis earlier texts, see Gassman 2007; Brindley 2009; Pines 2017b.

18   See respectively *Lunyu yizhu* 15.20: 166, 9.23: 94, 9.2: 88.

19   See, e.g., Makeham 1993, who elaborates on Xu Gan's views; cf. Roetz 1993: 181–183.

富與貴是人之所欲也；不以其道得之，不處也。貧與賤是人之所惡
也；不以其道得〔=去〕之，不去也。君子去仁，惡乎成名？

Riches and nobility are what every man desires; but if they cannot be
attained in accordance with the Way, do not accept them. Poverty and
base status are what every man detests. But if they cannot be avoided in
accordance with the Way, do not avoid them. If the noble man abandons
benevolence, how will he accomplish his name?[20]

The message is clear: while the quest for a name, just like the quest
for material benefits, is natural and laudable, it should be pursued
only in accordance with one's moral Way. The Master is well aware of
the difficulty of attaining the balance. Time and again he repeats that
one should concern oneself with one's own abilities rather than with
recognition from others.[21] Becoming famous is desirable but it is still a
secondary goal.

As we advance into the Warring States period, the importance of the
quest for a name increases, as is observable in a great variety of texts. Let
us take *Mozi* 墨子 as an example. The text repeatedly treats the quest for
renown and praise (*yu* 譽) as a singularly important factor in determining
the behavior of the elite members. Mozi (ca. 460–390 BCE) specifically
appeals to the rulers' quest for fame so as to encourage them to accept his
controversial advice; should the rulers do so, "their name will be handed
down to posterity."[22] The same quest for name and praise influenced the
behavior of the fellow *shi*. As distinct from Confucius, Mozi unequivocally
endorses this quest. In his seminal chapters on the principle of "elevating
the worthy" (*shang xian* 尚賢), Mozi explains how the worthies' quest for
renown should be addressed by the rulers. Monarchs should "enrich, honor,
respect, and praise" 富之、貴之、敬之、譽之 their aides; only "then will

---

20   *Lunyu yizhu* 4.5: 36.
21   *Lunyu yizhu* 1.16: 10, 4.14: 38–39, 14.30: 155.
22   垂名於後世. See, e.g., *Mozi jiaozhu* III.12: 121 ("Shang tong 尚同 zhong"); V.9: 218 ("Fei gong
      非攻 xia").

it be possible to gain [the service of] good *shi* in the state and increase their number" 然后國之良士，亦將可得而眾也。[23]

Mozi's suggestions are simple: like other specialists in different fields, "good *shi*" (*liang shi* 良士) are interested in acclaim and emoluments, and in order to attract them the ruler should generously subsidize them and flatter them. A *shi*'s quest for riches and fame does not diminish their worthiness in Mozi's eyes. Mozi surely dislikes unjustified renown (e.g., his opposition to the glorification of aggressive generals),[24] but worthy *shi* fully deserve the ruler's endorsement of their quest for a fine reputation.

We shall return later to Mozi's other considerations regarding one's quest for a name and its influence on individual behavior, but first let us explore some of the ideas of Confucius's followers. In general, these viewed the quest for a name in highly positive terms, although voices of caution that we encounter in the *Analects* recur in many later texts as well. In the *Mengzi* 孟子, for instance, the quest for a name appears in a highly positive context: "One who is fond of [a good] name is able to yield a thousand-chariot-sized state. If he is not such a person, his countenance will be uneasy even when giving away a basketful of food and a cup of soup."[25] Yet Mengzi (ca. 380–304 BCE) echoes Confucius's reservations about paying too much attention to external reputation and career success. Rather, the real nobility, renown, and fine reputation are "embedded" in one's self: they are not delivered by the outside world.[26] The quest for a name is a positive ethical factor, but it should not be the primary motivation of the noble man's action: priority should be given to one's inner satisfaction with one's own morality. Hence, discussions about attaining a good name remain marginal in *Mengzi*.

---

23   *Mozi jiaozhu* II.8: 66 ("Shang xian 尚賢 shang").
24   See *Mozi jiaozhu* V.7: 199 ("Fei gong 非攻 shang").
25   好名之人，能讓千乘之國。苟非其人，簞食豆羹見於色。*Mengzi yizhu* 14.11: 304. Note that Zhu Xi 朱熹 (1130–1200) reads this passage differently: a person may do a great gesture of yielding in search for praise, but actually his morality still remains flawed and his greed will transpire in small matters. See *Mengzi zhangju* 14: 366.
26   *Mengzi yizhu* 11.17: 251; see also Roetz 1993: 182; Goldin 2011: 54–55.

In sharp contrast to *Mengzi*, *Xunzi* 荀子 presents the most sophisticated discussion about the impact of the quest for a name on a noble man's ethical and political conduct. In discussing Xunzi's (ca. 310–230 BCE) views of names, I shall not focus on his philosophical explorations of the idea of "names" and their "rectification," which has been discussed elsewhere.[27] Let us move directly to the ethical and political meanings of the term *ming* in Xunzi. Here we can discern several distinct usages. First, much like in *Mozi*, a "name" (i.e., fame, good reputation) is a promise for rulers who would heed Xunzi's recommendations. Attaining a "name" on a par with actual achievements (*gong* 功) will be the hallmark of their success.[28] Yet the second level shows that the name does not always parallel one's achievements. As far as outstanding *shi* are concerned, good repute can arise not from a real success but as a compensation for the lack thereof. Xunzi clarifies this in one of the central chapters of the text, "Ru xiao" (儒效, "The Effectiveness of the Ru"):

故君子無爵而貴，無祿而富，不言而信，不怒而威，窮處而榮，獨居而樂，豈不至尊、至富、至重、至嚴之情舉積此哉！……故君子務脩其內，而讓之於外；務積德於身，而處之以遵道。如是，則貴名起如日月，天下應之如雷霆。故曰：君子隱而顯，微而明，辭讓而勝。《詩》曰：「鶴鳴于九皋，聲聞于天。」此之謂也。

Hence the noble man is esteemed without rank, rich without emoluments, trustworthy without words, awe-inspiring without anger. He lives in poverty but is glorious, dwells alone but is joyful—is it not that he accumulated the essence of the most respectable, the richest, the most important and the sternest? ... Hence the noble man is devoted to internal cultivation and yields externally, devotes himself to accumulating virtue in his body and dwells in it to comply with the Way. In this way, his noble name arises like the sun and moon, All-under-Heaven respond to him

---

27   Graham 1989: 265–267; Goldin 2011: 92–95; Fraser 2016; q.v. for further references.

28   See, e.g., *Xunzi jijie* V.9: 152 ("Wang zhi" 王制), VII.11: 216 ("Wang ba" 王霸); IX.14: 263 ("Zhi shi" 致士), *et saepe*.

as to a thunderbolt. Therefore it is said: the noble man is obscure, and yet is illustrious; he is hidden and yet is luminous; he is yielding and yet victorious. The *Poem* says: "The crane cries at the nine marshes, its voice is heard in Heaven." This is what is meant.[29]

The noble man does not depend on external circumstances; his internal cultivation suffices to counterbalance failures in pursuing his career. Accumulation of virtue allows him to attain the "noble name" even when he remains obscure and lacks rank and emolument. His name makes him the true leader of All-under-Heaven, the one to whom the people respond "as to the thunderbolt." Elsewhere, Xunzi clarifies further how the name compensates the noble man (or, more precisely, the best of the noble men—the Great Ru 大儒) for his failures in real life:

> 彼大儒者，雖隱於窮閣漏屋，無置錐之地，而王公不能與之爭名；用百里之地，而千里之國莫能與之爭勝；笞棰暴國，齊一天下，而莫能傾也——是大儒之徵也。……通則一天下，窮則獨立貴名，天不能死，地不能埋，桀、跖之世不能汙，非大儒莫之能立。

> This Great Ru, even when he lives in obscurity in an impoverished lane in a leaking house and has not enough space to place an awl, kings and dukes are unable to vie for a good name with him; when he has a territory of a hundred *li* squared, none of the states of one thousand *li* squared can vie for superiority with him. He beats down violent states, orders and unifies All-under-Heaven, and nobody is able to overturn him—this is the sign of the Great Ru. ... When he succeeds, he unifies All-under-Heaven; when he fails, he establishes alone his noble name. Heaven cannot kill it; Earth cannot bury it; the age of [tyrant] Jie and [Robber] Zhi cannot tarnish it: only the Great Ru can establish it like this.[30]

Here the "name" (i.e., good reputation) is posed as the supreme asset of the Great Ru, the possession of which is a recompense for the lack of attainments

---

29 *Xunzi jijie* IV.8: 127–128 ("Ru xiao"). The quoted poem is "He ming" 鶴鳴 (Mao 184).
30 *Xunzi jijie* IV.8: 117–118 ("Ru xiao").

in his real life. Obscure and impoverished, he is still able to contest successfully with self-proclaimed kings of the Warring States and with other territorial lords, because his noble name is the source of enormous moral power. This name reaches cosmic dimensions: neither Heaven, nor Earth, nor human evildoers can tarnish it. Possessing a "noble name" is depicted in this extraordinary panegyric to the Great Ru as coequal with the supreme political achievement of unifying All-under-Heaven, which was during the Warring States period the ultimate goal of competing thinkers.[31] In fact, Xunzi creates here two parallel hierarchies: one is crowned by real political achievements, and another one marked by the attainment of a "noble name."

Yet Xunzi, who was fully aware of the dangerous quest for glory as a self-contained goal of some *shi* (a topic that will be discussed in the next section), was careful to avoid it. Hence he introduces the third dimension to his discussion of name: its subordination to other moral values. Xunzi reminds his audience that renown attained by villains like Robber Zhi 盜跖 may match that of the sage emperor Shun 舜, but "the noble man does not value it, because it did not come from the midst of ritual and propriety."[32] Those men who seek reputation for the sake of reputation—e.g. through display of excessive moral purism—are villains. "To steal a name is worse than stealing property."[33] Real renown is attainable exclusively through following the path of morality:

> 故君子者，信矣，而亦欲人之信己也；忠矣，而亦欲人之親己也；脩正治辨矣，而亦欲人之善己也。慮之易知也，行之易安也，持之易立也，成則必得其所好，必不遇其所惡焉。是故窮則不隱，通則大明，身死而名彌白。

The noble man is trustworthy: and he also expects others to trust him. He is loyal: and he also expects others to be close to him. He cultivates his rectitude and puts in order his discriminative abilities: and he also

---

31 For this point, see Pines 2000a.

32 然而君子不貴者，非禮義之中也。*Xunzi jijie* II.3: 39 ("Bu gou" 不苟).

33 盜名不如盜貨。*Xunzi jijie* II.3: 52 ("Bu gou" 不苟).

expects others to be good to him. His thoughts are easy to understand, his behavior easily brings calm, what he adheres to is easy to establish. When he accomplishes his [goal], he will surely attain whatever he is drawn to and surely will not encounter whatever he detests. Therefore, even when impoverished, he is not obscure, and when he succeeds he becomes greatly illustrious. His body may die, but his name will be ever radiant.[34]

This passage adds three points to Xunzi's discussion of names. First, it unequivocally reiterates that only through moral self-cultivation can one attain real renown, which will make one's name "radiant" forever. Second, from the promise "even when impoverished, he is not obscure" we may infer that obscurity—viz., lack of a name—was more frightening for a noble man than economic hardship. And third, the last line implies that attaining a noble name was a means of transcending death: compensation not just for immediate misfortune but even for mortality itself. The transcendent qualities of posthumous fame—echoed in a few other moralizing texts, such as the "Black Robes" ("Ziyi" 緇衣) chapter of the *Liji* 禮記[35]—further elevate *ming* to the position of being the most valuable reward for one's goodness.

The above survey of different attitudes toward the noble man's quest for a name suffices to cover most invocations of the term "name" in discussions by the followers of Confucius and by other supporters of moralizing politics. A good name is a much-coveted goal of moral self-cultivation and of studying.[36] It is the natural prize for those who follow the Way (*Dao* 道)

---

34 *Xunzi jijie* II.4: 61 ("Rong ru" 榮辱).

35 "[The noble man] has substance behind his words and standards behind his actions; thus in life, he cannot be robbed of his will, and in death, he cannot be robbed of his [good] name" 言有物 而行有格也；是以生則不可奪志，死則不可奪名 (*Liji jijie* LII.33: 1330 ["Ziyi" 緇衣]; for a parallel passage in the Guodian manuscript of "Ziyi," see Cook 2012: 410–412).

36 Thus, *Lüshi chunqiu* 呂氏春秋 reminds one that although Confucius and Mozi failed to implement their great way, they at least succeeded in accomplishing "illustrious names" (*xian ming* 顯名) (*Lüshi chunqiu jiaoshi* 13.7: 722 ["Yu da" 諭大]). For identifying prominence and good name as one of the primary goals of learning and self-cultivation, see also *Lüshi chunqiu jiaoshi* 4.2: 195 ("Quan xue" 勸學), 4.3: 205 ("Zun shi" 尊師).

and "principle" (*li* 理): it cannot be attained by immoral power-holders.[37] In a somewhat simplistically optimistic passage, *Zhong yong* 中庸 (The doctrine of the mean) places "name" together with "position" (*wei* 位), "emoluments" (*lu* 祿) and longevity (*shou* 壽) as the four "musts" that will be surely attained by a possessor of "great virtue."[38] Other texts combine attaining a good name with filial obligations: most notably, the *Xiaojing* 孝經 (Canon of filial piety) proclaims in its opening paragraph:

> 身體髮膚，受之父母，不敢毀傷，孝之始也。立身行道，揚名於後世，以顯父母，孝之終也。
>
> One's body, hair, and skin are what one receives from one's parents. Not daring to hurt them is the starting point of filiality. To establish oneself, to implement the way, and to make a name for subsequent generations, thereby bringing prominence to one's parents: this is the final point of filiality.[39]

The last sentence adds one more dimension to the notion of a good name as the apex of the noble man's aspirations: attaining a name is related not just to one's self-cultivation, learning, and moral conduct, but is also the end point of one's filial obligations.[40] The quest for a name is not just legitimate; it is essential for a noble man. For a cultivated man of letters, it is the one—and, under unfavorable circumstances, the only—attainable goal. The quest for a glorious name becomes one of the major (if not *the major*) prime movers of the noble man's actions.

3. Dying for One's Name

In the above section we noticed concerns by Confucius, Mozi, and Xunzi that some people would attain undeserved renown not borne out by their

---

37   *Lüshi chunqiu jiaoshi* 2.1: 110–111 ("Gong ming" 功名).

38   *Zhong yong* 17, in *Si shu zhangju*, p. 25.

39   *Xiaojing yizhu* 1: 1 ("Kaizong mingyi" 開宗明義).

40   This point is echoed in *Lüshi chunqiu jiaoshi* 14.1: 733 ("Xiao xing" 孝行).

morality. Alas, their endorsement of the quest for a name might have contributed—even if inadvertently—precisely to the proliferation of name-seeking as its own goal. Actually, the entire atmosphere of the Warring States period was conducive to the transformation of a "name" into the most coveted asset. On the one hand, dissemination of meritocratic ideas and practices opened the routes of advancement to a great variety of aspiring men-of-service. On the other hand, there was no clear agreement as to which qualities made a man eligible for government service or patronage; nor was there agreement about how to select the worthy candidates.[41] Under these circumstances, gaining renown—through whatever possible means—was an excellent way of acquiring patrons or recommenders for an office. For many people the quest for a name was the first step toward employment, riches, and political influence.[42]

Aside from career considerations, the quest for a name was fueled by the transcendent promise of posthumous fame, as noted above in our discussion of *Xunzi*. The idea of attaining an immortal name was appealing enough to some *shi* to brave death in their search for eternal glory. This motive appears most prominently in stories of assassin-retainers, scattered throughout the *Zhanguo ce* 戰國策 (Stratagems of the Warring States) and later collected by Sima Qian 司馬遷 (ca. 145–90 BCE) in his *Shiji* 史記 (Records of the historian). Their differences aside, these stories have a common plot. A powerful patron "discovers" or "recognizes" a brave *shi* and entices him—usually through very lavish gifts—to kill the patron's enemy. The *shi* fulfills his promise, with varying degrees of success, but uniformly displays total commitment to the mission and readiness to self-sacrifice. Importantly, the stories neither provide moral or political

---

41   See more in Pines 2013; cf. Richter 2005.

42   One of the most peculiar offshoots of this quest for a name as a means of political advancement was the case of lofty recluses who ostensibly discarded political career, but actually gained thereby the renown due to moral purists and became even more welcome to occupy official positions. See Pines 2009: 152–161. Note that it is precisely these recluses' quest for a name which ignites Xunzi's ire (see note 33 above).

justification for the planned assassination, nor do they set much store by the success of an assassination attempt. Clearly, the focus of these stories lies elsewhere.

Let us illustrate this with two examples. The first is that of Yu Rang 豫讓, who was committed to avenging his dead master, Zhi Bo 知伯 (d. 453 BCE). Yu Rang is said to have once served Zhi Bo's enemies, heads of the Fan 范 and Zhonghang 中行 lineages,[43] but after those were eliminated by Zhi Bo, he served his new master faithfully. The latter treated him as a "state-level *shi*" (*guoshi* 國士), and hence deserved Yu's utmost loyalty: "A *shi* dies for the sake of the one who profoundly understands him" 士 為知己者死.[44] After Zhi Bo's defeat and posthumous humiliation by his arch-enemy, Zhao Xiangzi 趙襄子 (d. ca. 442 BCE), Yu Rang committed himself to revenge. He went to great lengths to hide his identity (resorting to self-mutilation), but was nonetheless apprehended by Zhao Xiangzi. Considering Yu Rang a "righteous *shi*" (*yishi* 義士), Zhao released him, but when Yu Rang was caught for the second time Zhao told him:

> 嗟乎，豫子！豫子之為知伯，名既成矣，寡人舍子，亦以足矣。子自為計，寡人不舍子。

> Alas, Master Yu! You, Master Yu, have already accomplished your name [by trying to avenge] Zhi Bo. And my previous release of you was enough as well. Think about this yourself: now I cannot release you.

To this Yu Rang replied:

---

43   The story is patently ahistorical here. The Fan and Zhonghang lineages were eliminated in 492 BCE by a coalition of Jin ministerial lineages led by Zhao Yang 趙鞅 (d. 475 BCE). One of the partners in this coalition was Zhi the Elder (Zhi Bo 知伯) by the name Li 躒, or, possibly, his son Zhi Jia 知甲. Zhi the Elder (Zhi Bo), who was killed in 453 BCE, was Zhi Jia's son, Yao 瑤, who played no role in the downfall of the Fan and Zhonghang lineages; and in any case it is highly implausible that Yu Rang was a servant of two different lineages forty years before the described events. Clearly, the authors of *Zhanguo ce* conflated different Zhi Elders and also embellished Yu Rang's biography.

44   *Zhanguo ce zhushi*, "Zhao ce 1" 18.4: 617.

臣聞明主不掩人之義，忠臣不愛死以成名。君前已寬舍臣，天下莫
不稱君之賢。今日之事，臣故伏誅，然願請君之衣而擊之，雖死不
恨。非所望也，敢布腹心。

I heard that a clear-sighted sovereign does not conceal the righteousness of
others; the loyal subject does not begrudge death in order to accomplish a
good name. That you, my lord, generously released me previously caused
everybody under Heaven to praise your worthiness. Now, I am ready
to be executed. As for today's events, I am of course ready to submit to
execution, but I wish to request to strike your garments, so that I shall
have no regret even if I die. This would be beyond my expectations; yet I
presume to lay bare my inmost heart.[45]

Yu Rang's request was granted: he struck Zhao's garments, shouting: "I
have avenged Zhi Bo," and then committed suicide. His heroic sacrifice
ended therefore in fiasco: or did it? Politically speaking, his case was
moribund: after all, his master, Zhi Bo was already eliminated, and revenge
could do nothing to restore Zhi Bo's hereditary house. Nor did the success
of his mission matter much to Yu Rang: the story tells of his rejection of a
friend's idea to enter Zhao Xiangzi's service and then to murder him—this
would contradict the basic principles of a retainer's loyalty! So what did
matter to Yu Rang? I think the final exchange clarifies this beyond doubt:
both Zhao Xiangzi and Yu Rang acted as actors in a historical spectacle, the
greatest prize of which was attaining fame—a "name"—in this life and in
the afterlife.

To check this assertion let us look at another assassin's story, that of
Nie Zheng 聶政. Nie's patron, a disgruntled Han 韓 noble, Yan Sui 嚴遂,
planned to assassinate his rival, Prime Minister Han Kui 韓傀 (d. ca. 397
BCE). Nie Zheng initially refused to enter Yan Sui's service, saying that he
should take care of his aged mother, but after her death he volunteered to
perform the assassination. Being careful not to let the plot be leaked even
posthumously so as to prevent punishment for his patron, Nie performed

---

45   *Zhanguo ce zhushi* 18.4: 618 ("Zhao ce 趙策 1").

the assassination alone. Not only did he stab the well-guarded Han Kui and kill many of the guards, he also managed to gouge out his own eyes and cut off his own face so as to die unrecognized.

Yet the genre cannot tolerate a nameless hero. Here enters Nie Zheng's elder sister, who travels to the state of Han, where her brother's body lies in the expectation that somebody will identify the murderer. She explains her motives: "As my younger brother is supremely worthy, I cannot, for the sake of cherishing my body, allow my brother's name to be eradicated: it was not his intention!"[46] Then, in Han, she makes the final performance. The brother is named as being in line with supreme heroes of the past:

今死而無名，父母既歿矣，兄弟無有，此為我故也。夫愛身不揚弟
之名，吾不忍也。

Now, he had died namelessly. Yet our parents are dead already, we have neither brothers nor sisters, so he [erased his identity] because of me. Yet to cherish my body and not extol the name of my younger brother: I cannot bear to do that![47]

Having said this, Nie Zheng's sister embraced her brother's body and committed suicide. Judging from political reasoning, this was a grave mistake: after all, Nie Zheng's avowed desire to preserve secrecy was out of concern for his employer, and his sister annulled her brother's achievement by identifying him. Yet this was not the judgment of the public opinion of that age, if we trust the *Zhanguo ce*:

晉、楚、齊、衛聞之曰：「非獨政之能，乃其姊者，以列女也。聶
政之所以名施於後世者，其姊不避菹醢之誅，以揚其名也。」

Having heard about this, [the people] in Jin, Chu, Qi, and [smaller] Wei all said: "Not only was [Nie] Zheng an able person, his sister was also

---

46 弟至賢，不可愛妾之軀，滅吾弟之名，非弟意也。(*Zhanguo ce zhushi* 27.22: 1035 ["Han ce" 韓策 2]).

47 *Zhanguo ce zhushi* 27.22: 1035 ("Han ce" 2).

an exemplary woman. The reason why Nie Zheng's name is transmitted to later generations is that his sister did not eschew the punishment of becoming mincemeat so as to extol her brother's name."[48]

Once again this finale clarifies that the assassination was primarily about getting a name for Nie Zheng (and eventually for his sister as well).[49] Assassination had no moral justifications, nor did it attain its political goal (presumably after Nie Zheng was identified, his patron could not escape the vengeance of the Han ruling house). What matters is that one more hero joined the pantheon of martyrs who died to sanctify their name.

It goes without saying that stories about assassin-retainers collected in the *Zhanguo ce* and in the *Shiji* were heavily embellished—or outright invented— by their anonymous authors. What did they want to attain? I believe that the major goal was to promote the peculiar idea of personal loyalty, the one that is due only to the one who "profoundly understands" the true value of a *shi* (*zhi ji* 知己, implying "to understand the other as you understand yourself"). Creating and circulating these stories was an important means of convincing potential patrons of the high value of a *shi*: should an employer "profoundly understand" his retainer or minister (usually through lavishly rewarding him), he may be sure that the minister would reciprocate by sacrificing his life for the employer's sake.[50] This self-sacrifice was not just an act of gratitude but was motivated by the transcendent value of attaining a glorious name "to be transmitted in later generations."

Assassin-retainers were just one group of heroes hailed for their readiness to sacrifice their lives for the sake of ultimate glory. To these

---

48 Ibid. "Becoming mincemeat" was the due punishment for those related to Nie Zheng. Nie's sister would have been turned into mincemeat had she not killed herself (or was she turned into mincemeat posthumously?).

49 Michael Nylan (1998–1999: 236–238) discusses this story in the context of Sima Qian's history writing. Oddly, she does not address at all the story's appearance in the *Zhanguo ce*, which in all likelihood served a source for Sima Qian. For a much more sophisticated discussion, which compares the *Zhanguo ce* and *Shiji*, see Durrant 1995: 105–110.

50 See more in Pines 2002b.

one can add another group of exemplary personages: moral purists who would starve themselves to death rather than accept morally contaminated emolument from contemporaneous rulers, or those willing to remonstrate on pain of death so as to preserve their integrity. These were represented by the imagined figures of Boyi 伯夷 and Shuqi 叔齊, who abandoned even the righteous King Wu of Zhou 周武王 (d. ca. 1042 BCE) when the latter's behavior were at odds with their lofty principles, or Bigan 比干, the courageous cousin of the Shang 商 tyrant Zhouxin 紂辛 (d. ca. 1046 BCE), who was cruelly executed for his upright admonitions. As I have argued elsewhere, their stories were aimed at promulgating a type of loyalty different from that of the assassin-retainers: loyalty not to a ruler-friend, but to the Way, i.e. to one's moral principles.[51] Yet going beyond these differences, one discovers a common trope of self-sacrifice (or sacrifice of one's career and of immediate material interests) not just out of commitment to one's principles but primarily as a means to attain glory and ensure thereby "commemorative immortality." Yu Rang and Nie Zheng differed tremendously from Boyi or Bigan, but each exemplified the common goal of the name seekers: "their body may be dead but their name is ever more radiant."[52]

4. Name or Body?

In the pluralistic world of the Warring States, few if any political or ethical principles remained uncontested and the quest for a name was not an exception. It came under attack from two directions. Politically, it was considered by some as detrimental to proper norms of meritocratic

---

[51] Pines 2002b: 53–62.

[52] It was Han Fei 韓非 (d. 233 BCE), the singularly perceptive political analyst, who discerned the similar logic behind these divergent stories: hailing loyal ministers who were lofty enough to sacrifice themselves but whose practical value for the ruler was close to nil. See *Han Feizi jijie* IV.14: 105–106 ("Jian jie shi chen" 姦劫弒臣). See also more below in the text.

appointment. The danger that an unscrupulous manipulator might attain a good name at the expense of truly meritorious servitors was broadly recognized even before our age of sophisticated PR campaigns. This topic will be addressed in the next section; here I want to focus on a different line of attacking the name-seekers: i.e., the ultimate folly of sacrificing one's body for an elusive name.

This line of reasoning is commonly associated with the so-called Daoist thought, and there is no doubt that it is most readily observable in such texts as *Laozi* 老子, *Zhuangzi* 莊子, and (a much later) *Liezi* 列子. *Laozi* is one of the earliest texts to focus on the body or the self (*shen* 身) as a legitimate focus of concern. It is also arguably the first to juxtapose body and name. *Laozi* rhetorically asks: "What is closer to you: body or name?" 名與身孰親？—and the answer is clear.[53] The search for fame and reputation pales in comparison with preserving one's life: to attain longevity one should "know what is sufficient" (*zhi zu* 知足) and "when to stop" (*zhi zhi* 知止), which may well be interpreted specifically as the need to limit political involvement.[54]

In *Zhuangzi*, a text that radically assaults the intellectuals' commitment to political involvement and denigrates career-seekers, the attack on the quest for a name becomes more vivid. Pursuing a name is dangerous; hence "The doer of good stays clear of a name (repute)" 為善無近名.[55] The quest for a name is characteristic of shortsighted and avaricious career-seekers, like Confucius and his disciples. In one of the anecdotes, a sagacious gardener criticizes Confucius's disciple, Zigong:

子非夫博學以擬聖，於于以蓋眾，獨弦哀歌以賣名聲於天下者乎？汝方將忘汝神氣，墮汝形骸，而庶幾乎！而身之不能治，而何暇治天下乎？子往矣，無乏吾事！

---

53 *Laozi* 44 cited from *Boshu Laozi*, 39–40; *Guodian Laozi* A, slip 35 (Cook 2012: 279).

54 For more on the *Laozi*'s role in prioritizing the "body" over political career, see Pines 2009a: 155–156.

55 *Zhuangzi jinzhu* 3: 94 ("Yang sheng zhu" 養生主); translation adapted from Graham 1981: 62.

Are not you the one who has learned extensively to resemble a sage, who huffs and puffs to lord it over the multitudes, the one who plucks the strings and sings mournfully all alone in order to peddle your name and renown in All-under-Heaven? You are one who forgets about your spirit and breath, destroys your body and bones, and only then can you approach [your goals]. You are unable to order your body: so where will you have spare time to order All-under-Heaven? Go away, do not disturb my job.[56]

Zigong's behavior is both immoral (showing off his abilities to attain renown) and stupid: his achievements come at the expense of bodily health, and are therefore meaningless. Elsewhere, the authors present a more concentrated assault against the common quest for external gains at the expense of one's body:

自三代以下者，天下莫不以物易其性矣。小人則以身殉利，士則以身殉名，大夫則以身殉家，聖人則以身殉天下。故此數子者，事業不同，名聲異號，其於傷性以身為殉，一也。

From the Three Dynasties on, everybody under Heaven is engaged in seeking [external] things at the expense of one's [innate] nature. Petty men sacrifice their bodies for profits, *shi* sacrifice their bodies for a good name; grandees sacrifice their bodies for their houses; sages sacrifice their bodies for All-under-Heaven. In all these cases, their undertakings are different and their appellations are distinct, but from the point of view of hurting their innate nature and sacrificing their bodies, they are all the same.[57]

This is a doubly sophisticated assault on the quest for a name. Not only is this quest considered harmful for one's body, it is also ominously close to the profit-seeking of petty men. Recall that Confucius and his followers clearly distinguished between the term "benefit/profit" (*li* 利) with its

---

56   *Zhuangzi jinzhu* 12: 318 ("Tian di" 天地).
57   *Zhuangzi jinzhu* 8: 239 ("Pianmu" 駢拇).

negative emotive meaning[58] and "name," the emotive meaning of which remained overwhelmingly positive. By contrast, Zhuangzi places both terms in dangerous proximity: they are "all the same" not just from the point of view of bodily harm they incur but possibly in terms of their moral value as well.

We shall return in the last section to the impact of *Laozi*'s and *Zhuangzi*'s views on the subsequent criticism of name-seekers in the imperial period; here I want only to note that awareness of the potential conflict between "body" and "name" was not limited to these two thinkers but was quite widespread. One indication of this is an interesting anecdote in the *Zhanguo ce*. It tells of a meeting between the powerful—but due-to-be-demoted—chancellor of Qin, Fan Sui 范雎 (d. 255 BCE) and his aspiring successor, Cai Ze 蔡澤.[59] Cai Ze tries to convince Fan Sui to resign by pointing to the mounting personal dangers for any gifted leader who ignores the advantages of a timely retreat. Fan Sui, aware of Cai's rhetorical trap, rebuffs him:

故君子殺身以成名，義之所在，身雖死，無憾悔，何為不可哉？

Thus, for a noble man to die in order to attain a name is where duty lies; even if I die, I shall have nothing to regret—why should I avoid it?[60]

This statement—which is very audacious in light of the above passages from *Laozi* and *Zhuangzi*—invokes the transcendent qualities of a good name: death pales in comparison with the attainment of lasting renown. Yet Cai Ze is well prepared for this argument. He reminds Fan that one can attain a good name even without sacrificing oneself. "If one can establish one's loyalty and achieve a name only after dying, then even Weizi was not benevolent enough, Confucius was not sage enough, and Guan Zhong was

---

58 For "benefit," see Defoort 2008. For "emotive meaning," see Defoort, this volume.

59 For in-depth analysis of this anecdote, see Pines 2018. Fan Sui's name is written either with character 雎 (Sui) or 雎 (Ju). My reading follows Bai Guohong 2015.

60 *Zhanguo ce zhushi* 5.18: 204 ("Qin ce 秦策 3").

not great enough."[61] Having heard this, Fan Sui is willing to reconsider his adamant stance: if he could preserve both the name and the body it is surely preferable to a heroic but meaningless death. Yet the authors of the anecdote leave open the question as to which of the two—name or body—should be given priority.

5. Name and Politics

Aside from philosophical and ethical implications, the widespread quest for a good name had far-reaching political consequences. On the most immediate level, it posed the problem of fraudulent reputation. Insofar as many appointments were determined on the basis of one's repute, it was increasingly important for policy makers to distinguish between an appointee's deserved and underserved prominence. On a deeper level, some thinkers noticed that the quest for a name could be utilized to strengthen rather than weaken the political order. As we shall see, the latter idea had far-reaching practical consequences.

Criticism of the unjustified quest for a name is explicit both in Mozi's philippics against the renown of the supporters of aggressive wars and in repeated warnings by Confucius and his disciples that true repute should be based on moral principles alone. However, neither Mozi nor Confucians explained how underserved prominence came about. It was the opponents of moralizing discourse in politics, Shang Yang 商鞅 (d. 338 BCE), Han Fei 韓非 (d. 233 BCE), and other contributors to the books attributed to them (the *Shangjunshu* 商君書 [hereafter, *Book of Lord Shang*] and *Han Feizi* 韓非子),

---

61 夫待死之後可以立忠成名，是微子不足仁，孔子不足聖，管仲不足大也。(*Zhanguo ce zhushi* 5.18: 204 ["Qin ce 3"]). Weizi was the minister of the last Shang tyrant, Zhouxin; he fled the state to avoid persecution. Confucius considered him a paragon of benevolence (*Lunyu* 18.1). Guan Zhong (d. 645 BCE) was the architect of hegemony of Lord Huan of Qi 齊桓公 (r. 685–643 BCE). Weizi, Guan Zhong, and Confucius had established their reputation without suffering persecution.

who exposed the reasons for this unwelcome phenomenon. The *Book of Lord Shang* ridicules the prevailing discourse of "elevating the worthy" as follows:

> 夫舉賢能，世之所以治也；而治之所以亂。世之所謂賢者，言正也；所以為言正者，黨也。聽其言也，則以為能；問其黨，以為然。故貴之，不待其有功；誅之，不待其有罪也。

> Elevation of the worthy and the able is what the world considers orderly rule: that is why orderly rule is in turmoil. What the world calls a "worthy" is one who is defined as upright; but those who define him as good and upright are his clique. When you hear his words, you consider him able; when you ask his associates, they approve it. Hence, one is ennobled before one has any merits; one is punished before one has committed a crime.[62]

The authors are unequivocal: a person's reputation is related neither to his abilities nor to his uprightness but is rather fabricated by one's partisans. These partisans, the despised "peripatetic eaters" (*youshizhe* 游食者) who travel from one court to another and get emoluments in exchange for their skillful argumentation, are singled out in the text as "caterpillars" (*ming* 螟) who confuse the ruler with their doctrines, mislead the population at large and endanger the social and political order.[63] Since one's reputation is created by these unscrupulous individuals, it clearly cannot serve as a means of selecting and promoting officials. Those "who are appointed on account of their reputation or [after] having requested an audience" should never "be allowed to become rich and noble."[64]

Han Fei echoes these sentiments: one's reputation should not serve as the basis of one's appointment and promotion. Rather, the ruler should promote his subjects exclusively in accord with strict and uniform rules: "discuss them according to their tasks, check them according to their performance, assess them according to their merits."[65] These rules will

---

62 *Book of Lord Shang* 25.1 (Pines 2017a: 240).

63 See e.g., *Book of Lord Shang* 3.6, 3.10 (Pines 2017a: 137–140).

64 任譽、清濁(=請謁)，不可以富貴 · *Book of Lord Shang* 17.4 (Pines 2017a: 211).

65 論之於任，試之於事，課之於功 (*Han Feizi jijie* XIV.38: 375 ["Nan san" 難三]).

replace the misguided reliance on one's renown with objectively observable criteria that will allow the evaluation of one's real merits and determine one's career.[66]

The opposition of Shang Yang and Han Fei to the idea of promotions based on an individual's reputation is not surprising; but does this mean that these thinkers are opposed in principle to an individual's quest for a name? Not necessarily. Actually, Shang Yang put forward a brilliant and counterintuitive idea: the individual's quest for a name (and riches) should become the foundation of a good political order. Insofar as one is motivated by the desire to attain renown, the ruler may be able to direct this motivation to socially and politically acceptable goals. Mozi might have been the first to outline this idea. In his promulgation of the controversial concept of "universal love" (or "caring for everyone," *jian ai* 兼愛), he reminded the rulers that they are able to direct people even to "kill themselves for the sake of a name" 殺身而為名; so, naturally, it would be easier to encourage subjects to engage in such a beneficial way of life as caring for everyone.[67] Yet this idea was never developed in full in the *Mozi*. For Shang Yang, by contrast, it became the cornerstone of a new social order.

The *Book of Lord Shang* postulates that individuals are selfish, but this is not necessarily a bad thing. It is precisely the selfishness of individuals and their covetous inborn nature (*xing* 性) that can be utilized so as not to jeopardize but rather to strengthen political order. The authors explain:

> 民之性，饑而求食，勞而求佚，苦則索樂，辱則求榮，此民之情也。民之求利，失禮之法；求名，失性之常。奚以論其然也？今夫盜賊上犯君上之所禁，下失臣子之禮，故名辱而身危，猶不止者，

---

66 For Han Fei's opposition to promotions based on reputation, see, e.g., *Han Feizi jijie* V.18: 118 ("Nan mian" 南面), V.19: 127 ("Shi xie" 飾邪); for Han Fei's recommendations about the appropriate ways of promotion, see *Han Feizi jijie* XIX.50: 460 ("Xian xue" 顯學). See also Yuan Lihua 2005; Pines 2013: 182–184.

67 *Mozi jiaozhu* IV.15: 160 ("Jian ai 兼愛 zhong").

利也。其上世之士，衣不煖膚，食不滿腸，苦其志意，勞其四肢，傷其五臟，而益裕廣耳，非性之常，而為之者，名也。故曰名利之所湊，則民道之。

The nature of the people is to seek food when they are hungry, to seek respite when they work hard, to seek joy when they are embittered, to seek glory when they are humiliated: this is the people's disposition. In seeking benefit, the people lose the standard of ritual,[68] in seeking a name (=repute), they lose the constant of their nature.[69] How can I demonstrate this? Now, criminals violate the prohibitions of rulers and superiors above, and lose the ritual of subjects and sons below; hence their name is dishonored and their body endangered, but they still do not stop: this is because of benefit. In the generations of old, there were men-of-service (*shi*) who did not have enough clothes to warm their skin, nor enough food to fill their bellies. They exerted their four limbs and injured their five internal organs, but behaved ever more broad-heartedly: this is not the constant of [human] nature, yet they did it because of a [good] name. Hence it is said: wherever the name and benefit meet, the people will go in this direction. [70]

This discussion is one of the earliest systematic analyses of human nature in Chinese history. Two major factors influencing human behavior are the quest for riches and the quest for a name. The first causes the people to transgress against moral and legal norms; the second even transcends their quest for life and causes them to endanger themselves. Yet while the "name" here may refer to a transcendent force that causes the people to sacrifice their bodily well being, this usage is of secondary importance in the *Book of Lord Shang*. Generally, the text equates "name" as fame and

---

68 The combination *li zhi fa* 禮之法 ("standard of ritual") is peculiar to the *Book of Lord Shang*; it implies here the essential norms of behavior embedded in the broader concept of ritual. For different meanings of the term *li* 禮 (ritual) in pre-imperial discourse, see Pines 2000b.

69 The "constant of one's nature" (*xing zhi chang* 性之常) refers here to the fear of death. In seeking name, the people are ready to sacrifice their lives.

70 *Book of Lord Shang* 6.4 (Pines 2017a: 160).

repute with "name" as social status. The quest for a name is in the final analysis the quest for social prestige and the ensuing social and economic benefits. Shang Yang considers this quest entirely legitimate, as long as it is realizable exclusively through routes approved by the state. The historical Shang Yang famously replaced the aristocratic social order with a new one based on ranks of merit.[71] These ranks—and the adjacent social, economic, and political privileges—were bestowed by the ruler on meritorious soldiers and diligent tillers. The text explains how this system should turn the quest for a name into the foundation of social order:

> 主操名利之柄，而能致功名者，數也。……夫農，民之所苦；而戰，民之所危也。犯其所苦，行其所危者，計也。故民生則計利，死則慮名。名利之所出，不可不審也。利出於地，則民盡力；名出於戰，則民致死。

> When the sovereign holds the handles of a (good) name and benefit and is able to bring together the name [only] to the meritorious, this is the method. ... Farming is what the people consider a hardship; war is what the people consider dangerous. Yet they brave what they consider bitter and perform what they consider dangerous because of the calculation [of a name and benefit]. Thus, in [ordinary] life, the people calculate benefits; [facing] death, they think of a (good) name. One cannot but investigate whence the name and benefit come. When benefits come from land, the people fully utilize their strength; when the name comes from war, the people are ready to die.[72]

The idea that the name "comes from war" refers to Shang Yang's policies of granting ranks primarily (or exclusively) for merit attained on the

---

71 The system of ranks of merit had been studied intensively in China, Japan, and in the West, especially since new paleographic discoveries that clarified aspects of its functioning and the magnitude of its social impact. I discuss this system in the context of the ideology of the *Book of Lord Shang* in Pines 2016b; q.v. for further references.

72 *Book of Lord Shang* 6.5 (Pines 2017a: 161).

battlefield.[73] Yet the point is not only to bestow ranks on meritorious soldiers (or, elsewhere, diligent tillers), but also to prevent the people from attaining a "name" outside the state-mandated rank system. This understanding stands in the background of the *Book of Lord Shang*'s assault on privately gained reputation. When "those who have privately established a name are deemed illustrious" (*siming xian zhi* 私名顯之), this is "a licentious way" (*yin dao* 淫道). The text recommends the unification of "the gates of prominence and glory" (*xianrong zhi men* 顯榮之門), preventing anybody outside the state-mandated system of ranks to enter these gates. Those "who do not fight but attain glory, who have no rank but are respected" (不戰而榮，無爵而尊) are called "villains" (*jianmin* 姦民).[74] Glory, respect, renown—all should be inseparable from the ranks of merit bestowed by the state.

An instrumentalist approach to the quest for name and its equation with the quest for social status in the *Book of Lord Shang* may appear simplistic, but Shang Yang's insight into the mechanics of human motivation was validated by the success of his reforms. The system of ranks of merit introduced by Shang Yang reshaped not just Qin's social structure but even social mores, becoming the major motivating force for Qin's soldiers. As soldiers knew that valiant fighting and cutting off enemy's heads would bring about not just material but social, legal, and even political privileges, they exerted themselves, contributing to Qin's eventual supremacy. In retrospect, Shang Yang's reform, based as it was on the state's monopolization of both the sources of material wellbeing ("benefit") and social prestige ("name"), appears as a singularly successful—albeit morally dubious—experiment in social engineering.[75]

---

73 See more in Pines 2016a.

74 See respectively *Book of Lord Shang* 22.1, 6.10, and 18.6 (Pines 2017a: 228–29, 164–65, and 218).

75 See more in Pines 2016b.

6. Status or Repute?
Ming in Politics and Historiography

The military-based system of ranks of merit introduced by Shang Yang outlived its usefulness by the time of imperial unification in 221 BCE, and it atrophied under the Han dynasty (206/202 BCE–220 CE). Nonetheless, the idea that the state can use the people's quest for a name (viz., social status and prestige) so as to direct them towards desirable modes of behavior retained its validity. The *Book of Lord Shang* anticipates the potential utilization of its insights for different ends: it mentions that by manipulating the bestowal of benefits (and by extension of the "name"), the rulers would be able to direct the subjects to any ends—from tilling and fighting to studying the canonical *Poems* and *Documents*.[76] This observation was prophetical. In the Han dynasty, as universal military service was discontinued,[77] and the sociopolitical system changed profoundly, the Qin goal of turning the entire population into tillers cum soldiers was no longer relevant. Rather, the Han rulers, starting with Emperor Wu 漢武帝 (r. 141–87 BCE) were in need of a new *modus vivendi* with the reviving local elites. This *modus vivendi* was based on the promulgation of certain virtues associated with Confucian teaching. The nascent system of recommendations cum examinations encouraged the people to adopt norms of behavior that the state singled out as socially desirable, viz. filiality and incorruptibility (*xiaolian* 孝廉). From then on, following these norms, rather than displaying military valor, opened the routes up the social ladder.

The results of this experiment were no less remarkable than Qin's introduction of the system of military-based ranks of merit. Members of the Han elites were ready to go to great extremes to be named filial and incorruptible.[78] Excessive mourning periods for deceased parents,

---

76   *Book of Lord Shang* 23.3 (Pines 2017a: 233).

77   Lewis 2000.

78   See Makeham 1994: 99–111; Nylan 1996.

lavish burials, acts of self-denial, such as refusals to accept government nominations—all these became inseparable parts of the new political ethos, especially under the Latter Han dynasty (25–220 CE). As these "eccentricities, distortions, and outright abuses"[79] became commonplace, they generated heated debates about the correspondence (or the lack thereof) between the "name" (*ming* 名) and "actuality" (*shi* 實) in sociopolitical life. Criticism notwithstanding, attempts to utilize the quest for a name to generate politically or socially desirable behavior continued throughout the imperial period. This can be exemplified by the practice of bestowing tokens of status and honor on filial sons and chaste women. This practice continued throughout the imperial millennia and accelerated under the Qing dynasty (1636/44–1912). Whether or not these tokens of honor and commemoration (both physical—such as towering arches—and literary, most notably commemoration in local gazetteers, as discussed by Epstein in Chapter 6) were the primary motivating force that prompted excessive displays of chastity and filiality is debatable, but surely at least some filial sons and chaste widows were enticed by the desire to attain immediate and lasting fame.[80]

The imperially orchestrated bestowal of ranks and tokens of honor remained a potent means by which rulers utilized their subjects' quest for a name in ways that suited their own agenda; but this was neither the only, nor, arguably, the primary way of attaining a good name. In the long run, Shang Yang's desire to maintain the state monopoly over *ming* as both repute and as social status was unattainable. The court could determine one's status; but one's reputation was established primarily by other members of the educated elite, most notably those involved in history writing. From the Han dynasty on, it was up to historians to provide "commemorative immortality," which proved to be of exceptional importance for the literati, and even for many rulers themselves.

---

79   Makeham 1994: 107.

80   See Elvin 1996; for a different view, see Epstein, this volume.

Using history writing to determine one's reputation can be linked to the *Annals*, but the real rise in the importance of historical texts in this context starts with Sima Qian's *Shiji*. Specifically, Sima Qian's invention of the biographic genre was of primary importance. Since this invention has been discussed in the past, including by the present author, I shall confine myself to a few brief observations.[81] First, it is highly likely that Sima Qian was the first to systematically commemorate outstanding individuals in his "Arrayed traditions" (*Lie zhuan* 列傳).[82] Second, among many reasons for his apparent invention of this genre, the primary one—discussed by Sima Qian in the first chapter of the "Arrayed traditions"—can be called religious. By commemorating outstanding individuals whose fate was often cruel and unjust, the historian compensates them for injustice inflicted on them by Heaven. In Stephen Durrant's words, "the historian thereby becomes the savior, those attached to him are saved, living on through the power of his writing brush."[83] An afterlife in a historical text is viewed as a compensation for under-appreciation or failure in real life. Third, Sima Qian's invention of the biographic genre shaped China's history writing for millennia to come. Commemoration in a historical text became the major means of attaining a sort of transcendent justice. It turned composing biographies into the most thriving part of history writing. Not incidentally, the lion's share of historical texts recorded in the bibliographic section of *Suishu* 隋書 (History of the Sui dynasty) (discussed by Durrant, Chapter 3) consisted of biographies.

---

81 See Pines 2009b: 333–340. For a sample of earlier studies to which I am particularly indebted, see Li Wai-yee 1994 and Durrant 1995. For a focused study on the concept of "name" in Sima Qian's work, see Ruan Zhong 2003.

82 Li Wai-yee (1994: 378–79, n. 55) raises the possibility that the biographic genre first appeared in the now lost late Warring States compilation, *Shi ben* 世本; cf. Twitchett 1962: 96.

83 Durrant 1995: 25. The first of Sima Qian's "arrayed traditions" tells the fate of two legendary righteous hermits, Boyi 伯夷 and Shuqi 叔齊, whose failure in real life illustrates Heaven's injustice. For a brilliant discussion of this chapter, see Durrant 1995: 20–27; see also Shan Shaojie 2005.

If my view of the *Shiji* is correct, it may be surmised that by creating commemorative immortality through recording a person's deeds in a historical book, Sima Qian solved the problem outlined with the greatest clarity in the *Xunzi* passages cited in section 2 above. Xunzi was aware of the impossibility of many "Great Ru," like himself, to fully realize their potential, and promised to compensate them with a noble name that would not be destroyed either by Heaven and Earth, or by other humans. Yet Xunzi did not clarify how this name would be formed and be perpetuated for generations to come. By recording people's deeds in his *Shiji* whose material appeared to be perishable but eventually proved to be indestructible, Sima Qian realized Xunzi's dream. Immortality enshrined in a historical text became more vivid than any other way of commemoration. Henceforth participants in historical spectacles—be these audacious assassin-retainers, brave remonstrators, or zealous purists who preferred death to filthy service—could rest assured: they would die but would never decay. Eight centuries after Sima Qian, the great critic of historical writings, Liu Zhiji 劉知幾 (661–721) summarized:

夫人寓形天地，其生也若蜉蝣之在世，如白駒之過隙，發端庸淺。猶且恥當年而功不立，疾沒世而名不聞。上起帝王，下窮匹庶，近則朝廷之士，遠則山林之客，諒其於功也、名也，莫不汲汲焉，孜孜焉。夫如是者何哉？皆以圖不朽之事也。何者而稱不朽乎？蓋書名竹帛而已。

As a human finds a refuge between Heaven and Earth, his life is as short as that of a mayfly, or like a white colt's passing a crevice—its starting point is mediocre and shallow. In any case, he is ashamed that even at his prime he has failed to establish merit, and by the time of his demise, he has failed to make his name well known.[84] From thearchs and monarchs above to commoners below, from the men-of-service who stay close to the courts to the farthest sojourners in mountains and forests—everybody anxiously and incessantly thinks about his merit and name. Why is this?

---

84 A reference to *Lunyu* 15.20 discussed above in the text.

Because everybody thinks of how to avoid "decaying." What is called "not decaying"? It is to be recorded on bamboo and silk, and that is all.[85]

Liu Zhiji's passage reflects a consensus that crystallized in the aftermath of Sima Qian's magnum opus. One's immortality ("not decaying") is attainable primarily in a historical text. According to Liu Zhiji, the very formation of scribal offices in the past came to respond to the people's existential angst. Being recorded on bamboo and silk saves mortals from oblivion and makes their life meaningful.

Going from an individual to a political level, we may notice that the proliferation of historical commemoration altered the balance of power between the state and the educated elite. It effectively undermined Shang Yang's vision that the state alone would control one's "name." From Sima Qian on, one's transcendent name was determined neither by officials, nor by the court, but by historians, who—even if acting in their capacity of court historians—usually spoke on behalf of broader concerns of the educated elite rather than on behalf of narrow court agendas. This means that one's posthumous repute was in the final analysis determined by peers, not by rulers. The state remained an important source of social prestige, but it was no longer the exclusive determinant of a person's *ming*.

7. A Surrogate for Morality? Imperial Debates over Name-Seeking

This essay suggested a great variety of usages of one's "name" in early Chinese political and ethical discourse: from a means of encouraging personal self-cultivation, to an instrument of political control, to a transcendent category that compensated some of the zealous men-of-service for the inability to realize their lofty desires. We have seen that aside from moral loftiness,

---

85 *Shitong* 11.1: 303 ("Shiguan jianzhi" 史官建置).

the quest for a name generated manipulations and persistent attempts to fabricate a good reputation. The highly divergent usages of the term "name" and the differences in their social, political, and moral consequences explain why the quest for a name and for commemorative immortality, as well as debates about the legitimacy of this quest as a prime-mover of one's action, continued throughout the imperial millennia.

Criticisms of the manipulative search for reputation by undeserving individuals were voiced as early as the Han dynasty.[86] They can be illustrated by a single example: the "Yang Zhu" 楊朱 chapter of the *Liezi* 列子, probably produced after the Han (in the 3rd or 4th century CE). The opening paragraph of this chapter ridicules the self-destructive quest for a name. It concludes with the following lines:

> 實無名,名無實。名者,偽而已矣。昔者堯舜偽以天下讓許由、善卷,而不失天下,享祚百年。伯夷、叔齊實以孤竹君讓,而終亡其國,餓死於首陽之山。實偽之辯,如此其省也。

> Reality has no name [in it]; a name has no reality. A name is just pretension. In the past, Yao and Shun pretended to yield All-under-Heaven to Xu You and Shan Juan, but they did not lose All-under-Heaven; rather they enjoyed ruling for a century.[87] Boyi and Shuqi really yielded the position of the lords of Guzhu, and in the end lost their state and died of starvation on Shouyang Mountain.[88] The distinction between reality and pretension should be examined in this way.[89]

---

86 See Makeham 1994.

87 According to the late Warring States period legend, paragon rulers Yao and Shun were ready to yield worldly rule to lofty hermits, but those refused to accept the gift (see, e.g., *Zhuangzi jinzhu* 1:18 ["Xiao yao you" 逍遙遊]; 28: 744–745 ["Rang wang" 讓王]). For a subversive reading of this story as that of fake yielding, see discussion in Pines 2005; cf. Allan 2016.

88 Boyi and Shuqi were sons of the ruler of Guzhu. The father bequeathed his rule to the younger, Shuqi, who then yielded to Boyi; yet Boyi refused to violate the father's will. Thus both sons fled their state and lost it forever. Eventually, they starved themselves to death to avoid eating "contaminated" grains of the Zhou house, the legitimacy of which they questioned. See *Shiji* 61: 2123.

89 *Liezi jishi* 7: 218 ("Yang Zhu" 楊朱).

Yang Zhu's conclusion is clear: name-seeking is deceptive by its nature; a name is just a matter of pretension, and the former paragons who got renown for their selfless behavior were nothing more than skillful manipulators. This discourse, which clearly borrows from the Warring States-period texts, such as *Zhuangzi* and *Han Feizi*, is reflective of the low esteem of the quest for a name among some of the critical-minded literati.

The assaults against name-seeking continued from the Latter Han dynasty and beyond, often combined with polemics over the so-called Doctrine of Names (*mingjiao* 名教), identified by Makeham as "ethos based on fostering reputation/name."[90] However, mainstream political thought rejected this assault. Throughout the entire imperial period, despite their awareness of inevitable abuses, the majority of thinkers remained adamant in their insistence that it is better to motivate the people through promises of fine reputation rather than through other, more dubious means. Three examples from three different periods suffice to demonstrate this persistently favorable view of the ongoing quest for a name.

Yan Zhitui 顏之推 (531–591) dedicated one chapter of his *Yanshi jiaxun* 顏氏家訓 (Family instructions of Mr. Yan) to "Name and Reality" ("Ming shi" 名實). He starts with admitting that "the best *shi* forget about their name, medium-ranked *shi* establish their name, and inferior *shi* steal their name."[91] Namely, the best is to be intrinsically moral, "to embody the Way" (*ti dao* 體道): for such a man, a name is meaningless. The worst case is the one who maintains "an honest appearance but is wicked deep inside" 厚貌 深姦: such a man strives to "steal a name," yet he will ultimately fail. For the rest, the majority of the average men-of-service, the quest for a name is the most efficient incentive for moral action. In answering a hypothetical query about the reasons for which the sages made use of the Doctrine of Names, Yan Zhitui explains:

---

90 Makeham 1994: 172–183. For a systematic study of the Doctrine of Names and debates about it from the Latter Han dynasty on, see Liu Zehua 1996, vol. 2: 333 ff.

91 上士忘名，中士立名，下士竊名 (*Yanshi jiaxun* IV.10: 303).

勸也，勸其立名，則獲其實。且勸一伯夷，而千萬人立清風矣；勸
一季札，而千萬人立仁風矣；勸一柳下惠，而千萬人立貞風矣；勸
一史魚，而千萬人立直風矣。

This was done to encourage [people]. When you encourage them to establish [good] name, you get real [improvement]. So, you encourage [through an example] a single Boyi, and myriad people establish the mores of purity; you encourage [through an example] a single Ji Zha, and myriad people establish the mores of benevolence; you encourage [through an example] a single Liuxia Hui, and myriad people establish the mores of integrity; you encourage [through an example] a single Scribe Yu, and myriad people establish the mores of straightforwardness.[92]

Yan Zhitui is unequivocal: one cannot expect an average man-of-service to attain the supreme moral qualities of former paragons; yet promulgation of these paragons' fame has a positive value of encouraging the people to behave morally. Even though this morality is motivated by a selfish desire to attain a good reputation, its real impact on one's behavior is highly positive. The quest for a name creates therefore a better and more moral world than would be possible otherwise.

Yan Zhitui's ideas are echoed in an essay "Jin ming lun" 近名論 ("On approaching the name") by the great Song (960–1279) statesman Fan Zhongyan 范仲淹 (989–1052). Fan polemicizes against Zhuangzi's dictum, cited above (p. 190): "The doer of good stays clear of a name." This view is a dead end of unruliness, asserts Fan. Rather, the former sage kings were right in making names into "a doctrine" (jiao 教). Although Fan admits that the best people are those who embody morality without considering their reputation, he recognizes the difficulty of attaining such a degree of selflessness:

---

92 *Yanshi jiaxun* IV.10: 312–313. For Boyi, see discussion above in the text; Ji Zha 季札 (fl. mid-6th century BCE) was a Wu 吳 prince renowned for his morality (he yielded the throne to his brothers) and sagacity; Liuxia Hui 柳下惠 (fl. late 7th century) was a Lu official, hailed as a paragon of modesty; Scribe Yu 史魚, Confucius' contemporary, was praised for his straightforwardness.

有性本忠孝者，上也；行忠孝者，次也；假忠孝而求名者，又次也。至若簡賢附勢，反道敗德，父叛君，惟欲是從，不復愛其名者，下也。人不愛名，則雖有刑法干戈，不可止其惡也。

The best are those whose natures are rooted in loyalty and filiality; second to them are those who act in accord with loyalty and filiality; then come those who borrow loyalty and filiality to seek name. The worst are those who despise the worthies and are attracted to power, those who oppose the Way and destroy virtue, those who assassinate their fathers and rebel against their lords, and those who follow only their desires and do not care about their name. When a person does not care for his name, neither punitive laws nor shields and halberds can stop his evildoing.[93]

Once again we discover a thinker who recognizes that the quest for a name is not the best of all motivations for moral action, but that it is still efficient enough and is much preferable to the cynical situation in which no one cares for his reputation. The same understanding is presented in a clearer way by one of the major thinkers of the late imperial period, Gu Yanwu 顧炎武 (1613–1682). In exploring various factors that determine the social and political behavior of humans, Gu observes:

君臣上下懷利以相接，遂成風流，不可復制。後之為治者宜何術之操？曰，唯名可以勝之。名之所在，上之所庸，而忠信廉潔者顯榮於世。名之所去，上之所擯，而怙侈貪得者廢錮於家。……《南史》有云：「漢世士務修身，故忠孝成俗。至於乘軒服冕，非此莫由。晉宋以來，風衰義缺。故昔人之言，曰名教，曰名節，曰功名，不能使天下之人以義為利，而猶使之以名為利，雖非純王之風，亦可以救積污之俗矣。」

When the ruler and the minister, superiors and inferiors interact on the basis of the quest for profit, it becomes habitual, and the situation can no longer be controlled. So which techniques should be used to bring about order then? I would say: only [the quest for a] name can overcome it [the quest for profit]. Whoever has [a good] name is employed by superiors:

93 *Fan Zhongyan quanji* 7: 131 ("Jin ming lun" 近名論).

then loyalty and trustworthiness, incorruptibility and purity become prominent in the world. Whoever loses his good name is discarded by his superiors: then those who rely on extravagance and avariciously seek gain are not employed and are confined to their own homes.

The *Nan shi* (*History of the Southern Dynasties*) says: "During the Han dynasty, men-of-service strived to cultivate themselves, hence, loyalty and filiality became their custom. Without [displaying] these, one could never mount an official's chariot and wear the official's robes. From the Jin [265–420] and Song [420–479] on, these mores declined and righteousness was impaired. That is why the 'doctrine of names' or 'names and principles,' or 'merits and name' that the ancients spoke of— although none of these could cause the people to treat righteousness as benefit—could at least cause them to treat name as benefit. Whereas this was not the pure mores of the True Monarch, it still sufficed to correct increasingly sullied customs."[94]

Writing with the advantage of accumulated historical experience, Gu Yanwu comes even more forcefully to the conclusion promoted centuries earlier by Yan Zhitui and later by Fan Zhongyan. Seeking reputation is not an ideal of pure morality; but in a benefit-driven world it is better that noble men take care of their fine reputation than focus on material gains alone. Using one's quest for a name as a prime mover for one's behavior is preferable to reliance on coercive measures to protect social order. The idea originally promoted by Shang Yang—namely, to utilize one's quest for a name so as to generate socially acceptable behavior—did not lose its appeal two millennia after it was originally put forward.

Yet this summary would be simplistic if it ignored the persistent skepticism regarding name-seeking. As I started with the greatest Ming (1368–1644) historical novel, *Sanguo yanyi*, which depicts Lord Guan's self-sacrifice for the sake of preserving his name unsullied, it is appropriate to end with the sister novel, *Shuihuzhuan* 水滸傳 (Water margins), which

---

94 *Rizhilu* 13: 478–479 ("Ming jiao" 名教). Citation is from *Nan shi* 74: 1851.

adds a different perspective on the quest for a name. The novel's hero, Song Jiang 宋江, enjoys unparalleled fame among the gallant fraternity. At first, the reader appreciates this renown and does not expect an ironic turn in the narrative. But then we get to chapters 36 and 37, in which Song Jiang repeatedly falls into traps set by different brigands, and is going to be robbed and killed. Time and again, at the last moment the bandits learn of his name, at which point they immediately release him, express their admiration, and offer assistance. One cannot escape feeling that this excessive repetition of similarly structured plots is designed to create an ironic effect, undermining the validity of name-seeking, associating it with the underworld of brigands, and ultimately ridiculing over-reliance on one's name in social life.

This last note brings me to the lesson I learned from Andrew Plaks's seminal *The Four Masterworks of the Ming Novel*.[95] Any noble value—or any philosophical and literary keyword—could be subject to scrutiny and potential deconstruction by the imperial literati. The quest for a name—the much hailed means of improving social mores under the less than perfect conditions of imperial rule—is not an exception. The counter-discourse that questioned, and at times ridiculed, the validity of lofty pronouncements can be considered subversive of the dominant ideology. Yet by highlighting tensions around pivotal social and political values, this counter-discourse might have allowed greater flexibility in the implementation of these values, ultimately contributing to the remarkable resilience of imperial political culture.

Bibliography

Adamek, Piotr. 2015. *A Good Son Is Sad if He Hears the Name of His Father: The Tabooing of Names in China as a Way of Implementing Social Values.* Sankt Augustin: Institut Monumenta Serica.

Allan, Sarah. 2016. *The Heir and the Sage: Dynastic Legend in Early China* (rev. ed.). Albany: State University of New York Press.

---

95   Plaks 1987.

Bai Guohong 白國紅. 2015. "Guanyu Fan Sui zhi ming de kaocha yu sisuo" 關於范睢之名的考察與思索. *Jiangxi shehui kexue* 江西社會科學 11: 114–120.

Book of Lord Shang. See Pines 2017.

Boshu Laozi jiaozhu 帛書老子校注. 1996. Compiled and annotated by Gao Ming 高明. Beijing: Zhonghua shuju.

Brindley, Erica. 2009. "'Why Use an Ox-Cleaver to Carve a Chicken?': The Sociology of the *junzi* Ideal in the *Lunyu*." *Philosophy East and West* 59.1: 47–70.

Cao Feng. 2008. "A Return to Intellectual History: A New Approach to Pre-Qin Discourse on Name." Translated by Joseph E. Harroff. *Frontiers of Philosophy in China* 3.2: 213–228.

Cao Feng 曹峰. 2017. *Zhongguo gudai 'ming' de zhengzhi sixiang yanjiu* 中國古代"名"的政治思想研究. Shanghai: Shanghai guji chubanshe.

Chunqiu Zuozhuan zhu 春秋左傳注. 1990. Annotated by Yang Bojun 楊伯峻. Beijing: Zhonghua shuju.

Cook, Scott. 2012. *The Bamboo Texts of Guodian: A Study and Complete Translation.* Vols. 1–2. Ithaca, NY: Cornell East Asia Series.

Defoort, Carine. 2008. "The Profit That Does Not Profit: Paradoxes with *li* in Early Chinese Texts." *Asia Major* (third series) 21.1: 153–181.

Duara, Prasenjit. 1988. "Superscribing Symbols: The Myth of Guandi, Chinese God of War." *Journal of Asiatic Studies* 47.4: 778–795.

Durrant, Stephen W. 1995. *The Cloudy Mirror: Tension and Conflict in the Writings of Sima Qian.* Albany: State University of New York Press.

Durrant, Stephen W., Li Wai-yee, and David Schaberg. 2016. *Zuo Tradition / Zuozhuan Commentary on the "Spring and Autumn Annals."* Seattle: University of Washington Press.

Durrant, Stephen W., Li Wai-yee, Michael Nylan, and Hans van Ess. 2016. *The Letter to Ren An and Sima Qian's Legacy.* Seattle: University of Washington Press.

Elvin, Mark. 1996. "Female Virtue and State in China." In Elvin, *Another History: Essays on China from a European Perspective*, 302–351. Sydney: Wild Peony.

Falkenhausen, Lothar von. 1993. "Issues in Western Zhou Studies: A Review Article." *Early China* 18: 139–226.

Fan Zhongyan quanji 范仲淹全集. 2004. By Fan Zhongyan 范仲淹 (989–1052). Compiled by Fan Nengjun 范能濬. Collated by Xue Zhengxing 薛正興. Nanjing: Fenghuang chubanshe.

Fraser, Chris. 2016. "Language and Logic in the *Xunzi*." In *Dao Companion to the Philosophy of Xunzi*, edited by Eric L. Hutton, 291–321. Dordrecht: Springer.

Gassmann, Robert H. 2007. "Die Bezeichnung *jun-zi*: Ansätze zur Chun-qiu-zeitlichen Kontextualisierung und zur Bedeutungsbestimmung im *Lun Yu*."

In *Zurück zur Freude: Studien zur chinesischen Literatur und Lebenswelt und ihrer Rezeption in Ost und West: Festschrift für Wolfgang Kubin*, edited by Marc Hermann and Christian Schwermann, 411–436. Monumenta Serica Monograph Series 57. Sankt Augustin: Institut Monumenta Serica.

Geaney, Jane. 2010. "Grounding 'Language' in the Senses: What the Eyes and Ears Reveal about *ming* 名 (Names) in Early Chinese Texts." *Philosophy East and West* 60.2: 251–293.

Goldin, Paul R. 2011. *Confucianism*. Durham, U.K.: Acumen.

———. 2013. "Han Fei and the *Han Feizi*." In *Dao Companion to the Philosophy of Han Fei*, edited by Paul R. Goldin, 1–21. Dordrecht: Springer.

———. 2016. "Women and Moral Dilemmas in Early Chinese Narrative." In *The Bloomsbury Research Handbook of Chinese Philosophy and Gender*, edited by Ann A. Pang-White, 25–35. London: Bloomsbury.

Gou Dongfeng 苟東鋒. 2013. "Rujia zhi 'ming' de san zhong neihan" 儒家之名的三重內涵. *Zhongguo zhexue* 中國哲學 8: 42–48.

Graham, Angus C. 1981. *Chuang-tzǔ: The Inner Chapters*. London: Unwin.

———. 1989. *Disputers of the Tao: Philosophical Argument in Ancient China*. La Salle, IL: Open Court.

Guanzi jiaozhu 管子校注. 2004. Compiled by Li Xiangfeng 黎翔鳳. Beijing: Zhonghua shuju.

Han Feizi jijie 非子集解. 1998. Compiled by Wang Xianshen 王先慎 (1859–1922). Beijing: Zhonghua shuju.

Karapet'iants, A. M. 1988. "Чуньцю и древнекитайский исторический ритуал." In *Этика и ритуал в традиционном Китае*, edited by L. S. Vasil'ev et al., 85–154. Moscow: Nauka.

Korolkov, Maxim. 2010. "Земельное законодательство и контроль над землей в эпоху Чжаньго и в начале раннеимперской эпохи (по данным обнаруженных законодательных текстов.)" Ph.D. thesis. Russian Academy of Sciences, Institute of Oriental Studies.

Lewis, Mark E. 2000. "The Han Abolition of Universal Military Service." In *Warfare in Chinese History*, edited by Hans Van de Ven, 33–76. Leiden: Brill.

———. Forthcoming. *Honor and Shame in Early China*. Cambridge: Cambridge University Press.

Li Wai-yee. 1994. "The Idea of Authority in the *Shi ji* (*Records of the Historian*)." *Harvard Journal of Asiatic Studies* 54.2: 345–405.

———. 2007. *The Readability of the Past in Early Chinese Historiography*. Cambridge, MA: Harvard University Asia Center.

Liezi jishi 列子集釋. 1991. Annotated by Yang Bojun 楊伯峻. Beijing: Zhonghua shuju.

Liji jijie 禮記集解. 1995. Compiled by Sun Xidan 孫希旦 (1736–1784). Edited by Shen Xiaohuan 沈嘯寰 and Wang Xingxian 王星賢. Beijing: Zhonghua shuju.

Liu Zehua 劉澤華 (ed.) 1996. *Zhongguo zhengzhi sixiang shi* 中國政治思想史. 3 vols. Hangzhou: Zhejiang renmin chubanshe.

Loy, Hui-chieh. 2003. "*Analects* 13.3 and the Doctrine of 'Correcting Names.'" *Monumenta Serica* 51: 19–36.

Lunyu yizhu 論語譯注. 1992. Annotated by Yang Bojun 楊伯峻. Beijing: Zhonghua shuju.

Lüshi chunqiu jiaoshi 呂氏春秋校釋. 1995. Compiled and annotated by Chen Qiyou 陳奇猷. Shanghai: Xuelin.

Makeham, John. 1990–1991. "The Legalist Concept of *Hsing-ming*: An Example of the Contribution of Archeological Evidence to the Re-Interpretation of Transmitted Texts." *Monumenta Serica* 39: 87–114.

———. 1991. "Names, Actualities, and the Emergence of Essential Theories of Naming in Classical Chinese Thought." *Philosophy East and West* 41.3: 341–363.

———. 1993. "The *Analects* and Reputation: A Note on *Analects* 15.18 and 15.19." *Bulletin of the School of Oriental and African Studies* 56.3: 582–586.

———. 1994. *Name and Actuality in Early Chinese Thought*. Albany: State University of New York Press.

Mao shi zhengyi 毛詩正義. (1815) 1991. Annotated by Zheng Xuan 鄭玄 (127–200) and Kong Yingda 孔穎達 (574–648). In *Shisan jing zhushu fu jiaokanji* 十三經注疏附校勘記, compiled by Ruan Yuan 阮元 (1764–1849), vol. 1, 259–629. Beijing: Zhonghua shuju.

Mengzi yizhu 孟子譯注. 1992. Annotated by Yang Bojun 楊伯峻. Beijing: Zhonghua shuju.

Mengzi zhangju 孟子章句. 2001. Annotated by Zhu Xi 朱熹 (1130–1200). In *Sishu zhangju* 四書章句. Beijing: Zhonghua shuju.

Mozi jiaozhu 墨子校注. 1994. Compiled and annotated by Wu Yujiang 吳毓江 (1898–1977). Beijing: Zhonghua shuju.

Möller, Hans-Georg. 1997. "The Chinese Theory of Forms and Names (*xingming zhi xue*) and Its Relation to a 'Philosophy of Signs.'" *Journal of Chinese Philosophy* 24.2: 179–208.

Nan shi 南史. 1997. Composed by Li Yanshou 李延壽 (fl. 620–660). Beijing: Zhonghua shuju.

Nylan, Michael. 1996. "Confucian Piety and Individualism in Han China." *Journal of the American Oriental Society* 116.1: 1–27.

———. 1998–1999. "Sima Qian: A True Historian?" *Early China* 23–24: 203–246.

Pines, Yuri. 2000a. "'The One That Pervades the All' in Ancient Chinese Political

Thought: The Origins of 'The Great Unity' Paradigm." *T'oung Pao* 86.4–5: 280–324.

———. 2000b. "Disputers of the Li: Breakthroughs in the Concept of Ritual in Pre-Imperial China." *Asia Major* (Third Series) 13.1: 1–41.

———. 2002a. *Foundations of Confucian Thought: Intellectual Life in the Chunqiu Period, 722–453 B.C.E.* Honolulu: University of Hawai'i Press.

———. 2002b. "Friends or Foes: Changing Concepts of Ruler-Minister Relations and the Notion of Loyalty in Pre-Imperial China." *Monumenta Serica* 50 (2002): 35–74.

———. 2005. "Disputers of Abdication: Zhanguo Egalitarianism and the Sovereign's Power." *T'oung Pao* 91.4–5: 243–300.

———. 2009a. *Envisioning Eternal Empire: Chinese Political Thought of the Warring States Era.* Honolulu: University of Hawai'i Press.

———. 2009b. "Chinese History-Writing between the Sacred and the Secular." In *Early Chinese Religion: Part One: Shang through Han (1250 BC–220 AD),* edited by John Lagerwey and Marc Kalinowski, Vol. 1: 315–340. Leiden: Brill.

———. 2013. "Between Merit and Pedigree: Evolution of the Concept of 'Elevating the Worthy' in Pre-Imperial China." In *The East Asian Challenge to Democracy: Political Meritocracy in Comparative Perspective,* edited by Daniel Bell and Li Chenyang, 161–202. Cambridge: Cambridge University Press.

———. 2016a. "A 'Total War'? Rethinking Military Ideology in the *Book of Lord Shang.*" *Journal of Chinese Military History* 5.2: 97–134.

———. 2016b. "Social Engineering in Early China: The Ideology of the *Shangjunshu* (*Book of Lord Shang*) Revisited." *Oriens Extremus* 55: 1–37.

———. 2017a. *The Book of Lord Shang: Apologetics of State Power in Early China.* New York: Columbia University Press.

———. 2017b. "Confucius's Elitism: The Concepts of *Junzi* and *Xiaoren* Revisited." In *A Companion to Confucius,* edited by Paul R. Goldin, 164–184. Wiley Blackwell.

———. 2018. "Irony, Political Philosophy, and Historiography: Cai Ze's Anecdote in *Zhanguo ce* Revisited." *Studia Orientalia Slovaca* 17.2: 87–113.

———. Forthcoming. *Zhou History Unearthed: The Bamboo Manuscript Xinian and Early Chinese Historiography.* New York: Columbia University Press

Plaks, Andrew. 1987. *The Four Masterworks of the Ming Novel.* Princeton, NJ: Princeton University Press.

Richter, Matthias, 2005. *Guan ren: Texte der altchinesischen Literatur zur Charakterkunde und Beamtenrekrutierung.* Bern: Peter Lang.

Rizhilu jishi 日知錄集釋. 1996. By Gu Yanwu 顧炎武 (1613–1682). Annotated by Huang Rucheng 黃如成. Collated by Qin Kecheng 秦克誠. Changsha: Yuelu shushe.

Roetz, Heiner. 1993. *Confucian Ethics of the Axial Age*. Albany: State University of New York Press.

Ruan Zhong 阮忠. 2003. "Sima Qian 'liming' jiqi *Shiji* de shixing yu shixing" 司馬遷「立名」及其《史記》的史性與詩性. *Gaodeng hanshou xuebao (zhexue shehui kexue ban)* 高等函授學報 (哲學社會科學版) 2: 5–7, 23.

Rubin, Vitalij (Vitaly). «Как Сыма Цянь изображал период Чуньцю.» *Народы Азии и Африки* 2: 66–76.

Sanguo yanyi 三國演義. 1996. By Luo Guanzhong 羅貫中 (ca. 1330–1400). Rearranged and commentary by Mao Zonggang 毛宗崗 (1632–1709). Shanghai: Shanghai guji chubanshe.

Schaberg, David. 2001. *A Patterned Past: Form and Thought in Early Chinese Historiography*. Cambridge, MA: Harvard University Asia Center.

Shan Shaojie 單少傑. 2005. "'Boyi liezhuan' zhong de gongzheng linian he yongheng linian" 《伯夷列傳》中的公正理念和永恒理念. *Zhongguo renmin daxue xuebao* 中國人民大學學報 4: 129–137.

Shiji 史記. 1997. By Sima Qian 司馬遷 (ca. 145–ca. 90 BCE) et al. Annotated by Zhang Shoujie 張守節, Sima Zhen 司馬貞, and Pei Yin 裴駰. Beijing: Zhonghua shuju.

Shitong tongshi 史通通釋. 1993. By Liu Zhiji 劉知幾 (661–721). Annotated by Pu Qilong 浦起龍. Taibei: Liren shuju.

Shuihuzhuan 水滸傳. 1993. By Shi Nai'an 施耐庵 (1296–1370) and Luo Guanzhong 羅貫中 (ca. 1330–1400). Rongyutang 容與堂 edition. Collated by Ling Geng 凌賡, Diao Ning 刁寧 and Heng He 恒鶴. Shanghai: Shanghai guji chubanshe.

Sishu zhangju ji zhu 四書章句集注. 2001. Annotated by Zhu Xi 朱熹 (1130–1200). Beijing: Zhonghua shuju.

Solomon, Bernard S. 2013. *On the School of Names in Ancient China*. Monumenta Serica Monograph Series 64. Sankt Augustin: Steyler Verlag.

Tavor, Ori. 2014. "Naming/Power: Linguistic Engineering and the Construction of Discourse in Early China." *Asian Philosophy* 24.4: 313–329.

Twitchett, Denis. 1962. "Chinese Biographical Writings." In *Historians of China and Japan*, edited by William G. Beasley and Edwin G. Pulleyblank, 95–114. London: Oxford University Press.

Van Auken, Newell Ann. 2007. "Could 'Subtle Words' Have Conveyed 'Praise and Blame'? The Implications of Formal Regularity and Variation in *Spring and Autumn (Chūn qiū)* Records." *Early China* 31: 47–111.

———. 2016. *The Commentarial Transformation of the Spring and Autumn*. Albany: State University of New York Press.

Xiaojing yizhu 孝經譯注. 1996. Annotated by Hu Pingsheng 胡平生. Beijing: Zhonghua shuju.

Xunzi jijie 荀子集解. 1992. Annotated by Wang Xianqian 王先謙 (1842–1917). Edited by Shen Xiaohuan 沈嘯寰 and Wang Xingxian 王星賢. Beijing: Zhonghua shuju.

Yang Jianqiang 楊建強 and Xiao Qunzhong 肖群忠. 2015. "Lun mingjie" 論名節. *Lunlixue yanjiu* 倫理學研究 7: 64–69.

Yanshi jiaxun jijie 顏氏家訓集解. 1993. By Yan Zhitui 顏之推 (531–591). Collated by Wang Liqi 王利器 (1912–1988). Rev. ed. Beijing: Zhonghua shuju.

Yuan Lihua 袁禮華. 2005. "Zhong xian bu shang xian, yong xian qie fang xian: Han Fei xiannengguan chutan" 重賢不尚賢 用賢且防賢——韓非賢能觀初探. *Nanchang daxue xuebao (renwen shehui kexueban)* 南昌大學學報（人文社會科學版）1: 59–63.

Zhanguo ce zhushi 戰國策注釋. 1991. Annotated by He Jianzhang 何建章. Beijing: Zhonghua shuju.

Zhao Shengqun 趙生群. 2000. *Chunqiu jing zhuan yanjiu* 春秋經傳研究. Shanghai: Shanghai guji chubanshe.

Zhuangzi jinzhu jinyi 莊子今注今譯. 1994. Annotated by Chen Guying 陳鼓應. Beijing: Zhonghua shuju.

Zuozhuan. See *Chunqiu Zuozhuan zhu.*

Virtue Keywords

6

Embodied Virtue: How Was Loyalty Edited and Performed in Late Imperial China?

Chiung-yun Evelyn Liu

The culture of *zhong* 忠 (loyalty) in late imperial China is a significant, complex and understudied subject. Following the rise of the Neo-Confucian school of the True Way (道學) in the Southern Song dynasty and its institutionalization as state orthodoxy in the early Ming period, the idea of loyalty, together with other moral virtues upheld by Neo-Confucian teachings, gradually penetrated into almost every aspect of late imperial life. Politically, loyalty defined the ruler-subject relationship and an official's responsibilities to the state, which in turn played a crucial part in the making of intellectual identity. Socially, the extent to which a person could carry out this moral ideal was closely tied to his *ming* 名 (reputation).[1] The reputation of loyalty, in the sense of selfless devotion to state affairs, was powerful cultural capital and could help to build and expand social networks. In terms of family relations, *zhong* is an extension of *xiao* 孝 (filial piety) according to *Xiaojing* 孝經 (The classic of filial piety). Even the non-elites, who theoretically were not bound by the ethos of *zhong*, became the readers and/or audience of numerous stories and plays that featured the heroic and gripping endeavors of historical and fictional loyal subjects.

---

1   On *ming*, see Chapter 5 in this volume.

In other words, loyalty in late imperial China was not just a concept; it was a culture that shaped people's mentality, words, and actions. It connected the family to the state and communal obligations to personal feelings; hence it could be both public and private, both exclusively elite and widely popular. How we can better understand this late imperial culture of loyalty remains a challenge. Historians have recently proposed to examine Confucian moralism during the Ming-Qing transition through the politics and media of image making,[2] and literary scholars have reassessed the nature of moral representation and exemplarity in Chinese vernacular fiction.[3] This essay focuses on two related media that significantly aided the transmission of the idea of loyalty—the moral story compendia and dramatic texts—and examines how they might have transformed the landscape of moral imagination from the late 13th century onward. Instead of seeing the late imperial practice of loyalty as a process of top-down indoctrination, I argue that these popular texts in fact constantly negotiate the balance between moral ideals and their affective reception, between the edifying intent of official and social elite and the preference of the wider population. With the aim to instruct as well as to entertain the reader/audience, these media, while promulgating moral codes, also reshape and reinvigorate them.

As it is impossible to cover the history of loyalty in one essay, in the next section, I will very briefly summarize the development of the idea of loyalty down to the Song dynasty, and then connect it to the subject of the current study, which will unfold in three parts. I will first examine the preface to *Xiaoxue riji qieyao gushi* 小學日記切要故事 (Important stories of the past to be recorded and remembered daily for elementary learning; hereafter *Riji gushi*), dated 1291. In this original preface to the earliest *Riji gushi*, the editor explains the organization, criteria for story selection, and expected effects of his compilation, providing a clear overview of its nature and texture. By comparing the presentations of loyal exemplars

2   Zhang Ying 2017.
3   Sibau 2018.

from Warring States texts with those included in the story compendia, I shall demonstrate how the late imperial editors attempted to soften or tone down the tension inherent in the earlier understanding of loyalty through ameliorating ruler-subject conflicts and shifting the focus to the loyal subjects' deep emotional concern about the fate of the state.

As the *Riji gushi* compiled in the Yuan dynasty is no longer extant, I will, in the second part, look into another contemporaneous story collection eulogizing loyalty, *Junchen gushi* 君臣故事 (Stories of rulers and subjects), in tandem with other late imperial editions of *Riji gushi*. By examining the rationale behind the selection and classification of these stories, I shall analyze how the categorizations, marking the multifarious dimensions of this moral virtue, connect with each other to form an arguably new structure of loyalty, and how the emotionally charged narratives become a dominant mode in illustrating loyalty. These developments redefine the teachings of loyalty as expounded in *Zhongjing* 忠經 (The classic of loyalty).

This will take us to the third part of the chapter, which investigates how the typology of loyalty presented in the moral story collections received further transformation in late imperial drama. Specifically, we will focus on the late 17th century *chuanqi* play, *Qian zhong lu* 千忠戮 (The slaughter of the thousand loyal ones) written by Li Yu 李玉 (1591?–1671?). In contrast to the so-called closet drama (*antou ju* 案頭劇), which was popular among the late imperial elite, *Qian zhong lu* was written for a general audience and widely performed.[4] Thus the ways in which the playwright engages the multiple loyalist types in dialogue with each other and incorporates the role of the commoners into the enterprise of loyalty merit our special attention. I shall demonstrate how the playwright both inherits and refashions existing modes of embodying loyalty, thereby eliciting the sympathies of the common people and also urging them to take action.

---

4   Yan Changke and Zhou Chuanjia 1985: 13–28; Liu Chiung-yun 2016: 3–5.

Preamble: Loyalty from Early to Late-Imperial China

There has been constant debate on the semantic range of loyalty, one of the cardinal virtues in China since the Spring and Autumn period (770–453 BCE). *Zhong* 忠, often in tandem with "trustworthiness" (*xin* 信), evolved as one of the most important values in early Chinese political and ethical thought, even before other main ethical and social ideas were proposed by the Confucians of the Warring States period (453–221 BCE). In early texts, *zhong* did not necessarily refer to loyalty to the ruler alone: it could be directed to the people, or, more commonly to the state (frequently identified as *sheji* 社稷, "the altars of soil and grain"). Personal loyalty directed at a retainer's master coexisted with more sophisticated notions of loyalty directed either at the state as a collective entity or at supreme moral principles or the Way (*dao* 道). During this period of political fragmentation, when ministers could frequently change their allegiance from one court to another, loyalty remained one of the most frequently debated virtues. These debates became less acute after the imperial unification of 221 BCE, but the importance of loyalty as one of the primary political virtues remained unchallenged through the Han dynasty (206/202 BCE–220 CE) and thereafter.[5]

The Song dynasty (960–1279) is often considered the second peak of interest in loyalty as a pivotal ethical virtue. It was then that the idea of unswerving loyalty to a single ruler was significantly strengthened. From the point of view of the Neo-Confucian School of the True Way, loyalty was by no means coterminous with servile obedience to the ruler. Rather, it was but the enactment of the selfless and magnanimous qualities of Heaven's

---

[5] The nature of *zhong* in the pre-imperial period has been studied extensively in recent years. See, e.g., Pines 2002b; Sato 2007, 2009, and 2010; Cook 2015. Note that the semantic field of *zhong* 忠 is not confined to "loyalty" alone (Goldin 2008). For more discussion of personal loyalty vis-à-vis loyalty to the state/the Way, see also Ge Quan 1998.

Way, the realization of one's innate moral goodness to the highest level.[6] In the complex political situation of the Song era, practical manifestations of loyalty could vary considerably—encompassing loyal martyrdom, eremitism, and compromise with Jurchen and Mongol conquerors while retaining loyalist sentiments. Eventually, however, it was the martyrs, such as Yue Fei 岳飛 (1103–1142) and Wen Tianxiang 文天祥 (1236–1283), who became the most celebrated figures of Song loyalism from the 14th century onwards.[7]

Further questions arise: If loyalty can be enacted in multiple ways, why did the martyr stand out and become the dominant representative of loyalty in late imperial China? What were the features highlighted in the making of loyalist models? How was the concept of loyalty illustrated and disseminated from the Song dynasty onward, as it eventually became a much-discussed topic in late imperial Chinese literature?

While the significance and contested meanings of loyalty have been widely studied in the field of pre-modern China,[8] the media that concretized and promulgated this particular moral value in late imperial China have been much less investigated. This essay fills in the lacuna by focusing on popular moral story compendia (*tongsu gushi leishu* 通俗故事類書) and dramatic texts. The moral story compendia were first compiled in the 13th century as popular textbooks, or primers, for teaching Confucian values to young children.[9] They were then extensively edited and reprinted during the 16th-century publishing boom, as evinced by the

---

6   Bol 1992.

7   For different views of loyalty during the Song period, see, e.g., Wang Gungwu 1962; James Liu 1972; Davis 1996; Standen 2007. For the proliferation of the loyalist martyr's image after the fall of the Song, see Jay 1991.

8   In addition to the studies cited above, most studies on loyalty in the late imperial period focus on the political culture and ethical dilemma facing particular historical figures. See He Guanbiao 1997; Hsieh 2004; Struve 2009; Zhao Yuan 2015: 259–299.

9   For a general introduction of the significance of these story compendia in post-imperial China, see Sakai 1958: 25–51 and 120–124.

more than twenty editions now surviving in Japan alone.[10] This corpus of materials is among the most important vehicles that transmitted the teachings of loyalty and other Confucian moral values during the late imperial period,[11] yet it has received little attention in English scholarship so far.

The promulgation of virtues through didactic anecdotes was a common feature of Chinese ethical discourse which can be traced back to the Warring State period.[12] This phenomenon is evident already in *Zuozhuan* 左傳 (Zuo tradition), as David Schaberg has demonstrated,[13] as well as in later anecdotal collections that proliferated during the Han dynasty. For instance, *Shuoyuan* 說苑 (Garden of persuasions) and *Lienü zhuan* 列女傳 (Traditions of illustrious women) group accounts of historical figures thematically, upholding their conduct as exemplary. The compilation of the late imperial popular story collections no doubt sprang from this cultural tradition, but their targeted readers, editing principles, and criteria for story selection changed significantly, reflecting in particular the emphasis on self-cultivation and the pedagogical methods promoted by Zhu Xi 朱熹 (1130–1200).

---

10   For an extensive investigation of these editions preserved in Japan, see Hashimoto 2006.

11   For example, as filial piety is considered a fundamental virtue for the further cultivation of loyalty, filial piety exemplars also comprise one part of the stories in *Riji gushi*. In several late Ming editions of *Riji gushi*, these filial piety stories are titled "*Ershisi xiao* 二十四孝" (Twenty-four exemplars of filial piety), an appellation first used by Guo Jujing 郭居敬 (fl. 1295–1321) for his edited work, *Quanxiang ershisi xiao shixuan* 全相二十四孝詩選 (Twenty-four exemplars of filial piety with complete images and selected poems). According to Osawa's study, the twenty-four filial piety stories in these *Riji gushi* editions were highly influential. They superseded Guo's original choice of twenty-four exemplars and became a relatively stable set of filial piety paragons from the late Ming down to the modern period. See Osawa 2002. On *Ershisi xiao*, see Chapter 7 in this volume.

12   Schaberg 2011; Van Els and Queen 2017.

13   Schaberg 2001: 10.

1. *Riji gushi* and the Problem with Loyalty

We know little about Yu Shao 虞韶 (fl. late 12th century), who first compiled *Riji gushi*. In Huang Zhongzhao's 黃仲昭 (1435–1508) *Bamin tongzhi* 八閩 通志 (General account of the eight districts in the Min area [Fujian]), the earliest document that mentions Yu Shao, he is grouped together with three other men of letters, Mao Zhifang 毛直方, Yu Tingshuo 虞廷碩 and Liu Bian 劉邊. All of them hailed from Jian'an 建安 (northwest of modern Fujian province), lived through the Song-Yuan transition, and made a living by teaching and compiling a wide variety of books for publication. None of them served the newly established Yuan dynasty.[14]

The original *Riji gushi* that Yu Shao compiled is no longer extant. However, his preface, preserved in a later *Riji gushi* edition (hereafter the 1566 edition),[15] clearly states the conception, purpose, and sources of his collection. He first singles out Zhu Xi's *Xiaoxue* 小學 (The elementary learning) as the main inspiration for his own work. In *Xiaoxue*, Zhu Xi designs the first three chapters—"establishing the teaching" (*lijiao* 立教), "clarifying cardinal human relationships" (*minglun* 明倫), and "revering the self" (*jingshen* 敬身)—as the essential principles (*gang* 綱); these are followed by another three chapters expounding on the principles with concrete examples—"examining antiquity" (*jigu* 稽古), "admirable sayings" (*jiayan* 嘉言), and "good deeds" (*shanxing* 善行). Teachings and examples complement each other.

Yu then explains that in order to collect these moral examples, he consulted historical and biographical records extensively, and also made selections from *Mingchen yanxing lu* 名臣言行錄 (Records of the sayings and deeds of celebrated officials) compiled by Zhu Xi. The stories are arranged according to the following principle:

---

14   *Bamin tongzhi* 65. 22b.

15   Hashimoto 1998.

……入則事親敬長，出則隆師親友，與夫行己治家，待人應物，以
達於忠君蒞官之際，一言一行，一是皆以聖賢行事為法條，分彙列
輯成一編。

At home, one should serve one's parents and respect one's elders. Outside
the home, one should honor one's teachers and care for one's friends. As
for conducting oneself, managing one's family, interacting with people
and responding to things, all the way up to serving one's ruler loyally and
fulfilling one's official duties, every word and every act is based on the
comportment of the sages and the worthies. I categorized and arranged
[these stories] to create a book.[16]

Yu no doubt had the teachings of *Daxue* 大學 (The great learning) in mind,
expecting his book to function as an important foundation that would
continue to nourish one's social and spiritual progress, from self-cultivation,
harmonizing the family, and governing the state, to attaining peace in
all under Heaven. The examples he collected from historical records not
only explicate what each moral virtue means, but also prescribe how one
should *practice* these virtues. From the beginning, *Riji gushi* exhibited
a dual emphasis on ethical education and historical precedents. On the
one hand, it continued the long tradition of using historical anecdotes
in political and philosophical discourses, combining descriptive and
prescriptive narrative functions. On the other hand, with the development
of print culture in northern Fujian in the 12th century, anecdotal narratives
took a more elementary and popular form, serving as a basis from which
some of its readers could move on to more complex Confucian classics
and historiography.

Since such a text invites its readers to emulate the examples contained
in it, what to include or exclude becomes a matter of importance. In
discussing his choice of stories on the virtue of loyalty in the preface, Yu
specifically mentions Yu Quan's 鬻拳 example of "forceful remonstrance"
(*qiangjian* 強諫) and its problem. Yu Quan, the minister of the state of

---

16   *Riji gushi* 1566: preface, 1b.

Chu 楚, once remonstrated with his lord, King Wen 楚文王 (r. 689–675 BCE), yet the king did not heed his advice. Yu Quan forced the king to acquiesce by threatening him with a weapon. To atone for this crime of insubordination and offensive self-assertion, he cut off his own feet. Later, when the king of Chu returned from an unsuccessful battle with another domain, Yu Quan refused to let him enter the capital city. The king was therefore forced to attack another domain, won the battle this time, but fell ill on his way home and died before long. Yu Quan buried his lord and committed suicide to accompany him to the netherworld. The comment of a noble man (junzi 君子) following these records in Zuozhuan goes: "Yu Quan can be said to have been devoted to his ruler. Through remonstrance he brought himself to punishment. And even after his punishment, he did not neglect to bring his lord to goodness" 鬻拳可謂愛君矣，諫以自納於刑，刑猶不忘納君於善.[17]

Contrary to the noble man's comment, which praises Yu Quan for being able to press his ruler to do the right thing while demanding no less of himself, Yu Shao considers Yu Quan's behavior "deviating from propriety while correcting a wrong" 矯枉害正. As much as Yu Quan loves his ruler, he cannot escape blame for "the crime of defying his superior" 陵上之罪. Yu's judgment can be understood as a continuation of the views held by Song-Yuan scholars and officials.[18] The best known among them is perhaps Zhu Xi's comment on Yu Quan: "his intention was loyal, but none of his actions abided by proper principles" 其意則忠，而其事皆非理.[19] While Yu Quan's case is still generally listed under the category of "loyalty" in the reference books (leishu 類書) of this period, it is often presented as an inappropriate kind of loyalty that should not be emulated in contemporaneous scholarly writings.[20] The eminent early Ming Confucian scholar Fang Xiaoru 方孝孺

---

17   *Zuozhuan*, Zhuang 19.1: 211. I follow the English translation in *Zuo Tradition* 1:187.

18   *Zhang xiansheng jiaozheng Yang Baoxue Yizhuan* 3.64; *Nanxuan ji* 31.8a; *Yanyuan ji* 12.176.

19   *Zhuzi yulei* 134. 61.

20   *Cefu yuangui* 739. 2a–2b; *Chongkan zengguang fenmen leilin zashuo* 3.3b–4a; *Gujin hebi shilei beiyao houji* 7.10b.

(1357–1402) wrote an essay specifically on Yu Quan, in which he elucidates the potential danger of such aberrant action: "To coerce the ruler and call it devotion to the ruler, this will enable treacherous officials and subversive traitors who intend to kill the ruler and usurp the throne to do so in the name of devotion" 劫君而謂之愛君，將使奸臣亂賊欲行篡弒之事者，皆挾愛君之名以自文.[21] This argument explains why the 15th-century scholar-official and bibliophile Ye Sheng 葉盛 (1420–1474) considered Yu Shao's exclusion of Yu Quan's story from his collection particularly laudable.[22] In contradistinction to the general practice of Song-Yuan *leishu*, which classifies Yu Quan as an example of loyalty, Yu Shao's choice of omission corresponded to the intellectual trends of his time that continued through the late imperial period. In the surviving story compendia, which all date after the mid-15th century, the story of Yu Quan basically disappears.

The eventual exclusion of Yu Quan's story, when examined together with other pre-Qin examples of loyalty and their presence or absence in the late imperial story collections, reveals the central issues surrounding the practice of loyalty that preoccupied Chinese intellectuals since the early period. What are the proper role(s) and duties of the ruler and of the ministers? How can ministers maintain the smooth operation of state affairs when the rulers are not judicious sages but ordinary men, or worse, immoral fools? How to negotiate between principle (*jing* 經) and expediency (*quan* 權)? In other words, to what extent does a principle that demands constant application leave room for its expedient modification?[23] Without delving too deeply into the rich scholarship on these important questions that preoccupied early thinkers in China, two passages from the chapter "The Way of the Minister" (Chen Dao 臣道) in *Xunzi* 荀子, which discuss the varieties and gradations of loyalty through historical examples, may offer a useful basis for comparison with later representatives in the story compendia.

---

21   *Xunzhizhai ji* 1979: 5.4a–5a.
22   *Shuidong riji* 1980: 131.
23   Vankeerberghen 2005–2006; Defoort 2015.

Xunzi begins his discussion by distinguishing the kinds of ministers who would benefit the ruler from their opposites with a succinct summary:

從命而利君謂之順，從命而不利君謂之諂，逆命而利君謂之忠，逆命而不利君謂之篡。

He who obeys orders and benefits the ruler is called compliant; he who obeys orders and does not benefit the ruler is called servile; he who contradict orders and benefits the ruler is called loyal; he who contradicts orders and does not benefit the ruler is called a usurper.[24]

Worse than all of the above, he who disregards the state and the ruler, caring only about personal gain, is nothing but the state's villain. Here the ruler's benefit, which overlaps with that of the state in Xunzi's view, is the key factor in determining the ruler-minister relationship. If the order benefits the ruler, the minister must comply. Yet if the ruler issues unwise orders, the minister will have to place the ruler's benefit above all else and contradict the ill-judged command. A minister should direct his loyalty not to the ruler's personal will, but to the welfare of the state and the sovereign. The virtue of loyalty requires the minister to oppose his ruler's order when necessary, so as to fulfill his duty to guard the security of the state.

Xunzi then explicates four ways in which different historical figures opted to contradict or correct their rulers' wrongdoings:

故諫、爭、輔、拂之人，社稷之臣也，國君之寶也。……伊尹、箕子，可謂諫矣；比干、子胥，可謂爭矣；平原君之於趙，可謂輔矣；信陵君之於魏，可謂拂矣。

Thus, people who engage in remonstrating, contending, supporting and assisting are the ministers of the altars of soil and grain, and treasures for the ruler ... Yi Yin and Jizi may be called remonstrating; Bigan and [Wu] Zixu can be called contending; Lord Pingyuan with the Zhao [ruler], can

---

24   *Xunzi* 9.13: 249. Here I follow Pines's English translation (Pines 2009: 178).

be called supporting; Lord Xinling with the Wei [ruler], can be called assisting.[25]

The first type of opposition, which Xunzi designates as "remonstrating" (*jian* 諫), is the gentlest and least adversarial. The loyal minister expresses his disagreement through verbal advice, and if the advice is not taken, he will discontinue his service to the lord, as exemplified by Yi Yin 伊尹 and Jizi 箕子. Yi Yin, who remonstrated with his ruler, the tyrant Jie 桀, to no avail, left Jie for Jie's rival, Tang 湯, who would eventually overthrow Jie. Jizi feigned madness to avoid persecution by another despot, King Zhòu 紂 of Shang (r. 1075–1046 BCE).[26] The second form of opposition also involves verbal remonstrance, but the minister's reaction to unheeded criticism is much more drastic. If his criticism is not taken, the minister will die trying to change his lord's mind, as in the cases of Bigan 比干 and Wu Zixu 伍子胥. Bigan served the same debauched King Zhòu, but instead of escaping, he remonstrated relentlessly until King Zhòu ordered to have his chest cut open so that he could display his loyal heart. Wu Zixu, the general who turned the state of Wu into a major power, warned his ruler, King Fuchai 夫差, about the danger posed by the neighboring state of Yue 越. The king ignored this warning and the relations between him and Wu Zixu deteriorated until the king ordered Zixu to commit suicide.[27] In both the third and forth cases, the ministers openly defied the rulers' orders. The "assisting" (*fu* 輔) minister, Lord Pingyuan 平原君 from the state of Zhao 趙, collaborated with other officials so as to force the ruler to change his policy. The "supporting" (or "opposing," *fu* 拂) minister, Lord Xinling 信陵君 of the state of Wei 魏, stole his king's

---

25 *Xunzi* IX.13: 250. Here I consulted Hutton's and Pines's English translations and made a few modifications (Hutton 2014: 135; Pines 2009: 179). Note that *fu* 拂 can mean either "opposing" or "assisting" (the latter meaning is attested in *Mengzi* 12.15 [see *Mengzi yizhu* 300n9]. Xunzi may have been consciously playing between the two meanings of the term: one who opposes the ruler is the one who truly assists him.

26 For more detailed account of these examples, see Hutton 2014: 134–135.

27 *Shiji* 66. 2179–2180.

army and defeated the powerful state of Qin to save Wei from the menace of Qin.

Among all the paragons Xunzi puts forth, only the two examples of contending ministers, Bigan and Wu Zixu, are occasionally included in the popular story compendia of late imperial period. In the 1594 edition *Riji gushi,* compiled by Peng Bin 彭濱 and Wu Zongzha 吳宗札 as a civil examination aide, Bigan's story is given the title "the minister who remonstrated directly and had his heart carved out" 剖心直諫臣. This story is very short compared to other narratives in this book, containing only forty-two characters. It outlines how Bigan "forcefully remonstrated" (*lijian* 力諫), enraging King Zhòu, who as a result killed Bigan in order to see his heart.[28] In another late Ming edition attributed to the official and famous calligrapher Zhang Ruitu 張瑞圖 (1570–1641), the story, titled "Killing Gan and Carving Out His Heart" (*sigan poxin* 死干剖心), is more elaborate. Instead of plain summary, the editor incorporated Bigan's saying recorded in *Shiji* into the narrative: "[if] the ruler errs but the minster does not remonstrate until he dies, what would happen to the people" 君有過而不以死諫, 則百姓何辜? (literally, "what wrongs would the people have done to deserve the baleful consequences?").[29] Possibly drawing from other Song dynasty works of historiography, he then added that Bigan prostrated himself before the king and requested him to "wash his heart and change his behavior" 洗心易行.[30] The two details constitute the main body of the narrative, making Bigan's concern about the people and the emotional intensity of his "direct remonstrance" the focal points of his loyalty.

---

28 *Dingjuan jiaozeng pingzhu wulun riji gushi daquan* 1.22b–23a.

29 *Shiji* 38.1610. The exact wording in *Shiji* is *yi si zheng* 以死爭. The text in the story compendia uses *jian* 諫 instead of *zheng* 爭.

30 *Xinqie leijie guanyang riji gushi daquan* 1990, 6: 22b. This detail seems to first appear in *Huangwang daji* 皇王大紀 (Great chronicle of emperors and kings) by Hu Hong 胡宏 (1105–1161), then quoted in *Zizhi tongjian qianbian* 資治通鑒前編 (Previous supplement to the comprehensive mirror to aid in government) by Jin Luxiang 金履祥 (1232–1303). See *Huangwang daji* 10.36b; *Zizhi tongjian qianbian* 5. 41a.

This is also the edition that includes Wu Zixu's story, but with a twist. While Wu Zixu is taken as a paragon of contending remonstrance in *Xunzi*, his story in this collection, as its title "Cannot Bear to See the State of Wu Destroyed" 不忍吳亡 indicates, emphasizes Wu Zixu's attachment to the state he had served rather than his staunch admonition of the king. The narrative briefly mentions that Wu Zixu remonstrated with King Fuchai because the latter had become infatuated with the femme fatale Xi Shi 西施 and neglected state affairs. The king did not take Zixu's advice, but instead ordered him to commit suicide by sending him a sword. Before taking his own life, Wu Zixu looked up to Heaven and exclaimed: "Once I die, the people of Yue will come to dig up the altars of soil and grain of Wu; how can I bear to see that?" 吾死越人掘吳社稷, 吾安忍乎?[31]

The following two-thirds of the narrative gives much attention to the supernatural feats Zixu's ghost conjured up to protect the state of Wu from Yue attacks: Zixu's head was cut off and placed on the southern tower of the city by the order of the King of Wu; his ghost rode on the tides coming back and forth, and raised the waves to beat against the shore so as to resist Yue invasion. When the Yue army approached,

> 望胥頭若車輪, 目若閃電, 鬚髮四張, 影射越軍, 暴風疾雨, 奔雷激電, 飛沙走石, 疾如弓弩。

> [They] saw Zixu's head [hanging on the wall] as big as a chariot wheel. His eyes flashed like lightening bolts. His hair and beard stuck out all around. His shadow loomed over the Yue army. The wind was violent, the rain tempestuous, thunder roared, lightening flashed. Sand and stones hurled through the air, swift as arrows from crossbows.[32]

Stunned by the power of the ghost, the Yue generals made obeisance to Wu Zixu's ghost, who then appeared in their dreams and said: "My heart cannot bear to see the state of Wu destroyed. But I can return your army

---

31 *Xinqie leijie guanyang riji gushi daquan* 7: 5a–5b.

32 Ibid. I consulted and modified David Jonhson's English translation (Johnson 1980: 142).

to you" 吾心不忍吳亡, 可還汝軍. The next day, the Yue army entered the capital of Wu and captured Fuchai. He lamented: "How can I face Zixu [in the underworld]" 何面目見子胥耶?

Much of the narrative on the Yue army's encounter with Wu Zixu's ghost is drawn from Zhao Ye's 趙曄 (fl. 1ˢᵗ century) *Wu Yue chunqiu* 吳越 春秋 (Spring and autumn of Wu and Yue) rather than *Shiji* 史記 (Records of the grand historian). However, whereas *Wu Yue chunqiu* includes Wu Zixu's vow of vengeance against Wu (as does *Shiji* and other sources), *Riji gushi* erases the vengeful side of Zixu and emphasizes how he "cannot bear" (*buren* 不忍) to witness Wu's destruction. Thus Fuchai's final lament, taken from "Wu yu" 吳語 in *Guoyu* 國語,[33] indicates his belated recognition of Zixu's loyalty.

The ways in which the Wu Zixu story is *re-presented* in this late-Ming story compendium show the compiler's preference for the theme of lasting attachment to the state while downplaying the ruler-minister conflict. This helps to explain why the other paragons of loyalty upheld in *Xunzi*, such as Lords Pingyuan and Xinling, could hardly make it into the late imperial popular story compendia. With varying degrees, the cases of Lord Xinling, Lord Pingyuan and Yu Quan all push the line between principle and expediency and raise the issue of how far a minister can go with his efforts to correct his ruler for the benefit of the state. In the eyes of Ming-Qing intellectuals, the transgressive means through which these ministers resolve the disagreement between ruler and minister were too dangerous and subversive.

To summarize the issue of selection and omission of loyalty stories from the *Riji gushi* collections, it is useful to revisit David Schaberg's discussion of the emergence and popularization of indirect remonstrance during the Han dynasty. Schaberg aptly juxtaposes direct and indirect remonstrance as two contrasting modes. The anecdotes of direct remonstrators such as Bigan and Wu Zixu represent the ideal of brave or even suicidal commitment to frank

---

33   *Guoyu* 19.7: 562.

communication with the ruler. Conversely, "tales of indirect remonstrance, featuring entertainers or ministers pretending to entertain, held up an ideal of tact, rhetorical cunning, and self-preservation."[34] With the establishment of the Han empire, when potential advisors were relegated to the position of dependence, remonstrance through riddles and verbal games provides a possible solution to the ever-difficult task of persuading the ruler.

Each of these two forms of remonstrance has its problems. While direct remonstrance often exacerbates the conflict between ruler and subject, indirect remonstrance, i.e. sugarcoating a moral message with playful rhetoric and pleasing theatricality, risks degrading the intellectual to the roles of jester and entertainer. Conversely, the practice of direct remonstrance, though dangerous, may evoke the lost pride of the *shi* (men of service, often synonymous with scholar-officials in later periods) when they enjoyed a much higher status in the ruler-subject relationship, as the courage as well as the responsibility to stand up against the ruler mark the core values of *shi* identity.[35]

The shifting criteria in choosing the models of loyalty lay out the sets of contending values surrounding the practice of loyalty: opposition versus submission, defiance versus compliance, and dedication versus resignation. Generally, the solution is to follow the middle way. On one end of the spectrum, the mode of indirect remonstrance through verbal art receives little representation, if at all. Direct remonstrance, even when suicidal (as in the cases of Bigan and Wu Zixu), is much more prized. On the other end, examples of remonstrance deemed too radical, such as those of Lord Pingyuan, Lord Xinling, or Yu Quan, are not featured in the Ming compendia either. The compendia compilers most widely favor the stories that highlight the courage and audacity of loyal subjects without undermining the authority of the ruler.

---

34   Schaberg 2005:196. See also Li 1993:17–23.
35   See Pines's analysis of Hai Rui 海瑞 (1514–1587) as an example (Pines 2012: 93–100).

2. Editing Loyalty: *Junchen gushi*

The power and problem of violence in remonstrance provide us with a key to understanding the organization and representation of loyalty in the story compendia *Riji gushi* and *Junchen gushi*. It should be noted that as the number of stories in these compendia range from nearly a hundred to over 300, my discussion here by no means exhausts the richness of this corpus of texts. The focus on violence and remonstrance in connection to the loyalty stories here aims primarily at bridging the story compendia with dramatic works discussed in the next section.

Also, since Yu Shao's original *Riji gushi* did not survive, and the expanded or reworked late Ming editions are too voluminous and textually complex to be properly managed within the scope of this chapter, the discussion in this section will focus mainly on *Junchen gushi* 君臣故事 (Stories of rulers and subjects), first published during the Yuan dynasty[36] (see Figure 1). Although *Riji gushi* and *Junchen gushi* bear different titles, the organization, categorization, and sizable overlapping of the stories indicate they are products of similar mentalities, that is, both set out to teach Confucian moral values on an elementary level. The only major difference is that as a compendium of stories on both rulers and subjects, *Junchen gushi* is divided into "the section on the way of rulers" 君道門 and "the section on the way of subjects" 臣道門, with the ruler's section being much shorter. Similar to *Riji gushi*, "the way of subjects" also begins with knowledge acquisition (Confucian arts 儒術), then proceeds to moral

---

36   A Gozan-ban 五山版 (Five-mountain edition) reprint of the Yuan dynasty edition, with the full title *Fenlei hebi tuxiang jujie junchen gushi* 分類合璧圖像句解君臣故事, (Categorized stories of rulers and subjects combined with illustrations and sentence explications), is preserved in the Sonkeikaku bunko 尊經閣文庫 of the Maeda Ikutokukai Foundation 前田育德會 in Tokyo. The Oriental Library (Tōyō Bunko 東洋文庫) holds another reprint of the same edition. Special thanks to Professor Oki Yasushi 大木康 of Tokyo University for helping me access this edition in the Oriental Library. For studies on *Junchen gushi* in the context of Yuan dynasty print culture, see Miya 2006: 114–116, 142–143.

cultivation through proper daily interactions with family and friends (human relationships 人倫), and finally to public service (bureaucratic system 官制). Individual life and sociopolitical self-realization connect with each other to function as a whole. The section on subjects in this text works like a compact version of *Riji gushi*, allowing us to more effectively extract from it the basic typologies of loyalty stories.

Aside from the categories of "Confucian arts" and "human relationships," which respectively cover the formative stage of a person's life and the five cardinal human relationships, three major aspects of loyalty are presented in *Junchen gushi*: remonstrance, good governance, and honorable death. Remonstrance as the key action that defines a minister's loyalty has been discussed in the previous section. For the other two aspects, a good elucidation is provided in *Zhongjing*, an apocryphal text arguably compiled either in the Tang or the Song dynasty.[37] Section 7 of *Zhongjing*, "Principles of Governance" 政理, states: "to transform [the people] through virtue is the highest realization of proper principle" 夫化之以德，理之上也,[38] while resorting to punishment is the least desirable choice. Honorable death is discussed in the next section "Military Preparation" 武備, which promises that a morally upright leader will "get the army to exert their hearts to the utmost, use all their strength, and [be ready] to give up their lives. Thus, attacks will succeed and defense will be solid" 故得師盡其心，竭其力，致其命，是以攻之則克，守之則固.[39] Echoing *Zhongjing*, the examples of good officials and death-defying military commanders occupy a significant portion in the representations of loyalty in the story compendia, be it *Junchen gushi* or *Riji gushi*. To a certain extant, these stories illustrate the principles enunciated in *Zhongjing*.

---

37   For *Zhongjing* and Ming dynasty print culture, see Liu Chiung-yun 2015 (pp. 318–319 for its dating).

38   *Zhongjing xiangjie* 7.481.

39   *Zhongjing xiangjie* 8.481–482.

But at the same time, the way *Junchen gushi* organizes the stories suggests a different conception of the relationships among the significance of remonstrance, good governance, and honorable death, the three major aspects of loyalty. In *Junchen gushi*, four stories on remonstrance open "the section on the ways of subjects," followed by six stories on death-defying generals. A few stories placed under the sub-categories such as incorruptible integrity 清廉, transformative governance 政化, hearing legal cases 聽訟, and leniency 寬恕 come next, while most stories on good governance are grouped together in the "bureaucratic system" section. This differs from the approach in *Zhongjing*. There the author specifically warns against overrating honorable death by posing the rhetorical question:

> 夫忠者，豈惟奉君忘身，徇國忘家，正色直辭，臨難死節而已矣？
>
> When it comes to loyalty, how can it be just about forgetting one's body in the service of the ruler, sacrificing for the state and forgetting about one's own family, offering forthright arguments in an uncompromising manner, and dying for one's principles when facing calamities, and nothing else?[40]

The highest kind of loyalty, *Zhongjing* argues, is "to orchestrate and manage [state affairs] with hidden aplomb and subtlety, to rectify oneself and pacify others, and to follow the principle of appointing the virtuous" 沉謀潛運，正己安人，任賢以為理.[41] It elevates good governance and considers honorable death a last resort. Following this logic, the stories on good governance should come before those on death-defying generals.

But instead, in *Junchen gushi* the stories of death-defying generals are placed right after those on remonstrance, the foremost duty of ministers and officials. Why such an arrangement? Narrative patterns and replacement mechanism may provide the clues to an answer. Although remonstrating officials and death-defying generals seem to represent two distinct aspects

---

40   *Zhongjing xiangjie* 3.480.

41   Ibid.

of loyalty, they actually share a similar narrative pattern upon closer inspection. Both center on confrontation. In the cases of remonstrance, the confrontation takes place between rulers and remonstrators: Boyi 伯夷 and Shuqi 叔齊 halted the horse of King Wu of Zhou 周武王 (d. ca. 1043 BCE) and remonstrate with him against overthrowing King Zhòu of Shang. Shentu Gang 申屠剛 remonstrates with Emperor Guangwu of Han 漢光武帝 (r. 25–57) against a hunting expedition by putting his head into a wheel of the emperor's carriage. Zhu Yun 朱雲 breaks a railing in the imperial court when he presses Emperor Cheng of Han 漢成帝 (r. 33–7 BCE) to execute the incompetent and fawning prime minister, Zhang Yu 張禹 (?– 5 BCE). Xin Pi 辛毗 (d. 235) remonstrates with Emperor Wen of Wei 魏文帝 (r. 221–226) against relocating 1,000 households during the time of famine by pulling the emperor's lapel from the back.[42]

Among the four stories above, the case of Boyi and Shuqi stands apart. While the remonstrators in the other examples are the emperors' ministers, these two former princes of Guzhu 孤竹 are described in the *Lunyu* 論語 (*The Analects*) and later texts as *yimin* 逸民 (recluses), i.e., those who strove to maintain their moral integrity and refused to serve unworthy rulers.[43] Strictly speaking, the recluses are subjects of neither Shang nor Zhou. But the compiler's efforts to focus on a moment of confrontation without disruptive consequences remain the same. In the annotations inserted in between the narratives, the compiler states: "King Wu ... was the virtuous ruler of Zhou. King Zhòu was the last ruler of Yin (Shang). He was self-indulgent and had lost the Way, therefore King Wu attacked him" 武王……有周之賢君；紂，殷之末君，沈湎無道，武王伐之.[44] The compiler feels

---

42 As the Yuan dynasty edition *Junchen gushi* is not easily accessible, to facilitate references, in the following I cite a later Japanese reprint (*wakokubon* 和刻本) edition dated 1674. This Japanese reprint differs from the Yuan dynasty edition mainly in the style of the illustrations and the general book layout. Other than a number of miswritten characters, the contents, categories and story orders in these two editions are the same. *Junchen gushi* 1990: 213–214.

43 *Lunyu* 18.8. Also see *Shiji* 61:2121–2123. See more in Rubin 1986.

44 *Junchen gushi* 1990: 213.

the need to justify Boyi's and Shuqi's remonstrance: "Although King Wu was saving the people from extreme suffering (literally, water and fire), the act of a subject killing his ruler ultimately violates the principles [of orderly government], hence the strenuous remonstrance" 武王雖救民於水火之中，然臣弒君，終為悖理，是故苦諫.[45] The narrative highlights Boyi's and Shuqi's adherence to high moral principles. At the same time, their resolute yet non-aggressive remonstrance does not truly challenge the authority of the ruler.

All four stories of confrontational remonstrance mentioned above can be read as modifications of Yu Quan's forcefulness. Particularly in Zhu Yun's case, conflict and reconciliation achieve a delicate balance. Zhu's actions and expressions mark him as an unflinching remonstrator. He first makes an audacious proposition urging the emperor to execute the emperor's mentor and highly favored minister, Zhang Yu. When the enraged emperor orders Zhu to be escorted out, Zhu rushes forward and tries to climb over the railing that separates him from the emperor, while yelling: "I will be content if I get to join the company of Longfeng and Bigan in the underworld!"[46] 臣得從龍逢、比干遊於地下足矣. The physical movement of climbing over the railing looks almost like an assault on the emperor, but the action stops right there. The railing is broken; the emperor is unharmed. When Zhu summons the spirits of Longfeng and Bigan, both renowned upright remonstrators killed by tyrants, the tension between the ruler and the minister reaches its climax in the narrative, for by comparing himself to these ministers, Zhu is equating the emperor with the Xia and Shang tyrants. Zhu Yun's comparison risks exasperating the emperor and he appears ready to die. At the same time, it gives the emperor the chance to prove that he is *not* the tyrant: he should just avoid punishing his minister for undaunted remonstrance.

---

45 Ibid.

46 *Junchen gushi* 1990: 214. Longfeng allegedly was a loyal martyr at the court of the last ruler of the Xia dynasty, Jie 桀.

Breaking the tension, another official in court, Xin Qingji 辛慶忌 (?–12 BCE), steps in and risks his own life to plead for Zhu. The shadow of death hovers momentarily, but is soon dispelled. All of Zhu Yun's transgressions, potentially violent but suppressed, are just enough to fortify his image as a loyal remonstrator without going overboard. The delicate balance[47] thus also demarcates a space for the ruler to play his part. Later, when the time comes to fix the broken railing, the emperor says: "Do not replace it. Just fix the broken part and leave the mark there to honor the upright minister" 勿易。因而輯之，旌直臣.[48] The example of Zhu Yun eventually became proverbial: "the subject who breaks the railing" (*zhejianchen* 折檻臣) came to be a common allusion in classical prose and poetry.

Story compendia, designed for readers with limited literacy, require their narratives to be succinct and pithy—most stories are between fifty and two hundred words. The analysis of the above case demonstrates how elements such as confrontation, (suppressed) violence, dramatic action, and hyperbolic language can be useful in orchestrating a gripping narrative that forcefully conveys the protagonist's loyal qualities without endangering the authority of the ruler. At the same time, Zhu Yun's story is perhaps the furthest a remonstrance narrative can go, if the ruler-subject power equilibrium is to be maintained. Remonstrance, as a manifestation of loyalty that aims at correcting the ruler, is a complex undertaking in which the ruler-subject power balance is constantly in tension. How to present proper examples of remonstrance could be a difficult task for the compilers of the story compendia. For the confrontational type of remonstrance, Zhu Yun's story marks the limit of what is acceptable.

This may explain the emergence of another mode of remonstrance emphasizing restraint in the 1566 edition of *Riji gushi*. While confrontational

---

47   The balance is precarious, for as much as Zhu Yun is considered a model of loyalty in the imperial period, the Eastern Han historian Ban Gu 班固 (32–92) still faults him for being "insubordinate to his superior" (*fanshang* 犯上). *Hanshu* 100: 4204–4205.

48   Ibid.

remonstrance stories such as the cases of Zhu Yun and Shentu Gang are still included, there appears a set of stories featuring Song dynasty ministers who remonstrate with emperors through restraint, composure and unrelenting perseverance. The best example of this mode of loyalty can be found in the story of Zhao Pu 趙普 (922–992), the prime minister of Song Taizu 宋太祖 (r. 960–976). The minister and the emperor disagree on the appointment of a certain official. Zhao continues to submit the memorial to recommend the same person every day, and each time, the emperor returns it. One day, the enraged emperor grabs the memorial, tears it into pieces and throws it on the ground. "Zhao Pu acted as if nothing had happened, slowly picked up pieces of the memorial, brought them home, patched them up and submitted the repaired memorial again the next day" 普神色自若，徐拾奏，歸補綴，明日復進[49] (see Figure 2). On seeing the memorial, the emperor finally heeds Zhao's recommendation. This narrative contrasts with the stories of Zhu Yun in many interesting ways. In Zhao Pu's case, his resolution to remonstrate is manifested through the act of reparation rather than transgression, and he effects change through tenacity rather than intensity.

While compilers of story compendia try to moderate or simply avoid direct conflict between the ruler and the subject, the motif of confrontation and violence thrives in the stories of death-defying generals. Under the category "the loyal and the righteous" 忠義 in *Junchen gushi*, each story features a wartime confrontation between an unyielding general in captivity and the leader of the enemy troops. The six stories in order are:

(1) Yan Gaoqing 顏杲卿 (692–756), captured by the rebel An Lushan 安祿山 (703–757), is tied to a pole and executed by slow slicing. During the process, Yan is made to eat his own sliced flesh. Even so, he continues to curse his enemy. Provoked, An cuts off his tongue and Yan "dies slurring his curse" 含糊而絕.[50]

---

49   *Riji gushi* 1566: 9.16b–17a.

50   *Junchen gushi* 1990: 214.

(2) Sun Kui 孫揆 (d. 890), captured by the Turkic Shatuo 沙陀 general Li Keyong 李克用 (856–908), humiliates his enemy by instructing Li's soldiers in the correct way of sawing himself apart. He yells: "You servants of dogs! Don't you know that when you try to saw a person apart, you need to first secure him between two planks!" 死狗奴，解人當以板，汝輩安知！[51]

(3) The Northern Song official Liu Ge 劉韐 (1067–1127), when facing the Jurchens urging him to surrender, drinks a cup of wine and commits suicide by hanging himself.

(4) Wang Yanzhang 王彥章 (863–923), a major general of the Later Liang 後梁 (907–923), chooses to commit suicide when given a chance to surrender. The narrative ends with Wang saying: "I have received favors from the Liang Dynasty. I cannot repay it except by death" 臣受梁恩，非死不能報.[52]

(5) Lin Yun 林蘊, when working under the Xichuan military commissioner 西川節度使 Liu Pi 劉闢 (d. 806), detects that Liu is preparing to revolt and remonstrates with him intensely. Liu, enraged, orders an executioner to threaten Lin by pressing and rubbing a sword against his neck. Lin reproaches the executioner: "Kill me if you want to! How dare you, a stupid slave, treat my neck as a whetstone!" 死即死，我項豈頑奴砥石耶。[53]

(6) Zhang Xun 張巡 (708–757) defends Suiyang 睢陽 during the An Lushan Rebellion. After Yin Ziqi 尹子琦, a general under An's command, breaks into the city, Zhang is captured and brought in front of Yin, who ridicules him by asking:

> 「聞君督戰，則眥裂血面，嚼齒皆碎，何至如是？」答曰：「吾欲氣吞逆賊，故力屈耳。」子琦怒，以刀抉齒。巡罵曰：「我為君父死，爾附賊，乃犬彘也。」

---

51   Ibid.
52   *Junchen gushi* 1990: 215.
53   Ibid.

"I heard that when you command troops in a battle, [you are so fierce that] your eyes bulge, your face is smeared with blood and that you clench your teeth till they crack. How did you come to this? [i.e., you are supposed to be fierce—why were you captured?] [Zhang] replied: "My spirit would fain devour the rebel—it was just that my strength gave way!"[54] Ziqi was enraged: he used a broad sword to knock out [Zhang's] teeth. [Zhang] Xun cursed him: "I die for my ruler and father; you attach yourself to a rebel—you are but a dog and a swine!"[55]

When the two parties of a confrontation shift from ruler-minister to general-enemy, especially when in several cases the enemies are "barbarian" rebels, it is as if a bar is lifted for the narrator to explore the uses of graphic violence and stirring verbal expressions to create compelling moral stories. In contrast to the stories of good governance, which are by nature less dramatic, such conflict-oriented narratives can easily build up to an arresting climax. This is a sensational text stoking excitement. The catchy four-syllable titles of these stories, such as "tied to a pole and dismembered" 縛柱節解, "fastened between planks and sawed" 束板鋸解, "Lin Yun having a sword rubbed against his neck" 林蘊磨頸, "Zhang Xun having his teeth knocked out" 張巡抉齒, further reinforce the image of the key action. The combination of action verbs and object-nouns encapsulates the climatic moment in the narrative and facilitates visualization. The story, the title, and very often the illustrations that accompany the narratives, work together to turn a conversation or a gesture into the synecdoche of a

---

54   The stories in these compendia are almost always taken from historical texts and re-written in simple classical Chinese. During the process, variances and mistakes may occur. Zhang Xun's biography in the *Jiu Tangshu* 舊唐書 records this sentence as 吾欲氣吞逆賊，但力不遂耳. Here the *Junchen gushi* seems to be based on *Xin Tangshu* 新唐書：吾欲氣吞逆賊，顧力屈耳, with the character *gu* 顧 meaning "but," yet mistakes it to be *gu* 故, which renders the meaning of this sentence less clear. The more proper formulation—to convey the meaning of "because"—would be 力屈故耳. The detail mentioned in these records, viz. that Zhang Xun killed his concubine to feed his soldiers during the siege, was omitted in the *Junchen gushi*, but was later widely included in the late-Ming edition *Riji gusji*.

55   *Junchen gushi* 1990: 215. For a study of the martyrdom of Zhang Xun, see Graff 1995.

protagonist's loyalty (see Figure 3). In the limited textual space of a page, the meaning of loyalty is condensed into a particular moment of vehement protest empowered by aggressive actions and heated, sometimes even vituperative, language in the cases of martyrs facing death.

The biography of one Madame Sheng, written by the 16th-century scholar-official Tang Shunzhi 唐順之 (1507–1560), grants a rare glimpse into how an educated female reader from an elite family responded to a text like *Riji gushi*.

> 孺人自少讀《小學》、《孝經》書，頗解意旨，故生平喜書。然獨不喜佛書。中饋有間，則取《小學日記故事》，稗官小説，家誦説之。每至古人壯節偉行，則擊手詫嘆，以為烈士當如是。

The honored lady[56] had read *Xiaoxue* and *Xiaojing* when she was young and understood them well. So she liked reading her whole life, although she did not care for Buddhist works. During moments of leisure from housework, she would take the *Xiaoxue riji gushi*, unofficial histories, and novels to recite and discuss the texts at home. Whenever she came to stories about the unyielding integrity and admirable deeds of historical figures, she would clap her hands and exclaim with amazement, saying that a heroic man should be like this![57]

Although works like *Riji gushi* and *Junchen guhi* are usually defined as primers, this passage tells us that their readership was by no means limited to children. In fact, to Madame Sheng, *Riji gushi*, unofficial history, and novels are comparable reading materials, and what attracts her especially in these books are the "unyielding integrity and admirable deeds of historical figures," which prompt her to "clap her hands and exclaim with amazement." These didactic materials are mentioned in the same breath as fiction, suggesting that they might be thought to share the same entertainment value.

---

56   *Ruren* 孺人 is the title given to wives and mothers of officials above the 7th rank.

57   *Jingchuan xiansheng wenji* 15. 305.

This account of a gentry woman reader's response indicates that the popularity of such stories needs to be understood in light of the combination of moral education, narrative strategy, and affective power. Despite their brevity and simplicity, the stories of death-defying loyalists are effective. Compared to the examples of good governance during peacetime, stories about dissenting remonstrators and death-defying generals are much more engaging and exciting. Often organized in consecutive order or close proximity, they constitute a significant part of the loyalty stories both in terms of quantity and length. Together, they create a panorama of loyalist drama, which conjoin the heroic action of civil ministers (*wenchen* 文臣) and that of military generals (*wujiang* 武將), operating on a few noticeable patterns with enough variation in details to keep the reader stirred and amazed. Similar thematic typologies also characterize dramatic works of the Yuan-Ming period, as the early Ming prince and dramatist Zhu Qian's 朱權 (1378–1448) classification indicates.[58]

Narratives and drama intersected and shared many similar motifs in the representations of loyalty. Indeed, the distinction between books for reading and drama for listening/viewing is blurred when we take into consideration the rich illustrations in the moral story compendia. Also, in addition to silent reading, texts like *Riji gushi* were much more often recited, memorized and told as stories in everyday life settings between teacher and students, mother and children, and family members.[59] Thus these story compendia and drama work together to entertain and to disseminate the idea and emotions of loyalty through visual, oral, and aural communication. Their reception among those of varying levels of literacy creates a cultural space of shared moral imagination.

---

58 Zhu Quan classifies northern drama (*zaju*) into twelve categories in *Taihe zhengyin pu* 太和正音譜 (A formulary of correct sounds for an era of great peace). Among them are "the ones who don (official) robes and hold memorial tablets" 披袍秉笏, with a note below in parentheses, "these are plays about rulers and ministers" 即君臣雜劇, "loyal subjects and heroic men of service" 忠臣烈士 and "chastising miscreants and rebuking slanderers" 斥奸罵讒. *Taihe zhengyin pu* 1959: 24.

59 *Tianma shanfang yigao* 1983: 3.477. For a full discussion of the readers and uses of *Riji gushi*, see Liu Chiung-yun 2019: 48–56.

3. Performing Loyalty

Among all the late imperial plays on the subject of loyalty, few integrate the ethical dilemma and the aesthetics of emotions as powerfully as the 17th-century *chuanqi* play *Qian zhong lu*.[60] Its setting is the 1402 Usurpation and its aftermath. A four-year war ended with the young Jianwen 建文 Emperor (r. 1398–1402) losing the throne to his ambitious uncle Zhu Di 朱棣 (1360–1424), who became the Yongle Emperor (r. 1402–1424). The play tells the story of the defeated former emperor, who escapes to the southwestern borderlands of the empire under the protection of his loyal subjects and hides there for over twenty years. (The historical Jianwen emperor disappeared and might have died in 1402.) The playwright uses three sets of characters, all officials who served the Jianwen emperor, to exemplify the martyr, the exile, and the repentant turncoat. Each captures a key dimension of loyalty. At the same time, these possible ways of "performing" loyalty were put in dialogue with each other, revealing the price, limitation or dilemmas inherent in the practice of this particular moral virtue. In this sense, the play to a certain extent echoes the design of loyalty typologies seen in the story compendia but further reshapes and complicates it in the form of a full-length dramatic work.

---

60   *Qian zhong lu* is among the dramatic works written by a group of professional playwrights active in Suzhou in 17th-century China. Unlike literati playwrights who sought appreciation in literati circles, these Suzhou playwrights' works were mostly performed in public spaces including temples, river ports, market places and public theaters. Because of their performance-oriented rather than author-oriented nature, many of these plays exist in the form of manuscripts in full or in selected scenes. The earliest extant manuscript of *Qian zhong lu* in full length, dated 1708, is reprinted and collected in Wang Wenzhang and Liu Wenfeng 2010, 17: 1–100. The quotations of *Qian zhong lu* discussed in this paper are based on this text. For a punctuated critical edition, see *Qian zhong lu* 1989. For discussions of the Suzhou playwrights, see Lu Eting 1980, Wang Anqi 1986, Li Mei 2000, Fox 2015. For a study of *Qian zhong lu*, see Liu Chiung-yun 2016.

3.1 The Martyr

The martyr and the exile, representing two groups of loyalists in *Qian zhong lu*, may be seen as a further transformation of the confrontational and moderating modes of loyalty discussed above. The former is represented by Fang Xiaoru 方孝孺 (1357–1402), who pays the price of having "ten categories of relatives and associates"[61] killed for his staunch loyalty to the dethroned Jianwen Emperor.[62] The latter is embodied by Cheng Ji 程濟, who accompanies the Jianwen Emperor throughout his twenty-three-year exile.

The famous scene "Drafting the Decree" 草詔, which stages Fang Xiaoru's death, employs a pattern already familiar to us. The martyr condemns the enemy, the enraged enemy inflicts torture, the martyr withstands it and continues to curse the enemy till the very end. However, in the play, this pattern is elaborately redesigned to become a death ritual that sublimates shocking violence as a passage to divinity. The transformative course begins with Fang Xiaoru being forced to enter the imperial court to meet the newly enthroned Yongle Emperor. On his way to meet Yongle, Fang Xiaoru passes the execution ground, where two of his former colleagues and leading advisors of the Jianwen Emperor, Qi Tai 齊泰 (d. 1402) and Huang Zicheng 黃子澄 (1350–1402), are about to be executed. The three men greet each other with smiles, calmly bid farewell, and envisage their meeting again soon in another world after death.

Fang Xiaoru walks further and sees the corpse of Jing Qing 景清 (d. 1402) wrapped in red cloth and paraded on stage by two executioners.[63] Jing Qing's attempt to assassinate Yongle after he ascended the throne is widely recorded in the unofficial histories of the Ming dynasty.[64] With incremental

---

61   The ten categories include nine degrees of kinship plus disciples and friends.

62   For a more detailed account of the 1402 Usurpation in history and an analysis of its aftermath, see Elman 1993; 2013: 28–33; Chan Hok-lam 2007: 75–158. For the transformation of the historical memory of 1402 Usurpation in the late Ming, see Liu Chiung-yun 2012: 61–117.

63   占、丑創子扛紅屍首上遶場走下。*Qian zhong lu* 2010: 29.

64   Liu Chiung-yun 2016: 11–12.

elaboration, his assassination has come to signify a kind of vengeful loyalty. According to a late Ming account, Jing Qing wore a red gown to attend the imperial audience one morning, planning to assassinate Yongle.[65] Forewarned by an astrological anomaly the previous day, Yongle became suspicious and discovered the sword Jing Qing had hidden under his clothes. Jing Qing, like all the martyrs we have discussed so far, condemned Yongle. The latter had Jing Qing's teeth knocked out. In return, Jing Qing advanced and spat the blood in his mouth at Yongle, an act that overlaps with the account of Fang Xiaoru's martyrdom in unofficial histories.[66] The exasperated Yongle consequently ordered not only Jing Qing's execution, but also the skinning of his corpse, which was then stuffed with straw and put up on the city gate as a warning against any similar attempt in the future. That night, Yongle dreamt of Jing Qing chasing him with a sword in the imperial court. The next morning, as Yongle's carriage went under the city gate, the stuffed corpse fell in front of Yongle and took three steps forward as if to attack him.

To have Jing Qing's corpse paraded on stage is therefore also to summon the ferocity and relentless demand for justice associated with this account. The corpse wrapped in red cloth foreshadows the violence that will take place later in the confrontation between Fang Xiaoru and Yongle. Also, the encounters with Qi Tai, Huang Zicheng and the corpse of Jing Qing connect Fang Xiaoru's actions with other loyalist endeavors preceding his own. It is like a procession of like-minded loyalists. More specifically, the overlapping narrative details in accounts of the death of Fang Xiaoru and that of Jing Qing, as well as the admiration of the former for the latter, make for mutual reinforcement.[67] The full power of this death ritual is achieved not only by Fang Xiaoru, but also by the memories of other undaunted and determined martyrs.

---

65   *Guochao dianhui* 2.88a–88b.

66   *Jiangshi mishi* 1. 294.

67   *Qian zhong lu* 2010: 29.

When Fang Xiaoru finally arrives at the court, the battle between Fang Xiaoru and Yongle begins. Fang meets Yongle in his white mourning gown, and refuses to draft the decree to endorse Yongle's rule. As the initially rather polite Yongle gradually loses his patience and threatens to call for troops to press Fang to write, Fang takes the brush and writes down the character for "usurp" 篡 three times on paper. These words, each like a stab to Yongle, announce a battle on the metaphoric level between the loyalist and the new emperor, and the battlefield is nowhere other than Fang Xiaoru's own body.

Yongle orders Fang Xiaoru's execution. But before the execution takes place, Fang pours out his complex emotions in song. Assuming Jianwen to have died in the burning palace when Yongle's troops broke in, he first addresses the spirits of emperors Hongwu and Jianwen, confidently reiterating his moral integrity; he then addresses his wife, lamenting that he has to sacrifice his lineage to fulfill his duty as a loyal subject; he harangues Yongle, again condemning his wrongdoing and cruelty; and finally he appeals to Heaven to seek divine justice. The idea that loyalty in its utmost realization has the power to move Heaven and Earth, as expounded in *Zhongjing*, is crucial for understanding the logic behind Fang's martyrdom. From a humanistic point of view, Fang Xiaoru's extreme form of loyalty can be very disturbing. As early as the mid-15th century, grand secretary Li Xian 李賢 (1408–1466) had commented: Had Fang committed suicide when the capital fell, he would not have had to confront and exasperate the Yongle Emperor, and thus would have been able to spare the lives of all his kin and friends. For him, Fang Xiaoru's martyrdom is "loyalty of the excessive kind" 忠之過者.[68]

Yet when the realm of Heaven and the power of divine retribution come into play, the death of Fang Xiaoru's kin and associates to the tenth degree, which could have been interpreted as a callous and "selfish" choice Fang made to fulfill or dramatize his own duty of loyalty, becomes a human

---

68   *Tianshun rilu* 1993: 1163.

being's maximal sacrifice to Heaven, an ultimate form of devotion. The *self* here, of course, has to be understood in an extended sense; the whole lineage is taken as "one." Divine justice is the last recourse for a loyalist in a defeated campaign against his enemy. The greater the sacrifice, the more powerfully the martyr can move Heaven and enlist the aid of divine retribution. Loyalty is a difficult virtue. Perhaps it is with deep understanding of such difficulty that the author of *Zhongjing* instructs: "Only Heaven can pass judgment on humans; it never fails to respond to their virtue or evil" 惟天鑒人，善惡必應.[69] The reward of performing loyal duties may not lie in this life, but in the long run Heaven will judiciously repay the virtuous and punish the treacherous. The final judgment of Heaven balances the possibly life-threatening price a loyal minister has to pay in this life. A minister holds fast to the principle of loyalty not just for the ruler, but ultimately to vindicate Heaven's justice.

Such is the belief that buttresses Fang Xiaoru's confidence in the efficacy of his "spirit of righteousness" 正氣. He does not see death as the end to his life, but the chance earned through martyrdom to plead his case to Heaven, as he sings: "In haste, I will hurry my soul to enumerate (the wrongs I suffer) to the blue yonder. No doubt the luminous heart of Heaven will distinguish the virtuous from the sinful" 急急的趕陰魂歷歷訴青霄。少不得天心炯炯分白皂.[70] The extremity of his sacrifice, with its awe-inspiring weight, will not only impress the human world with a formidable example of loyalty, but also immensely enhance the force of his plea in the world after death.

Eager to stop his overflowing accusations, Yongle orders that his teeth be knocked out and his tongue sliced off. Thus to Fang Xiaoru, the only means of attack left is the blood in his mouth. He spits the blood at Yongle and continues to "sing in a fashion without teeth and tongue" 無牙舌唱：

---

69   *Zhongjing xiangjie* 16: 484–5.
70   *Qian zhong lu* 2010: 31–32.

血噴腥紅難洗濯。受萬苦的孤臣粉身和碎腦……

這的是領袖千忠，一身兒千古少。

[*Coda*]

The spattered blood, pungent in scarlet red, is difficult to wash off.

The lone minister, having borne myriad sufferings,

Will have his body pulverized and his brain crushed ...

Truly this is the body that leads the thousand loyal ones—

a rarity through all ages.[71]

On the surface, or in light of the new order, Fang is a member of the defeated camp, the receiver of punishment. But his fierce attack at Yongle in this scene through written words, eloquent condemnation, and the exalted sense of integrity bolstered by the spirits of like-minded martyrs and the emperors he has served, redefine his suffering body. More specifically, the final spatter of blood that soils Yongle's imperial gown functions like a double symbol. It simultaneously marks the sanguinary beginning of Yongle's reign and the undying power of Fang's loyalist fervor. As the play unfolds, the spirit of Fang Xiaoru, accompanied by that of the Hongwu Emperor, will return to claim Yongle's life.

3.2 The Exile

If spattered blood in the imperial court signifies the martyr's loyalty, the scene of the snowy night in *Qian zhong lu* aptly illustrates the nature of those loyalists who follow the Jianwen emperor into exile. Several contrasting pairs characterize the two types of loyalty. Geographically, Fang Xiaoru, a high official in the capital, dies in the imperial court under political spotlight, whereas those who accompany Jianwen to wander in the wilderness at the margin of the empire hide their true identities. Temporally, Fang Xiaoru dies a spectacular death soon after the end of the civil war, while the mission of the wandering loyalists is to endure all

71 Ibid.

sorts of predicaments in everyday life to help Jianwen survive. The former demands publicity, or even theatricality to ensure remembrance of the martyr and the reign he defends.[72] The latter lives by keeping quiet, hidden and indistinct.

Such is the atmosphere the playwright creates in scene twelve, "Temple Encounter" 廟遇. The scene begins with Jianwen and Cheng Ji wandering in the mountainous region of southwest China on a snowy night. Before the snowstorm strikes, in the last scene, the former ruler and his official, now disguised respectively as a Buddhist and a Daoist monk, have just been robbed of all their food and belongings. While trying to find a shelter, wearing the last remaining layer of their gowns, Jianwen sings about the unrelenting coldness of the snow:

【絳都春序】千山冷雪。嘆狂飆凜然，侵入肌裂。高下瀰漫〔難走介〕痛步履傾欹行欲跌。雪呀，你把江山白佔寒威裂，斷送我歧途肘掣。

[*Preface to Spring in the Crimson City*]
Boundless mountains, freezing snow.
I lament that the whirling wind is so fierce
that it pierces through my body, splitting flesh.
Above and below, one expanse of snow. [He stumbles with difficulty.]
I endure pain with every tottering step as I stumble along.
Oh, Snow!
You take over rivers and mountains and turn them all pale with an
    overpowering painful chill.
You block my way, leaving me on the wrong path, holding me back in
    every way and making me feel as if my elbows are held back.[73]

Every line in this lyric carries double meanings. The pun *baizhan* 白佔, which respectively means "white color" (*bai* 白) and "to occupy" (*zhan* 佔),

---

72   On martyrdom and theatricality in late imperial China, see Wakeman 1984: 631–665.

73   *Qian zhong lu* 2010: 46–47.

refers both to the snow that covers the whole landscape, and to Yongle, who unjustly takes over the state formerly ruled by his nephew. The merciless, all-pervasive, and penetrating chill results from the snowstorm and symbolically, also from Yongle, who has ordered the capture of the former emperor, now on the run. Having descended to fugitive status, Jianwen now faces all the perils any ordinary person may have to go through: robbers, cold, hunger, and lack of shelter. The dethroned emperor and the commoner now share a common fate, having to fight with all sorts of natural and human threats in order to meet the very basic need to survive.

The fall of the Jianwen Emperor shifts the locus of ruler-subject relationship from the imperial court to the wilderness, and with the shift, the playwright presents another mode of loyalty hitherto rarely seen. As the image of the overpowering snowstorm suggests, Jianwen is in no position to regain power. The privileges and duties of a ruler are all lost to him. The *ruler* 君 has become merely a nominal title with no substance, which means that those who choose to follow their former ruler in exile have to forfeit all that officialdom could have offered: emoluments, social status, family prosperity, and the honor and gratification of serving the state. Divested of public and ceremonial aspects, the relationship between Jianwen and his followers is stripped down to basic personal loyalty. This personal loyalty does not involve any material benefits bestowed by the ruler in return for the service of his subjects, as discussed by Yuri Pines on the personal loyalty of Chunqiu retainers toward their masters.[74] Rather, in the barest state of existence, the loyalists display a ruler-subject relationship rooted in personal bonding and affection.[75]

The essence of this mode of loyalty is best captured by the encounter between the two pairs of exiles: Jianwen and Cheng Ji, and Wu Chengxue

---

74 Pines 2002a: 154–161.

75 The affectionate relationship between Jianwen and his subjects can be understood as another manifestation of the late Ming culture of *qing* 情 (sentiments, emotions). Li 1993: 47–88; Epstein 2001: 61–119; Gōyama 2006: 14–29.

吳成學 and Niu Jingxian 牛景先. The latter two, having forsaken their own families, positions and secure lives, have been searching for the dethroned emperor in the hope of aiding him or providing for him whenever circumstances permit. On that snowy night, the two groups of wanderers chance to find shelter in the same deserted temple. Wu and Niu settle down in the west wing of the building. Soon after, Jianwen and Cheng Ji seek shelter in the east wing. In a somnolent state, Wu Chengxue hears the sound of repressed sobbing: the tone of grief and desolation reminds him of his former emperor. Walking gently toward the east wing with Niu Jingxian, by the faint moonlight, the two are thrilled at the sight of Jianwen.

As soon as Wu and Niu confirm their true identities to Jianwen, the two kneel down and kowtow to pay respect to Jianwen. The former emperor, surprised, helps them up while singing: "On hearing this, hearing this, my spirit and soul tremble. [He looks at them.] As I gaze and scrutinize, gaze and scrutinize, my sadness and melancholy turn into joy" 聽説罷，聽説罷，神魂震越。〔看末、付介〕重凝覷，重凝覷，悲愁變悦.[76] This is a moment of mutual recognition. Regardless of the reality that Jianwen is no longer the emperor, but a displaced man who has lost everything, Wu and Niu adhere to the formal etiquette that reaffirms the bond between an emperor and his subjects. At a dilapidated temple in the wilderness, when the former emperor and his loyalist officials have all been relegated to the state of anonymous wanderers, Wu and Xiu insist on recognizing the former relationship and honoring its significance to the fullest extent. Loyalty, represented in this context, is conscientious recognition of and appreciation for any kindness and favor one once received in the past. The loyalists do not abandon or forget about Jianwen because they once received emoluments from him 食君之祿. Loyalty here is unconditional devotion based on requital and personal bond.

This mode of loyalty is an ironic counterpart of the efforts to moderate the ruler-subject conflicts discussed in the previous sections. In the

---

76   *Qian zhong lu* 2010: 48.

affectionate and touching relationship between the dethroned emperor and his loyalist followers, conflicts are removed at the cost of actual power. Intimate companionship between the ruler and the subject, as depicted in *Qian zhong lu,* can only be realized when the ruler is dethroned and exiled. If Fang Xiaoru's case represents martyrdom in the extreme, these loyalists in exile seem to embody, at the other end, another extreme development, which directly eliminates the ruler-subject hierarchy.

One may be tempted to see such a design as the result of imperial power rising to new heights: an ideal ruler-subject relationship can only be imagined through a dethroned emperor. However, the emperor as an ordinary man and the ruler-subject companionship also present a form of loyalty much more humane and accessible to the wider audience of public theater. It offers another possibility complementary to the superhuman martyrdom embodied by Fang Xiaoru. Moreover, as the playwright designs it, the fall of Jianwen actually opens up a space that invites the role of the commoner to participate in the debate on loyalty.

3.3 The Turncoat and Commoner

Scene nineteen, "Break Open the Cart 打車," stages the confrontation between Cheng Ji and the turncoat Yan Zhenzhi 嚴震直 (1344–1402). Yan, a former official of Jianwen now serving Yongle, has captured Jianwen and is taking him to the capital in a wooden cart. Cheng Ji, who has been pursuing them, has finally caught up with them. He demands that Yan releases Jianwen and chastises him for his treacherous act. He recalls aloud how Yan was once among the leaders of Jianwen's officials, standing in the front row during audience with the former emperor and receiving ample emoluments from him. The turncoat and the loyalist start to debate, each standing on one side of the imprisoned former emperor. Yan argues that even though the emperor has changed, uncle and nephew belong to the same imperial house. Someone like him, who has the ambition to establish a career, has to follow a master on the rise. Seeing that Yan has no intention of releasing Jianwen and lacking any other means to fight the imperial force, Cheng sings an emotionally intense song that mixes despair, woe, indignation, and hatred. He laments that Jianwen has lost his wife and son, mother and brother due to Yongle. Despite all the sufferings Jianwen has gone through, Heaven shows no mercy for the good and kind. At the emotional climax of his song, he condemns Yan's unprincipled pursuit of self-interest, and asks how Heaven can allow such injustice. Finally, he promises that his spirit will continue to accompany Jianwen in the other world, as he is unable to save him in this world after all.

Throughout the debate, the soldiers are standing and watching from the sidelines. At the end of Cheng's song, they are struck dumb. Silence. Then a commotion arises, and they shout:

> 這等看起來，我每都是差的了！我每眾人那一個不是建文皇帝的子民？那一個不吃建文皇帝糧餉？今日倒幫了別人，拿他去斷送性命。天理何在？天理何在？還要做什麼人！
>
> It looks like we are all wrong! Which one of us is not the son and subject of the Jianwen Emperor? Which one of us did not eat the grains and provisions of the Jianwen Emperor? Yet today we are helping others to capture him and send him to be killed. Where is Heavenly justice? Where is Heavenly justice? How can we go on as human beings![77]

The soldiers are given a crucial role. They take off their uniforms and put down their weapons, leaving the stage while singing "We discard armor and throw away halberds and return to the fields in our villages. How can we help a violent persecutor kill a benevolent master" 棄甲拋戈歸田里，怎去助強梁把恩主戕？[78] The idea of loyalty is rendered simplistically here, but not without clear force. To hurt someone who had been kind to you is against the very fundamental principle of being human. In the eyes of the soldiers, Jianwen's defeat and sufferings, as well as the sharp contrast

---

77   Ibid. 75–76.

78   *Qian zhong lu* 2010: 76.

between how he is treated by Yan and by Cheng, can only be judged in terms of basic reciprocity in human relations.

The awakening of the supposedly crude and uneducated soldiers puts Yan to shame. The sharp contrast is best visualized in the lyric sung by Cheng: "All of a sudden their conscience radiates luminously, and the soldiers leave the army's ranks. This is immensely better than a monkey dressed in official garb—one with the heart of jackals and wolves" 一霎裹良心炯炯棄戎行，絕勝卻沐猴冠帶狼豺狼.[79] On the one hand are the uneducated soldiers, whose awakening reveals their clear conscience. The act of taking off their armor signifies their return to the original pure state of humanity, relinquishing unjust material gain. On the other hand, Yan, wearing the magnificent garb of a high official, is left alone facing his former emperor and the devoted loyalist Cheng Ji. Triggered by the soldier's acts, Yan repents, bows to Jianwen and Cheng Ji, and commits suicide. Thus, at the apparent dead end when even Cheng Ji's eloquent reproach achieved no effect, the moral transformation of the soldiers functions as the key that moves Yan to repent and accordingly saves the life of Jianwen.

The locus of loyalty, which earlier has been shifted, geographically, from the imperial court to the wilderness at the margin of the empire, now further expands to the lower stratum of society. While normally loyalty is a virtue that is expected only of officials and aspiring officials, especially the higher officials who receive greater emoluments from the emperor, a scene like "Break Open the Cart" manifests the playwright's efforts to incorporate the voices of commoners into his design of loyalist models and indicates the appeal such incorporation might have had for the audience. Those not bound by the duty of loyalty are nevertheless excited and inspired by the devotion of the loyalists to the emperor. Although not obligated to sacrifice their lives for the emperor, they contribute to the loyalist enterprise. The commoners in this play cease to exist as the vulgar populace. Instead, their conscience becomes instrumental in the fulfillment of proper ruler-subject

---

79   Ibid.

relationships and holds a small yet indispensable position in the whole ethical structure.[80]

Conclusion

This chapter aims to enrich existing scholarship on loyalty by shifting the focus from the writings of scholars and officials to cultural productions designed for a wider audience. By examining the moral story compendia and drama together, it illuminates how the idea of loyalty, which started out as an ethical precept directed particularly to those who hold official positions, captured popular imagination and engaged their audience beyond the elite in the late imperial period. It highlights *how* the idea of loyalty is embodied in the actions of historical figures and dramatic characters, and draws attention to the affective power generated through these representations. I argue that the development of the idea of loyalty in the late imperial period is by no means as simple as a top-down indoctrination process. Rather, it has always been a cultural arena where various factors negotiate with each other. Among these, storytelling, narrative pattern, and dramatic performance continue to affect and shape the expressions as well as the meanings of loyalty.

The simple narratives in the popular moral story compendia often give the impression that these stories are repetitive, trite, and therefore

---

80   This emphasis on plebian heroes recurs in late Ming and early Qing writings. Some would argue that this glorification of the commoner's virtue characterizes the Suzhou playwrights. Specifically on the themes of commoners rescuing loyal officials or their family members, another Suzhou playwright Zhu Zuochao 朱佐朝 also wrote a play on the 1402 usurpation, *Xieying shi* 血影石 (The rock with shadows of blood). Li Yu has another play titled *Qingzhong pu* 清忠譜 (Registers of the pure and the loyal) which, based on an actual political event that took place in Suzhou in 1626, features five commoners, so indignant at the corruption of the powerful eunuch Wei Zhongxian 魏忠賢 (1568–1627) that they sacrificed their lives to save the righteous official Zhou Shunchang 周順昌 (1584–1626), who was persecuted by Wei because of his outspoken criticism of the eunuch's faction.

insignificant. However, my analysis has demonstrated that these texts in fact constitute a dynamic site where pedagogical goals, commercial interests, and entertainment converge and interact. By examining editorial principles, selection of sources, and narrative strategies, I discuss two prominent features in the representations of loyalty: the use of stylized violence to empower the loyal minister and the attempt to moderate the tension inherent in the ruler-subject relationship.

In *Qian zhong lu*, each direction is pushed further. With the dramatic literary form that incorporates narrative, song, and a much more complex plot structure, the play profoundly captures the predicaments and pathos of loyal subjects. In the direction of using violence to empower the loyal minster, the play, through Fang Xiaoru's martyrdom, illustrates that loyalty acquires its most stunning theatricality, hence strongest potency, in the form of ritualized violence. In the direction of moderating the tension between ruler and subjects, the play presents a deeply moving ruler-subject bond, which ironically also indicates that the tension between ruler and subject may never be completely resolved unless the ruler ceases ruling. While the ideal ruler-subject relation seemed almost impossible to attain, the agency of the commoner rose to become a literary theme explored by Li Yu and other contemporary writers. With the wide dissemination of heroic and stimulating stories of loyal exemplars in story compendia, drama and storytelling in the late Ming and early Qing period, writers, readers and audiences together participate in the cultural exercise of shaping the meaning of loyalty, exploring the power and limitations of this ethical value and the possible ways of reformulating it.

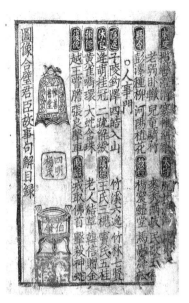

Figure 1. The last page of the table of contents in *Fenlei hebi tuxiang jujie junchen gushi* 分類合璧圖像句解君臣故事 (Categorized stories of rulers and subjects with illustrations and explications), reprint of a Yuan dynasty edition. (Reproduced with permission from Tōyō Bunko （公財）東洋文庫, Tokyo.)

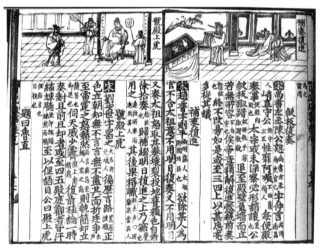

Figure 2. "Bu zou fu jin 補奏復進" (Patch up the memorial and submit it again), in *Xinzeng tuxiang xiaoxue riji gushi daquan* 新增圖像小學日記故事大全 (Stories of the past to be recorded and remembered daily for elementary learning with newly added illustrations), 1566 edition. (Reproduced with permission from Hōsa Bunko 蓬左文庫, Nagoya.)

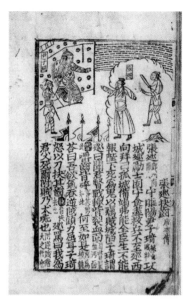

Figure 3. "Zhang Xun juechi 張巡抉齒" (Zhang Xun having his teeth knocked out), in *Fenlei hebi tuxiang jujie junchen gushi* 分類合璧圖像句解君臣故事. (Reproduced with permission from Tōyō Bunko, Tokyo.)

Bibliography

Bol, Peter. 1992. *This Culture of Ours: Intellectual Transition in T'ang and Sung China*. Stanford: Stanford University Press.

Bamin tongzhi 八閩通志. 1955. By Huang Zhongzhao 黃仲昭 (1435–1508). In *Siku quanshu cunmu congshu* 四庫全書存目叢書, vol. *shibu* 史部 178. Tainan: Zhuangyan wenhua.

Cefu yuangui 冊府元龜. 1983. Compiled by Wang Qinruo 王欽若 (962–1025) et al. In *Wenyuange Siku quanshu* 文淵閣四庫全書, vol. 915. Taipei: Taiwan shangwu yinshuguan.

Chan, Hok-lam. 2007. "Legitimating Usurpation: Historical Revisions under the Ming Yongle Emperor (r. 1402–1424)." In *The Legitimation of New Orders: Case Studies in World History*, edited by Philip Yuen-sang Leung, 75–158. Hong Kong: Chinese University Press.

Chongkan zengguang fenmen leilin zashuo 重刊增廣分門類林雜説. 1997. Compiled by Wang Pengshou 王朋壽 (fl. 1165). In *Xuxiu siku quanshu* 續修四庫全書, vol. *zibu* 子部 1219. Shanghai: Shanghai guji chubanshe.

Chunqiu Zuozhuan zhu 春秋左傳注. 1981. Annotated by Yang Bojun 楊伯峻. Beijing: Zhonghua shuju.

Cook, Scott. 2015. "The Changing Role of the Minsiter in the Warring States: Evidence from the *Yanzi chunqiu* 晏子春秋." In *Ideology of Power and Power of Ideology in Early China*, edited by Yuri Pines, Paul R. Goldin and Martin Kern, 181–210. Leiden: Brill.

Davis, Richard L. 1996. *Wind Against the Mountain: The Crisis of Politics and Culture in Thirteenth-Century China*. Cambridge, MA.: Harvard University Press.

Defoort, Carine. 2015. "Heavy and Light Body Parts: The Weighing Metaphor in Early Chinese Dialogues." *Early China* 38: 55–77.

Dingjuan jiaozeng pingzhu wulun riji gushi daquan 鼎鐫校增評註五倫日記故事大全. 1594. Preserved in Sonkeikaku Bunko 尊經閣文庫, Maeda Ikutoku kai 前田育德會, Tokyo, Japan.

Ditmanson, Peter. 2007. "Venerating the Martyrs of the 1402 Usurpation: History and Memory in the Mid and Late Ming Dynasty." *T'oung Pao* 93.1: 110–158.

Elman, Benjamin A. 1993. " 'Where is King Ch'eng?' Civil Examination and Confucian Ideology during Early Ming, 1368–1415." *T'oung Pao* 79.1: 23–68.

_____. 2013. *Civil Examinations and Meritocracy in Late Imperial China. Cambridge*. MA: Harvard University Press.

Epstein, Maram. 2001. *Competing Discourses: Orthodoxy, Authenticity and Engendered Meanings in Late Imperial Chinese Fiction*. Cambridge, MA: Harvard University Press.

Fenlei hebi tuxiang jujie junchen gushi 分類合璧圖像句解君臣故事. Date unknown. Reprint of Yuan edition preserved in Tōyō Bunko 東洋文庫, Tokyo, Japan.

Fenlei hebi tuxiang jujie junchen gushi 分類合璧圖像句解君臣故事. 1990. In *Hekeben leishu jicheng* 和刻本類書集成, compiled by Nagasawa Kikuya 長澤規矩也 vol. 3. Shanghai: Shanghai guji chubanshe.

Fletcher, George P. 1993. *Loyalty: An Essay on the Morality of Relationships*. New York: Oxford University Press.

Fox, Ariel. 2015. "Southern Capital: Staging Commerce in Seventeenth Century Suzhou." Ph.D. dissertation. Harvard University.

Ge Quan 葛荃. 1998. *Zhengde zhi* 政德志. Shanghai: Shanghai renmin chubanshe.

Goldin, Paul R. 2008. "When *Zhong* Does Not Mean 'Loyalty.'" *Dao: A Journal of Comparative Philosophy* 7: 165–174.

Goyama Kiwamu 合山究. 2006. *Min Shin jidai no josei to bungaku* 明清時代の女性と文学. Tokyo: Kyuko Shoin.

Graff, David A. 1995. "The Meritorious Cannibal: Chang Hsün's Defense of Sui-yang and the Exaltation of Loyalty at the Age of Rebellion." *Asia Major* (Third Series) 8.1: 1–17.

Gujin hebi shilei beiyao houji 古今合璧事類備要後集. 1983. Compiled by Xie Weixin 謝維新 (fl.1257). In *Wenyuange Siku quanshu* 文淵閣四庫全書, vol. 939. Taipei: Taiwan shangwu yinshuguan.

Guochao dianhui 國朝典彙. 1955. Compiled by Xu Xueju 徐學聚 (*jinshi* 1583). In *Siku quanshu cunmu congshu* 四庫全書存目叢書, vol. *shibu* 史部 264. Tainan: Zhuangyan wenhua.

Guoyu jijie 國語集解. 2002. Compiled by Xu Yuangao 徐元誥. Beijing: Zhonghua shuju.

Hanshu 漢書. 1962. By Ban Gu 班固 (32–92), et al. Annotated by Yan Shigu 顏師古 (581–645). Beijing: Zhonghua shuju.

Hashimoto Soko 橋本草子. 1998. "Nichi koji no kanpon ni tsuite" 日記故事の版本について. *Kyoto Joshi Daigaku jinbun ronso* 京都女子大學人文論叢 46: 33–58.

⸻. 2006. "Nichi koji no genzon kanpon oyobi sono shuppan no haikei ni tsuite" 日記故事の現存刊本及びその出版の背景について. *Chūgoku: shakai to bunka* 中國: 社會と文化 21: 108–124.

He Guanbiao 何冠彪. 1997. *Sheng yu si: Ming ji shidafu de jueze* 生與死：明季士大夫的抉擇. Taipei: Lianjing.

Hsieh, Andrew 謝正光. 2004. "Qingchu zhongjun dianfan zhi suozao yu heliu: Shandong Laiyang Jiangshi xingyi kaolun" 清初忠君典範之塑造與合流: 山東萊陽姜氏行誼考論. In *Ming Qing wenxue yu sixiang zhong zhi zhuti yishi yu shehui. Xueshu sixiang pian* 明清文學與思想中之主體意識與社會 (學術思想篇), edited by Chung Tsai-chun 鍾彩鈞 and Yang Chin-lung 楊晉龍, 291–343. Taipei: Zhongyang yanjiuyuan.

Hutton, Eric L. 2014. *Xunzi: The Complete Text*. Princeton: Princeton University Press.

Jay, Jennifer W. 1991. *A Change in Dynasties: Loyalty in Thirteenth-Century China*. Bellingham, WA: Western Washington University.

Jiang Qing 姜清. 2000. *Jiangshi mishi* 姜氏秘史. In *Yuzhang congshu* 豫章叢書, edited by Tao Fulu 陶福履 and Hu Sijing 胡思敬, vol. *shibu* 史部 1. Nanchang: Jiangxi jiaoyu chubanshe.

Jingchuan xiansheng wenji 荊川先生文集. 1979. By Tang Shunzhi 唐順之 (1507–1560). Reprinted in *Sibu congkan* 四部叢刊. Taipei: Taiwan shangwu yinshuguan.

Junchen gushi 1990. See *Fenlei hebi tuxiang jujie junchen gushi* 1990.

Johnson, David. 1980. "The Wu Tzu-hsü Pien-wen and Its Sources." *Harvard Journal of Asiatic Studies* 40.1–2: 93–156; 465–505.

Li Mei 李玫. 2000. *Ming Qing zhi ji Suzhou zuojia qun yanjiu* 明清之際蘇州作家群研究. Beijing: Zhongguo shehui kexue chubanshe.

Li Wai-yee. 1993. *Enchantment and Disenchantment: Love and Illusion in Chinese Literature*. Princeton, N.J.: Princeton University Press.

_____. 2014. *Women and National Trauma in Late Imperial Chinese Literature*. Cambridge, MA: Harvard University Press.

_____. 2013. "Riddles, Concealment, and Rhetoric in Early China." In *Facing the Monarch: Modes of Advice in the Early Chinese Court*, edited by Garret P. S. Olberding. Cambridge, MA: Harvard University Asia Center.

Lin Su-chuan 林素娟. 2005. "Handai fuchou yiti suo tuxian de junchen guanxi ji zhongxiao guannian" 漢代復仇議題所凸顯的君臣關係及忠孝觀念. *Chengda zhongwen xuebao* 成大中文學報 12: 23–46.

Liu, James T. C. 1972. "Yüeh Fei (1103–1141) and China's Heritage of Loyalty." *Journal of Asian Studies* 31.2: 291–297.

Liu Chiung-yun 劉瓊云. 2012. "Diwang huanhun: Mingdai jianwendi liuwang xushi de yanyi" 帝王還魂: 明代建文帝流亡敘事的衍異. *Xin shixue* 新史學 23.4: 61–117.

_____. 2015. "Tiandao zhishu shangpin: *Zhongjing* zhi chuban yu mingdai zhong wenhua" 天道、治術、商品：《忠經》之出版與明代忠文化. In *Tushu zhishi jiangou yu wenhua chuanbo* 圖書、知識建構與文化傳播, edited by Hu Siao-chen 胡曉真 and Li Sher-shiueh 李奭學, 313–365. Taipei: Hanxue yanjiu zhongxin.

_____. 2016. "Qingchu *Qian zhong lu* li de shenti shengqing yu zhongchen jiyi" 清初千忠錄裏的身體、聲情與忠臣記憶. *Xiju yanjiu* 戲劇研究 17: 1–40.

_____. 2019. "Women keyi cong mingdai daode gushi leishu zhong du chu sheme: Zhishi bianji, wenhua wangluo yu tongsu zhongguan" 我們可以從明代道德故事類書中讀出什麼？知識編輯，文化網絡與通俗忠觀. *Xin shixue* 新史學 30.3: 1–73.

Lu Eting 陸萼庭. 1980. *Kunju yanchu shigao* 崑劇演出史稿. Shanghai: Shanghai wenyi chubanshe.

Lunyu yizhu 論語譯注. 1992. Annotated by Yang Bojun 楊伯峻. Beijing: Zhonghua shuju.

Mengzi yizhu 孟子譯注. 1992. Annotated by Yang Bojun 楊伯峻. Beijing: Zhonghua shuju.

Miya Noriko 宮紀子. 2006. *Mongoru jidai no shuppan bunka* モンゴル時代の出版文化. Nagoya: Nagoya Daigaku Shuppankai.

Nanxuan ji 南軒集. 1983. By Zhang Shi 張栻 (1133–1180). In *Wenyuange Siku quanshu* 文淵閣四庫全書, vol. 1167. Taipei: Taiwan shangwu yinshuguan.

Osawa, Akihiro 大澤顯浩. 2002. "Mingdai chuban wenhua zhong de 'ershisi xiao': lun xiaozi xingxiang de jianli yu fazhan" 明代出版文化中的「二十四孝」：論孝子形象的建立與發展. *Mingdai yanjiu tongxun* 明代研究通訊 5: 11–33.

Pines, Yuri. 2002a. *Foundations of Confucian Thought: Intellectual Life in the Chunqiu Period (722–453 B.C.E.)*. Honolulu: University of Hawai'i Press.

_____. 2002b. "Friends or Foes: Changing Concepts of Ruler-Minister Relations and the Notion of Loyalty in Pre-Imperial China." *Monumenta Serica* 50: 35–74.

_____. 2009. *Envisioning Eternal Empire: Chinese Political Thought of the Warring States Era*. Honolulu: University of Hawai'i Press.

_____. 2012. *The Everlasting Empire: The Political Culture of Ancient China and Its Imperial Legacy*. Princeton: Princeton University Press.

Qian zhong lu 千忠錄. 1989. By Li Yu 李玉 (ca.1590–ca.1660). Edited by Zhou Miaozhong 周妙中. Beijing: Zhonghua shuju.

Qian zhong lu 千忠錄. 2010. By Li Yu 李玉 (ca.1590–ca.1660). In *Fu Xihua cang gudian xiqu zhenben congkan* 傅惜華藏古典戲曲珍本叢刊, edited by Wang Wenzhang 王文章 and Liu Wenfeng 劉文峰. Beijing: Xueyuan chubanshe.

Rubin, Vitaly A. 1986. "A Chinese Don Quixote: Changing Attitudes to Po-i's Image." In *Confucianism: The Dynamics of Tradition*, edited by Irene Eber, 155–184. New York: Macmillan.

Sakai Tadao 酒井忠夫. 1958. "Mindai no nichiyō ruisho to shomin kyōiku" 明代の日用類書と庶民教育. In *Kinsei Chugoku kyōikushi kenkyū* 近世中國教育史研究, edited by Hayashi Tomoharu 林友春, 25–154. Tokyo: Kokudosha.

Sato Masayuki 佐藤將之. 2007."Guojia sheji cunwang zhi daode: Chunqiu zhanguo zaoqi 'zhong' he 'zhongxin' gainian zhi yiyi" 國家社稷存亡之道德: 春秋戰國早期「忠」和「忠信」概念之意義. *Qinghua xuebao* 清華學報 37.1: 1–33.

_____. 2009."Zhanguo zhongwanqi 'zhong' guannian zhi yanbian yu zhuanzhe ji qi sixiang yiyi" 戰國中晚期「忠」觀念之演變與轉折暨其思想意義. *Zhongyang daxue renwen xuebao* 中央大學人文學報 39: 55–98.

_____. 2010. *Zhongguo gudai zhong lun yanjiu* 中國古代忠論研究. Taipei: Guoli Taiwan daxue chuban zhongxin.

Schaberg, David. 1997. "Remonstrance in Eastern Zhou Historiography." *Early China* 22: 133–179.

_____. 2001. *A Patterned Past: Form and Thought in Early Chinese Historiography Cambridge*. MA: Harvard University Press.

_____. 2005. "Playing at Critique: Indirect Remonstrance and the Formation of *Shi* Identity." In *Text and Ritual in Early China*, edited by Martin Kern. Seattle: University of Washington Press.

_____. 2011 "Chinese History and Philosophy." In *The Oxford History of Historical Writing*, vol.1, edited by Andrew Feldherr and Grant Hardy, 395–414. Oxford and New York: Oxford University Press.

Shiji 史記. 1959. By Sima Qian 司馬遷 (ca. 145–90 BCE). Annotated by Pei Yin 裴駰, Sima Zhen 司馬貞 and Zhang Shoujie 張守節. Beijing: Zhonghua shuju.

Shuidong riji 水東日記. 1980. By Ye Sheng 葉盛 (1420–1470). Annotated by Wei Zhongping 魏中平. Beijing: Zhonghua shuju.

Sibau, Maria Franca. 2018. *Reading for the Moral: Exemplarity and the Confucian Moral Imagination in Seventeenth-Century Chinese Short Fiction*. Albany: State University of New York Press.

Standen, Naomi. 2007. *Unbounded Loyalty: Frontier Crossing in Liao China*. Honolulu: University of Hawai'i Press.

Struve, Lynn A. 2009. "Self-Struggles of a Martyr: Memories, Dreams, and Obsessions in the Extant Diary of Huang Chunyao." *Harvard Journal of Asiatic Studies* 69.2: 343–394.

Taihe zhengyin pu 太和正音譜. 1959. By Zhu Quan 朱權 (1378–1448). In *Zhongguo gudian xiqu lunzhu jicheng* 中國古典戲曲論著集成. Beijing: Zhongguo xiju chubanshe.

Tianma shanfang yigao 天馬山房遺稿. 1983. By Zhu Zhi 朱湽 (1486–1552). In *Wenyuange Siku quanshu* 文淵閣四庫全書, vol. 1273. Taipei: Taiwan shangwu yinshuguan.

Tianshun rilu 天順日錄. 1993. By Li Xian 李賢 (d. 1466). In *Guochao diangu* 國朝典故, compiled by Deng Shilong 鄧士龍. Edited by Xu Daling 許大齡 and Wang Tianyou 王天有, vol.2. Beijing: Beijing daxue chubanshe.

Van Els, Paul and Sarah A. Queen (eds.). 2017. *Between History and Philosophy: Anecdotes in Early China*. Albany: State University of New York Press.

Vankeerberghen, Griet. 2005–2006. "Choosing Balance, Weighing ("Quan" 權) as a Metaphor for Action in Early Chinese Texts." *Early China* 30: 47–89.

Wakeman, Frederic Jr. 1984. "Romantics, Stoics and Martyrs in Seventeenth-Century China." *The Journal of Asian Studies* 43.4: 631–665.

Wang Anqi 王安祈. 1986. *Mingdai chuanqi zhi juchang ji qi yishu* 明代傳奇之劇場及其藝術. Taipei: Taiwan xuesheng shuju.

Wang Gungwu. 1962. "Feng Tao: An Essay on Confucian Loyalty." In *Confucian Personalities*, edited by Denis Twitchett and Arthur F. Wright, 123–145. Stanford: Stanford University Press.

Wang Wenzhang 王文章 and Liu Wenfeng 劉文峰 (eds.) 2010. *Fu Xihua cang gudian xiqu zhenben congkan* 傅惜華藏古典戲曲珍本叢刊. Beijing: Xueyuan chubanshe.

Wang Zijin 王子今. 1999. *Zhong guannian yanjiu: yizhong zhengzhi daode de wenhua yuanliu yu lishi yanbian* 忠觀念研究：一種政治道德的文化源流與歷史演變. Changchun: Jilin jiaoyu chubanshe.

Wu Xinlei 吳新雷. 1996. *Zhongguo xiqu shilun* 中國戲曲史論. Nanjing: Jiangsu jiaoyu chubanshe.

Wuyue chunqiu 吳越春秋. 1989. In *Sibu congkan* 四部叢刊, *chubian* 初編 vol. 51. Shanghai: Shanghai shudian.

Xinke taicang cangban quanbu hexiang zhushi dazi riji gushi 新刻太倉藏板全補合像註釋大字日記故事. 2011. Compiled by Yang Qiao 楊喬 (Ming dynasty, date unknown). In *Mingdai tongsu riyong leishu jikan* 明代通俗日用類書集刊, vol. 14. Chongqing: Xinan shifan daxue chubanshe.

Xinqie leijie guanyang riji gushi daquan 新鍥類解官樣日記故事大全. 1990. Compiled by Zhang Ruitu 張瑞圖 (1570–1644). In *Hekeben leishu jicheng* 和刻本類書集成, compiled by Nagasawa Kikuya 長澤規矩也, vol. 3. Shanghai: Shanghai guji chubanshe.

Xinzeng tuxiang xiaoxue riji gushi daquan 新增圖像小學日記故事大全. 1566. Compiled by Yu Shao 虞韶 (fl. late 12th century). Expanded by Guan Xu 管昫 (fl. late 15th century). Preserved in Hōsa Bunko, Nagoya, Japan.

Xunzhi zhai ji 遜志齋集. 1979. By Fang Xiaoru 方孝孺 (1357–1402). In *Sibu congkan* 四部叢刊, vol. *zhengbian* 正編 73. Taipei: Taiwan shangwu yinshuguan.

Xunzi jijie 荀子集解. 1992. Annotated by Wang Xianqian 王先謙 (1842–1917). Edited by Shen Xiaohuan 沈嘯寰 and Wang Xingxian 王星賢. Beijing: Zhonghua shuju.

Yan Changke 顏常珂 and Zhou Chuanjia 周傳家. 1985. *Li Yu pingzhuan* 李玉評傳. Beijing: Zhongguo xiju chubanshe.

Yan Dunyi 嚴敦易. 1982. *Yuan Ming Qing xiqu lunji* 元明清戲曲論集. Zhengzhou: Zhongzhou shuhuashe.

Yanyuan ji 剡源集. 1985. By Dai Biaoyuan 戴表元 (1244–1310). In *Congshu jicheng chubian* 叢書籍成初編, vol. 2056. Beijing: Zhonghua shuju.

Yushi xueji 虞氏學記. Date unknown. Manuscript. Preserved in National Library of Korea, Seoul, Korea.

Zhang xiansheng jiaozheng Yang Baoxue Yizhuan 張先生校正楊寶學易傳. 2013. By Yang Wanli 楊萬里 (1127–1206). In *Zhongguo yixue wenxian jicheng* 中國易學文獻集成, vol. 31. Beijing: Guojia tushuguan chubanshe.

Zhang Ying. 2017. *Confucian Image Politics: Masculine Morality in Seventeenth-Century China*. Seattle: University of Washington Press.

Zhao Yuan 趙園. 2015. *Zhidu-yanlun-xintai: Ming Qing zhiji shidafu yanjiu xubian* 制度·言論·心態：明清之際士大夫研究續編. Beijing: Beijing daxue chubanshe.

Zhongjing xiangjie 忠經詳解. 1995. Attributed to Zheng Xuan 鄭玄 (127–200). Annotated by Tao Yuanliang 陶原良 (fl. early 17th century). In *Xuxiu siku quanshu* 續修四庫全書, vol. *zibu* 子部 933. Shanghai: Shanghai guji chubanshe.

Zhuzi yulei 朱子語類. 1986. By Zhu Xi 朱熹 (1130–1200). Compiled by Li Jingde 黎靖德 (fl. 1270). Edited by Wang Xingxian 王星賢. Beijing: Zhonghua shuju.

Zuo Tradition / Zuozhuan: Commentary on the "Spring and Autumn Annals". 2016. Translated and introduced by Stephen Durrant, Wai-yee Li, and David Schaberg. 3 vols. Seattle: University of Washington Press.

Zuozhuan. See *Chunqiu Zuozhuan zhu*.

7

Filial Piety as an Emotion in Late Imperial China

Maram Epstein

Given the foundational importance of filial piety (*xiao* 孝) to premodern Chinese constructions of self, there has been surprisingly little critical interest in reassessing the May Fourth judgment against filial piety as a despotic and anti-humanistic Confucian value that held China back from modernization.[1] Shortly after Lu Xun 魯迅 (1881–1936) published *Kuangren riji* 狂人日記 (Diary of a madman), Wu Yu 吳虞 (1872–1949) published "Chiren yu lijiao" 吃人與禮教 (Cannibalism and Confucian ethics), in which he discussed several instances of cannibalism in order to argue for the urgency of family reform.[2] Wu quickly followed with a series of essays that explicitly targeted filial piety as the ideology that underpinned the despotic nature of traditional Chinese society and government. In his essay, "Jiazu zhidu wei zhuanzhizhuyi zhi genju lun," Wu Yu described the traditional parallel ideologies of filial piety and loyalty as oppressive for the young and socially inferior.[3] In his 1920 essay "Shuo xiao" 說孝 (On filial piety), Wu Yu blamed the clan system and "inhumane rites" for injustice and for destroying lives over thousands of years.[4]

---

1   Notable exceptions include Hsiung Ping-chen 1994; Kutcher 1999; Chan and Tan 2004; Knapp 2005; Lu Miaw-fen 2005 and 2011; Brown 2007; Kindall 2016; Zhang Ying 2017.

2   Both were published in 1919. In Lu Xun 1981, vol. 1: 422–433; in Wu Yu 1990: 66.

3   家族制度為專制主義之根據論 (On the traditional family system as the basis for despotism), published 1917. In Wu Yu 1990: 7.

4   Published 1924. In Wu Yu 1990: 17.

Though largely forgotten now, Wu Yu was an influential May Fourth figure who was championed by Hu Shi 胡適 (1891–1962) as "the old hero from Sichuan who attacked Confucius and sons single-handedly" 四川省隻手打孔家店的老英雄; Hu Shi's phrase gave rise to the slogan "Down with Confucius and sons and save Confucius [from the misrepresentation of Confucianism]" 打倒孔家店，救出孔夫子.[5] Wu described filial piety as a ritual obligation that locked adult children into a subservient relationship with their parents and as a social structure that focused family resources on caring for the most senior generation of the family. He explicitly identified the need to produce a male heir to maintain ancestral lines, central to the concept of *xiao*, as being responsible for the twin evils of arranged marriage and polygyny. In his view, filial piety was inimical to social progress and the development of a modern nation state.

No doubt because of his acrimonious relationship with his father, Wu Yu went further than other May Fourth radicals in singling out filial piety as a symbol for all that was wrong with Confucian ideology.[6] However, he was not an exception. In another essay published in *Xin qingnian* 新青年 (New youth), Zhang Yaoxiang 張耀翔 (1893–1964) wrote a scathing attack on the absolute authority of parents to sell, kill or sacrifice their children and treat them like chattel rather than grant them personhood.[7] Perhaps the best-known May Fourth critique of filial piety is Lu Xun's reminiscence of reading an illustrated copy of the *Twenty-Four Exemplars of Filial Piety* when he was a child. He found the image of Old Master Lai 老萊子 humiliating (he plays the child and rolls on the floor so that his parents would not feel their age), but it was the illustration of Guo Ju 郭巨 digging a grave for his infant son in order to conserve dwindling resources for his mother that filled the child Lu Xun with horror: he feared his own father might want to demonstrate his filial loyalty to his mother in a similar fashion.[8]

---

5   Chow Tse-tsung 1994: 294.

6   Stapleton 2008: 135.

7   Zhang Yaoxiang 1918: 637.

8   Lu Xun, *Zhaohua xishi* 朝花夕拾 (1926). In Lu Xun 1981, vol. 2: 254–256.

The polemical rhetoric used by May Fourth writers presents the ritualized cardinal bonds that define Confucian ethics as artificial and dehumanizing, and frames ritual in an oppositional relationship to the genuine expression of emotions. Among the most artificial aspects of filial piety were mourning rites, an aspect of ritual life that was synonymous with *xiao*.[9] Shortly after the death of his mother in 1919, Hu Shi published an essay in *Xin qingnian* calling for the need to reform mourning rites. He treats the wearing of mourning robes as a metonym for mourning and as synonymous with the concept of filial piety itself. He declared: "My mother is the person I have revered and loved most in my life" 我生平最敬愛的一個人, but his discussion of mourning focuses only on the technical aspects of ritual, not its function in channeling emotions and making one's grief socially legible.[10] He comments that the wearing of mourning robes is a superficial remnant of the ancient rites, that it's just a way for people to put on a façade "to deceive themselves and others" 自欺欺人.[11] Only when people ask themselves why they are behaving in certain ways, and, in response, "strip away clean all manner of hypocritical ceremonies left by ancient funereal rituals" 把古喪禮遺下的種種虛偽儀式刪除乾淨 will they arrive at a system of mourning rites that approximates human emotions.[12] At no point in the essay does Hu Shi allow that mourning rites are a means to channel profound emotions and make them socially legible; they are merely an inherited set of practices that no longer meet the needs of modern life. This epistemological binary treating ritual performance as separate from the sincere expression of emotions continues to inform many modern views of traditional Chinese mourning practices.

---

9   One of the common meanings of *xiao* is "mourning apparel." For a description of ritualized mourning devoid of feelings in a May Fourth text, see Ba Jin's *Jia* 家 (Family, 1933). See Ba Jin 1962: 375–378.

10 Hu Shi 1919: 574.

11 Hu Shi 1919: 574.

12 Hu Shi 1919: 576.

Ever since the Han Emperor Hui 惠帝 (r. 195–188 BCE) first used filial piety as a standard for evaluating men's suitability to serve in the imperial bureaucracy, emperors claimed to "rule the world by filial piety" (*yi xiao zhi tianxia* 以孝治天下) to a greater or lesser degree. The system of imperial rewards established during the Han dynasty (206/202 BCE–220 CE) promoted the culture of self-abnegation and sacrifice associated with filial piety. Interest in the representation of filial piety, especially extreme acts exemplified by "exceeding the rites" (*guoli* 過禮), martyrdom, and child sacrifice, flourished during the Han and the Six Dynasties (220–589).[13] Buddhism introduced one of the most striking post-Han innovations to filial practices: based on Jataka tales that illustrate how the Buddha and his adepts transcend an attachment to the physical plane through acts of self-inflicted violence, desperate sons and daughters embraced flesh-slicing (*gegu* 割股) as a spiritual practice that enabled them to use their own flesh to prepare medicinal broths for parents suffering from seemingly incurable conditions.[14] Late-imperial writers often referred to flesh slicing as *yuxiao* 愚孝, a term that is typically translated as "ignorant filiality." However, a less biased reading of late-imperial sources reveals strong support for this practice, even among the elite, suggesting that a more accurate translation may be "common," as in the sense of unschooled filiality.[15]

Even as May Fourth ideology has trained us to be suspicious of filial piety as an artificial tool of social control promoted by the imperial state, a vastly different image of the place of filial piety in premodern China emerges when we read traditional texts. This is particularly true of the late-imperial period due to the survival of so many personal writings. The vast majority of late-imperial texts present filial piety—the values and practices

---

13   For exceeding the rites, see Knapp 2005: 137–164. For a sampling of cynical readings of these acts, see Elvin 1984; Holzman 1998; T'ien Ju-kang 1988: 159–161.

14   Qiu Zhonglin 1995; Yu Jimmy Yung Fung 2012: 62–68; Knapp 2014.

15   Chaves 1986: 454–460 and 466–468.

that define the bond between child and parent—as a core expression of the ethical and affective self, not as an externally imposed obligation.

Due to the impossibility of treating the complex history of filial piety in one essay, this chapter will focus primarily on the late-imperial period, with an emphasis on the 16th to 19th centuries. I have chosen this timeframe because of the extensive body of scholarship that discusses filial piety in early China, and because, until recently, filial piety has not been identified as a particularly important keyword for understanding the late-imperial period, except as a tool of state ideology. As more scholars are beginning to focus on the late-imperial meanings and practices of *xiao*, it is becoming apparent that rather than being a holdover virtue from earlier periods that was on its last gasp, filial piety reemerged as a vital and dynamic cultural value during the Ming (1368–1644) and Qing (1636/1644–1912) dynasties.[16]

1. *Xiao* in Early China

In its earliest usages in pre-Confucian China, *xiao* was closely related to ancestral sacrifices and was primarily used in its verbal sense meaning "to make offerings to the dead."[17] In contrast to the Shang (ca. 1600–ca. 1046 BCE), when sacrifices were typically directed toward a distant ancestor, during the Western Zhou (ca. 1046–771 BCE) these sacrifices began to be directed toward deceased figures closer to those performing the ritual. Named recipients included parents and ancestors, as well as brothers, friends, and matrimonial relatives; unnamed spirits could also receive sacrifices.[18] These early *xiao* rites had both political and ritual functions. In addition to ensuring the happiness of the ancestors, and thereby bringing

---

16   Although filial piety was an important aspect of women's virtue during this period, there is only enough space here to focus on its place in male culture. For discussions of filial daughters, see Epstein 2011 and Epstein 2019.

17   Knapp 1995: 197–200.

18   Ikezawa 1994: 19; Knapp 1995: 201.

physical and political good fortune to their living descendants, these rites also established political authority in ways that subordinated kinship to political structures.[19] As an extension of its emphasis on feeding the dead, *xiao* also took on the meaning of the feeding and support (*xiaoyang* 孝養) of living parents.[20] With the broadening of *xiao* from lineage rites to service to one's parents, it became a value shared by the elites and commoners.

Even as early Ru thinkers redefined filial piety as an innate capacity for affective and ethical actions, filial piety remained integral to the political order. As recorded in the *Lunyu* 論語 (hereafter, the *Analects*), *xiao* is associated with an internalized state of reverence (*jing* 敬) and the desire to emulate the ancestors and carry on their affairs as expressed in the phrase "filial thoughts" (*xiaosi* 孝思). The following passage illustrates how the *Analects* radically shifts the meaning of *xiao* away from the ritual act of providing food to the son's interior affective state:

> 子游問孝。子曰:「今之孝者,是謂能養。至於犬馬,皆能有養;
> 不敬,何以別乎?」

> Ziyou asked about *xiao*. The Master said: "The *xiao* of today is called being able to feed (*yang* 養) [your parents]. But dogs and horses are both able to get fed (*yang*). If there is no respect (*jing*), what is the difference?"[21]

This passage gave rise to the concept of reverent feeding (*gongyang* 供養) as a filial act.[22] The *Analects* also justified the three-year mourning period as being roughly parallel to the time that a child would be nursed ("held in his parents' bosom" 父母之懷). "Having received three years of loving care from parents" 三年之愛於其父母, the superior person loses all taste for pleasures for the three years after they die.[23] Another passage from the

---

19 Pines 2002: 190–197.

20 Knapp 1995: 201–202.

21 *Lunyu* 2.7. Also see *Shijing*, "Xia wu" 下武 (Mao 243); Knapp 1995: 204; and Defoort, Chapter 1 in this volume.

22 For a discussion of reverent feeding as a classical form of filial devotion, see Knapp 2005: 113–115.

23 *Lunyu* 17.21.

Analects defines *xiao* in purely ritual rather than affective terms. "When your parents are alive, serve them according to the rites. When they die, bury them according to the rites; make sacrifices to them according to the rites" 生事之以禮；死葬之以禮，祭之以禮.[24]

Mencius (ca. 4th century BCE) went further than the *Analects* in categorizing filial piety not as a subcategory of ritual behavior but as something innate to human nature.[25] In the passage which describes the "inherent abilities" and "inherent knowledge" (良能良知) that define the self as innately ethical, Mencius explains that an infant's love for its parents is innate and is the basis for that person's ability to love others. "There are no children carried in their parents' arms who do not know how to love their parents, or when grown, how to respect their elders. Loving one's parents, that is humanity" 孩提之童，無不知愛其親者；及其長也，無不知敬其兄也。親親，仁也.[26] This love of parents (or more literally, "treating them as one's most intimate relations,") is both an innate ability and a form of knowledge; as such, it is related to Mencius' vision of affective ethics, the "four sprouts" (*siduan* 四端) that are the basis for his doctrine that human nature is inherently good.[27] Mencius privileges childhood as a time when everyone has access to this innate moral knowledge; he defines the great person as one who has not lost his "childlike mind" 赤子之心.[28]

Even as *The Analects* and *Mencius* present filial piety as a core aspect of people's innate capacity to embody affective and ethical norms, other Warring States (453–221 BCE) and Han texts debate the relative status of filial piety and political loyalty. For Xunzi 荀子 (3rd c. BCE), in a chapter entitled "Zi Dao" 子道 (The way of a son), filial piety holds only the status of a minor virtue.[29] In keeping with Xunzi's belief that human nature is

---

24   *Lunyu* 2.5. Translation based on Leys and Nylan 2014: 5.
25   Izekawa 1994: 82–92.
26   *Mengzi* 13.15: 283–284.
27   *Mengzi* 3.6: 72–73 and 12.6: 262–263.
28   *Mengzi* 8.12: 174.
29   *Xunzi* 29: 529 ("Zi Dao" 子道).

driven by selfish urges and desires, no one, including fathers and lords, can be assumed to be morally infallible. The highest virtues are following the Way and righteousness; a filial son must be willing to disobey his father to help him avoid making any mistakes.[30] The contradiction between the two virtues of filial piety and loyalty was exposed most forcefully by Han Fei 韓 非 (d. 233 BCE), who attacked preoccupations with filial piety as "selfish" (*si* 私) and inimical to the common interests (*gong* 公) of the state: "a filial son to his father is a traitorous subject to his ruler" 夫父之孝子，君之背 臣也.[31] Among the followers of Confucius there was considerable debate about the relative status of loyalty to father and to ruler.[32] The *Lüshi chunqiu* 呂氏春秋 (composed ca. 239 BCE) and the highly influential *Xiaojing* 孝經 (Classic of filial piety), both roughly contemporaneous with the *Han Feizi*, tried to rectify the potential tension between loyalties to family and state by establishing the two as parallel.[33]

The Han rulers, under whose auspices *Xiaojing* was canonized, promulgated the vision of filiality as coterminous with demands of political loyalty. The establishment of filial piety as the foundational virtue in imperial China cannot be separated from the efforts of Han Emperor Wu 漢武帝 (r. 141–87 BCE) to legitimate his rule through the adoption of Confucianism as state ideology in 136 BCE. It was from this point that the *Xiaojing* was given canonical status and was circulated widely as a work of

---

30 *Xunzi* 29: 530 ("Zi Dao").

31 *Han Feizi* 49: 449 ("Wu du" 五蠹). Also see Nylan 1996: 3, and Goldin 2013: 7.

32 For the texts that postulate the superiority of mourning obligations to the ruler, see Brown 2007: 30–32. For examples of texts that prioritize mourning to one's father, see the "Liu de" 六德 manuscript from Tomb 1, Guodian 郭店, slips 26–29 (translated in Cook 2012: 791). On the relationship between filial piety and political loyalty, see also Liu, Chapter 6 in this volume.

33 Cf. Pines' discussion of *Xiaojing*, Chapter 5 in this volume. Although the exact relationship of these two texts is unclear, there are clear parallels between the *Xiaojing* and the much shorter "Xiaoxing" 孝行 chapter of the *Lüshi chunqiu* (14.1: 731–733). Both foreground filial piety as the root of a well-ordered society, promote filial piety as a means of achieving fame, and warn against harming the body that was given by one's parents. The strongest parallel is found in the "Tianzi" 天子 chapter of the *Xiaojing*.

Confucius, even though the text appeared relatively late and its teachings share very little with the personal ethical focus of the *Analects*. Schools employed specialists in the *Xiaojing*, and rewards were given to those who memorized the text.[34]

The construction of filial piety in the *Xiaojing* shifts the focus away from the Mencian emphasis on the natural emotions of the childlike mind. The *Xiaojing* canonized filial piety and political loyalty as parallel values by emphasizing the continuity between personal obligations to the family and public obligations to the state. Reflecting the construction of filial piety and loyalty as parallel, during the Han dynasty mourning clothes could be donned both for one's parents and one's patrons. Even before the Han state encoded fixed mourning periods for parents, it was a legal requirement that "former officials" mourn their bureaucratic sponsors for three years, effectively defining *xiao* as a political act.[35] During the late Han, it was still commonplace for men to carry mourning staffs, a ritual gesture reserved for the mourning of a parent, when mourning their patrons.[36] It was not until the 1st century CE that personal mourning for parents began to be practiced as the definitive filial act, and it was not until the 2nd century CE that the observance of three years of mourning for both mother and father was to become normative among the elite.[37]

After exemplary filial behaviors were made a core component of the "behavioral dossiers" (*xingzhuang* 行狀) compiled for candidates for official positions, ambitious men competed to participate in the new culture of extreme filial piety.[38] The more abject and impassioned the display of filial

---

34 Nylan 1996: 8.
35 Nylan 1996: 10.
36 Nylan 1996: 16; Brown 2007: 61–63.
37 Brown 2007: 22. In her review of extant Western Han records, Brown found only seven accounts of men observing the three-year mourning period for parents.
38 For examples, see Knapp 2005: 144–154; Holzman 1998: 192–195.

devotions, the more likely it was to bring fame.[39] Moreover, unique acts were read as demonstrations of sincerity rather than the rote following of ritual prescriptions. By the Eastern Han, the competitive culture of filial devotions as a route to fame encouraged sons to endure hardship or danger to provide for a parent's needs and desires. The wife of Jiang Shi 姜詩 (fl. 60 CE) sent her son to get river water for her mother-in-law because she liked to drink it. When he drowned, Jiang Shi's wife told the mother-in-law that her grandson had left to study so that she would not grieve for him.[40] During the Wei-Jin period, the elites recorded in the *Shishuo xinyu* 世說新語 (A new account of tales of the world) distinguished themselves from earlier worthies by rejecting ritual formalism as the standard of filial piety in favor of the unrestrained expressions of emotions.[41]

For most of the Han, the political loyalty owed one's patron trumped the personal loyalties owed parents or family. Because *xiao* mourning often referred to expressions of loyalty to patrons, Han usage of the term occludes distinctions between the political and the personal. This began to shift during the Eastern Han; shortly after the fall of the Han, Cao Pi 曹丕 (187–226) sparked a court debate when he asked to whom one should give the last dose of medicine when both one's father and lord were ill. By the end of the Wei, there was growing consensus that a greater loyalty was owed one's father than one's lord.[42] During the Six Dynasties, a period of political upheaval when Buddhism was establishing itself in China, the political and cultural capital associated with filial piety began to decline. By the early Tang (618–907), the elite had largely lost interest in compiling

---

39 For a discussion of fame, see the essay by Pines in this volume; on funerary ethics, see the essay by Graziani.

40 *Hou Hanshu* 84. 2783.

41 That Ruan Ji 阮籍 (210–263), one of the most eccentric sages of the bamboo grove, ignores convention when mourning his mother and consumes meat and wine but is nonetheless recognized as wracked by grief, confirms the importance of emotional expression over ritual formalism in Liu Yiqing's 劉義慶 (403–444) construction of sincere filiality. See *Shishuo xinyu* 548–550 (23.2), 552 (23.9), and 553 (23.11).

42 Tang Changru 1983: 236.

accounts of exemplary filial piety,[43] and the state had stopped using filial piety as a measure of a man's suitability for official service.[44] In the meanwhile, Confucian ethicists continued to promote the importance of *xiao* as crucial to lineage building, and neo-Confucian writers embraced it as a necessary ritual aspect of self-cultivation. By the Ming dynasty, filial piety was being increasingly framed in affective terms.

2. *The Twenty-Four Exemplars of Filial Piety* and the Popularization of Affective Filial Piety

Central to the sinicization of Buddhism was its adoption of filial piety. The Buddhist construction of filial piety frames it not as a ritual act but as an expression of love. The 7th-century *Fumu enzhong jing* 父母恩重經 (Sutra on the profound kindness of parents) states:

母見兒歡。兒見母喜。二情恩悲親愛。慈重莫復。

> When the mother sees the son, she is happy. When the son sees the mother, he is happy. The two feel kindness (*en* 恩), compassion, intimacy, and love [for each other]. There is nothing stronger than this kind of love (*ci* 慈).[45]

Buddhist filial narratives foreground the intimate emotional bonds between parents and children as the basis for filial piety. The narrative of the lachrymose Mulian who travels to Hell to rescue his mother's soul not only illustrates how sons are responsible for their mother's well-being after death, but more importantly introduced a new mode of filial heroism to China.[46] Despite the injunctions in the *Xiaojing* against harming the body given by one's parents, devoted sons and daughters borrowed techniques of self-inflicted violence

---

43   Knapp 2005: 61–70.

44   Xiao Qunzhong 2002: 93–96.

45   Translation from Cole 1998: 138.

46   Cole 1998: 159–191, esp. 176.

from Buddhism, such as blood writing and flesh cutting, and established them as filial acts endowed with powerful spiritual meanings.[47] Their goal was not to demonstrate transcendence of the physical plane as it was in Buddhism, but to use their own bodies to extend their parents' lives.

One of the most influential texts in popularizing the affective turn in filial narratives is *Ershisi xiao* 二十四孝 (Twenty-four exemplars of filial piety, hereafter *Twenty-Four Exemplars*); attributed to Guo Jujing 郭居敬 (fl. 1295–1321).[48] Illustrated versions of the *Twenty-Four Exemplars* were remarkably successful in promoting filial piety as a set of virtuous behaviors accessible to people from all levels of society. Although the biographies are drawn from famous early collections that emphasize the willingness of sons to sacrifice for filial ends, the versions in the *Twenty-Four Exemplars* shift the meaning of *xiao* away from its ritual roots. There are no biographies that focus on mourning rites per se or the kinds of abject self-denial that served as an index of virtue in early filial accounts. For example, in the earliest versions of the Guo Ju tale that had so scared young Lu Xun, Guo decides to sacrifice his newborn son in anticipation of how the boy might impede his ability to provide care for his mother and how she might be tempted to share her meager food with him; there is no threat of imminent starvation.[49] A 4th-century version preserved in the collection of supernatural tales *Soushen ji* 搜神記 notes that filial Guo had been born into a wealthy family and that his brothers were still wealthy.[50] This early Guo Ju acts out of a moral fanaticism in his unwillingness to approach his brothers for help. In contrast, the Guo Ju of the *Twenty-Four Exemplars* decides to sacrifice his son out of hopeless desperation.

---

47 Yu Jimmy Yung Fung 2012: 1, 62–88. The legend of the princess Miaoshan 妙善 exemplifies how the spiritual act of self-inflicted violence was incorporated into a mode of heroic filial sacrifice. See Jiang Zhiqi 2001: 31–44.

48 The earliest known use of the *Ershisi xiao* title appears in a manuscript found in Dunhuang dating to the Five Dynasties (907–960). See Knapp 2005: 197n21.

49 Yōgaku 2003: 56–57.

50 *Soushen* ji 11.82.

Unlike earlier accounts, the majority of biographies in the Yuan version of the *Twenty-Four Exemplars* focus on filial piety as a quotidian expression of emotional intimacy and caring. The collection introduces two exemplars not found in earlier compilations of filial accounts dating from the Six Dynasties and Tang dynasty. These narratives foreground simple gestures of caring rather than grand gestures of self-sacrifice: Lu Ji 陸績 sneaks oranges home to present to his mother rather than enjoy them himself, and Wang Pou 王裒 rushes to his mother's grave to comfort her spirit whenever there is a storm because she had feared thunder when alive. Although filial piety had not been particularly associated with childhood before this time, fourteen of the stories feature an exemplar who is a child or begin by mentioning that the protagonist had lost a parent when he was very young, effectively locating filial piety in the emotional bond between young child and the surviving parent. By claiming that the motivation for being filial is rooted in a young child's naïve feelings of love for a parent, these narratives position the exemplary filial acts as sincere rather than calculated, and as an expression of intimate family bonds rather than an expression of public ambitions.

3. Reformulations of Filial Piety during the Late Imperial Period

Those historians who approach the late imperial era for the ways it anticipates the modern have tended either to overlook late-imperial reformulations of filial piety, or discuss them in disparaging terms. One comprehensive study, which takes a generally positive view of filial piety as a unique feature of Chinese culture and ethics, summarizes the views of filial culture in late-imperial China as "becoming more extreme, despotic, and backward, enabling people to appreciate, based on their own actual life experiences, the bleakness and artifice of the feudal family system."[51] From

---

51   Xiao Qunzhong 2002: 113.

a teleological perspective that takes the modern concept of the autonomous individual as the ideal, the late-imperial culture of filial piety does look repressive. However, a recent body of scholarship reveals the extent to which filial piety was central to people's construction of themselves as ethical and affective subjects during the late Ming and Qing.[52]

Although filial piety was used as a powerful ideological tool of statecraft during the Ming and Qing dynasties, it also took on new philosophical and social meanings that could be used to resist state hegemony. Much of the renewed interest in the ritualized aspects of filial piety during this period, mourning rites in particular, can be traced to the adoption of the Cheng-Zhu 程朱 School of Principle (*lixue* 理學), commonly referred to as Neo-Confucianism, as state ideology by Ming Taizu 明太祖 (r. 1368–1398). Ritual, as a tool of self-cultivation, is particularly important to Cheng-Zhu Neo-Confucianism as a means of enabling individuals to overcome their subjective natures (a negative source of bias) and actualize the transcendent ideals associated with Principle (*li* 理). After the 16th century, a small minority among the elite promoted certain mourning practices associated with Neo-Confucianism, especially the use of mourning huts (*lumu* 廬墓), to bolster their local power and ritual superiority over their neighbors.[53] Some gazetteers began to honor "following the Confucian mourning rites" (*ruli* 如禮) as the definitive filial act.

However, the mid-Ming also witnessed a reaction against the hegemony of Cheng-Zhu teachings that was most powerfully articulated by Wang Yangming 王陽明 (1472–1529), who followed Mencius in grounding morality in human relationships.[54] This revived a philosophical interest in filial piety as an affective state that is innate to all children. By the late Ming and through the Qing, filial piety was being increasingly referenced in local

52   Hsiung 1994; Kutcher 1999; Lu Miaw-fen 2005, 2006, 2011; Lu Weijing 2013; Kindall 2016; Zhang Ying 2017.

53   Brook 1989: 481–482; Lu Weijing 2013.

54   Chow Kai-wing 1994: 3, 24, 44–46; Lu Weijing 2013: 21–48; Xiao Qunzhong 2002: 100–104; Kutcher 1999: 45–73; Lu Miaw-fen 2011: 35–46, 339–347; Zhang Ying 2013: 57.

gazetteers, personal writings, and fiction as a primary index of a person's affective ethics, a reformulation of the cardinal Confucian bonds as innate and rooted in the subjective mind rather than an external ideal derived from heavenly Principle. Late-imperial discourse increasingly framed filial actions in affective and subjective terms, although skeptical modern readers may regard the supposedly sincere displays of filial devotion from emperors and commoners alike merely as attempts to manipulate image and opinion.

The increasing philosophical and cultural importance of subjective emotions in Ming thought is conventionally traced to the influence of the School of the Mind, a philosophical movement that grew out of Wang Yangming's claim that the individual mind is the site of a morally perfect "innate knowledge" (*liangzhi* 良知). Scholarship in Western languages has tended to emphasize the importance of the School of the Mind as the starting point for the counterhegemonic Taizhou 泰州 School and the formation of the cult of *qing* 情 (emotions).[55] Significantly, however, Wang Ji 王畿 (1498–1583), a disciple of Wang Yangming who founded the Zhezhong 浙中 school, identified the idealized affective ethical values of "filial piety, fraternal love, loyalty, and trustworthiness" (孝弟忠信) as the emotions that are innate to all men and women.[56] As recently discussed by the intellectual historian Lu Miaw-fen, a group of mainstream scholars from the Zhejiang area identified the subjective site of moral consciousness as synonymous with filial piety.[57] Among these men was Luo Rufang 羅汝芳 (1515–1588; *jinshi* 1553), a philosopher who is well known to literary scholars because of his influence on Tang Xianzu 湯顯祖 (1550–1616), the author of the paean to *qing, Mudan ting* 牡丹亭 (Peony pavilion). In terms that will be familiar to those who know Tang Xianzu's preface to *Mudan ting*, Luo borrowed from Mencius and neo-Confucian cosmological thinking to construct filial piety as both an innate emotion and a transcendent cosmic

---

55   de Bary 1970.

56   Cited from Lu Miaw-fen 2011: 120n82.

57   Lu Miaw-fen 2006: 13; 2011: 120–121, 133–168.

force with generative powers.[58] Luo developed Wang Yangming's "pure knowing" into the "childlike mind" (*chizi zhi xin* 赤子之心) capable of manifesting "filial piety, fraternal love, and parental love" (*xiao, ti, ci* 孝弟 慈) without study and without effort.[59]

There are obvious parallels between Luo Rufang's concept of filial piety as an innate emotion, source of ethical action, and autonomous cosmic force, and the late-Ming cult of *qing*.[60] Feng Menglong 馮夢龍 (1574–1646) makes explicit the connection between filial piety and *qing*. In the first preface to his compendium *Qingshi leilüe* 情史類略 (Classification of love), he writes that *qing* is necessary for the sincere expression of the ritualized bonds of loyalty, filiality, chastity, and martyrdom:

情史氏曰：自來忠孝節烈之事，從道理上做者必勉強，從至情上出 者必真切。

The Historian of *qing* says: It has always been that acts of loyalty, filiality, chastity, and martyrdom are of necessity forced if they are performed out of principle, but will certainly be authentic if they emerge from absolute *qing*.[61]

Rather than identify *qing* as being in opposition to ritual norms, this passage characterizes *qing* as the subjective emotional energy that animates loyalty, filiality, chastity, and martyrdom in their ideal forms. By the 18th and 19th centuries, this construction of *qing* as being consistent with the cardinal Confucian bonds became mainstream in literati fiction.

The fall of the Ming dynasty raised the ideological importance of filial piety as a symbol of personal virtue and a tool of statecraft. The promotion of the core virtues of filial piety and chastity were central to the Qing government's self-legitimation, and the state expanded the scope of the

---

58 Lu Miaw-fen 2006: 6–12.

59 Cited from Lu Miaw-fen 2006: 23.

60 See Plaks, Chapter 8, and Li, Chapter 9 in this volume.

61 *Feng Menglong quanji* 20, 1: 41b. Patrick Hanan dates the compilation to before 1631, Hanan 1981: 95.

jingbiao 旌表 award system for the chaste and the filial. These imperial testimonials, monumentalized in arches and shrines, helped disseminate moral values in local communities.[62] However, interest in filial piety extended well beyond China's rulers and bureaucrats. Some members of the Han elite turned to mourning rites as a symbol of resistance during early Qing.[63] *Xiao* also became fully disseminated downward and the state encouraged local officials to seek out filial exemplars from among commoners. As a result, local gazetteers began to include highly sympathetic biographies of commoners (including beggars) who devoted themselves to the welfare of their parents. Auto/biographical writings and fiction included references to filial acts as details with outsized narrative significance.

3.1 Enacting Filial Piety at the Court

Even though both the Ming and Qing states embraced Neo-Confucianism, a philosophical system that emphasized ritual regulation in the expression of emotions, official discourse increasingly emphasized the affective basis for filial piety. The first Ming emperor (Ming Taizu) promoted Zhu Xi's 朱熹 (1130–1200) *Jiali* 家禮 (Family rituals) as the ritual standard for the practice of domestic rites, followed the prescriptions of *Jiali*, and had an altar, called the "Ancestral Worship Hall" (Fengxian dian 奉先殿), constructed to the left of the primary Qianqing Palace 乾清宮. There, again following *Jiali*, he made daily visits to present incense, and offered formal sacrifices at the new and full moon, festival days, and anniversary days.[64] Instead of focusing on such acts as Confucian ritual restoration after the Ming overthrew the Mongol Yuan dynasty, the official records foreground

---

62   Elvin 1984: 135–138; Rowe 2001: 433–440; Theiss 2004: 7, 39, and *passim*; Weijing Lu 2008: 4, 85–86 and *passim*.

63   Kutcher lists five studies on mourning produced by scholars born between 1368–1610, and seventy-nine works produced by scholars born between 1610–1780. Kutcher 1999: 73–87.

64   *Ming shi* 52: 1331.

the expression of natural emotions. The "Filial Thoughts" section of *Ming Taizu baoxun* 明太祖寶訓 (Veritable records of the Ming Taizu) describes a sacrifice Ming Taizu made on the anniversary of his mother's death. The entry records the emperor's personal reminiscences about his mother's final instructions to her sons when he was seventeen, long before the emperor established the new dynasty. As recorded, the emperor concluded his speech:

> 「今大業垂成，母不及見，語猶在耳，痛不能堪也。」因悲咽泣下，群臣莫不感惻。

> "Now the great enterprise is close to being completed, but my mother did not get to see it. Her words are still in my ears, and the pain is more than I can bear." He then cried in grief and shed tears, and all the officials were without exception moved and felt great sympathy.[65]

Although this may have been no more than mere performance on the part of an emperor known for acts of sadistic cruelty, the discursive attention in the official record to the affective details of how the rites were performed points to the cultural importance of these filial emotions. The emperor is depicted as an "everyman" feeling the loss of his mother; the final detail of the officials' reaction serves as rhetorical evidence of the emperor's sincerity. A separate entry recording the anniversary of his father's death states that the emperor "could not stop crying" (*qixia buzhi* 泣下不止).[66] The description of the emperor crying is significant; as Christoph Harbsmeier has written, "crying" (*qi*) is a personal and uncontrollable expression in contrast to "wailing" (*ku* 哭), which is public, ritualized, and deliberate.[67] It should be noted that this representation of Ming Taizu indulging in crying rather than wailing for his deceased father long predates the late Ming valorization of the natural emotions as the appropriate foundation for

---

65   "Xiaosi" 孝思 in *Ming shilu* 1:14a.

66   *Ming Taizu baoxun*, "Xiaosi" in *Ming shilu* 1: 13b–14a.

67   Harbsmeier 1999: 317–318.

ritual performance.[68] The "Filial Yearnings" section of *Ming Taizu baoxun* chronicles Taizu's dreams of his parents, dreams that caused him to cry out in his sleep.[69] These spontaneous and unmediated outbursts signaled the sincerity of emperor's filial devotion.

Taizu also encouraged his officials to give added consideration to the expression of the natural emotions in the Ming redaction of the ritual code. After the death of his beloved consort Chengmu 成穆 (1343–1374), Taizu directed that the code be revised so that every son could mourn his mother for the full twenty-seven-month mourning period even if she had been a concubine and even when his father was still alive. Although Zhu Xi's *Jiali* permitted an extended mourning period for mothers, the emperor mandated this change as justified by the natural affections.[70] The rescript justifies the necessity of changing the prescriptions found in the *Zhouli* 周禮 and *Yili* 儀禮, which permit only one year of mourning for a mother when the father is still alive: "The kindness of fathers and mothers is the same, and to differ to such degrees (in mourning) is truly at odds with human feelings" 父母之恩一也，而低昂若是，不情甚矣.[71] This statement shifts the emphasis of mourning rites from ritual, patrilineal duty to the natural emotions.

The natural emotions as a crucial aspect of filial piety were again central to the Great Rites Controversy (*da liyi* 大禮議), a major political struggle that pitted the newly enthroned Jiajing 嘉靖 emperor (r. 1521–1567) against many court officials. When the Zhengde 正德 emperor (r. 1506–1521) died without an heir, his young cousin was placed on the throne. However, rather than recognize his uncle, the Hongzhi 弘治 emperor (r. 1488–1506), as his imperial deceased father, and his natural parents as imperial uncle and aunt—as would have been politically expedient and ritually correct (as

---

68   For example, the late Ming official Lü Kun 呂坤 (1536–1618) wrote that the prescribed wailing detailed in the *Jiali* distorts the natural emotions; cited from Zhu Xi 1991: 82n53.

69   *Ming Taizu baoxun*, "Xiaosi," in *Ming shilu* 1: 15b–16a.

70   Ebrey 1991: 153.

71   *Ming shi* 60: 1493.

argued by the majority of officials at court)—the Jiajing emperor wished to raise his father's rank posthumously. In 1538, he finally succeeded in placing his father's spirit tablet in the Imperial Ancestral Temple, an honor reserved for emperors. Zhang Cong 張璁 (1475–1539), one of the officials who supported the emperor's position, argued that ritual sacrifices needed to be rooted in proper feelings (*renqing* 人情) in order not to be false.[72] Although the debates about natural emotions were rooted in a context of fierce partisan struggles, it is nonetheless significant to recognize the ways in which filial piety was being redefined in affective terms.

During the Qing dynasty, there was an expansion and intensification of the trends established during the Ming. Social and cultural historians have noted the ideological value of filial piety as a means for both the central state and local elites to order society and strengthen communities. This instrumental view of ritual as a tool of statecraft was articulated by the Qing censor Chen Zizhi 陳紫芝 (*jinshi* 1679), who advised that "for managing the world and pacifying the people there is nothing greater than ritual."[73] Filial piety was central to the vision of governing espoused by the Kangxi 康熙 emperor (r. 1661–1722). When mourning his grandmother, the Empress Dowager Xiaozhuang 孝莊, the deeply grieving emperor stated: "We rule the empire with filial piety. That is why I want to exemplify this principle for my ministers and my people—and for my own descendants."[74] However, as has been noted of the chastity cult, the Qing court was less focused on developing a universal and coherent orthodox interpretation of filial piety and mourning rites, than in deploying a flexible approach to promote its avowed mission of moral transformation (*jiaohua* 教化).[75]

The apogee of Qing efforts to govern by moral instruction has been dated to roughly 1725–1775, years that cover the Yongzheng (雍正,

---

72   Fisher 1990: 56, 58, 148, and 150.

73   Cited Smith 1990: 288.

74   *Qinding da Qing huidian*, j. 403, Kangxi 37. Translation cited from Silas Wu 1979: 52.

75   Elvin 1984: 135–138; Rowe 2001: 2–3, 433–440; Theiss 2004: 3, 7, 39, and *passim*.

1723–1735) and early Qianlong (乾隆, 1736–1795) reign periods when the state was extending its control over indigenous peoples on the northwest and southeast frontiers.[76] During this period, the state turned its attention to the moral transformation of the population as part of its efforts to maximize state control over economic resources, the official elites, and the multi-ethnic population. The Yongzheng emperor in particular fashioned his imperial role as activist; he saw the goal of the state as the "teaching and cultivation" (*jiaoyang* 教養) of the people.[77] At levels that exceeded the structures already put in place during the early Ming, the state invested in local administration and the establishment of local schools, granaries, community shrines, and systems of imperial rewards to inculcate virtue among the populace.[78] As part of his efforts to cultivate specific ethical behaviors, the Yongzheng emperor ordered the expansion of the *jingbiao* award system for chaste women and filial sons. Although vastly overshadowed by the chastity cult, state support for the cult of filial piety was robust; an average of thirty-one awards per year were made to filial sons between the years 1696–1873, a total of 5,533 awards.[79]

Compared to their predecessors, Qing rulers held a fundamentally different understanding of how the ritual code should function as a tool of ideological control. From a Confucian perspective, proper ritual performances had an important symbolic function. Not only are they important for confirming the Heavenly mandate, they also exemplified a basic respect for the Confucian ritualized hierarchies upon which the entire social order was based. No one, at any level of society, was exempt from mourning rituals; as a universal ethical expectation, mourning rites helped construct a sense of cultural coherence that unified the center and margins of the empire. The early Manchu emperors, however, treated the

---

76   Rowe 2001: 1, 434–438 and *passim*.

77   Theiss 2004: 35.

78   See Zelin 1984; Theiss 2004: 30, 44.

79   Lu Miaw-fen 2011: 36.

performance of mourning rites as an expression of personal bonds; Han officials, in response, saw this as a rejection of core Confucian beliefs about the ethical and religious power of ritual performance. Han court officials objected strenuously in 1688 when the Kangxi emperor rejected ritual protocol—he insisted on honoring his grandmother by cutting off his queue, a Manchu rite reserved for the mourning of a father or grandfather, and he violated Chinese precedents by mourning her for a full twenty-seven months, rather than the twenty-seven days as was the established practice from previous dynasties.[80] The eclectic blend of mourning rites employed by the Kangxi emperor highlighted the personal and private nature of his mourning as an expression of his affections; it also revealed his comparative lack of concern for the hierarchical distinctions undergirding mourning rites, especially public state mourning.[81] Han officials viewed the Manchu failure to respect the existing ritual practices as an attack on Han culture; this had the effect of transforming mourning rites into a potent symbol of Han-Manchu political and cultural differences.

The Manchu cultural emphasis prioritizing the expression of emotions over ritual norms may explain the Qianlong emperor's personal cult of filial piety directed at his mother.[82] In 1735, following the deaths of his formal mother, Empress Xiaojingxian 孝敬憲 (d. 1731), and his father, the Yongzheng emperor (d. 1735), the Qianlong emperor honored his birth mother, a consort who had entered the imperial harem at a relatively low status, as Empress Dowager Chongqing 崇慶 (1692–1777).[83] His filial ministrations to her, commemorated in painted albums he commissioned, helped define the moral tenor of his reign; in this, he consciously modeled himself on his grandfather, the Kangxi emperor, for whom filial piety was "an intensely felt emotional commitment" and a means to express his

---

80   Silas Wu 1979: 52

81   Kutcher 1999: 92–97.

82   Crossley 1999: 141.

83   Chen Baozhen 2014: 134.

"intense love and respect" for his grandmother.[84] Since the Kangxi emperor had taken his grandmother on his imperial tours, the Qianlong emperor too made his mother central to the symbolism of four of his extravagant southern tours, the first of which was planned to coincide with her 60th birthday in 1751. The emperor arranged for his mother to accompany him on many of his travels and he arranged for her to stay near him whenever he traveled to and from the court.[85] In Beijing, at the site of the Summer Palace, he created an elaborate vista, building her a Buddhist temple at the renamed Longevity Mountain (Wanshoushan 萬壽山). For her 70th birthday, he spent over 70,000 taels constructing and rebuilding temples in the suburbs around Beijing.[86] One historian describes the Qianlong emperor's celebrations of his mother's birthdays toward the end of her life as "veritable orgies of filial solicitude."[87]

Even as the Manchu emperors made their personal filial practices central to how they fulfilled their public roles as ruler of all under Heaven, they developed a new policy of "observing mourning at one's post" (*zairen shouzhi* 在任守制) in order to prioritize the service of high officials to the state over the observance of their personal filial obligations. While the policy of *duoqing* 奪情 that enabled an official "to cut short his emotions" and petition to return to his post before the twenty-seven-month mourning period was over can be traced to the Tang, its use was considered exceptional and had been largely limited to military officials during times of crises.[88] While some officials were no doubt happy to hold on to their positions, the refusal of the Qing state to allow high officials leave to mourn their parents was an inflammatory affront to Han sensibilities: not only was mourning viewed as a moral obligation to one's parents, but mourning leave was considered a right. The policy of curtailing or suspending an official's

---

84   Wu, Silas 1979: 9.
85   Kahn 1971: 88–92; Chen Baozhen 2014: 110.
86   Chen Baozhen 2014: 130–131.
87   Kahn 1971: 96.
88   Kutcher 1999: 25.

personal mourning for a parent became fully standardized under the Yongzheng emperor; on a case by case basis, officials would be given leave to return home or be told to "observe mourning at their posts."[89] Although the Qianlong emperor repeatedly published edicts stating his desire to limit the practice of "observing mourning at one's post," in practice, his court continued to deny mourning leave to local officials, such as those responsible for collecting taxes.[90]

Tensions over how mourning was to be observed signaled a clear breakdown of the accepted understanding of filial piety and loyalty to the state as parallel and mutually constitutive values.[91] Earlier in the dynasty, Ming loyalists had viewed the Manchu attack on mourning rites as an assault on Han culture, and there had been a marked surge of interest in research on mourning rites even by scholars who came of age after the fall of the Ming. The political and cultural climate of the Qing focused attention on mourning rituals as a powerful symbol of Chinese identity.[92] Seen from this perspective, evidential research on mourning rites came to represent a highly personal and local expression of resistance to the Qing state appropriation of filial discourse and practices. Thus, rather than framing individual performances of filial piety during the late-imperial era as an extension of state ideology, it may be more productive to focus on its local and personal meanings.

3.2 Representations of Filial Piety in Fiction

It is easy to dismiss invocations of filial piety in the official record as no more than acts of image politics; the frequency with which writers used filial piety as a theme in less regulated discourses suggests its cultural and sentimental resonance. Although filial piety appears as a minor theme in

---

89   Kutcher 1999: 142.
90   Kutcher 1999: 150n100.
91   Kutcher 1999: 120.
92   Chow Kai-wing 1994: 44 and 91.

many 16th-century novels, sometimes as a marked absence—most notably in *Jin Ping Mei* 金瓶梅—it became much more prominent by the 17th and 18th centuries.[93] The dystopian late-Ming, early-Qing novel *Xingshi yinyuan zhuan* 醒世姻緣傳 (Marriage bonds to awaken the world), a work likely influenced by *Jin Ping Mei*, places idealized depictions of the filial son Chao Liang 晁梁 in structurally significant chapters.[94] By the 18th century, filial piety became a dominant theme in many literati novels. The Manchu imperial cult of filial piety directed at mothers seems to be reflected in the 18th-century literati novel *Yesou puyan* 野叟曝言 (A country codger's words of exposure; by Xia Jingqu 夏敬渠, 1705–1787), a rambling work that features a heroic Confucian protagonist who makes his filial devotions to his mother central to his political vision for saving the empire.[95] *Qilu deng* 歧路燈 (Lantern at the crossroad; by Li Lüyuan 李綠園, 1707–1790) places filial piety at the center of its narrative about moral regeneration. Although *Rulin waishi* 儒林外史 (The scholars; by Wu Jingzi 吳敬梓, 1701–1754) has traditionally been interpreted as a satire of 18th-century China, it takes ritual, especially mourning rites, seriously.[96] Wu Jingzi rewrote the Wang Mian 王冕 character of the prologue chapter to make him an exemplary filial son; the depictions of how characters observe mourning for parents forms a figural chain that links many of the scenes. Du Shaoqing 杜少卿 is the character in *Rulin waishi* who has been identified as an autobiographical projection of Wu Jingzi. The motif that animates Shaoqing's characterization is his eagerness to respond when someone appeals to his filial sensibilities.

Although Cao Xueqin's 曹雪芹 (c. 1715–c. 1763) unfinished manuscript *Shitou ji* 石頭記 (Story of the stone) erases many aspects of normative

---

93   Despite the absence of filial piety as an explicit theme in *Jin Ping Mei*, the commentator Zhang Zhupo 張竹坡 (1670–1698) imposes a filial reading in his prefatory essay "Kuxiao shuo" 苦孝説 [On unrelenting filial piety] in order to argue for the moral and literary seriousness of the novel. *Zhang Zhupo piping Jin Ping Mei*, 19.

94   Epstein 2001: 134. See *Xingshi yinyuan zhuan*, chapters 36 and 49.

95   Epstein 2001: 236–238.

96   Shang Wei 2003.

filial culture from its rich descriptions of life in the elite Jia family, the last forty chapters of the 120-chapter *Honglou meng* 紅樓夢 (Dream of the red chamber; published 1791), as well as its earliest sequel, *Hou Honglou meng* 後紅樓夢 (Later dream of the red chamber; published 1796, by Xiaoyaozi 逍遙子), reintegrate filial piety into descriptions of the quotidian life of the Jia family.[97] The 19th-century novels *Jinghua yuan* 鏡花緣 (Flowers in the mirror; by Li Ruzhen 李汝珍, ca. 1763–1830) and *Ernü yingxiong zhuan* 兒女英雄傳 (A tale of heroic lovers; by Wen Kang 文康, fl. 1821–1850, first extant edition dated 1879), which were influenced by *Honglou meng*, also make expressions of filial piety central to their fictional worlds.[98] The *tanci* 彈詞 novel *Tianyuhua* 天雨花 (The heavens rain flowers, published 1804) presents the daughter-father bond as more important than the female protagonist's relationship with her husband.[99]

There is only space here to analyze the depiction of filial piety in one early-Qing short story written by Li Yu 李漁 (1610–1680), an author who is known for his witty reversals of narrative clichés. Li Yu's fiction reflects the importance of the cult of *qing* values in the promotion of romantic love as a life goal and in his many playful inversions of normative gender and sexual roles. Li Yu's seemingly preposterous story, "The Nativity Room" (*Shengwo lou* 生我樓; dated to 1657 or 1658) depicts filial piety as a powerful technology of self, a means to actualize one's adult identity.[100]

In the story, an adult orphan named Yao Ji 姚繼 sees an impoverished old man selling himself in the market and out of compassion decides to adopt him as a father. Yin Hou 尹厚, the old man, is actually a wealthy but childless farmer; he had built a tower in which to conceive a son, but when the boy was a toddler he disappeared, seemingly the victim of a wild animal.

---

97   For a discussion of the treatment of the theme of filial piety in these texts, see Epstein 2019, Chapter 5.

98   Guida 2006; Epstein 2001: 297–299.

99   Epstein 2011; Hu Siao-chen 2005; Li Wai-yee 2014, 207–230.

100 For a translation of the story, see Hanan 1992: 221–249. The translation of the title here follows Hanan. The term "technology of the self" comes from Foucault 1997: 223–251.

In order to ensure that he finds an heir who will not "deceive him with false affections," Yin Hou dresses as a poor beggar, travels to a market so distant that he will not be recognized, and puts himself up for sale as a father for the outrageous sum of ten taels.[101] Despite Yin Hou's self-presentation as a useless, penniless, and cantankerous old beggar, Yao Ji is delighted to establish him as his father since Yao Ji sees himself as incomplete, socially and morally. As an orphan, Yao Ji feels the lack of a father who could help him "be a good person" (*zuo ge haoren* 做個好人). Furthermore, without a parent to negotiate for him, Yao Ji has been unable to marry and establish a family of his own. When the two become separated during the chaos at the end of the Song dynasty, Yao Ji is forced to buy one of the many women who have been bundled up in sacks in a "human market." Hoping to find a wife, Yao Ji selects one of the sacks. When he discovers that the woman inside the sack is too old to be suitable as a wife, Yao Ji establishes her as his mother. By the end of the story, Yao Ji's willingness to embrace the role of filial son has not only gained him a mother and father, but it also reunites him with the girl with whom he had fallen in love but had been unable to marry because of his orphan status. In the kind of plot twist common to *huaben* stories, when Yao Ji finally arrives at Yin Hou's home, he discovers that the old woman he had purchased is Yin Hou's wife, and, through a birth defect, it is revealed that he is Yin Hou's biological son.

The odd title of the story, *Shengwo lou*, which might more literally be translated as "the tower of giving birth to myself/ the tower where I gain life," or "the tower where I procreate," raises the question of who, exactly, is being reproduced in this story. At first reading, the "I" seems to refer to the father Yin Hou, since he builds the tower precisely to reproduce and to live on as an ancestor through the son he hopes to sire. However, the "I" even more logically refers to the son who has suffered from a truncated identity until he completes himself by becoming a filial son. With no identifiable father, Yao Ji had lost both his social and ritual identities and would be

---

101 *Li Yu quanji* 4: 254.

cut off from future progeny. As suggested by the title, Yao Ji's creation of himself as a filial son is ultimately generative: his parents may have given birth to his physical body, but he is born into his adult identities as son, husband, and father, only through his innate desire to be filial. It is this act, more than his marriage, that literally enables him to "be a good person." "The Nativity Room" illustrates how filial piety functions positively as a technology of self that enables Yao Ji to transform himself into a fully realized social male endowed with affective and ethical subjectivity.

3.3 Filial Narratives in Qing Local Gazetteers: From Ritual to Sentiment

There is likely no better source for identifying what acts were associated with exemplary filial piety during the late-imperial period than local gazetteers. Even though local gazetteers were produced to meet both local and state needs, they largely reflect local interests.[102] Because gentry at the local level had a fair degree of editorial autonomy in their selection and presentation of the types of acts they wished to honor as exemplary, comparing roughly contemporaneous gazetteers produced in different areas can provide data on regional variations in the representation of filial piety. Gazetteers also enable us to see to what extent filial piety existed as a lived value beyond the elite strata of society during the late-imperial period. Many modern scholars are rightfully suspicious of the reliability of official records and point to the broad gap between discourse and practice.[103] While I agree that we should be careful not to confuse the written record with actual practice, it is possible to use gazetteers to demonstrate that during the 18th

---

102   Dennis 2015: 3, 64–70.

103   For example, in a study of the representation of filial piety in gazetteers from the Jiangnan area, historian Yu Xinzhong argues that the increased presence of filial exemplars in local gazetteers is primarily a response to the official efforts to promote filial piety and should not be taken as evidence that people had become more filial than they had been during the Ming. See Yu Xinzhong 2006: 21.

and early 19th centuries, local gazetteers increasingly focused on the affective and personal meanings of exemplary filial acts. Although filial piety was promoted in a top-down effort by the state, local biographies show that it found a receptive audience and was embraced at all levels of society as a lived and deeply personal value.

In order to highlight broad patterns in regional differences appearing in local gazetteers, I draw examples from two regions: the more ritually conservative Tai'an prefecture in Shandong, and several counties in Jiangnan.[104] Because Tai'an prefecture lies fifty miles to the north of Qufu, the birthplace of Confucius and the center of the cult of Confucius, and is home to Mount Tai, one of the five sacred mountains of imperial China, it is not surprising that the gazetteers produced here reflect a proudly conservative construction of filial piety that foregrounds ritual practice. As shown in Table 1, a diachronic reading of six Tai'an gazetteers printed between 1554 and 1929 illustrates the increasing interest, peaking in the mid-18th century, in documenting filial piety as a category of virtue. The right hand column of the table documents the number of filial exemplars who are honored for acts of ritualized mourning, living in a mourning hut and/or observing, at a minimum, the full twenty-seven month mourning period.

Table 1: Tai'an Gazetteers

Year	Section title	Number of filial biographies/Total number of biographies	Percentage of filial exemplars honored for ritualized mourning
1554	Personages 人物	1/34 (3%)	100%
1671	Filial and Righteous 孝義	7/7 (100%)	57%
1760	Filial and Righteous	77/152 (51%)	48%
1782	Filial and Righteous	23/55 (42%)	39%
1828	Filial and Righteous	7/8 (87.5%)	57%
1929	Filial and Righteous	38/144 (26%)	29%

---

104   Epstein (2019) contains more extensive discussions of the regional and diachronic differences in biographies of filial sons and daughters compiled in local gazetteers.

The 1554 Ming gazetteer contains just one section of male biographies grouped under the generic title "Personages" (*Renwu* 人物); of the thirty-four biographies, only the final entry is memorialized for his filial behavior. Zhang Yi, a scholar, fulfilled a number of ritualized filial acts: he was studious and sincere in his labors to care for (*laoyang* 勞養) his parents, never tiring during winter or summer. He retreated to a mourning hut for the full twenty-seven-month period for both his father and mother.[105] The editors of the 1671 edition insert a subheading entitled "Filial and Righteous," which appears in all subsequent editions of the gazetteer.

The ritual practice of withdrawing to a mourning hut is one of the most common filial practices recorded in the Tai'an and Qufu gazetteers. Although the term *lumu* 廬墓 does not appear in the earliest compilations of rites, the ritual basis for the practice was established in the *Liji*, which details that male mourners should live in a hut (*lu*) covered in grasses, and sleep on a straw mat, using a clod of earth for a pillow.[106] According to Lu Weijing, there was a resurgence of interest in the practice of *lumu* during the 17th century. She cites the efforts of Feng Shaoxu 馮少墟 (1556–1627), an official and follower of Wang Yangming, who attracted large audiences to his public lectures in which he highlighted filial piety as a concrete way to pursue the way of the sage kings Yao and Shun. For Feng, the practice of living in mourning huts was a core expression of how to be filial, and he disseminated the names of both elite and non-elite men who observed the practice.[107] J. J. M. de Groot (1854–1921), an historian of Chinese religions who was in the Xiamen area in the 1880s, commented that he neither saw nor heard of anyone living in a mourning hut during his time in China, and suggests that the practice might have been replaced by keeping watch over the corpse and sleeping on mats beside the coffin until the burial.[108] Infrequent references to mourning huts

---

105 *Taishan zhi* 1554, 4: 30a.
106 *Liji jijie* VIII.3: 202 ("Tan Gong shang" 檀弓上).
107 Lu Weijing 2013: 164–170.
108 de Groot 1989 (1894), vol 2.1: 794.

do appear in the Qianlong-era Tingzhou and the 1830 Zhanping gazetteers of Fujian. As we shall see, the ritual and social importance of residing in a mourning hut differed by region, but the data from sets of gazetteers from the same region supports de Groot's observation that the practice was much less central to mourning observances by the late 19th century.

Interest in documenting exemplary filial piety peaked in the 1760 Tai'an gazetteer. The "Filial and Righteous" section of the 1760 gazetteer contains over 150 biographies, about half of them commemorating filial sons. Of these, the majority focuses on some aspect of ritualized mourning, particularly the practice of living in a mourning hut (37%), becoming gaunt with grief (as prescribed in the *Liji*), or observing the full twenty-seven-month period of mourning. It is noteworthy, however, that in comparison to the two earlier editions, a number of the biographies reflect the narrative influence of the *Twenty-Four Exemplars*. The following biography is modeled after the story of Dong Yong 董永, who indentured himself to buy a coffin for his father:

> 趙成美新泰人。幼孤，貧為人傭工。跣足裸體而母之衣 [illegible] 無缺。母瞽不能自爨。每晨起作食食母，然後為出力。作數十年無怠。母死典身買棺以葬。
>
> Zhao Chengmei of Xintai lost his father when young. He was very poor and worked for others as a servant. Though he went barefoot clothed in tattered rags, his mother did not lack for [food and] clothing. His mother was blind and could not cook for herself. He got up every morning and prepared food for his mother and then left to go to work. He did this for several decades without tiring of it. When his mother died, he indentured himself to buy a coffin in order to bury her.[109]

This biography contains no references to ritualized acts of filial piety; instead it heightens the pathos of Chengmei's filial acts by focusing on his devotions to his blind mother despite his poverty.

---

109 *Tai'an fu zhi* 1760, 18: 52b–53a.

Similar to narratives in the *Twenty-Four Exemplars*, providing food for one's parents is a major theme of the biographies in the Tai'an gazetteers. One son provided his mother with delicacies (*ganzhi* 甘旨) and shielded her from knowledge of the famine of 1615 while he and his wife subsisted on tree leaves and bark.[110] One of the most unusual features of this gazetteer is that even though it contains three examples of sons who slice their flesh for a parent, the narratives frame it as a type of reverent feeding, explaining that the sons were too poor to purchase meat for their ill mothers who craved a nourishing broth.

Despite the ritual focus of most filial biographies in the Tai'an gazetteers, by 1760 the compilers began to show greater interest in the emotional motivations behind filial acts, as in the following biography. When his parents fell ill in 1657, the student Wang Changji served them both tirelessly. He even tasted his father's feces–mimicking Yu Qianlou 庾黔婁 of the *Twenty-Four Exemplars*. After his parents died, Changji stamped his feet, wailed, refused food for several days, all as prescribed by the *Liji*, and then fell ill. On the day of the burial, Changji faced their grave and could not bear to return home. In the depth of winter, when there was snow and ice everywhere, members of his lineage urged him to return home, but he did not comply. In what is surely an embellishment to the story, since he was likely to be the only one staying out at the lineage cemetery during the harsh winter, the biography describes Changji opening his eyes wide and staring for a long time; he then repeatedly called for his parents and died. He received official honors in 1732.[111] Even though Wang Changji fulfilled a number of conventional ritual acts associated with mourning, the narrative focus is on his affective state. His decision to stay at the cemetery is motivated by his emotions ("he could not bear

---

110   *Tai'an fu zhi* 1760, 18: 40b. A similar detail appears in scene 21 of Gao Ming's 高明 (?1305–?1369) opera *Pipa ji* 琵琶記 in which the filial Zhao Wuniang gives her parents-in-law rice while she eats chaff.

111   *Tai'an fu zhi* 1760, 18: 49a–b.

to return home," *bu ren gui* 不忍歸) rather than a commitment to ritual prescription. By dramatizing the tension between Changji and the relatives who want to protect him, the narrative highlights his passionate resolve to stay beside his parents' tombs, despite the frigid weather. The detail that he dies calling out to his parents is a motif repeated in many narratives that focuses the readers' attention on the primary affective bond connecting adult child to parent. Although a son's most important filial role was to maintain ancestor worship, through his own efforts and those of his son(s), a dramatic focus on the death of the filial child was becoming increasingly foregrounded as a powerful expression of the affective filial bond in exemplary biographies.

A comparison of gazetteers from different regions demonstrates the extent to which filial culture was localized. The records of filial sons included in the gazetteers from Wujin 武進 and Yanghu 陽湖 counties reveal striking contrasts with the biographies in the Tai'an gazetteers because of their relative lack of interest in filial piety as a ritual act. Wujin and Yanghu counties, part of Changzhou prefecture in Jiangsu province, are nestled in China's cultural core on the northwest corner of Lake Taihu, between Suzhou and Yangzhou. A diachronic look at the gazetteers published here illustrates the tremendous explosion of interest in compiling filial exemplars during the Qing.

Table 2: Wujin-Yanghu Gazetteers[112]

Year	Number of filial biographies in the "Filial and Fraternal" (*xiaoyou* 孝友) section	Number of references to mourning huts	Number of references to flesh-slicing (*gegu* 割股)
Wanli 1573–1620	17/29 (59%)	2/17 (12%)	4/17 (24%)
1765	40/47 (85%)	4/40 (10%)	16/40 (40%)
1842	285/310 (92%)	26/285 (9%)	185/285 (65%)
1888	27/30 (90%)	2/27 (7%)	6/27 (22%)

---

112   In order to save space, I refer to these counties as a unit since they published a joint gazetteer in 1842 and 1888. The Wanli and 1765 gazetteer are limited to Wujin county.

The striking increase of filial exemplars in the 1842 edition is largely due to the appended list of 142 names of men who committed *gegu* for parents, stepmothers, grandparents and even a teacher.[113]

Most modern discussions of flesh-slicing condemn it as a heterodox and marginal practice. The evidence from gazetteers from the Jiangnan area as well as non-official elite writings, however, reveals widespread elite sympathy and support for the practice. One of the most intriguing findings of a comparative reading is the range of attitudes toward filial flesh-slicing in gazetteers from different regions. Even though the imperial state tried repeatedly to ban flesh-slicing, it is one of the dominant forms of exemplary filial piety recorded in gazetteers from the Jiangnan area. In 1652, the court of the Shunzhi emperor issued a rescript continuing the ban on granting *jingbiao* awards to those who practiced filial flesh-cutting or other acts that might endanger life.[114] In 1728, the Yongzheng emperor wrote a lengthy memorial debating whether to grant *jingbiao* honors to a son who had died after cutting out part of his liver to make a stew for his mother. He refers to the practice of cutting out a piece of the thigh or liver to save a dying parent as *yuxiao*, "common/ignorant filial piety," and cites Han Yu 韓愈 (768–824), Zhu Xi, the *Xiaojing*, Mencius, and Confucius, to argue that the practice of filial flesh-cutting is unorthodox. However, despite this marshaling of arguments against harming the body given to each child by his or her parents, the memorial ends up sympathizing with the son: "his urgent desire to save his mother was indeed exceptional" 而其迫切救母之心，實屬難得.[115] Toward the end of the memorial, the Yongzheng emperor observes sympathetically: "It is true that for chaste martyrs who take their lives and for those who slice their thighs and livers out of unschooled filial piety, their actions are comparable" 誠以烈婦損生與割肝割股之愚孝其事相類.[116]

---

113 *Wujin Yanghu xian he zhi* 1842, 27: 42b–53b.
114 *Qinding da Qing huidian* 403, Shunzhi 9: 501–502.
115 *Qinding da Qing huidian* 403, Yongzheng 6: 506.
116 *Qinding da Qing huidian* 403, Yongzheng 6: 507.

Although the memorial ultimately decides against granting a *jingbiao* award in this case so as not to promote a practice of taking life lightly, in equating the filial slicing of flesh with chaste suicides, it anticipates the late Qing recognition of filial martyrdom as an expression of virtue. The widespread support for chaste martyrs was literally bleeding into filial culture. The 1842 Wujin-Yanghu gazetteer presents a fully sympathetic view of filial martyrdom; 7% of the 285 biographies of filial sons culminate in the death of the son. The biography of Qian Minqi presents him as a filial martyr. Minqi made it his mission in life and death to serve his father, who suffered from a chronic disease. When his father died, Minqi passed out from grief. After reviving, he said: "I will serve my father in the underworld" 吾將事吾父於地下矣. He then ordered his family to prepare his hemp mourning clothes, rush sandals, and a shroud. Minqi called out to his father several times and then died.[117] Minqi's ability to predict his own death echoes the hagiographies of Buddhist and Daoist saints and encourages us to read his death as a spiritual act.

Rather than emphasizing ritualized filial acts, some biographies in other Jiangnan gazetteers honor adult men for their ability to tap into the filial sentiments of a child.

> 程煒字闇章，上元人。性誠樸，早葬偶不再娶。侍父寢三十年，親滌溺器，裏衣垢必親浣。父年九十歿，煒老矣，猶孺子泣.
>
> Cheng Wei, styled Anzhang, hailed from Shangyuan. By nature honest and sincere, he lost his wife early and did not remarry. He served his father who was bedridden for thirty years, personally washing his chamber pot, and when his inner garments were soiled he would wash them himself. His father was ninety when he passed away, and though Wei was old, he still wept like a child.[118]

---

117 *Wujin Yanghu xian he zhi* 1842, 27: 40b.
118 *Chongkan Jiangning fu zhi*, 1880 (1811), 35: 19a.

Fang Bingzhao was also celebrated for "serving his mother with great contentment and with childlike attachment, for the rest of her life" 事其母陶陶遂遂終身如赤子.[119] As illustrated in the *Twenty-Four Exemplars*, unscripted shows of grief and affection are the unmediated expressions of a childlike heart.

Compared to the biographies from the Tai'an and Qufu gazetteers, many of which are brief formulaic records of ritualized mourning, the portraits of filial sons in the Wujin-Yanghu gazetteers seem to borrow from the individualized and hybrid characterizations common in popular fiction, particularly in the ways they depict protagonists as *duoqing* 多情, simultaneously rich in sentiment and heroic. Given the proximity of Wujin and Yanghu counties to Suzhou, a center of commercial publishing, the impact of fiction on gazetteer biographies should not be surprising. As shown in Table 2, the downplaying of ritual performance as the core of filial piety in the Wujin-Yanghu gazetteers is reflected in the relative lack of attention paid to the practice of mourning huts. When the practice of *lumu* is referenced, it is typically a background detail in a narrative that highlights the expression of emotions. For example, the following biography, set during the Wanli reign period and published in the 1765 gazetteer, frames the son's ritualized mourning within highly sentimental and activist expressions of devotion to his parents.

> 陳都性至孝。父燧為怨家搆陷。都時十六，斷指瀝血叩臺白父冤。屢遭箠楚，絕復甦。聘而不昏者。廿載冤竟得白。母鄒氏病劇，割股和丸食之，病良已。父母歿結廬墓旁榜曰松廬，常坐壙側，烈風暴雨不歸。每一號哭哀動路人。先是，母病思食桃，以非時不可得，遂終身不食桃。

Chen Du was by nature extremely filial. When Du was sixteen, his father Sui was implicated in a legal matter by an enemy. Du cut off a finger, and, dripping blood, submitted his case at court to protest his father's

119   *Wujin Yanghu xian he zhi*, 1842, 27: 39a–b.

innocence. He was repeatedly caned, and would pass out and then revive. Although he was betrothed, Du did not marry and eventually, after twenty years, cleared his father of the injustice. When his mother Zou was seriously ill, Du cut flesh from his thigh to make a remedy and her condition improved. When his parents died, he constructed a mourning hut beside their graves, calling it his pine cottage, and was always there sitting beside their grave mounds, not returning home even in gusty winds and stormy rain. Every time he wailed and cried, passersby were moved by his grief. Once, his mother, when ill, had wanted to eat peaches, but he could not obtain any because it was the wrong season. As a result, he did not eat peaches for the rest of his life.[120]

The dramatic attempt to clear his father's name, with the detail of him cutting off a finger presumably to make a blood oath, his refusal to marry, and his commitment over twenty years to fulfill his pledge, all attest to Chen Du's heroic nature. The biography concludes on a highly sentimental note with details on the affective power of Chen Du's wailing and on his refusal to eat peaches as a way to embody his bond to his mother.

An essay included in a 1668 Jiangning gazetteer provides an explanation for the striking regional differences between those gazetteers that foreground orthodox mourning rites and those that highlight *gegu*. As the brief essay argues, mourning rites evolved over time: Confucius himself said that "in the past, they made graves only but not burial mounds" 古也墓而不墳.[121] As the writers suggest, while they find it acceptable to expand upon the practices of the rites, it is not acceptable to scale back. The compilers then justify their inclusion of *gegu*, even though it was not eligible for official honors, by explaining that they include it to encourage a culture of filial piety since "mourners value 'ritualized mourning' (*xiao*) less than acts of loving compassion (*ci* 慈) for their parents" 喪民多薄於孝

---

120   *Chongxiu Wujin xian zhi* 1765, 10: 35b.

121   *Liji jijie* VII.3: 168–169 ("Tan Gong shang").

而厚於慈親之極.[122] This pairing of the two types of filial deeds establishes them as poles demarcating categories of exemplary filial action: residing in mourning huts is associated with ritualized mourning, while *gegu* represents an affective expression of "loving compassion." This affective valence justifies the widespread inclusion of flesh-slicing and filial martyrdom, acts that contradict a more narrow ritual definition of filial piety, in the Jiangnan gazetteers. The compilers of a Qianlong-era gazetteer from Wujiang County, Jiangsu, similarly disparage flesh-slicing as dangerous and improper, even while admiring it as a powerful expression of love for one's parents that would inspire others:

> 其愛親之極，殺身不顧。一念之精誠，足以感人心脾。
>
> [Those who slice their flesh] love their parents to such an extreme that they have no regard for their own lives. The absolute sincerity of their single focus suffices to move people at a visceral level.[123]

As the comment concludes, not only is the willingness to make the ultimate sacrifice for one's parents a compelling expression of loving care, it also has a powerful somatic effect on those who hear about it. Although flesh-cutting contravenes one of the most basic injunctions from the *Xiaojing* against harming the body given by one's parents, it was ultimately endorsed during the late-imperial period as a sincere expression of loving care.

Conclusion

The centrality of filial piety as a keyword for understanding the culture and politics of early China has been long accepted in China studies. Much less scholarly attention has been paid to it as a dynamic and multivalent term

---

122   *Jiangning fu zhi* 1668, 34: 26a–b.

123   *Wujiang xian zhi*, Qianlong, "*Xiaoyou*" j. 30. Cited from Yu Xinzhong 2006: 20.

in later eras. As we have seen, the meanings of and practices associated with *xiao* evolved unevenly. As with so many other key terms, philosophers and rulers exploited the cultural power associated with *xiao* and used it as a signifier to mask profound cultural tensions. It could serve to strengthen the bonds of political loyalty or to augment the lineages at the expense of the state; it could be viewed as a set of fixed ritual obligations or as an innate expression of the affective ethical self. It could be associated with quotidian care for the parents, but could also become a heroic virtue, generating extreme behaviors that contradict its philosophically and ritually derived meanings.

Even as filial piety remained a core value through all of China's imperial history, the specific importance of filial piety to the culture and politics of the late-imperial period is only beginning to be appreciated. By the Qing, government policies extended the reach of Confucian ideology to all levels of society in a way that was unprecedented. So many actors embraced filial piety as a hypergood that no one group had a monopoly on defining its meanings. Certain Neo-Confucian elites were successful in rebranding "following the rites" as exemplary, as reflected in local gazetteers; other elites embraced popular expressions of filial piety, such as the Buddhist-inspired practice of *gegu* or martyrdom and expressions of affective care. Among the most significant developments in the late-imperial culture of filial piety was its affective turn. In contrast to earlier periods, which often illustrate a fanatical commitment to filial piety as an ideal, the late-imperial construction of filial piety became sentimentalized to such a degree that mundane expressions of filial love and caring were elevated to a new level of cultural significance. New Culture writers have taught us to see filial piety as an ideological tool of despotic government and as a ritual obligation that distorted natural emotions and desires. However, it is impossible to ignore that the vast majority of references to filial piety that appear everywhere in the late-imperial discursive record depict it positively and increasingly focus on it, not as a ritual obligation, but as an expression of the affective and ethical self.

Bibliography

Ba Jin 巴金 (1904–2005). 1962. *Jia* 家. Beijing: Renmin wenxue chubanshe.

de Bary, Wm. Theodore. 1970. "Individualism and Humanitarianism in Late Ming Thought." In *Self and Society in Ming Thought*, edited by Wm. Theodore de Bary, 145–247. New York: Columbia University Press.

Brook, Timothy. 1989. "Funerary Ritual and the Building of Lineages in Late Imperial China." *Harvard Journal of Asiatic Studies* 49.2: 465–499.

Brown, Miranda Dympna. 2007. *The Politics of Mourning in Early China*. Albany, NY: State University of New York Press.

Chan Alan Kam-leung and Sor-hoon Tan (eds.). 2004. *Filial Piety in Chinese Thought and Culture*. London and New York: RoutledgeCurzon.

Chaves, Jonathan. 1986. "Moral Action in the Poetry of Wu Chia-chi (1618–1684)." *Harvard Journal of Asiatic Studies* 42.2: 387–469.

Chen Baozhen 陳葆真. 2014. "Qianlong huangdi dui Xiaosheng taihou de xiaoxing he ta suo xianshi yiyi" 乾隆皇帝對孝聖太后的孝行和它所顯示意義. *Gugong xueshu jikan* 故宮學術集刊 31.1: 103–154.

Chongkan Jiangning fu zhi 重刊江甯府志. 1811. Reprinted 1880.

Chongxiu Wujin xian zhi 重修武進縣志. 1765.

Chow Kai-wing. 1994. *The Rise of Confucian Ritualism in Late Imperial China: Ethics, Classics, and Lineage Discourse*. Stanford CA: Stanford University Press.

Chow Tse-tsung. 1960. "The Anti-Confucian Movement in Early Republican China." In *The Confucian Persuasion*, edited by Arthur F. Wright, 288–312. Stanford, CA: Stanford University Press.

Cole, Alan. 1998. *Mothers and Sons in Chinese Buddhism*. Stanford, CA: Stanford University Press.

Cook, Scott Bradley. 2012. *The Bamboo Texts of Guodian: A Study & Complete Translation*. Ithaca, NY: Cornell University Press.

Crossley, Pamela Kyle. 1999. *A Translucent Mirror: History and Identity in Qing Imperial Ideology*. Berkeley: University of California Press.

Dennis, Joseph. 2015. *Writing, Publishing, and Reading Local Gazetteers in Imperial China, 1100–1700*. Cambridge, MA: Harvard University Asia Center.

Ebrey, Patricia. 1991. *Confucianism and Family Rituals in Imperial China: A Social History or Writing about Rites*. Princeton, NJ: Princeton University Press.

Elvin, Mark. 1984. "Female Virtue and the State in China." *Past and Present* 104: 111–152.

Epstein, Maram. 2001. *Competing Discourses: Orthodoxy, Authenticity, and Engendered Meanings in Late-Imperial Chinese Fiction*. Cambridge, MA: Harvard University Press.

———. 2011. "Patrimonial Bonds: Daughter, Fathers, and Power in *Tianyuhua*." *Late Imperial China* 32.2: 1–33.

———. 2019. *Orthodox Passions: Narrating Filial Love in the High Qing*. Cambridge, MA: Harvard University Press.

Feng Menglong quanji 馮夢龍全集. 1993. By Feng Menglong 馮夢龍 (1574–1646). Shanghai: Shanghai guji chubanshe.

Fisher, Carney T. 1990. *The Chosen One: Succession and Adoption in the Court of Ming Shizong*. Sidney: Allen and Unwin.

Foucault, Michel. 1997. *Ethics, Subjectivity and Truth*. Edited by Paul Rabinow. New York: The New Press.

De Groot, J. J. M. 1989 (1894). *The Religious System of China: Its Ancient Forms, Evolution, History and Present Aspect, Manners, Custom and Social Institutions Connected Therewith*. Taipei: Southern Materials Center.

Goldin, Paul Rakita. 2013. "Han Fei and the Han Feizi." In *Dao Companion to the Philosophy of Han Fei*, edited by Paul Rakita Goldin, 1–21. Berlin: Springer.

Guida, Donatella. 2006. "*Ai* 愛 versus *xiao* 孝: The Expression of Love in the Novel *Jinghua yuan* 鏡花緣. A Preliminary Approach." In *Love, Hatred, and Other Passions: Questions and Themes on Emotions in Chinese Civilization*, edited by Paolo Santangelo and Donatella Guida, 301–313. Leiden: Brill.

Fumu enzhong jing 父母恩重經. 2002. Zhonghua dianzi Fodian xiehui (CBETA) http://buddhism.lib.ntu.edu.tw/BDLM/sutra/chi_pdf/sutra25/T85n2887.pdf.

Han Feizi jijie 非子集解. 1998. Compiled by Wang Xianshen 王先慎 (1859–1922). Beijing: Zhonghua shuju.

Hanan, Patrick. 1981. *The Chinese Vernacular Story*. Cambridge, MA: Harvard University Press.

Harbsmeier, Christoph. 1999. "Weeping and Wailing in Ancient China." In *Minds and Mentalities in Early Chinese Literature*, edited by Halvor Eifrig, 317–422. Beijing: Culture and Art Publishing House.

Holzman, Donald. 1998. "The Place of Filial Piety in Ancient China." *Journal of the American Oriental Society* 118.2: 185–199.

Hou Hanshu 後漢書. 1995. By Fan Ye 範曄 (398–445) et al. Beijing: Zhonghua shuju.

Hsiung Ping-chen. 1994. "Constructed Emotions: The Bond Between Mothers and Sons in Late Imperial China." *Late Imperial China* 15.1: 87–117.

Hu Shi 胡適. 1919. "Wo duiyu sangli de gaige" 我對於喪禮的改革. *Xin qingnian* 新青年 6.6: 568–577.

Hu Siao-chen. 2005. "The Daughter's Vision of National Crisis: *Tianyuhua* and a Woman Writer's Construction of the Late Ming." In *Dynastic Crisis and Cultural Innovation*, 200-31, edited by David Wang and Shang Wei. Cambridge, MA: Harvard University Asia Center.

Ikezawa, Masaru. 1994. "The Philosophy of Filial Piety in Ancient China: Ideological Development of Ancestor Worship in the Zhanguo Period." Ph.D. dissertation, University of British Columbia.

Jiang Zhiqi (1031–1104). 2001. "Biography of the Great Compassionate One of Xiangshan." Translated by Chün-fang Yü. In *Under Confucian Eyes: Writings on Gender in Chinese History*, edited by Susan Mann and Chen Yu-Yin, 31–44. Berkeley: University of California Press.

Jiangning fu zhi 江寧府志. 1668.

Kahn, Harold. 1971. *Monarchy in the Emperor's Eyes: Image and Reality in the Ch'ien-lung Reign*. Cambridge, MA: Harvard University Press.

Kindall, Elizabeth. 2016. *Geo-Narratives of a Filial Son: The Paintings and Travel Diaries of Huang Xiangjian (1609–1673)*. Cambridge, MA: Harvard University Asia Center.

Knapp, Keith. 1995. "The Ru Reinterpretation of *Xiao*." *Early China* 20: 195-222.

———. 2005. *Selfless Offspring: Filial Children and Social Order in Medieval China*. Honolulu: University of Hawai'i Press.

———. 2014. "Chinese Filial Cannibalism: A Silk Road Import?" In *China and Beyond in the Mediaeval Period: Cultural Crossings and Inter-regional Connections*, edited by Dorothy Wong et al., 135–149. Amherst, NY: Cambria Press.

Kutcher, Norman. 1999. *Mourning in Late Imperial China: Filial Piety and the State*. Cambridge and New York: Cambridge University Press.

Lee, Pauline C. 2012. *Li Zhi, Confucianism, and the Virtue of Desire*. Albany, NY: State University of New York Press.

Leys, Simon, and Michael Nylan. 2014. *The Analects: The Simon Leys Translation, Interpretations*. New York and London: W.W. Norton.

Li Wai-yee. 2014. *Women and National Trauma in Late Imperial Chinese Literature*. Cambridge, MA: Harvard University Asia Center.

Li Yu. 1992. *A Tower for the Summer Heat*. Translated by Patrcik Hanan. New York: Ballantine Books.

Li Yu quanji 李漁全集. 1991. By Li Yu 李漁 (1611–1680). Hangzhou: Zhejiang guji chubanshe.

Liji jijie 禮記集解. 1995. Compiled by Sun Xidan 孫希旦 (1736–1784). Edited by Shen Xiaohuan 沈嘯寰 and Wang Xingxian 王星賢. Beijing: Zhonghua shuju.

Lu Miaw-fen [Lü Miaofen] 呂妙芬. 2005. "Wan Ming *xiaojing* lunshu de zongjiao xingyi han: Yu Chuanxi de xiao lun ji qita wenhua mailuo," 晚明《孝經》論述的宗教性意涵：虞淳熙的孝論及其他文化脈絡." *Zhongyang yanjiuyuan jindai yanjiusuo jikan* 中央研究院近代研究所集刊 48: 1–46.

———. 2006. "Religious Dimensions of Filial Piety as Developed in Late Ming Interpretations of the *Xiaojing*." *Late Imperial China* 27.2: 1–37.

———. 2011. *Xiao zhi tianxia: Xiaojing yu jinshi Zhongguo de zhengzhi yu wenhua* 孝治天下：《孝經》與近世中國的政治與文化. Taipei: Zhongyang yanjiuyuan.

Lu Weijing. 2008. *True to her Word: The Faithful Maiden Cult in Late Imperial China.* Stanford, CA: Stanford University Press.

———. 2013. "Reviving an Ancient Filial Ideal: The Seventeenth-Century Practice of *Lumu* 廬墓." *Chinese Historical Review* 20.2: 159–179.

Lu Xun 魯迅 (1881–1936). 1981. *Lu Xun quanji* 魯迅全集. Beijing: Renmin chubanshe.

Lunyu yizhu 論語譯注. 1992. Annotated by Yang Bojun 楊伯峻. Beijing: Zhonghua shuju.

Lüshi chunqiu jiaoshi 呂氏春秋校釋. 1995. Compiled and annotated by Chen Qiyou 陳奇猷. Shanghai: Xuelin.

Mair, Victor. 1985. "Language and Ideology in the Written Popularizations of the *Sacred Edicts*." In *Popular Culture in Late Imperial China*, edited by David Johnson et al., 325–359. Berkeley, CA: University of California Press.

Mengzi yizhu 孟子譯注. 1992. Annotated by Yang Bojun 楊伯峻. Beijing: Zhonghua shuju.

Ming Taizu baoxun 明太祖寶訓. 1967. Taipei: Zhongyang yanjiuyuan.

Mingshi 明史. 1974. By Zhang Tingyu 張廷玉 (1672–1755) et al. Beijing: Zhonghua shuju.

Nylan, Michael. 1996. "Confucian Piety and Individualism in Han China." *Journal of the American Oriental Society* 116.1: 1–16.

———. 2001. *The Five "Confucian" Classics.* New Haven: Yale University Press.

Pines, Yuri. 2002. *Foundations of Confucian Thought: Intellectual Life in the Chunqiu Period (722–453 B.C.E.).* Honolulu: University of Hawai'i Press.

Qinding da Qing huidian shili 欽定大清會典事例. 1991. Beijing: Zhonghua shuju.

Qiu Zhonglin 邱仲麟. 1995. "Buxiao zhi xiao—Tang yilai gegu liaoqin xianxiang de shehuishi chutan" 不孝之孝——唐以來割股療親現象的社會史初探. *Xinshixue* 新史學 6.1: 49–94.

Rowe, William T. 2001. *Saving the World: Chen Hongmou and Elite Consciousness in Eighteenth-Century China.* Stanford, CA: Stanford University Press.

Shang Wei. 2003. *Rulin waishi and Cultural Transformation in Late Imperial China.* Cambridge, MA: Harvard University Asia Center.

Shishuo xinyu jiaojian 世說新語校箋. 1969. By Liu Yiqing 劉義慶 (403–444) et al. Edited by Yang Yong 楊勇. Hong Kong: Hong Kong dazhong shuju.

Smith, Richard J. 1990. "Ritual in Ch'ing Culture." In *Orthodoxy in Late Imperial China*, edited by Liu Kwang-ching, 281–310. Berkeley, CA: University of California Press.

Soushen ji 搜神記. 1957. By Gan Bao 干寶 (d. 336). Shanghai: Shangwu.

Stapleton, Kristin. 2008."Generational and Cultural Fissures in the May Fourth Movement: Wu Yu (1872–1949) and the Politics of Family Reform." In *Beyond the May Fourth Paradigm: In Search of Chinese Modernity*, edited by Chow Kai-wing et al., 131–148. Lanham, MD: Lexington Press.

Tai'an fu zhi 泰安府志. 1760.

Taishan zhi 泰山志. 1554.

Tang Changru 唐長孺. 1983. *Wei Jin Nan Bei chao shilun shiyi* 魏晉南北朝史論拾遺. Beijing: Zhonghua shuju.

Tao Zhenhuai陶貞懷 (fl. 1650). 1984. *Tianyuhua* 天雨花. Zhengzhou: Zhongzhou guji chubanshe.

Theiss, Janet. 2004. *Disgraceful Matters: The Politics of Chastity in Eighteenth-Century China*. Berkeley: University of California Press.

T'ien Ju-k'ang. 1988. *Male Anxiety and Female Chastity: A Comparative Study of Chinese Ethical Values in Ming-Ch'ing Times*. Leiden: E. J. Brill.

Wu Silas. 1979. *Passage to Power: K'ang-hsi and his Heir Apparent, 1661–1722*. Cambridge, MA: Harvard University Press.

Wu Yu 吳虞 (1872–1949). 1990. *Wu Yu wenlu* 吳虞文錄. In Minguo congshu 民國叢書, series 2, vol. 96. Shanghai: Shanghai shudian (reprint of 1927 edition).

Wujin Yanghu xian he zhi 武進陽湖縣合志. 1842.

Xiao Qunzhong肖群忠. 2002. *Zhongguo xiao wenhua yanjiu* 中國孝文化研究. Taipei: Wunan tushu chuban.

Xiaojing zhushu 孝經注疏. 1999. Edited by Li Xueqin 李學勤. Beijing: Beijing daxue chubanshe.

Xunzi jijie 荀子集解. 1992. Annotated by Wang Xianqian 王先謙 (1842–1917). Edited by Shen Xiaohuan 沈嘯寰 and Wang Xingxian 王星賢. Beijing: Zhonghua shuju.

Yōgaku no Kai 幼學の會. (ed.) 2003. *Kōshiden chūkai* 孝子傳注解. Tokyo: Kyūko shoin.

Yu, Jimmy Yung Fung. 2012. *Sanctity and Self-Inflicted Violence in Chinese Religions, 1500–1700*. Oxford: Oxford University Press.

Yu Xinzhong 余新忠. 2006. "Ming Qing shiqi xiaoxing de wenben jiedu—yi Jiangnan fangzhi jizai wei zhongxin" 明清時期孝行的文本解讀——以江南方志記載為中心. *Zhongguo shehui lishi pinglun* 中國社會歷史評論 7: 1–23.

Zelin, Madeleine. 1984. *The Magistrate's Tael: Rationalizing Fiscal Reform in Eighteenth-Century Ch'ing China*. Berkeley: University of California Press.

Zhang Yaoxiang 張耀翔 (1893–1964). 1918. "Lun wuguo fumu zhi zhuanheng" 論吾國父母之專橫. *Xin qingnian* 新青年 5.6: 637–640.

Zhang Ying. 2013. "The Politics and Practice of Moral Rectitude in the Late Ming: The Case of Huang Daozhou (1585–1646)." *Late Imperial China* 34.2: 52–82.

————. 2017. *Confucian Image Politics: Masculine Morality in Seventeenth-Century China*. Seattle: University of Washington Press.

Zhang Zhupo piping Jin Ping Mei 張竹坡批評金瓶梅. 1991. Annotated by Zhang Zhupo 張竹坡 (1670–1698). Collated by Wang Rumei 王汝梅, Li Zhaoxun 李昭恂 and Yu Fengshu 于鳳樹. Jinan: Qi Lu shushe.

Zhu Xi. 1991. *Chu Hsi's Family Rituals*. Translated by Patricia Ebrey. Princeton, NJ: Princeton University Press.

Keywords of the Self

8

Before the Emergence of Desire*

Andrew Plaks

Every reader of classical Chinese texts—at least those paying attention to the precise meanings of key words as they vary through different periods, genres and prose contexts—will be aware that the character *qing* 情 occurs in a broad range of usages for which the familiar sense of "feelings" or "emotions" is frequently inapplicable. In Chinese philosophical discourse, from the pre-imperial period through the Late Imperial period, the term *qing* conveys what may seem to be an entirely different set of semantic values, covering such things as essential nature, actual conditions, reality—even simply "truth."[1] This obvious bifurcation in the meaning of the word has been discussed by not a few scholars in China and the West. In Chinese critical scholarship (where, setting aside its centrality in works on poetry and drama theory, the word is most significantly highlighted in writings on the concept of "human nature" in Confucian thought),[2] the character may be presented without additional explication or it may be elucidated with reference to various modern compound expressions. But in Western-language Sinological writings it is generally necessary to unpack the connotations of the term by means of

---

* Author's note: This essay is essentially a reworking in written form of my introductory lecture presented at the conference on Keywords in Chinese Philosophy and Literature, setting forth an initial outline of the analytic scheme of my ongoing study of the concept of *qing*, through a series of close readings of selected passages in foundational texts that deal with this issue.

Editors' note: A number of the author's pointed renderings of key expressions in translated passages have been simplified to standard equivalents for the convenience of non-specialists.

1   These senses of the word *qing* are reflected in such common modern locutions as "affairs" 事情, "conditions" 情況, "information, intelligence" 情報, and the like.

2   The most prominent contemporary example being Xu Fuguan 1984.

translation (unless of course one opts to leave it in opaque transliteration), and it is frequently reduced to knee-jerk renderings such as "feeling" or vague expressions about inner essence.[3]

This paper is based on a comprehensive review of the use of the word *qing* in a variety of philosophical and literary texts from the Warring States (453–221 BCE) through the Ming (1368–1644) and Qing (1636/1644–1912) periods, with the aim of clarifying the changing signification of the term as it diverges over time. Unfortunately, this trajectory cannot be simplistically defined in terms of a steady transformation from a zero-degree basic core of meaning in the direction of more complex usages. In this case, there is no "original" form of the word to be unearthed using the tools of linguistic archeology or with reference to archaic script forms.[4] Significantly, while senses associated with truth or reality tend to predominate in early philosophical prose,[5] and notions of sentiment and love become preponderant in later literary and cultural contexts, we find too many counterexamples of each type at the respective ends of the spectrum to allow for a simplistic conclusion of one-way semantic transformation. With this in mind, I will attempt in this essay to map out a more nuanced typology of the apparently unrelated meanings of *qing*, with an eye toward bringing out a certain common ground of meaning running through many of these differential usages.

As we shall see, any pursuit of the essential signification of *qing* as a philosophical term must focus not on its occurrences as an isolated lexical unit, but rather on the ways in which it is linked to other characters in compound locutions—either as co-ordinate nouns or in noun-verb

---

3   See for example, Graham 1967; Puett 2004; Bruya 2001, among others.

4   The early use of the graph 青 as a phonetic marker, or a synthetic ideogram composed of the graph 化 over the element 心—among other more arcane forms—provide no appreciable assistance in this regard.

5   For occurrences of *qing* in the simple sense of "veracity" or "truth," see, e.g., "If those in power show preference for veracity, then the people will not dare to withhold the *truth*" 上好信，則民莫敢不用情 (*Lunyu yizhu* 13.4: 135; translation follows Kong Yingda's 孔穎達 [574–648] reading); Zhu Xi's 朱熹 [1130–1200] reading is: "If those in power show preference for good faith, then the people would not dare *to be dishonest*"; *Lunyu zhangju* 13: 142). Or: "One's arguments should not overstate the *truth*; and the *truth* should not exceed the bounds of correct behavior" 辭不越情，情不越義 (*Kongcongzi* 4: 79 ["Xing lun"刑論]), and so forth.

constructions—or how it is counter-posed to related terms of intellectual discourse, particularly innate nature (*xing* 性), heart/mind (*xin* 心) and principle/pattern (*li* 理). When *qing* is introduced as the object of one or another verbal expression, the perspective is shifted from that of a fixed element in a paradigm to a dynamic context of processes or relations—either affirmative or detrimental in nature. For example, various Chinese thinkers speak of "nurturing," "understanding," "ordering," "distinguishing," "gauging," "engaging with," "restoring," or "stabilizing" one's *qing*, while others emphasize the danger of "failing to grasp" it, or "harming" it, "discarding" it, among similar phrases.[6] The idea that one's *qing* requires a process of constant perfecting is articulated in one of our earliest datable treatises, the excavated text from the site of Guodian 郭店, known by the synthetic title *Xing zi ming chu* 性自命出 (paralleled by another excavated text from the Shanghai Museum collection, known as *Qing xing lun* 情性論).[7] In *Xing zi ming chu*, we are enjoined to put our *qing* in order[8]—a notion echoed in a passage in the presumably later "Fisherman" 漁父, one of the "Miscellaneous Chapters" of the *Zhuangzi* 莊子[9]—and we are told that "men of noble character" (as I prefer to translate *junzi*) succeed in acting upon their *qing* and bringing it to perfection 君子美其情.[10]

---

6   See for example "nurturing *qing*" 養情 (*Xunzi jijie* 191 349 ["Li lun" 禮論]); "to order the *qing* of liking and disliking" 理好惡之情 (*Zhuangzi jishi* 31:1031 ["Yu fu" 漁父]); "to understand one's *qing*" 知其情 (*Liji jijie*, 9:606 ["Li yun" 禮運]); "the noble man goes against his *qing*" 君子反情 (*Liji jijie*, 19:1003 ["Yue ji" 樂記]); "does not lose his *qing* inside" 內不失其情 (*Huainan honglie jijie* 1.11 ["Yuan Dao" 原道訓]); "to oppress one's innate nature and go against *qing*" 迫性拂情 (*Huainan honglie jijie* 7.241 ["Jingshen" 精神訓]); "to ignore the *qing* (of the situation)" 失諸情 (*Huainan honglie jijie* 10.331 ["Miu cheng" 繆稱訓]); "to be at peace with one's *qing* and innate nature" 安其情性 (*Huainan honglie jijie* 6.214 ["Lan ming" 覽冥訓]); "to harm *qing*" 虧情 (*Lüshi chunqiu jiaoshi*, 8: 85 "Qing yu" [情欲]); "must gauge its *qing* (the *qing* of heaven and earth)" 當察其情 (*Lüshi chunqiu jiaoshi*, 24: 657 "You shi" [有始]); to distinguish its *qing* 別其情 (*Chunqiu fanlu* 11: 143 ["Zheng guan" 正貫]); "to assess one's *qing*" 料其情 (*Guiguzi* 1: 3, ["Bai he" 捭闔]), and so forth.

7   For *Xing zi ming chu*, its translation, and its comparison with the Shanghai Museum manuscript, see Cook 2012: 667–750; all the references below are to this edition.

8   "To order *qing* by drawing it out and reimplanting it" 理其情而出入之 (slips 17–18; translation modifies Cook 2012: 712).

9   "To order the *qing* of liking and disliking" 理好惡之情, see n. 6 above.

10 Slip 20; Cook (2012: 715) translates: "The noble man regards the affections (*qing*) as beautiful."

Let us now begin our review of passages that mark out the semantic range of the term *qing* in Chinese thought, from emotional experience to metaphysical speculation, at the human end of the scale. As previously stated, there is no lack of moments in the philosophical corpus in which the common modern meaning of the word *qing* as "feelings" is indeed what is intended. This is patently clear where the character *qing* is linked to *yu* 欲 indicating human desire, as seen in any number of passages from *Zhuangzi*[11] or *Lüshi chunqiu*,[12] through the dialectics on *tianli* 天理 (heavenly principles) and *renyu* 人欲 (human desires) in Song Neo-Confucian writings and Late Imperial thought.[13] The use of *qing* to refer to the emotional core of human experience has particular relevance to speculation on the theoretical foundations of ritual, a point already made in the *Xing zi ming chu* manuscript,[14] repeated by Xunzi[15] and *Guanzi*,[16] and given canonic formulation in the *Liji*.[17]

---

11 E.g., "Taking the reduction and devaluation of one's feelings and desires as one's inner guide" 以情欲寡淺為內 (*Zhuangzi jishi* 31.1084 ["Tianxia" 天下]).

12 "Desires should have true feelings (*qing*) at their base, and feelings should have proper measure" 欲有情，情有節 (*Lüshi chunqiu jiaoshi* 8: 84 ["Qing yu" 情欲]); "it is basic to human feelings (*qing*) to desire long life and abhor untimely death, to desire comfort and abhor calamity" 人之情，欲壽而惡夭，欲安而惡危 (*Lüshi chunqiu jiaoshi* 24: 272 ["Shi yin" 適音]).

13 The opposition of *tianli* and *renyu* recur in Zhu Xi's writings (e.g., *Zhuzi yulei* 13: 224–227; 15: 287, 301, 30: 774; 42: 1071–1079). For some Ming-Qing examples, see, e.g., *Ming jingshi wenbian* edited by Chen Zilong 陳子龍 (1608–1647) et al., (95: 834, 171: 1748–1749); see also Wang Fuzhi's 王夫之 (1619–1692), *Du Sishu daquan shuo* 5: 278, 296, 352, 8: 519, 576.

14 "Ritual arises from [the ground of] human feelings" 禮作於情 (slip 18; Cook 2012: 714).

15 "The essence of sacrifice lies in the human feelings underlying attitudes, opinions, thoughts, and preferences" 祭者、志意思慕之情也 (*Xunzi jijie* 19: 375 ["Li lun"]).

16 "Ritual is grounded in human feelings and linked to the principles underlying correct behavior; it is that which gives it proper measure and mode of expression" 禮者，因人之情，緣義之理，而為之節文者 (*Guanzi jiaozhu* 36:770 ["Xin shu shang" 心術上]).

17 To give a few examples among many: "As a general principle, music arises in the human heart. One's feelings are stirred within and are thereby given form in patterns of sound." 凡音者，生人心者也。情動於中，故形於聲 (*Liji jijie* 19: 976 ["Yue ji" 樂記]); "the term 'music' is derived from the word 'joy'; it is an inevitable part of the expression of human feelings" 夫樂者樂也，人情之所不能免也 (*Liji jijie* 19:1032); "Ritual is grounded in human feelings and gives it the proper measure and mode of expression" 禮者，因人之情而為之節文 (*Liji jijie* 30: 1281 ["Fang ji" 坊記]).

The association of *qing* with human feelings is most obvious in those numerous passages itemizing the archetypal emotions "joy, wrath, grief, delight" (喜怒哀樂). From early on, this particular enumeration became primarily formulaic, and—with the exception of those points referring to an actual numerical category[18]—this and similar formulations serve for the most part as markers for the full repertoire of human emotional response,[19] and by extension, the entire realm of human experience as an object of metaphysical contemplation.

At the simplest level, "philosophical" definitions of *qing* may amount to nothing more than flat statements defining it as the ground of the human condition. See for instance the following passages:

---

18   E.g., "joy, wrath, grief, fear, affection, dislike, and desire, these are the seven feelings" 喜怒哀懼愛惡欲七者 (*Liji jijie* 9: 606 ["Li yun"]).

19   Examples of this sort of formulation are observed by the Warring States and Han periods. See *Xing zi ming chu* slips 42–43: "grief and joy are the most intense forms of feelings given full expression" 用情之至者，哀樂為甚 (cf. translation in Cook 2012: 732); "attraction, distaste, pleasure, wrath, grief and joy of the innate nature are examples of human feelings" 性之好、惡、喜、怒、哀、樂，謂之情 (*Xunzi jijie* 22:412 ["Zheng ming" 正名]); "when preference, dislike, joy, wrath, grief and joy are properly expressed, that is what is called natural feelings" 好惡、喜、怒、哀、樂臧焉，夫是之謂天情 (*Xunzi jijie* 17: 309 ["Tian lun" 天論]); "When one succeeds in setting aside anxiety, joy, delight, wrath, desire and concupiscence, one's inner self becomes settled. The feelings of such a person find advantage in ease and become restful. Without disturbance and disorder, harmony is thus realized on its own." 能去憂樂喜怒欲利，心乃反濟。彼心之情，利安以寧，勿煩勿亂，和乃自成 (*Guanzi jiaozhu* 49: 931 ["Nei ye" 業]); "Human life is full of responses in the form of pleasure, wrath, grief and joy." 人生有喜怒哀樂之答 (*Chunqiu fanlu* 41: 318 ["Wei ren zhe tian" 為人者天]); "the category of human feelings comprises distaste, pleasure, grief and joy" 情有好惡喜怒哀樂 (*Lunheng jiaoshi* 13: 132 ["Ben xing" 本性]). Such formulations appear with equal currency through the later Neo-Confucian writings, including those of Wang Yangming's 王陽明 (1472–1529) *Chuanxi lu* 傳習錄 ("pleasure, wrath, grief and joy, these are the emotional manifestation of one's inborn nature") 喜怒哀樂，性之情也 (*Wang Yangming quanji* 1:68 ["Da Lu Yuanjing shu" 答陸原靜書]); Wang Fuzhi: "pleasure, wrath, grief and joy represent the lower level of human feelings" 喜怒哀樂是情下半截 (*Du Sishu daquan shuo* 讀四書大全說 8: 555), and Dai Zhen 戴震 (1724–1727): "the emotions that spring from one's innate ground of feeling take the form of pleasure, wrath, grief and joy" 發乎情者，喜怒哀樂也 (*Mengzi ziyi shuzheng*, *juan* xia 下, 40]).

人見其禽獸也，而以為未嘗有才焉者，是豈人之情也哉。

When people observe their animalistic behavior, they assume that they never had the capacity for moral perfection, but is this, indeed, the essential human condition?[20]

是非仁人之情也。

A sense of right and wrong is the natural state of the man of compassion.[21]

夫貴為天子，富有天下，是人情之所同欲也。

It is a universal desire ingrained in the human condition to be honored as the Son of Heaven and possess the wealth of the entire world.[22]

多方駢枝於五藏之情。

... like excess growth and joined appendages with respect to the natural state of the human constitution.[23]

At times, *qing* appears as the basic condition of "things":

夫物之不齊，物之情也。

Lack of uniformity is the basic state of things.[24]

疏觀萬物而知其情。

To grasp the true nature of all things by general observation.[25]

人之有所不得與, 皆物之情也 。

The fact that this is beyond the ability of man to affect is entirely due to the essential nature of things.[26]

Qing may also refer to the basic conditions of the entire world and cosmic order:

---

20   *Mengzi yizhu* 11.8: 263 ("Gaozi shang" 告子上).

21   *Xunzi jijie* 3: 52 ("Bu gou" 不苟).

22   *Xunzi jijie* 4: 70 ("Rongru" 榮辱).

23   *Zhuangzi jishi* 8: 311 ("Pian mu" 駢拇).

24   *Mengzi yizhu* 5.4: 126 ("Teng Wengong shang" 滕文公上).

25   *Xunzi jijie* 21: 397 ("Jiebi" 解蔽).

26   *Zhuangzi jishi* 6: 241 ("Da zongshi" 大宗師).

包於四海之內，天壤之情，陰陽之和，莫不有也。

Nothing within the compass of the four seas is lacking: nothing in the realm of existence between Heaven and Earth, nothing governed by the harmonious interchange of *yin* and *yang*.[27]

彼道之情，惡音與聲。脩心靜音，道乃可得。

It is the essential state of the Dao to abhor sound and noise. Cultivate the mind and silence the sound—then one can obtain the Dao.[28]

Alternatively, *qing* may indicate the proper condition, the correct state, of human behavior:

故聲聞過情，君子恥之。

Thus when one's reputation goes beyond the proper state, it is a cause for shame to the man of noble character.[29]

聖人修節以止欲，故不過行其情也。

The sage cultivates a sense of proper measure to check his desires, thus he does not act in excess of the proper state.[30]

在己與人皆謂之情，無過情無不及情之謂理。

The term *qing* refers to those common feelings shared by oneself and others, and the term *li* means neither exceeding nor failing to reach the proper measure of feelings.[31]

When the semantic field embraced by discussions of *qing* is stretched to signify the entire ground of concrete existence, its meaning tends to merge with that of *xing* as an indicator of the essential nature of either finite beings, or "being" as a whole. Often *qing* and *xing* are simply conjoined

---

27 *Mozi jiaozhu* 6: 48 ("Ci guo" 辭過).
28 *Guanzi jiaozhu* 49: 935 ("Neiye"). Zhang Peilun 張佩綸 (1848–1903) proposes emending *qing* 情 in this sentence to *jing* 精 essence (*Guanzi jiaozhu*, 936n4).
29 *Mengzi yizhu* 8.18: 190.
30 *Lüshi chunqiu jiaoshi* 8: 84 ("Qingyu" 情欲).
31 *Mengzi ziyi shuzheng, juan* shang 上, 2.

to form a single binomial compound, in which the original distinction between the two terms becomes more or less irrelevant.[32] Elsewhere, the two dimensions may be presented in parallel phrases that give little ground for differentiating the separate concepts, as for example in the following line in the *Xunzi*: "This being the case, one follows one's inborn human nature, and conforms to the ground of human feelings" 然則從人之性，順人之情.[33]

This topic becomes more compelling when thinkers go on to consider the precise relation between these two terms of ontological analysis. In pursuing the position of *qing* within their metaphysical system, Confucian thinkers often resort to positing an elemental distinction between *xing* as the fixed, latent aspect of being, and *qing* as its manifestation in dynamic movement, as, for example, in Zhu Xi's (朱熹, 1130–1200) definition: "*qing* is the dynamic aspect of *xing*" 情者，性之動,[34] or Chen Chun's 陳淳 (1159–1223) further reductive explication of the terms in his *Beixi ziyi* 北溪字義: "that which is at rest and unmoving is *xing*; that which responds to stimuli and interacts with them is *qing*" 然不動是性，感而遂通是情.[35] Such formulations may imply the attribution of a certain sequential order

---

32   See *Xunzi*: "to repress *qing* and *xing*" 忍情性 (*Xunzi jijie* 5: 91 ["Fei shier zi" 非十二子]), and "one corrects one's *qing* and *xing* by straightening and enhancing them, one guides one's *qing* and *xing* by intervening and transforming them" 以矯飾人之情性而正之，以擾化人之情性而導之也 (*Xunzi jijie* 23: 435 ["Xing'e" 性惡]); *Zhuangzi*: "when outer form destroys substance and breadth undermines one's inner core, then the people lapse into confusion and chaos, and lose their capacity to revert to their inborn nature and recover their pristine state" 文滅質，博溺心，然後民始惑亂，無以反其性情而復其初 (*Zhuangzi jishi* 16:552 ["Shan xing" 繕性]); *Lunheng*: "Dong Zhongshu read the books of Xunzi and Mengzi and formed his theory of *qing* and *xing*: the primary infrastructure of the cosmos is the alternation of yin and yang, one following the other, and the primary infrastructure of human existence is the interaction of *qing* and *xing*. *Xing* arises from yang and *qing* arises from yin." 董仲舒覽孫、孟之書，作情性之說曰：「天之大經，一陰一陽，人之大經，一情一性。性生於陽，情生於陰 (*Lunheng jiaoshi* 13: 139 ["Ben xing" 本性]), and many more.

33   *Xunzi jijie* 23: 434–435 ("Xing e").

34   *Zhuzi yulei* 5: 89.

35   *Beixi ziyi* 1: 21.

proceeding from *xing* to *qing*, a proposition unequivocally stated in more than one passage in the *Xing zi ming chu*: "*qing* is produced by *xing*" 情生於性, or "*qing* is brought forth from *xing*" 情出於性.[36]

This raises more profound philosophical issues when we turn from a sense of temporal priority to various conceptions of the *logical* priority, or hierarchical ordering, of these two dimensions of being.[37] Once again, such statements may be limited to unexplained formulations of the subordination of *qing* to *xing*, such as in *Huainanzi*: "Thus, he who understands *qing*, the existential reality of *xing*, will not expend effort on that which cannot be effected by virtue of *xing* alone, and he who understands the existential reality of *ming* will not be troubled by the fact that *ming* is beyond human control" 故知性之情者，不務性之所無以為；知命之情者，不憂命之所無奈何.[38] In this light, I find significant Zhu Xi's reformulation of the crucial distinction between the latent and manifest states of existence obliquely expressed in the opening passage in the *Zhongyong* 中庸 (there put in terms of the archetypal markers of emotional states 喜怒哀樂), to define *qing* as the "emergence" or actualization" of the intrinsic nature of things: "the four 'incipient states' belong to the dimension of *qing*; *xing* is tantamount to *li,* which, when it emerges into concrete form, is *qing*" 四端，情也，性則理也，發者，情也; "no sooner does *xing* emerge into reality, than it becomes *qing*" 性纔發，便是情.[39] (I will return to the implications of this point at the conclusion of this chapter).

Another approach to the differentiation of *xing* and *qing* may be observed in attempts to assign a more contingent axiological status to the latter term.

---

36 Slips 2 and 39; cf. Cook 2012: 700 and 730.

37 Cf. *Xunzi*: "*Xing* is the culmination of the natural order, and *qing* is the substance of *xing*. *Yu* is the responsive manifestation of *qing*" 性者，天之就也, 情者、性之質，欲者，情之應也 (*Xunzi jijie* 22: 428 ["Zheng ming"正名]) and Zhu Xi: "*Li* is the infrastructure of the natural order, and *ming* is the application of *li*. *Xing* is that with which man is endowed from birth, and *qing* is the manifest dimension of *xing*." 理者，天之體；命者，理之用。性是人之所受，情是性之用 (*Zhuzi yulei* 5: 82).

38 *Huainan honglie jijie* 14: 465 ("Tai zu xun" 泰族訓).

39 *Zhuzi yulei* 5: 90. On the four "incipient states," see *Mengzi yizhu* 3.6: 80.

This is how I read the seminal passage in the *Mengzi* in which Mencius concedes that the potential perfection of inborn moral consciousness is of necessity compromised by the exigencies of the actual human condition:

乃若其情，則可以為善矣，乃所謂善也。若夫為不善，非才之罪也。

With respect to one's essential reality (*qing*), one has the capacity to do good; that is what is meant by the phrase "is good." As for instances in which one acts contrary to the good, these cannot be blamed on one's natural endowment.[40]

Li Ao 李翱 (772–841), in his seminal essay "Fu xing shu shang" 復性書 上 (Recovery of innate nature) (Part One), seems at first to apply an unforgiving dichotomy of moral value to *xing* and *qing*:

人之所以為聖人者，性也；人之所以惑其性者，情也。喜、怒、哀、懼、愛、惡、欲，七者皆情之所為也，情既昏，性斯匿矣；非性之過也，七者循環而交來，故性不能充也。

That whereby a man can become a sage is his innate nature, and that whereby a man is led astray is his existential condition. The seven emotions: delight, wrath, grief, fear, affection, dislike and desire are brought about by one's existential condition (*qing*). When one's existential condition is confused, one's innate nature is hidden: innate nature is not to blame. The seven emotions take turn to come from different directions: that is why innate nature (*xing*) cannot fulfill its potential.[41]

Having said this, Li Ao goes on to suggest that the two dimensions are in fact inseparably interwoven, such that one cannot exist without the other:

性與情不相無也，雖然無性則情無所生矣，是情由性而生；情不自情，因性而情；性不自性，由情以明。性者，天之命也，聖人得之而不惑者也；情者，性之動也，百姓溺之而不能知其本者也。

---

40 *Mengzi yizhu* 11.6: 259.
41 *Quan Tang wen* 637: 6433.

Xing and *qing* cannot exist one without the other, but in the absence of *xing* there is no source from which *qing* can come into being. That is to say, *qing* arises from *xing*. *Qing* does not constitute *qing* of its own accord—it is what it is by virtue of *xing*. *Xing* does not constitute *xing* of its own accord—it is visibly manifest through the dimension of *qing*. *Xing* is the basic endowment of the cosmic order; the sages attain *xing* and are free of confusion. *Qing* is the dynamic stirring of *xing*; the common people are drowned in *qing* and cannot know from whence it originates.[42]

Li Ao's striking play on words here ("*Qing* does not constitute *qing* of its own accord—it is what it is by virtue of *xing*. *Xing* does not constitute *xing* of its own accord—it is visibly manifest through the dimension of *qing*" 情不自情，因性而情，性不自性，由情以明), i.e., reading the characters *qing* and *xing* as verbs with the sense of fully realizing the potential significance of first the one and then the other, is replicated in a penetrating essay by the versatile Ming literatus Yang Shen 楊慎 (1488–1559):

不性其情何以久行其正……君子性其情，小人情其性。性，猶水也。情，波也。

If one does not incorporate one's human situation (*qing*) into one's innate moral disposition (*xing*), how then can one persevere in acting correctly ... the man of noble character incorporates his existential reality into his innate moral disposition, whereas the man of mean character does the opposite, he adapts his innate moral disposition to his existential reality. If *xing* can be likened to a body of water, then *qing* are the waves.[43]

---

42   *Quan Tang wen* 637: 6433. Cf. *Xing zi ming chu*: "its *xing* and *qing* are nearly equivalent" 其性情相近也 (slip 29; cf. Cook 2012: 720).

43   Yang Shen, "Xing qing shuo" 性情説, in *Sheng'an ji* 升庵集 5.13. As Yang Shen points out, the phrase *xing qi qing* first appears in Wang Bi's 王弼 (226–249) commentary to the *Book of Changes* (*Zhou Yi zhengyi* 周易正義, 26). Zhu Xi notes that Cheng Yi 程頤 (1033–1107) takes his cue from Wang Bi in adopting this phrase (*Zhuzi wenji* 53: 2520). He also argues that Cheng Yi's formulation is an improvement on Li Ao's (*Zhuzi yulei* 59: 1381). In *Mengzi*, Gaozi compares *xing* to flowing water to emphasize its malleability (*Mengzi yizhu* 11.2: 254). Here the analogy of *xing* with (still) water may be taken from Hu Hong 胡宏 (1105–1161), who calls *qing* "ripples" 水之瀾 and *yu* "waves" 水之波浪 (*Zhuzi yulei* 101.2589–2590).

Yang Shen's discussion also turns on a creative use of the two words as verbs, here apparently signifying "relating to one's *qing* as *xing*," and vice versa.[44] What I understand from this clever turn of phrase is the proposition that the capacity to internalize one's existential reality and integrate it into one's true nature, or the obverse—subjecting one's inborn moral potential to the demands of external reality—is what distinguishes the true "man of noble character" from the "man of mean character." Li's argument that *qing* is but the visible outer form of *xing*, building on the analogy of waves and water, finds expression in a variety of Chinese philosophical texts, from the *Xing zi ming chu*[45] all the way to the leading early Qing thinkers—in line with the common, though somewhat misleading, characterization of their thought as a form of "materialism"—who similarly argue that intrinsic principles can only be brought to realization through the medium of material reality.[46]

Sorting out the elements that govern Confucian attempts to define the essential ground of being becomes all the more complex when we take into

---

44 The concatenation of nominal and verbal uses of these words reminds one of the terms *natura naturata* and *natura naturans* in medieval and renaissance European Neo-Platonist discourse, best-known in the writings of Spinoza.

45 "The material substrate of pleasure, wrath, grief and sadness is one's inborn nature. When it reaches the point of external visibility, then it takes the form of concrete things" 喜怒哀悲之氣，性也。及其見於外，則物取之也 (slip 1; Cook 2012: 700). The text contends that one's innate predispositions cannot be actualized except in the context of external "things."

46 See, for example, Wang Fuzhi: "It is a fact that one's *xing* operates through the medium of one's *qing* .... when *one's* qing is activated independently, separate from one's *xing*, one then has the capacity to act in a manner contrary to the good." 性固行於情之中也……離性而自為情，則可以為不善矣 (*Du Sishu daquan shuo* 8.573); and again: "some people mistakenly assume that *qing* is equivalent to *xing* ... when *xing* is articulated in proper measure, that which constitutes its state of equilibrium is *qing*—in other words, *qing* is that which keeps *xing* in balance" 或人誤以情為性……性者節也，中之者情也，情中性也 (ibid., 8.574). Or Dai Zhen: "When one uses one's own *qing* to gauge that of others, one does not miss the mark, and can truly fulfill the intrinsic principles underlying one's behavior" 以情絜情而無爽失，於行事誠得其理矣. See also the quote from Dai Zhen on p. 330. See also Huang Zongxi 黃宗羲 (1610–1695): "The workings of *xing* cannot be observed except in the context of *qing*" 離情無以見性 (*Huang Zongxi quanji* 1: 136 ["Mengzi shi shuo" 孟子師説]).

account the parallel terms that figure in a variety of formulations. Chief among these is the word *xin* 心, whose significance in philosophical contexts generally indicates the seat of innate or acquired moral consciousness. Despite the clear lexical distinction between *xin* as commonly understood in the sense of "heart" or "mind," and the automatic glossing of *xing* as "nature," in certain contexts *xin* and *xing* become virtually interchangeable, most visibly in Mencius' discussion of the "full realization of the heart" (*jin qi xin* 盡其心),[47] in a sense identical to that expressed in numerous other Confucian arguments on the sagely state of attainment *jin qi xing* 盡其性 ("to fully realize one's innate disposition."). Zhu Xi and others also relax the distinction between *xin* and *xing* on occasion. Thus Zhu Xi explains: "there is nothing in one's inborn nature that is not good; that which emerges from one's core of being is *qing*, though there may be something not good in it" (性無不善，心所發為情，或有不善).[48] Instinctively, we assume that *xin* represents but one aspect of innate disposition, its "seat" or "locus," or the "core" of one's inner being. It is striking, therefore, when many of the leading voices of Song (960–1279) and later Neo-Confucian metaphysics, following Zhang Zai 張載 (1020–1077), elevate *xin* as an all-inclusive dimension that "governs" or "unites" *xing* and *qing*.[49]

Similar mental gymnastics can be observed with respect to the relation between *qing* and *li*. Thus, the crucial focus of Neo-Confucian debates initiated by Cheng Yi's 程頤 (1033–1107) provocative claim that *xing*, the inherent nature of things, is coterminous with the "principles" underlying

---

47   *Mengzi yizhu* 13.1: 301.

48   *Zhuzi yulei* 5: 92.

49   See Zhu Xi: "*Xing* embodies the substrate of principle at the core of one's being; *qing* equals the dynamic state of *xing*; one's inner core of being governs both one's *xing* and *qing*." 性者，心之理；情者，性之動；心者，性情之主 (*Zhuzi yulei* 5: 89). Much of the discourse on this issue revolves around Zhang Zai's 張載 (1020–1077) oft-quoted statement: "*Xin* totally encompasses *xing* and *qing*" 心，統性情 (*Zhang Zai ji*, 339). A similar inversion of the expected hierarchy seems to underlie *Guanzi*'s use of the phrase, the essential *qing* at the core of one's being 心之情 (*Guanzi jiaozhu* 49: 931 ["Nei ye"]).

their intrinsic structure of intelligibility (性即理也)[50] easily slides into identically-formulated polemic statements to the effect that it is *qing* or *xin* that constitutes the essential ground of being (*li* 理) 情即理也，心即理也, a claim frequently voiced in the thought of Wang Yangming 王陽明 (1472–1529) and others.[51] Dai Zhen 戴震 (1724–1777) goes as far as to profess the literal identity of *qing* and *li*:

> 以情絜情而無爽失，於行事誠得其理矣。情與理之名何以異?
>
> When one uses one's own *qing* to gauge that of others without missing the mark, one can truly fulfill the intrinsic principles underlying one's behavior. How, then, can one distinguish the two terms *qing* and *li*?[52]

The times of these latter thinkers, after all, saw the heightened focus on *qing* as feeling or sentiment—often synonymous with "love"—in the literary imagination, to the extent that scholars frequently speak (with a certain degree of hyperbole) of the "cult of *qing*" at the heart of late Ming and early Qing literati culture. It is important, therefore, to recognize that a writer such as Tang Xianzu 湯顯祖 (1550–1616)—whose romantic play *Mudan ting* 牡丹亭 (Peony pavilion) is often understood as a paean to the power of *qing* to countervail the logic of *li*—insists, in his preface to the play, on an

---

50   *Er Cheng ji*, 292.

51   Wang Yangming, *Chuanxi lu* (*Wang Yangming quanji*, vol. 2). Cf. Wang Fuzhi's pointed adaptation of the phrase in the following two formulations: "With respect to sages, their desires are congruent with the principles of things; *qing* is equivalent to the entire dimension of *xing*" 若聖人，則欲即理也，情一性也 (*Du Sishu daquan shuo* 4: 246); "Given the fact that *xing* is observed within the context of *qing*, it can also be expressed with the term *xin*. *Xin* totally encompasses *xing* and *qing*; from the perspective of its essential endowment, this is manifest in the state of actualization of *xing*; it comes into being through the vehicle of *qing*. We are speaking of *xin*, so that means that *xing* exists within *xin*, such that *xing* is the basic ground and *xin* is its dynamic operation" 性之於情上見者，亦得謂之心也。心統性情，自其函受而言也。此於性之發見，乘情而出者言心，則謂性在心，而性為體，心為用也 (*Du Sishu daquan shuo* 8: 554–555).

52   *Mengzi ziyi shuzheng, juan* shang 上, 2.

essentially non-dialectical balance between *qing* and *li*.[53] The same may be said of Cao Xueqin 曹雪芹 (ca. 1715–1764), whose incomparably profound exploration of the depths of human feeling in *Hongloumeng* 紅樓夢 (The Dream of Red Mansions) is infused with ambivalent, yet unmistakable intimations of the deeper truths of the human condition. This topic has been discussed in depth in numerous recent studies, including my own, and need not be rehearsed here.

At the start of this chapter, I suggested that the apparent dichotomy between the two separate semantic fields covered by the term *qing* in seminal Chinese texts may be resolved, in some sense, within a common semantic ground. I argued that this commonality goes beyond the simple observation that the two sets of meanings are often commingled across a broad spectrum of texts, from Early to Late Imperial China, such that one cannot posit a straight-line pattern of lexical development from a hypothetical "original" sense to later derived usages. Perhaps the clearest articulation of the conceptual merging of the notion of "feelings" with the idea of "essential reality" is found in the opening section of the canonic *Zhongyong* text, drawing its essential metaphysical distinction between a level of being in which the archetypal markers of the world of concrete experience, expressed in terms of human emotional states, remain pure potentialities, i.e. they have "not-yet emerged" into manifestation, and one in which they are actualized in concrete reality (this passage, of course, provided the inspiration for the title of the present chapter). As I have discussed here and elsewhere, the use of the formula of the four emotional states is not merely a rhetorical convention, but rests upon a broad understanding in Confucian metaphysical discourse, according to which the ultimate ground of being is inseparable from the essential reality of the world of human experience. Over the thousand-year span of what we

---

53   See the ambiguous final line of the preface: "Those who do not possess unimpeded vision always take this in opposition to moral principle. Nonetheless, even if one proclaims that *li* has no effective presence, how can one know that *qing* must necessarily exist?" (自非通人，恆以理相格耳。第云理之所必無，安知情之所必有邪? *Mudan ting*, 1 ["Tici" 題辭]).

sometimes call "Neo-Confucian" philosophy—from late Tang and Song through Ming and Qing—the most profound thinkers are at pains to define the complex relations among such terms as the intrinsic nature of existence (*xing* 性), the underlying patterns of intelligibility (*li* 理), and the core of being (*xin* 心), all of which overlap and intersect with the dual signification of the term *qing*, as an indicator of both the experiential reality—the "feelings," so to speak—and the ultimate "truth" of essential reality.

Bibliography

Beixi ziyi 北溪字義. By Chen Chun 陳淳 (1483–1544). E-*Siku quanshu* edition.

Bruya, Brian. 2001. "Qing and Emotion in Early Chinese Thought." *Ming Qing yanjiu* 10: 151–176.

Chunqiu fanlu yizheng 春秋繁露義證. 1992. Composed by Su Yu 蘇輿 (1874–1914). Beijing: Zhonghua shuju.

Cook, Scott. 2012. *The Bamboo Texts of Guodian: A Study and Complete Translation.* Vols. 1–2. Ithaca, NY: Cornell East Asia Series.

Du Sishu daquan shuo 讀四書大全說. 1989. By Wang Fuzhi 王夫之 (1619–1692). Beijing: Zhonghua shuju.

Graham, Angus C. 1967. "The Background of the Mencian Theory of Human Nature." *The Tsing Hua Journal of Chinese Studies* 6: 215–274.

Guanzi jiaozhu 管子校注. 2004. Compiled by Li Xiangfeng 黎翔鳳. Beijing: Zhonghua shuju.

Guiguzi 鬼谷子. 1989. With commentaries by Tao Hongjing 陶弘景 (456–536). Taipei: Shangwu yinshu guan.

Er Cheng ji 二程集. 1981. By Cheng Hao 程顥 (1032–1085) and Cheng Yi 程頤 (1033–1107). Punctuated by Wang Xiaoyu 王孝魚. Beijing: Zhonghua shuju.

Huainan honglie jijie 淮南鴻烈集解. 1989. With commentaries and annotations by Liu Wendian 劉文典 (1889–1958). Edited by Feng Yi 馮逸 and Qiao Hua 喬華. Beijing: Zhonghua shuju.

Huang Zongxi quanji 黃宗羲全集. 2005. By Huang Zongxi 黃宗羲 (1610–1695). Edited by Wu Guang 吳光 and Shen Shanhong 沈善洪. Hangzhou: Zhejiang guji chubanshe.

Kongcongzi jiaoshi 孔叢子校釋. 2011. Edited by Fu Yashu 傅亞庶. Beijing: Zhonghua shuju.

Liji jijie 禮記集解. 1998. With commentaries compiled by Sun Xidan 孫希旦 (1736–1784). Edited by Shen Xiaohuan 沈嘯寰 and Wang Xingxian 王星賢. Beijing: Zhonghua shuju.

Lüshi chunqiu jiaoshi 呂氏春秋校釋. 2002. With annotations by Chen Qiyou 陳奇猷. Shanghai: Shanghai guji chubanshe.

Lunheng jiaoshi 論衡校釋. 1990. By Wang Chong 王充 (27–97). Edited by Huang Hui 黃暉. Beijing: Zhonghua shuju.

Lunyu yizhu 論語譯注. 1992. Annotated by Yang Bojun 楊伯峻. Beijing: Zhonghua shuju.

Lunyu zhangju 論語章句. Annotated by Zhu Xi 朱熹 (1130–1200). In *Sishu zhangju* 四書章句. Beijing: Zhonghua shuju.

Mengzi yizhu 孟子譯注. 1992. Annotated by Yang Bojun 楊伯峻. Beijing: Zhonghua shuju.

Mengzi ziyi shuzheng 孟子字義疏證. 1982. By Dai Zhen 戴震 (1724–1777). Edited by He Wenguang 何文光. Beijing: Zhonghua shuju.

Ming jingshi wen bian 明經世文編. 1987. By Chen Zilong 陳子龍 (1608–1647) et al. Beijing: Zhonghua shuju.

Mozi jiaozhu 墨子校注. 1994. Compiled and annotated by Wu Yujiang 吳毓江 (1898–1977). Beijing: Zhonghua shuju.

Mudan ting 牡丹亭. 1978. By Tang Xianzu 湯顯祖 (1550–1616). Annotated by Xu Shuofang 徐朔方. Beijing: Renmin wenxue chubanshe.

Puett, Michael. 2004. "The Ethics of Responding Properly: The Notion of *Qing* in Early Chinese Thought." In *Love and Emotions in Traditional Chinese Literature*, edited by Halvor Eifring, 37–68. Leiden: Brill.

Quan Tang wen 全唐文. 1976. Compiled by Dong Gao 董誥 (1740–1818) et al. Beijing: Zhonghua shuju.

Sheng'an ji 升庵集. By Yang Shen 楊慎 (1488–1529). E-*Siqu quanshu* edition.

Wang Yangming quanji 王陽明全集. 1991. By Wang Shouren 王守仁 (Wang Yangming 王陽明, 1472–1529). Edited by Wu Guang 吳光 et al. Shanghai: Shanghai guji chubanshe.

Xing zi ming chu 性自命出. See Cook 2012.

Xu Fuguan 徐復觀. 1994 (1952, rev. 1969). *Zhongguo renxing lun shi* 中國人性論史. Taipei: Shangwu.

Xunzi jijie 荀子集解. 1992. Annotated by Wang Xianqian 王先謙 (1842–1917). Edited by Shen Xiaohuan 沈嘯寰 and Wang Xingxian 王星賢. Beijing: Zhonghua shuju.

Zhang Zai ji 張載集. 1985. By Zhang Zai 張載 (1020–1077). Edited by Zhang Xichen 章錫琛. Beijing: Zhonghua shuju.

Zhou Yi zhengyi 周易正義. 2009. Commentaries by Wang Bi 王弼 (226–249), Han Kangbo 韓康伯 (4th c.), and Kong Yingda 孔穎達 (574–648). Punctuated by Huang Kan 黃侃 (1886–1935). Beijing: Zhigong chubanshe.

Zhuangzi jishi 莊子集釋. 1995. Compiled by Guo Qingfan 郭慶藩 (1844–1896). Punctuated by Wang Xiaoyu 王孝魚. Beijing: Zhonghua shuju.

Zhuzi yulei 朱子語類. 1986. By Zhu Xi 朱熹 (1130–1200). Compiled by Li Jingde 黎靖德 (late 13th c.). Edited by Wang Xingxian 王星賢. Beijing: Zhonghua shuju.

Zhuzi wenji 朱子文集. 2000. By Zhu Xi 朱熹 (1130–1200). Edited by Chen Junmin. Taipei: Yuncheng wenhua.

9

Looking for the True Self

Wai-yee Li

My ruminations on the problem of "the true self" are inspired by an entry in Gu Yanwu's 顧炎武 (1613–1682) *Rizhi lu* 日知錄 (Record of knowledge accrued daily). In that passage he laments late Ming moral decline, as evinced by (possibly unconscious) allusions to *Zhuangzi* 莊子in examination essays.[1] Gu points out that "the word *zhen* 真 (genuine, real, true, authentic)[2] does not exist in the Five Classics; it first appears in the writings of Laozi and Zhuangzi" 五經無真字，始見老莊之書.[3] He goes on to parse the associations of *zhen* with death, transformation, immortality, transcendence, and mystical experience in Daoist writings (*Laozi* 老子, *Zhuangzi*, *Liezi* 列子), *Shuowen* 説文, and the accounts of aspirants to immortality and Daoist transcendence. Gu argues that the other common meanings of *zhen*—truth, reality, fact—emerged only in the Han dynasty, when the issue was often the correspondence or the gap between the name

---

1   Gu Yanwu, "Po ti yong Zhuangzi" 破題用莊子, in *Rizhi lu*, 18.659.

2   Of course these words have different valences in English, but instead of adhering to one English translation of the word *zhen*, I will use different words depending on the context.

3   The word *zhen* also does not appear in the *Analects*, *Mengzi* 孟子, and *Liji* 禮記.

or the appearance and the reality.[4] This set of meanings engage him less, however, than the notion of a person's inwardness or "true core."

For Gu Yanwu, the symbolic harbinger of the fall of the Ming dynasty was a model examination essay from 1568, in which the examiner expounds the idea of knowledge by drawing from *Zhuangzi*: "The Sage teaches the worthy man about true knowledge, which is nothing more than refusing to block his heart and mind" 聖人教賢者以真知，在不昧其心而已. Gu concludes darkly: "Scholars of our times avowedly adopt Mencius' 'innate moral knowledge' but secretly embrace Zhuangzi's 'true knowledge'" 今之學者明用孟子之良知，暗用莊子之真知.[5]

Taking my cue from Gu Yanwu, I will examine the reverberations of the word *zhen* in late Ming (late 16th to mid-17th century) culture and literature, juxtaposing confident assertions of spontaneity and freedom with hidden anxieties and uncertainties. In looking for the roots this dialectic, I will explore notions of the "true being" (*zhenren* 真人) and "true knowledge" (*zhenzhi* 真知) in *Zhuangzi*. Such a radical temporal gap is in part justified by the resurgence of interest in *Zhuangzi* during the late Ming.

1. The Problem of the True Self in Late Ming Culture

When Gu Yanwu decries allusions to the idea of "true knowledge" in *Zhuangzi*, perhaps he has in mind some version of Daoist transcendence

---

4   Gu Yanwu quotes examples from *Shiji* 史記. The context of adjudicating value or telling the real from the fake also underlies the discussions of *zhen* in other Han texts. In *Chunqiu fanlu* 春秋繁露, the context is often the relationship between "name" and "reality" (*Chunqiu fanlu yizheng*, 35.290–293, 36.312–313). In *Lunheng* 論衡, the word is embedded in discussions of nature and cultivation (*Lunheng jiaoshi*, 7.60–62, 67, 8.70, 75–77), knowledge and judgment, truth and falsehood (ibid. 2.19, 5.37, 16.167, 31.474, 63.887, 83.1174, 84.1179–1181), and affective responses to mere images or representations (ibid. 26.363, 27.381, 32.511, 47.694–706, 50.722, 64.923–924).

5   The terms *liangzhi* 良知 and *zhenzhi* are often used interchangeably in Wang Yangming's 王陽明 (1472–1529) writings. For Gu, this mixing of vocabulary meant that Ming Confucianism was "contaminated" by Daoism and Buddhism. All translations in this essay are mine.

that hides the pitfalls of self-indulgence, self-obsession, the abeyance of tangible moral concerns, or the severance of ties with socio-political order. He implies that the discourse of the quest for inner truth and genuine self-expression, so pervasive in late Ming culture, is morally problematic, not least because of its roots in non-Confucian writings. Gu's critique, typical of early Qing retrospection on the late Ming, emphasizes the deleterious effects of the quest for the "true self," which is precisely what comes to be celebrated in modern views of that cultural moment.[6] Histories of late Ming culture and literature are still filled with truisms on "individualism," "romanticism," "authenticity," and "freedom of spirit."[7] Such epithets suggest excess, confidence, and spontaneity, but even a cursory survey would show that late Ming writers are keenly aware of the problems and paradoxes in the celebration of genuineness.

1.1 Inward and Outward Trajectories

Genuineness seems least problematic when it is identified as the goal of moral self-cultivation, as in the discourse of innate moral knowledge in the "learning of the heart and mind" (*xinxue* 心學) propounded by Wang Yangming 王陽明 (1472–1529) and his followers. Wang defines "true core" (*zhenwu* 真吾) as "innate moral knowledge," the opposite of the "selfish core" (*siwu* 私吾) dominated by worldly concerns and desires.[8] In response to a disciple's qualms about the difficulty of "overcoming the self" (*keji* 克己), Wang Yangming urges the recognition of the "true self" (*zhenji* 真己) as "the master of the body" 軀殼的主宰 and the potential realization of "heavenly principle" (*tianli* 天理).[9] In a letter to his friend Lu Cheng 陸澄 (dated 1521), Wang redirects the latter's interest in the "genuine me" (*zhenwo* 真我) as enshrined in Daoist practices to Confucian self-cultivation: "As for

---

6   See, e.g., Wu Chengxue and Li Guangmo 2002.

7   There are also critiques of this position, e.g., Gong Pengcheng 2008.

8   Wang Yangming, "Congwu Daoren ji" 從吾道人記 (*Wang Yangming quanji* 王陽明全集 1: 250).

9   Wang Yangming, *Chuanxi lu* 傳習錄 (*Wang Yangming quanji* 1: 35–36).

what you call the 'genuine me,' so long as one can indeed be vigilant even with what is not seen, fearful even with what is not heard, and focus one's intent on this [i.e., inner power], then spirit, vital energy, and essence will all go the same way" 原靜所云真我者，果能戒謹不睹，恐懼不聞，而專志於是，則神往氣往精往. Wang implies that the Daoist "genuine me" has a more compelling Confucian version: the inner moral resources whereby one can attain transcendence.[10]

Wang Yangming's invocation of lines about vigilant mindfulness from the *Zhongyong* 中庸 (The mean)[11] reminds us that the idea of spontaneous illumination or direct access to inner truth is built on internalizing unremitting focus (*gongfu* 工夫). Thus Wang Yanming's disciple Wang Ji 王畿 (1498–1583) describes innate moral knowledge as "the spiritual root of moral nature" 性之靈根: "it is the true face and form that has always been there; it does not need to depend on cultivation to become perfect" 本來真面目，固不待修證而後全. However, this "true face and form" is not to be confused with mere impulses: "But if one only follows impulses and regards that as abiding by one's moral nature, relies on emotions and judgments and regards that as communing with subtle truths, and fails to attain constant focus so that it can become the guiding force, then one would change from one moment to the next, becoming adrift with no place of return." 若徒任作用為率性，倚情識為通微，不能隨時翕聚以為之主，倏忽變化，將至於蕩無所歸.[12] In a similar spirit, he commends the "true

---

10 Wang Yangming, "Yu Lu Yuanjing" 與陸原靜 (*Wang Yangming quanji* 1: 187). For Lu Cheng (1517 *jinshi*), see Huang Zongxi 黃宗羲, *Mingru xue'an* 明儒學案 (Huang *Zongxi quanji* 7: 335–336).

11 *Zhongyong* 1 (*Zhuzi zhangju* numbering): "That is why the noble man is vigilant even with what is not seen, fearful even with what is not heard." 是故君子戒慎乎其所不睹，恐懼乎其所不聞 (*Sishu jizhu*, 17).

12 Wang Ji, "Shu tongxin ce juan" 書同心冊卷 (*Wang Ji ji* 王畿集, 121–123). *Benlai mianmu* is a Buddhist term that first appears in the *Tan jing* 壇經 (Platform Sutra); the emphasis on self-cultivation here may be a deliberate amelioration of the Chan overtones. Wang Yangming equates *benlai mianmu* with "innate moral knowledge;" see *Chuanxi lu* (*Wang Yangming quanji* 1: 67). References to Buddhist and Daoist ideas are even more pervasive in Wang Ji's writings (Chung 2010).

naturalness" 真自然 of King Wen as the realization of these lines from the *Shijing* 詩經 (Classic of poetry): "With mindful vigilance, he serves the god on high" 小心翼翼，昭事上帝.[13] He compares the recovery of one's "true original nature" (*benlai zhenxing* 本來真性) from the crust of worldly concerns and desires to the process of smelting metal. Just as gold buried in ore requires the application of a strong flame, one's true nature can only be liberated from worldly desires by self-examination and self-cultivation.[14]

The analogy of metallurgy or alchemy is useful for visualizing the inward trajectory of attaining or recovering one's true moral nature in *xinxue* discourse. It provides an illuminating contrast with writings more concerned with the expression or communication of "the true self." Li Zhi 李贄 (1527–1602), known for writings that sometimes articulate subversion and iconoclasm, often presents "true nature" as something that needs to be expressed rather than attained—that is, the trajectory is outwards rather than inwards. Expression comes with the burden of confronting potential misunderstanding. It is not surprising, therefore, that Li Zhi's essay "The Childlike Mind" (Tongxin shuo 童心説),[15] usually celebrated as a paean to the true self, should focus on questions of evaluation and misjudgment (rather than self-cultivation).

The essay begins with an apologetic statement from Li Zhi's friend Jiao Hong 焦竑 (1540–1620), who wrote (under the pseudonym Longdong shannong 龍洞山農, Mountain Farmer of the Dragon Cave) in his 1582 preface to the Yuan play *Xixiang ji* 西廂記 (The western chamber, ca. 14ᵗʰ century): "Those with real understanding must not say that I still have a childlike mind" 知者勿謂我尚有童心可也. Here "childlike mind" is negative: the reader recalls examples of classical usage, such as the dire prediction for Lord Zhao of Lu 魯昭公 (r. 542–510 BCE, exiled 517 BCE)

---

13   Wang Ji, "Lun xue shu" 論學書, cited in Huang Zongxi's *Mingru xue'an* (*Huang Zongxi quanji* 7: 291). The lines are from "Da ming" 大明 (Mao 236).

14   Wang Ji, "Nanqiao bieyan" 南譙別言 (*Wang Ji ji*, 685–686).

15   *Li Zhi quanji zhu* 1: 276–277. For translations of this essay, see de Bary, "The Childlike Mind-and-Heart," in de Bary 1999, 867–868; Handler-Sptiz, Lee, Saussy 2016, 106–113.

in *Zuozhuan* 左傳 as one who "would not be able to come to a good end" 不終 because he "still had a childlike mind" 猶有童心 even at the age of nineteen, as evinced by his ritual impropriety during his mother's funeral.[16] Li Zhi refutes this implicit denigration of "the childlike mind" by upholding it as "the genuine mind" (*zhenxin* 真心), the untarnished beginning of consciousness:

夫童心者，絕假純真，最初一念之本心也。若失卻童心，便失卻真人。人而非真，全不復有初矣。

The childlike mind cuts off all fakery and is pure genuineness—it is the original mind behind the first glimmer of consciousness. If one loses the childlike mind, then one loses the genuine mind. To lose the genuine mind is to lose the genuine person. If a person is not genuine, then he will no longer recover his beginning.

At first glance, "the childlike mind" echoes "the heart and mind of the newborn child" 赤子之心 in *Mengzi*, an idea valorized by Wang Yangming and his followers, notably Wang Gen 王艮 (1483–1541), Wang Ji, and most pointedly Luo Rufang 羅汝芳 (1515–1588).[17] It is also possible that the image of the child here evokes associations with Daoist transcendence, as with the baby in *Laozi* and the one called a child because he is "the companion

---

16   "By the time of the burial, he had changed his hempen mourning clothes three times, but the hempen lapels still looked soiled." See *Zuozhuan*, Xiang 31.4: 1186; *Zuo Tradition*, 3: 1275.

17   Wang Yangming emphasizes the child's moral nature in *Chuanxi lu* (*Wang Yangming quanji* 1: 34). Wang Ji suggests that the Confucian notion of the "newborn child" encompasses analogous Buddhist and Daoist ideals ("Nan you hui ji" 南遊會記, *Wang Ji ji*, 154). Luo Rufang identifies the "heart of the newborn child" as "heavenly principle" (*Mingru xue'an*, in *Huang Zongxi quanji* 8:6). Li Zhi wrote about Wang Ji and Luo Rufang with deep admiration (*Li Zhi quanji zhu* 1: 327–329, 335–346). He referred to Wang Gen's son Wang Bi 王襞 (1511–1587) as his teacher (*Li Zhi quanji zhu* 3: 276). Huang Zongxi did not include Li Zhi in his history of Ming Confucian scholars, *Ming ru xue'an*, but Ji Wenfu 嵇文甫 (1895–1963) put him in the category of "Radical Wing of the Wang Yangming School" 王學左派 (Ji Wenfu 2013). Cf. Zuo Dongling 2000: 336–377, 405–437, 545–601; Luo Zongqiang 2006: 265–343.

of heaven" 與天為徒 in *Zhuangzi*.[18] But it soon becomes obvious that Li Zhi is not interested in "the childlike mind" as the goal of quest or as the impetus for moral action. The beginning polemical stance (arguing against a negative understanding of "the childlike mind") persists throughout the essay. This oppositional mood underlies the diatribes against "fake people" (*jiaren* 假人), "fake words" (*jiayan* 假言), "fake deeds" (*jiashi* 假事), and "fake writings" (*jiawen* 假文). Li Zhi does not explain how one reaches the childlike mind, except perhaps by implication through the process of its "unblocking" by removing obstacles such as acquired principles and information (*daoli wenjian* 道理聞見) and the desire to gain a good name or to avoid a bad one. Instead he celebrates how this childlike mind produces great works as unconscious craft, the "natural generation of finely patterned writing" (*ziwen* 自文).[19] This elision comes about because his prime concern is the manifestation (rather than the attainment) of "the childlike mind" and its opposite as well as the authority to elevate one and decry the other.

Li Zhi's essay is famous for its valorization of *Xixiang ji*, *Shuihu zhuan* 水滸傳 (Water margin), and Ming examination essays[20] as being rooted in "the childlike mind" and its heretical rejection of the canonical classics ("Six Classics, *Analects*, *Mengzi*") as "topics and excuses for Confucian scholars, the gathering place for fake people" 道學之口實，假人之淵藪. While the praise of fiction and drama recurs in his oeuvre, his condemnation of canonical classics is obviously belied by his extensive commentaries on these works. Why then did he strike this pose? Perhaps contemporary hypocrisy drove him to extremes.[21] Perhaps he obeyed the dictate of his

---

18 *Laozi* 55 (*Laozi jiaoshi*, 39); *Zhuangzi jishi* 4.143 ("Ren jian shi" 人間世). The child commanding transcendent perspectives also appears in *Zhuangzi jishi* 24.830–833 ("Xu Wugui" 徐無鬼).

19 Li Zhi also eulogizes untrammeled literary creation in "Zashuo" 雜説, "Du lü fushuo" 讀律膚説 (*Li Zhi quanji zhu* 1: 272–276, 364–365).

20 The inclusion of examination essays (*juziye* 舉子業) may seem incongruous, but it fits into Li Zhi's argument pitting contemporary and recent genres against hallowed ancient ones.

21 A provocative and paradoxical stance can encourage critical judgment (Handler-Sptiz 2017).

oppositional stance vis-à-vis society—the very titles of his books, *Fen shu* 焚書 (A book to be burned) and *Cang shu* 藏書 (A book to be hidden), convey defiance. What seems obvious is that while being genuine seems to imply the spontaneous manifestation of "the childlike mind," its expression is inevitably mediated by the anticipation of how one's words and actions are perceived. It also involves a sense of radical difference, the awareness of the gap between one's views and "consensual opinion" and of the corollary struggle to claim the authority of judgment.

In that sense Li Zhi's essay is intensely dialogic and proleptic: the argument proceeds by refuting its imagined detractors. It is an act of communication that presumes misunderstanding, hence the concluding line: "Alas, how can I get to have a word about writing with the true great sage, the one who has not yet lost his childlike mind"? 嗚呼！吾又安得真正大聖人童心未曾失者而與之一言文哉. It echoes the last line of "External Things" (Waiwu 外物) in *Zhuangzi*: "How can I get to have a word with one who has forgotten words?" 吾安得乎忘言之人而與之言哉?[22] The paradox of transcending language through language in *Zhuangzi* becomes the paradox of spontaneity and mediation, individual difference and authority in Li Zhi's essay. The question becomes: How can the genuine core that defies external constraints find external validation?

Declarative intent can thus be fraught with irony when the focus shifts to the authority of speaking and the context of communication. These latent issues in "The Childlike Mind" are more self-consciously articulated in "Rhapsody on Crossing the River" (*Shejiang fu* 涉江賦) by the poet, playwright, painter, and calligrapher Xu Wei 徐渭 (1521–1593):[23]

爰有一物	There is this one thing:
無罣無礙	Without cares, without burdens,
在小匪細	Not so trivial when it comes to smallness,

---

22   *Zhuangzi jishi* 26.944.

23   *Xu Wei ji* 1: 1–2.

在大匪泥	Not so implacable when it comes to greatness.
來不知始	Coming, one knows not how it begins,
往不知馳	Leaving, one knows not whence it veers.
得之者成	He who obtains it succeeds,
失之者敗	He who loses it is defeated.
得亦無攜	Obtain it and there is nothing to carry,
失亦不脫	Lose it and there is no casting off.
在方寸間	Existing in the heart and mind,
周天地折	It encompasses heaven and earth.
勿謂覺靈	Do not call awakening numinous—
是為真我	This is the genuine me.[24]
覺有變遷	Awakening comes with changes,
其體安處	Where will its body find a place?
體無不含	There is nothing the body does not encompass,
覺亦從出	And from it awakening also emerges.
覺固不離	Awakening is of course not detached from the body,
覺亦不即	But it is also not attached to it.[25]

This "genuine me" can be lost if not properly guarded: "The external bandit is easy to fend off, / The stealth uprising cannot be borne" 外寇易防，竊發莫支. Nurturing it is like building a high terrace: "Of imposing height, but missing one basket of earth, / It finally becomes a mere mound. / This is what I worry about, / How can anything else grieve me?" 九仞一虧，終為阜丘。予斯之憂，他奚愴懷？ The idea of inner naturalness ("Without cares, without burdens") that nevertheless requires careful nurturing is reminiscent of *xinxue* writings.[26]

---

24 The term "genuine me" (*zhenwo* 真我) first appears in Buddhist sutras (ca. 4th century).

25 *Yuanjue jing* 圓覺經 (p. 30): "Not attached, not detached; no binding, no letting go" 不即不離，無縛無脫.

26 Xu Wei develops similar ideas in "Du 'Long ti shuo'" 讀龍惕説 (*Xu Wei ji* 2: 677–679). Ji Ben's 季本 (1485–1563) "Long ti shuo" emphasizes the need to balance "naturalness" (*ziran* 自然) with "vigilance" (*ti* 惕), and Xu Wei further elaborates on their convergence.

Xu Wei wrote this rhapsody in 1552 on his way home to Shanyin (Zhejiang) after failing in the provincial examination. He begins by invoking Pan Yue's 潘岳 (247–300) "Rhapsody on Autumn Meditation" 秋興賦 (*Qiuxing fu*). Despite similarities of circumstances (both Pan and Xu were thirty-two when they composed their pieces, both suffered adversities and lamented graying hair), Xu notes a basic difference: whereas Pan remains attached to mundane glory and pleasures while professing a desire for withdrawal, Xu is sincere in avowing detachment.[27] The details of Xu Wei's life suggested otherwise. Stung by injustice, repeated failures in the civil service examination, and the calumny surrounding his patron Hu Zongxian 胡宗憲 (1512–1565), Xu Wei was driven by passionate engagement and rancor. Madness, self-mutilation, attempted suicide, the verdict of murder, and incarceration dogged his tragic life. Although that biographical context had yet to unfold, Xu Wei's disappointment even here is unmistakable. "Crossing the River" abides by, but ultimately eludes, the convention of "the consolation of philosophy," whose prototype may be Jia Yi's 賈誼 (200–169 BCE) "Rhapsody on the Owl" (*Funiao fu* 鵩鳥賦), in which Jia Yi calls upon the supposedly inauspicious bird to help him transcend worldly vicissitudes.[28]

Deliberation on the attributes of the "genuine me" (*zhenwo* 真我), cast in the form of a riddle reminiscent of Xunzi's proto-rhapsody, is framed by an almost comical exchange between Xu Wei and his older cousins.[29] They spot his gray hair and try to pull it; he slips away before submitting. They urge equanimity about his recent failure, and he responds with a defensive

---

27 Pan Yue's insincerity is famously portrayed in Yuan Haowen's 元好問 (1190–1257) "Lun shi sanshi shou" 論詩三十首 (6th poem): "The lofty feelings of the 'Rhapsody on Reclusion' last for a thousand years, / Who could have believed that Anren (Pan Yue) groveled in the roadside dust?" 高情千古閒居賦，爭信安仁拜路塵 (*Yuan Haowen quanji*, 338).

28 *Shiji* 84.2496–2500. The title is a later addition.

29 *Xunzi* 26 consists of a series of riddles presented in a question-and-answer form (*Xunzi jijie* 26.472–484). Its beginning line ("There is this great thing" 爰有大物) is only slightly modified in Xu Wei's rhapsody. The term *bozhong* 伯仲 usually means older brothers, but by this point both of Xu Wei's half-brothers had died.

excursus replete with Daoist and Buddhist allusions. Xu Wei claims to care only about the "genuine me," but instead of simply upholding it like an indomitable spirit capable of transcendent perspectives, he ends up affirming its corporeality. How then can one "rise above" physical decline? The piece ends with comic dismay and a quasi-apology. "Heaven-endowed lack" 稟其缺 makes him look forty-eight at age thirty-two:

又予視髮	Again I look at my hair:
玄綢白希	It's mostly dark, with a few white strands—
遠窺不得	From afar almost imperceptible,
逼視始知	Discernible only upon close inspection.
不審其變	One does not know the time or season
在何歲時	When this change came about.
豈以茲秋	How can you seize on this autumn
謂予憂為	And say that it's the cause of my sorrow?

Most modern interpreters read Xu Wei's celebration of the "genuine me" as a profession of faith and a bulwark against the lack of external validation.[30] He honored his cousin Wang Ji and Ji Ben 季本 (a follower of Wang Yangming) as teachers. Their close association began four or five years earlier,[31] and the "genuine me" here can thus be read as the fruit of a spiritual quest. It also tallies with Xu Wei's emphasis on "the true color" (*bense* 本色), sincerity, and the rejection of imitation in his literary prefaces and postscripts.[32] However, although Xu seems to uphold assiduous self-cultivation with the image of building a terrace, he also juxtaposes (and implicitly qualifies) the transcendent "genuine me" with circumstantial

---

30 See, e.g., Zhou Qun and Xie Jianhua 2006: 139–159.

31 Xu Wei, "Ji pu" 畸譜, in *Xu Wei ji* 4: 1328, 1332. For Xu Wei's biographies of Ji Ben, see *Xu Wei ji* 2: 628–629, 643–650. The poems Xu Wei addressed to Wang Ji are *gatha*-like summaries of *xinxue* principles (*Xu Wei ji* 1: 228, 2: 348–349). Ji Yun 紀昀 (1724–1805) characterized Xu Wei as the "transmitter of the expansive, unrestrained side of Wang Yangming" 傳姚江縱恣之派 (*Siku quanshu zongmu* 178.1606).

32 Xu Wei, "*Xiaofu shi* xu" 肖甫詩序, "Shu *Caoxuan tang gao* hou" 書草玄堂稿後, "Zeng Cheng weng xu" 贈成翁序, "*Xixiang* xu" 西廂序 (*Xu Wei ji* 2: 534–535, 579, 3: 907–908, 4: 1089).

constraints and ineluctable mundaneness and corporeality. The impetus behind defining the "genuine me" is to protest the misunderstanding that he is so small-minded as to succumb to self-doubt or frustration because of his failure in the examination in 1552. Xu Wei is trying to explain himself to his interlocutors, and the rhetorical context of self-justification and self-revelation is important to many formulations of genuineness.

1.2 Self-Division

As a corollary of the "outward trajectory" outlined above, works like "The Childlike Mind" or "Crossing the River" pointedly address the implied or represented reader. Does this sense of audience compromise genuineness? In Xu Wei's case, sometimes the original target audience (his patron) sets limits on "the true self" he hopes to convey to an ideal audience. How much "genuineness" can one express in commissioned writings? Xu Wei reflects on this question in the prefaces for collections of his writings composed during his tenure as Hu Zongxian's secretary (1557–1564).[33] Li Zhi often declares that he is following his own inclinations as he defies conventions or that he is writing only for his own pleasure,[34] yet the obsession with how he will be judged or understood (or misjudged and misunderstood) is never far from the surface. Li Zhi maintains that to be "self-consciously natural" 有意為自然 is no different from "forced correction" 矯強.[35] The discourse of innate moral nature is filled with images of spontaneity and continuity. This emphasis may be rooted in Mencius' idea that "acting from humaneness and dutifulness" 由仁義行 is superior to "acting humanely and dutifully" 行仁義[36]—that is,

---

33 See Xu Wei, "Chao dai ji xiao xu" 抄代集小序, "Mu chao xiao xu" 幕抄小序, "Chao xiao ji zixu" 抄小集自序, in *Xu Wei ji* 2: 536–537.

34 See, e.g., Li Zhi's letter to Yuan Zongdao (1592): "In general my books were all written for my pleasure; they were not written for others" 大凡我書皆為求以快樂自己，非為人也 ("Ji Jing you shu" 寄京友書, *Li Zhi quanji zhu*, 1: 171).

35 Li Zhi, "Du lü fushuo," in *Li Zhi quanji zhu*, 1: 364–365.

36 *Mengzi yizhu* 8.19: 191.

virtue should ideally be a natural motivating force rather than a goal-oriented code. But what if naturalness and the ideal moral action fail to converge?

The sage king Shun 舜, upheld as the paragon of "natural virtue" in *Mengzi*,[37] raises the issue of defining genuineness as intention or as natural force for Li Zhi. In a letter dated 1596 sent to Yuan Zongdao 袁宗道 (1560–1600), Li Zhi argues that Shun's love for his evil brother Xiang 象 is fake and genuine at the same time. In *Mengzi*, Wanzhang 萬章 asks Mencius: is Shun's happiness fake when his brother Xiang sees him and assumes the appearance of comity, having been foiled in his plot to murder Shun and to take over his property and wives? Mengzi claims that Shun knows about Xiang's plot because of his complete fraternal empathy with Xiang: "When Xiang worries, he worries; when Xiang is happy, he is happy" 象憂亦憂，象喜亦喜. "He (Xiang) has come by [assuming] the way of fraternal love, that is why Shun is sincerely happy about it. How can it be fake?" 彼以愛兄之道來，故誠信而喜之，奚偽焉?[38] Li Zhi disputes this in his letter to Yuan:[39]

> 若如軻言，則是舜不知象之殺己，是不智也；知其欲殺己而喜之，是喜殺也，是不誠也……故僕謂舜為偽喜，非過也。
>
> If it is as Meng Ke (Mencius) says, then Shun, being unaware that Xiang is trying to murder him, is unwise. If he is happy knowing that Xiang wants to murder him, then he is happy being murdered and is insincere ... That is why it is not wrong for me to say that Shun's happiness is fake.

But Li Zhi equivocates:

> 夫舜明知象之欲殺己也，然非真心喜象則不可以解象之毒，縱象之毒終不可解，然舍喜象無別解之法矣。故其喜象是偽也，其主意必欲喜象以得象之喜是真也。

---

37 See, e.g., *Mengzi yizhu* 8.19: 191; 13.30: 314.

38 *Mengzi yizhu* 9.2: 210.

39 Li Zhi, "Yu youren shu" 與友人書, *Li Zhi quanji zhu*, 1: 181–182. Yuan Zongdao was the oldest of the three Yuan brothers famous for their advocacy of the "natural spirit" (xingling 性靈) in literature.

For Shun knows full well that Xiang wants to kill him, but unless he is genuinely happy with Xiang, he cannot dispel Xiang's venom. Even if Xiang's venom cannot ultimately be dispelled, there is no other way to dispel it except by being happy with Xiang. That is why while his happiness with Xiang is fake, his recognition that it is imperative to be happy with Xiang in order to make Xiang happy with him is genuine.

Here logical reasoning introduces discontinuities, and genuineness undergoes an inevitable bifurcation as natural, emotional reaction and moral intention.

Shun's fraternal love involves the overcoming of aversion. Such intermediary steps sometimes get lost in the exaltation of the "true self." "Anybody can be Yao and Shun" 人皆可以為堯舜:[40] but if natural expression takes priority over conscious effort to imitate the sages, how is the transformation going to be achieved? Li Zhi's account of the "True Being" (*zhenren* 真人) as one moving between receptive "emptiness" (*xu* 虛) and steadfast "substantiveness" (*shi* 實) seems somehow abstract.[41] If the childlike mind gives rise to works that celebrate desire and rancor such as *Xixiang ji* and *Shuihu zhuan*, then it by definition encompasses emotions and impulses outside the parameters of pristine moral consciousness. Elsewhere Li Zhi links sensual desires (*haose* 好色) and the desire for gain (*haohuo* 好貨) to "the original heart and mind" (*benxin* 本心) and "simple and immediate words" (*eryan* 邇言).[42] He also affirms self-interest (*si* 私) and "the heart concerned with power and profit" (*shi li zhi xin* 勢利之心) as "endowed nature" (*bingfu zhi ziran* 稟賦之自然).[43] His critic quotes him: "For becoming Buddha and attaining sagehood, the only thing that matters is illuminating the mind. If the original mind is illumined, then to accept a thousand pieces of gold in one day is not avarice; to have coitus with ten women in one night is not licentiousness" 成佛證聖，唯在明心。本心若

---

40   *Mengzi yizhu* 12.2: 276.
41   Li Zhi, "Xu shi shuo" 虛實說 (*Li Zhi quanji zhu* 1: 287–289).
42   Li Zhi, "Da Deng mingfu" 答鄧明府 (*Li Zhi quanji zhu* 1: 94–101).
43   Li Zhi, "Deye ruchen houlun" 德業儒臣後論; *Daogu lu* 道古錄 10 (*Li Zhi quanji zhu* 6: 526, 14: 255).

明，雖一日受千金不為貪，一夜御十女不為淫.[44] Designed to malign Li, the quotation may or may not be authentic, but it does not sound too different from his affirmation of self-interest or sensual desires cited above.[45] Despite his ostentatious unconventionality, Li Zhi did not seem to have been guilty of real licentiousness. Yet he flaunted the negative epithets his critics inflicted on him to dramatize the odds he faced, fulfilling their label of him as "heretic" (*yiduan* 異端) to "let those fools make their name" 成 彼豎子之名 so that he could despise them even more.[46] Some questions remain unresolved: How exactly does the frank avowal of worldly desires lead to moral transcendence? Does inner illumination combined with outward transgression amount to self-division? What "true self" is Li Zhi claiming by reveling in the gap between the two?

The sense of deliberate paradox in Li Zhi is mixed with heightened emphasis on pleasure in the writings of the Yuan brothers from Gong'an 公 安 (Hubei), proponents of the so-called "natural spirit" (*xingling* 性靈) in literary creation. One of them, Yuan Hongdao 袁宏道 (1568–1610), younger brother of the aforementioned Yuan Zongdao, links ineffable "élan" (*qu* 趣) to genuine self-expression in a preface (1597) to his friend Chen Suoxue's 陳所學 collection. Those who master the ornaments of literati culture with self-conscious refinement or engage in abstruse philosophical speculations are said to be far from such élan. Instead Yuan upholds the child's joyous, unself-conscious movements as its epitome. He mentions Mencius' "heart of the newborn child" and Laozi's "baby" as the highest order of such élan. Recluses living the life of freedom are said to approximate it. Yuan seems most interested, however, in the élan of the defiantly unconcerned:

---

44 Zhou Yingbin 周應賓, *Shixiao lu* 識小錄, quoted in Zhang Jianye 2013, 107.

45 Cf. Li Zhi, "Shu Xiaoxiu shoujuan hou" 書小修手卷後 (1601): "All the wine, lust, and wealth of this world cannot pollute me in the least" 凡世間酒色財半點污染我不得 (*Li Zhi quanji zhu* 3: 201–202). Li was responding to his friend Yuan Zhongdao's 袁中道 (sobriquet Xiaoxiu 小修, the youngest of the three Yuan brothers) request that he should abide by a vegetarian diet. At that point Li Zhi had shaven his pate (although he kept his beard) and was living in a Buddhist monastery.

46 Li Zhi, "Yu Jiao Ruohou (Jiao Hong)" 與焦若侯 (*Li Zhi quanji zhu* 1: 152–153).

愚不肖之近趣也，以無品也，品愈卑故所求愈下，或為酒肉，或為聲伎，率心而行，無所忌憚，自以為絕望於世，故舉世非笑之不顧也，此又一趣也。

The stupid and worthless can come close to élan by being without standards. The lower their standards, the baser their quest—it could be wine and meat or entertainers and courtesans; they follow their heart and act without any inhibitions. Having no more to ask of the world, they can therefore be oblivious even if the whole world laughs at them or censures them. This too is a kind of élan.[47]

It is easy to read this simply as a testament to the late Ming "spirit of rebellion," whereby shedding inhibitions allows the true self to unfold. However, by using the same word (*qu*) to characterize moral and philosophical transcendence as well as defiant sensuality, Yuan points to secret affinities linking these disparate categories. It is this pose of mastery (i.e., the ability to claim that indulgence is not *merely* indulgence) that hints at anxiety, as much as Yuan's renunciation of sensual excess in his later writings that would justify the conception of self-division behind the celebration of self-expression.

1.3 Sickness, Flaws, Obsessions

The presumed gap between one's genuine core and social or conventional expectations leads to the glorification of flaws and deviance. Thus Zhang Dafu 張大復 (1544–1630):

木之有癭，石之有鸜鵒，皆病也。然是二物者，卒以此見貴於世。非世人之貴病也。病則奇，奇則至，至則傳。天隨生有言：「木病而後怪，不怪不能傳其形。文病而後奇，不奇不能駭於俗。」

---

47 Yuan Hongdao, "Xu Chen Zhengfu *Huixin ji*" 敍陳正甫會心集 (*Yuan Hongdao ji jianjiao* 1: 463–464). He offers a similar logic in his letter to his uncle Gong Weichang 龔惟長: he claims that "there are five kinds of true happiness" 真樂有五, among which he counts intellectual and sensual pleasures as well as shameless revelry in having wasted one's patrimony (*Yuan Hongdao ji jianjiao* 1: 205–206).

For trees to have swellings and for stones to have "mynah eyes" are all flaws. But for these two things, they are ultimately prized by the world because of these flaws. It is not because people of this world prize flaws. To be flawed is to be extraordinary, to be extraordinary is to be extreme, to be extreme is to be transmitted. Tiansui Sheng once said, "A tree becomes strange only with flaws; without being strange it will not succeed in having its form transmitted. Writings become extraordinary only if they are flawed; without being extraordinary they cannot startle the world."[48]

The cross section of a tree's "swelling" (i.e., the outgrowth on its trunk close to its roots) yields interesting patterns, just as unusual patterns of "mynah eyes" indicate the potential to become a superior ink-stone. Zhang must be aware that the very designation of the swelling or the "mynah eyes" as "flaws" or "sickness" is itself based on an arbitrary human perspective. But instead of dwelling on that, he chooses another line of reasoning: deviation from norms is the source of value and by implication conveys essential truths. One of his cognomens is "Sick Layman" (Bing jushi 病居士). He quotes the 9th-century poet Lu Guimeng's 陸龜蒙 (sobriquet Tiansui Sheng 天隨生 or "The Follower of Heaven") "Encomium on the Painting of the Strange Pine" (*Guaisong tu zan* 怪松圖贊).[49] Lu praises the twisted and bent pine as the symbol of indomitable life force that overcomes adversities. Zhang seems to go further and lauds deviance itself as the source of value.

Yuan Hongdao also articulates the idea that flaws confirm a person's genuine emotions and individual spirit in his preface (1596) to his younger brother Yuan Zhongdao's 袁中道 (1570–1623) poetry collection:[50]

> 大都獨抒性靈，不拘格套，非從自己胸臆流出，不肯下筆……其間有佳處，亦有疵處，佳處自不必言，即疵處亦多本色獨造語。然予

---

48   *Meihua caotang bitan* 1: 235–336.

49   *Quan Tang wen*, j. 801, 8410–8411. Instead of "having its form transmitted" 傳其形, Lu has "having its likeness painted" 圖其真.

50   Yuan Hongdao, "Xu Xiaoxiu shi" 敘小修詩 (*Yuan Hongdao ji jianjiao* 1: 187–190).

則極喜其疵處，而所謂佳者，尚不能不以粉飾、蹈襲為恨，以為未能盡脫近代文人習氣故也。

In the main he stands alone in expressing his natural spirit without being bound by modes and conventions. Unless it is something that flows forth from his heart, he refuses to write about it ... There are excellent parts but also flawed parts in it. The merits of the excellent parts go without saying, but even the flawed parts are full of his distinctive, original words. But I am especially partial to its flawed parts, for one cannot help regretting the adornment and imitation in what is considered excellent, because in such cases he cannot fully free himself from the habits of the literati in recent times.

Yuan then disparages advocates of classical literary models, predicting the oblivion of imitators and applauding contemporary popular songs: "they are still created by genuine persons unburdened by knowledge and learning, that is why genuine sounds still prevail" 猶是無聞無識真人所作，故多真聲.[51] If this may be compared to his brother's "true poetry" 真詩, it is because of the unself-conscious flaws in the latter's voice of rancor. It is "overly explicit" 過露: but Yuan Hongdao argues that in apparently flouting precepts of restraint and order, Zhongdao is but inheriting Qu Yuan's 屈原 plaint and embodying the "Chu style" 楚風. (The Yuan brothers hailed from Hubei, which was part of the ancient Chu kingdom.) Flaws confirm immediacy and genuine spirit because individuation is conceived of as deviation from the norm.

---

51   Yuan compares his own style, laced with colloquialisms, to that of popular songs. Cf. Feng Menglong's 馮夢龍 (1574–1645) preface to his collection of "mountain songs": "Although we are now in a declining age, there are only fake poetry and prose, no fake mountain songs. For mountain songs are not vying for fame with poetry and prose, hence they don't deign to be fake. If they don't deign to be fake, would it not be acceptable for us to use them to preserve what is genuine?" 且今雖季世，而但有假詩文，無假山歌，則山歌不與詩文爭名，故不屑假。苟其不屑假，而吾藉以存真，不亦可乎？(*Feng Menglong quanji* 10: 1). Proponents of the idea that "true poetry is to be found among the common people" 真詩乃在民間 include the defender of ancient literary models Li Mengyang 李夢陽 (1472–1529), the playwright and scholar-official Li Kaixian 李開先 (1502–1568), and the literatus and critic He Yisun 賀貽孫 (1605–1688).

The pursuit of genuineness thus leads to the valorization of follies and obsessions (*chi* 癡, *pi* 癖) as tokens of superior sensibility. Zhang Dai 張岱 (1597–1679) famously declares: "One cannot befriend a person without obsessions, for he would lack deep feelings. One cannot befriend a person without flaws, for he would lack the spirit of genuineness." 人無癖不可以交，以其無深情也。人無疵不可以交，以其無真氣也.[52] Yuan Hongdao explains:

嵇康之鍛也，武子之馬也，陸羽之茶也，米顛之石也，倪雲林之潔也，皆以僻〔癖〕而寄其磊傀俊逸之氣者也。余觀世上語言無味、面目可憎之人，皆無癖之人耳。若真有所癖，將沈湎酖溺，性命生死以之，何暇及錢奴宦賈之事？

The way Ji Kang was with forging iron, Wang Ji (Wuzi) with horses, Lu Yu with tea, Mi Fu (the Mad Mi) with rocks, or Ni Zan (Yunlin) with cleanliness—in all these cases they were using their obsessions to lodge their uncompromising, distinct, soaring spirit. From what I have seen, the ones whose words are insipid and whose countenances are unappealing are all people without obsessions. If one is truly obsessed with something, then one would immerse and indulge in it, one would put life and soul to realize it—how could one have time to spare for things such as money, servants, officialdom, or trade?"[53]

A well-known anecdote from *Shishuo xinyu* 世說新語 (A new account of tales of the world, 5th century) describes how the famous poet Ji Kang 嵇康 (223–262) "hammered away without stopping, as if there were no one around him" 揚槌不輟，傍若無人 when his political enemy, the aristocrat Zhong Hui 鍾會 (225–264), visited him. Ji Kang, defiantly absorbed in "forging iron," challenges Zhong Hui to respond to his refusal to communicate. Zhong has enough wit to bolster his dignity with an evasive

---

52   Zhang Dai, "Wu yiren zhuan" 五異人傳 (*Zhang Dai shiwen ji*, 267–268); *Tao'an mengyi*, 80.

53   Yuan Hongdao, *Ping shi* 瓶史 (*Yuan Hongdao ji jianjiao* 1: 826).

and non-committal reply.[54] Wang Ji 王濟 (3rd century), a discerning judge of horses, also humanizes them.[55] Lu Yu 陸羽 (733–804) is famous for his *Cha jing* 茶經 (Classic of tea). The great painter and calligrapher Mi Fu 米芾 (1051–1107) was obsessed with strangely shaped rocks, so much so that he would don official robes and bow to an interesting rock, calling it "elder brother." Another great artist, Ni Zan 倪瓚 (1301–1374), is featured in a number of stories detailing his obsessive fear of contamination. Yuan Hongdao is thus linking obsession to a range of attributes, including political defiance (Ji Kang), empathetic understanding (Wang Ji), connoisseurship (Lu Yu), and artistic powers (Mi Fu and Ni Zan). Their common denominator is the idea of a self inventing its own order that displaces the vulgar concerns shared by the common run of humanity.

Single-minded focus on an external object seems to purge the self of contingencies, yet this is ultimately about the vagaries of the self. Feng Menglong 馮夢龍 (1574–1645), in his collection *Tan gai* 談概 (Basics of conversation), includes Yuan Hongdao's comment on Mi Fu's love of rocks: "Chrysanthemums for Tao Yuanming, plum blossoms for Lin Bu, or rocks for Mi Fu are not about loving chrysanthemums, plum blossoms, or rocks—in all these cases it is the self loving the self" 陶之菊、林之梅、米之石，非愛菊、梅與石也。皆吾愛吾也.[56] Obsessions are said to mark a person's genuineness, which is thereby realized in unmediated value judgments that defy social norms and sometimes even rational understanding. Yet a possible dimension of self-regard qualifies the supposed immediacy and urgency.

---

54 "Moments passed and they did not exchange any word. Zhong [Hui] rose to leave, and [Ji] Kang said, 'What have you heard that made you come? What have you seen that made you leave?' Zhong Hui replied, 'By coming, I have heard what I heard. Upon leaving, I have seen what I saw.'" 移時不交一言。鍾起去，康曰：「何所聞而來，何所見而去？」鍾曰：「聞所聞而來，見所見而去。」(*Shishuo xinyu jianshu* 24.3: 767–768).

55 *Shishuo xinyu* 20.4, *Yulin* 語林, cited in Liu Xiaobiao's notes on the entry (*Shishuo xinyu jianshu*, 705).

56 Feng Menglong, *Tan gai*, in *Feng Menglong quanji*, 6: 152.

Yuan Hongdao uses the word *ji* 寄 (lodge) to describe the ways whereby restless discontent and proud defiance seek solace and recompense in obsessions. The word *ji* suggests a temporary abode, a choice to come and go as one pleases—quite the contrary of the idea of a person succumbing to obsessions. In other words, with *ji* the self regains a measure of control. The obsessing self tries to banish the flux and uncertainties of existence in order to forge its own logic or system; the observing self veers between validating this as "higher order" and being detached from it. Indeed, the imagination of ultimate control and the fear of real disequilibrium underline the discourse on eccentricity, passions, extreme emotions, and obsessions during the late Ming. In Yuan Hongdao's affirmation of obsession cited above, for instance, the context is "obsession with flowers" (*huapi* 花癖), of which he absolves himself. Those with a true passion for flowers brave dangers and hardships to acquire rare specimens, observe every phase of flowering with intensity, and gain vast and intuitive knowledge about flowers. Yuan considers such persons "true connoisseurs" (*zhen haoshi* 真好事) whom he cannot emulate:

若夫石公之養花，聊以破閒居孤寂之苦，非真能好之也。夫使其真好之，已為桃花洞口人矣。尚復為人間塵土之官哉。

As for the way I keep flowers, I just use them to dispel the affliction of withdrawal and solitude. It is not that I can be truly passionate about it. If I could, I would have become the one by the entrance to the Peach Blossom Cave! Why would I be still an official in the dusty human realm![57]

Yuan's treatise details necessary choices and rules of taste with methodical meticulousness typical of obsession, yet he is claiming the cultural space of shared taste and eschewing the radical subjectivity of the truly obsessed. The self-observation, the concern with control, and the social dimension of aesthetic standards are symptomatic of intrinsic divisions in the idea of obsession.

---

57 *Yuan Hongdao ji jianjiao*, 1: 826.

1.4 Self-Conscious Fictionality and Theatricality

Self-division is sometimes the implicit theme in the many genres of autobiographical writings (e.g., self-account 自傳, self-accusation 自訟, self-elegy 自祭文, encomium on one's portrait 自贊、自題小像, and funereal essay or tomb inscription for oneself 生壙自志、自題墓誌銘) that flourished from the late Ming to early Qing, as evinced by the frequent pose of bafflement in such writings.[58] The writer claims to fail to grasp his constant and unpredictable transformations or to be struck by how his contradictions escape categorical judgments. Sometimes he focuses on the gap between the self as the source of judgment and its object. There are moments of deliberate disconnection between the subject of autobiography and his interlocutor (e.g., Li Zhi, in *Zhuowu lun lue* 卓吾論略 [A brief account of Zhuowu], uses an obviously allegorical narrator whose name implies that he is either deceptive or authoritative),[59] of a break between the speaker and his articulated opinions (e.g., Xu Wei's *Ziwei mu zhiming* 自為墓誌銘 [Tomb inscription for myself]),[60] and of elaborate fantasies deemed necessary for truth telling (e.g., Chen Jiru's 陳繼儒 [1558–1639] account of choreographing his mourners and his postmortem magical transformation in *Kongqing xiansheng mu zhiming* 空青先生墓誌銘 [Tomb inscription for Master Kongqing]). To what extent can "the true self" accommodate inconstancy, inconsistency, or contradictions? If one is torn by conflicting motives and desires, which "true self" does one express? One can of course characterize (or even dramatize) the process of conflict as itself the "stuff" of

---

58   On 16th- and 17th-century autobiographical writings, see Du Lianzhe 1977; Wu Pei-yi 1990; Nakatani 2010; Chen Baoliang 2014: 269–294.

59   *Li Zhi quanji zhu* 1:233–235. Zhuowu was Li Zhi's sobriquet. The narrator, Kong Ruogu 孔若谷, is a supposed friend who explains Li Zhi's life, but the name does not appear elsewhere in Li Zhi's writings and seems transparently allegorical. It has been glossed as "an aperture as large as a valley" (Wu Pei-yi 1990: 21). But "Kong Ruogu" may also imply the voice of wisdom (with Kong suggesting Confucius) and humility (as in the expression *xu huai ruo gu* 虛懷若谷). In other words, Li Zhi is positing a narrator who is at the same time unreliable and wisely empathetic.

60   *Xu Wei ji* 2: 638–640. Xu Wei attempted to sum up his contradictions as he prepared for suicide.

genuine expression (as indeed seems to be the case with the aforementioned authors of autobiographical writings), but that is not admissible if the genuine is valorized as something pristine, indivisible and "expressible," as in Li Zhi's essay on the childlike mind.

The late Ming was the great age of Chinese drama and fiction, genres for which ideas about masking, delusion, self-deception, and self-transformation are endemic. Authors may profess lyrical self-expression or claim to represent characters who enact such ideals, but self-conscious theatricality and fictionality often introduce inevitable irony. Take for example Xu Wei's one-act play *Kuang gushi* 狂鼓史 (The mad drummer), which glorifies the literatus Mi Heng's 禰衡 (173–198) confrontation with the warlord Cao Cao 曹操 (155–220).[61] Historical and anecdotal sources tell the story of Mi Heng's defiance of Cao Cao, who in revenge brings about Mi's death.[62] The scene of Mi Heng cursing Cao Cao while beating the drum thus celebrates the poetic vindication of the disempowered, righteous man. However, Xu Wei sets his play in the underworld, where the ghosts of Mi Heng and Cao Cao reenact the drumming and cursing for the edification and amusement of the infernal judge. Past, present, and future perspectives converge to infuse the actions of Mi Heng and Cao Cao with memories and foreknowledge, charging immediacy with the specter of self-division. Tang Xianzu's 湯顯祖 (1550–1616) *Mudan ting* 牡丹亭 (Peony pavilion), widely recognized as the paean to untrammeled passion, nevertheless offers a complex picture on facets of desire, and its heroine answers different modes of self-expression and self-realization.[63] Perhaps the image of Monkey in *Xiyou bu* 西遊補 (Supplement to *Journey to the West*) by Dong Yue 董説 (1620–1686) best sums up the ambiguities in the quest for

---

61 The full title of the play is *Kuang gushi yuyang san nong* 狂鼓史漁陽三弄, *Xu Wei ji* 4: 1177–1185. For recent studies of the play, see Kwa 2012, He Yuming 2008.

62 *Sanguo zhi* 10.311, *Hou Hanshu* 80B.2652–2658, *Shishuo xinyu jianshu* 2.8: 64.

63 On this issue, see, e.g., Li Wai-yee 1993, 2010; Lu 2000; Chapter 8 in this volume.

the true self.[64] In this novella, Monkey enters a dream world with a Tower of Myriad Mirrors, where endless worlds open up. Almost as a response to this multiplicity, Monkey also undergoes confusing and sometimes involuntary transformations, turning into his own impersonator, confronted with stories of his supposed past that he cannot remember, losing control of the very "hair-monkeys" that used to symbolize the infinite expansion of his powers in *Xiyou ji* 西遊記 (*Journey to the West*).

Suffice it to say that these works reflect intrinsic divisions in the idea of *zhen* (or *zhenwo*). Our earlier examples show tensions between aspects of the "true self" as transcendent and mundane (as in Xu Wei's "Crossing the River"), as impulse and intention (as in Li Zhi's discussion of Shun's relationship with Xiang), as unconscious unfolding and deliberate valorization (as in Li Zhi's discourse of the childlike mind), as self-evident manifestation or hidden constraint and aspiration (as in Yuan Hongdao's discussion of obsession). "The one who acts by following innate nature can be called a genuine person" 率性而行，是謂真人: this apparently straightforward adage becomes complicated when embedded in the social context of mutual evaluation.[65] Genuineness should signal a single-minded relationship with oneself and with others, yet the pervasive concern with genuineness also breeds the hermeneutics of suspicion. To hold genuineness as an ideal has the potential for self-division, since to articulate and seek this ideal is to be already removed from it. Late Ming writers like to unmask

---

64   *Xiyou bu* tells of Monkey's dream, induced by the breath of the *qing* fish, after the pilgrims cross the Flaming Mountain by borrowing the fan from Princess Iron Fan (chapter 61 in *Journey to the West*). Some scholars suggest that *Xiyou bu* might have been written partly by Dong Yue's father Dong Sizhang 董斯張 (1587–1628). Interesting recent studies include Li Qiancheng 2004; Zhao Hongjuan 2006; Yang Yucheng 2013; Struve 2019.

65   Yuan Hongdao, "Shi Zhang Youyu zhenming hou" 書張幼于箴銘後 (1596) (*Yuan Hongdao ji jianjiao* 1: 193). *Xing* in *shuaixing* here does not imply moral core (as it does in *Zhongyong*). Zhang Xianyi 張獻翼 (sobriquet Youyu 幼于) was defiantly eccentric, but Yuan praised him for forthrightly following his modest and careful nature. Elsewhere he argued with Zhang about whether his description of Zhang as *diankuang* 顛狂 (mad, wild) should be considered a compliment (*Yuan Hongdao ji jianjiao* 1: 145–146, 1: 501–504).

the ostentatiously genuine, target the conventionally unconventional, and establish the distinction between themselves and others whom they accuse of bad faith and pretension. Not infrequently, they also turn the irony upon themselves. There are also moments of stringent self-criticism. Yuan Hongdao, in his later writings, criticizes his own glibness and sensual indulgence from a Buddhist perspective. In a letter to Qian Qianyi 錢謙益 (1582–1664), Yuan Zhongdao ruefully upholds the "genuineness" born of going against oneself. One seeks pleasures beyond the world, he writes, because worldly pleasures are unattainable or dangerous: "There are many instances when, being hunchbacked, one assumes the attitude of respect, which then becomes genuine respect." 因傴為恭，遂成真恭，世多有之.[66] Genuineness can be a nexus of correspondences driven by circumstance; it may yet be something imposed from without rather than emanating from within.

2. Beginnings of the Pursuit of Genuineness

Gu Yanwu offers a scathing critique of Li Zhi in *Rizhi lu*, but does not mention late Ming literati such as Xu Wei or the Yuan brothers.[67] His retrospection on allusions to *Zhuangzi* in late Ming examination essays is part of a broader critique of *xinxue*—his real target is how the idea of "true knowledge" or "true core" masks insidious Daoist and Buddhist influence on the discourse of Confucian moral self-cultivation.[68] In other

---

66 Yuan Zhongdao, "Da Qian Shouzhi" 答錢受之 (*Kexue zhai ji* 珂雪齋集 3: 1025).

67 For Gu's critique of Li Zhi, see *Rizhi lu* 18.660–662, 667–668. Gu also directed vitriol against Zhong Xing 鍾惺 (1574–1625), who was influential because of his popular poetry anthologies and commentary editions (*Rizhi lu*, 18.668–669).

68 On Gu Yanwu's critique of Wang Yangming and *xinxue*, see *Rizhi lu*, 18.653–657. Gu claimed that Ming scholars used the methods and mentality of Wei-Jin (220–420) "abstruse conversations" (*qingtan* 清談) to approach Confucian texts ("The abstruse conversations of time past talk about Laozi and Zhuangzi, the abstruse conversations of these days talk about Confucius and Mencius" 昔之清談談老莊，今之清談談孔孟, *Rizhi lu* 7.240).

words, he sets out to reveal the moral and metaphysical pitfalls of bringing the valence of truth, reality, and substance to a word (*zhen*) rooted in the quest for transcendent experience. Mere literati antics on "being genuine" are thus for him beyond the pale (and not even worth attacking). In that sense one may question whether there is any justification in conjoining the above discussion (which often addresses materials that devolve into some version of "to thine own self be true") with the uses of the word *zhen* in *Zhuangzi*. Mere assertion of influence would be vapid: *Zhuangzi* was of course familiar to any educated person. There were more commentaries on *Zhuangzi* produced during the 16th and 17th centuries than any other period in Chinese history, including quite a few by the authors mentioned above.[69] Their explicitly articulated arguments about *Zhuangzi*, however, may not be the best guide to their true affinities with *Zhuangzi*. (For example, an author's "transcendent reading" may be belied by dramatized angst and unresolved contradictions in his writings.) My modest question is simply this: is there any room for mutual illumination when we juxtapose issues in the above discussion with the meanings of the word *zhen* in *Zhuangzi*? Would it help us chart a trajectory of "the quest for the true self" as a self-consciously articulated problem?

2.1 Paradoxes of *Zhen* in *Zhuangzi*: True Arbiter, True Ruler, True Being, True Knowledge

One of the most famous passages on the idea of *zhen* as being related to interiority is the problematic proposition of transcendence in "The Discourse on Making Things Equal" (Qiwu lun 齊物論) in *Zhuangzi*. It comes in the wake of the enumeration of myriad, ever-changing mental states, like "music rising out of emptiness (i.e. empty holes), vaporous mist forming mushrooms" 樂出虛，蒸成菌—their source is elliptically designated as "this" (*ci* 此), which commentators gloss variously as the

---

69 For a comprehensive list, see Fang Yong 2008 and 2015.

heart-mind, the natural course (*ziran* 自然) or external things (*waiwu* 外物).[70] "This" seems to have become "that" in what follows:

非彼無我，非我無所取。是亦近矣，而莫知其所為使。若有真宰，而特不得其朕。可行己（已）信，而不見其形。有情而無形。百骸、九竅、六藏，賅而存焉，吾誰與為親？汝皆説之乎？其有私焉？如是皆有為臣妾乎？其臣妾不足以相治乎？其遞相為君臣乎？其有真君存焉。如求其情與不得，無益損乎其真。一受其成形，不亡以待盡。與物相刃相靡，其行盡如馳，而莫之能止，不亦悲乎？終身役役而不見其成功，苶然疲役而不知其所歸，可不哀邪。人謂之不死，奚益。其形化，其心與之然，可不謂大哀乎？人之生也，固若是芒乎？其我獨芒，而人亦有不芒者乎？

Without "that" there is no "me," without "me" there is nothing to draw from. This seems close enough, and yet one does not know what brings this about. It is as if there is a True Arbiter, yet one is singularly unable to get its signs.[71] What one believes of it can be put into action, and yet one does not see its form. There is truth but no form. The hundred bones, nine apertures, and six organs exist in all their completion. To which should I be kin? Do you take delight in all of them? Is there any partiality? In that case, should all be treated as subjects and concubines? And do subjects and concubines not have what it needs to govern each other? And do they take turns to be ruler and subject? Is there a True Ruler in existence? Whether one seeks to obtain the truth or fails to do so does not add to or diminish its genuineness.

The defined form, once received, cannot be changed as one waits for the end. Chipping and grinding against things, one speeds forward as if galloping, without being able to stop—is that not lamentable! One toils the whole life without seeing what has been accomplished. Desolate and

---

70   See comments by Guo Xiang 郭象 (252–312) and Cheng Xuanying 成玄英 (608–669) (*Zhuangzi jishi* 2.56); Hu Yuanjun 胡遠濬, cited in *Zhuangzi zuanjian* 莊子纂箋, 12; Wang Fuzhi 王夫之, *Zhuangzi jie* 莊子解 (*Chuanshan quanshu* 13: 98).

71   Cf. *Huainanzi*: "All things have signs, only the Way has no signs. The reason why it has no signs is because it does not have a constant configuration and direction" 凡物有朕，唯道無朕。所以無朕者，以其無常形勢也 (*Huainan honglie jijie* 15.493).

worn out, one does not know where to return, how can it not be woeful! What good would it do for people to say that one does not perish? The form changes, and the heart and mind go along with it, how can this not be called the great woe? Do humans live only to be so benighted? Or am I alone in being benighted and there are others who are not benighted?[72]

I quote this passage at some length to draw attention to the rhetorical functions of *zhen*, which may matter more than its paraphraseable meanings.[73] The argument gains momentum not by definition but by unanswered (or unanswerable) questions. The True Arbiter 真宰 or True Ruler 真君 is posited as a response to the conundrum of conceptualizing an absolute determinant beyond the mutual dependence of the "self" and an activating force. How can one ascertain the existence or attributes of this True Arbiter when it has no tangible manifestations? How does its "truth" or "reality" (*qing* 情) correspond to the components of a person? The implied speaker poses a series of questions to himself and his imagined interlocutor: how does one adjudicate the claims of the different constituents of a person? How does one part control another? The idea that a True Ruler may exist seems no more than a tentative attempt to resolve the sense of anarchy and contradictions emerging from a vision of a multifarious entity arbitrarily designated as a "self." This may be the first time in Chinese thought that the search for the ultimate source of being yields only hypothetical analogies of political hierarchy (master and subject). The True Arbiter and True Ruler are introduced to forestall greater disorder, not to bring real resolution. The tone then shifts and becomes declarative: whether one can determine the "reality" of this elusive higher explanation or not does not affect its "genuineness" (*zhen*). This statement about *zhen* is more emphatically affirmative, yet it is followed by lamentations of inevitable death, oblivion, and misunderstanding. We are presented with the promise of an absolute akin to a true core within the self (the sense of interiority being heightened

---

72   *Zhuangzi jishi* 2.56–57.

73   On the formal realization of the idea of change and reversal in *Zhuangzi*, see Graziani 2011.

by references to physical components of the body), and yet it is a quest dogged by inevitable negativity. Indeed, the sense of the struggle between, as well as the mutual implication of, transcendence and mortality is much stronger in the "Inner Chapters" than in the later chapters.

The same sense of rhetorical necessity drives the description of the True Being (*zhenren* 真人) in "Great and Venerable Teacher" (Da zongshi 大宗師). Perhaps more than other sections in *Zhuangzi*, this chapter relentlessly confronts the implacability of death and the limits of knowledge. It begins by grandly affirming the supremacy of "knowing how heaven works" 知天之所為 and "knowing how humans work" 知人之所為 but proceeds to skepticism.

> 雖然，有患。夫知有所待而後當，其所待者，特未定也。庸詎知吾所謂天之非人乎？所謂人之非天乎？且有真人而後有真知.
>
> However, there are worries. For knowledge has to depend on something in order to become pertinent, and that which it depends on cannot yet be fixed. How can one know that what I call heaven is not human? That what I call human is not heaven? Further, only when there is a True Being can there be True Knowledge."[74]

The True Being is thus posited to facilitate the conception of True Knowledge, the counterpoint to the preceding avowal of uncertainty. He embodies the point of reference that always anticipates the next question or negation—he must remain abstract and elliptical. The question "What can be called a True Being" 何謂真人 is answered through negation,[75] implied

---

74 *Zhuangzi jishi* 6.224–226.

75 "He does not reject the meager, he does not crow over achievement, he does not plan how affairs unfold" 不逆寡，不雄成，不謨士; "Sleeping, he does not dream; awakened, he has no worries; eating, he takes no pleasure" 其寢不夢，其覺無憂，其食不甘; "He does not know about being enamored of life, he does not know about abhorring death" 不知說生，不知惡死; "He does not forget where he begins, he does not seek where he ends" 不忘其所始，不求其所終; "This is called not using his heart and mind to diminish the Way, not using human efforts to aid Heaven" 是之謂不以心捐道，不以人助天 (*Zhuangzi jishi* 6.226–229).

conditionals,[76] semblance,[77] and paradoxical combinations.[78] The function of going beyond opposites and fixity seems to take precedence over the actual existence of the True Being. Thus Wang Fuzhi 王夫之 (1619–1692):

夫真人者豈真見有人，真知者豈真有其知哉？人皆天也，知皆不容知也，乃可恍惚而遇其知于滑湣.

As for the True Being, how can it be as if one truly sees such a being? Or for True Knowledge, how can it be as if one truly has such knowledge? All things human are also of heaven; in all cases, knowledge cannot be known. One can only, in uncertainty, encounter such knowledge at Flowing Dimness.[79]

---

76 "Being like that, he exceeds the limits without regrets and matches his lot without self-satisfaction. Being like that, he scales heights without fear, enters water without getting wet, enters fire without being burnt" 若然者，過而弗悔，當而不自得也。若然者，登高不慄，入水不濡，入火不熱; "Being like that, his mind is focused, his mien, still, his forehead, austere; he is melancholy like autumn, warm like spring; his joys and anger commune with the four seasons, finding things fitting without knowing their limits" 若然者，其心志，其容寂，其顙頯，淒然似秋，煖然似春，喜怒通四時，與物有宜，而莫知其極 (Zhuangzi jishi 6.226, 230–231). On the emendation of zhi 志 ("his mind is focused") as wang 忘 ("his mind forgets"), see Zhuangzi jiaoquan 莊子校詮, 1: 212; Zhuangzi zuanjian, 48. For arguments against that reading, see Wang Fuzhi, Zhuangzi jie (Chuanshan quanshu 13: 160). Guo Xiang glosses kui 頯 as "austere" but explains it as "protruding and impressive" in "Tian dao" 天道.

77 "Shining bright, he seems to be glad" 邴邴乎似喜乎, "afflicted, he seems to be like the rest of the world" 崔乎其似世乎, "connected, he seems to like closing up" 連乎其似好閉也 (Zhuangzi jishi 6.234).

78 "He seems inadequate but will not receive more. Moving easily, he stands alone but is not firm. Opening up, he is empty but has no outward glory" 若不足而不承，與乎，其觚而不堅也。張乎，其虛而不華也; "That is why what he is fond of is one, and what he is not fond of is also one. His oneness is one, and his negation of oneness is also one. In his oneness, he is the companion of Heaven. In his negation of oneness, he is the companion of man. When Heaven and man do not overcome one another, that is called the True Being" 故其好之也一，其弗好之也一。其一也一，其不一也一。其一與天為徒，其不一與人為徒。天與人不相勝也，是之謂真人。(Zhuangzi jishi 6.234–235). I read jian 堅 as gu 固, following Guo Xiang and Cheng Xuanying. Yao Nai reads this line as jian er bu gu 堅而不觚, "firm but not standing alone," cited in Zhuangzi jiaoquan, 1: 216–218.

79 Wang Fuzhi, Zhuangzi jie (Chuanshan quanshu 13:157). The term huanghu (in uncertainty) refers to the Way in Laozi 21 (Laozi jianshi, 88). "Flowing Dimness" 滑湣, like "the illumination of Flowing Doubt" 滑疑之耀 (Zhuangzi jishi 2.75), use the image of slippery ground and ambiguity to designate transcendent positioning.

In the "Outer Chapters" and "Miscellaneous Chapters," we have mostly more straightforward definitions of the True Being: paradoxes are often stated rather than played out through rhetoric. "Sharpening the Will" 刻意, for example, delineates different ways of being in the world and concludes with a definition of the True Being as one "who can embody unalloyed purity" 能體純素.[80] Tian Zifang 田子方 in the eponymous chapter describes his teacher Dongguo Shunzi 東郭順子: "His way of being is true. Human in appearance, he yet has heavenly emptiness. Compliant, he preserves his genuineness. Pure, he accommodates things" 其為人也真。人貌而天虛,緣而葆真,清而容物.[81] "Xu Wugui" 徐無鬼 offers more elliptical formulations reminiscent of "Great Venerable Teacher" but also adopts declarative statements: "He embraces virtue and nourishes harmony in order to go along with the world. This is called a True Being" 抱德煬和,以順天下,此謂真人.[82] *Huainanzi*, even while paraphrasing or quoting *Zhuangzi*, manages to purge the *zhenren* of paradoxes in creating a transcendent image.[83] In accounts of the quest for immortality in *Shiji* and "biographies of immortals" that flourished from about the 3rd century onwards, *zhenren* simply means a transcendent immortal or being who has reached perfection.[84]

2.2 *Zhen* in *Zhuangzi*: Performance, Communication, Sincerity

Anecdotes about conveying the quality of *zhen* or about the *zhenren* in action are premised on the gap between appearance and meaning—this

---

80 *Zhuangzi jishi* 15.546. Cheng Xuanying: "who can intuitively understand unalloyed purity."

81 *Zhuangzi jishi* 21.702.

82 *Zhuangzi jishi* 24.865. I read *yang* 煬 (burn) as a loan word for *yang* 養 (nourish), following Xi Tong 奚侗 (*Zhuangzi zuanjian*, 207).

83 *Huainan honglie jijie*, 2.50, 58, 61–62, 71, 6.193, 210, 7.227, 230, 8.260–261, 14.631. The term appears once in *Lüshi chunqiu*, where it refers to a sage of great virtue (*Lüshi chunqiu jiaoshi*, 3.144).

84 In Chan writings, the True Being or the True Being Without Position 無位真人 is the enlightened one who flouts all attempts to define him; see *Taishō shinshū Daizōkyō* 大正新修大藏經 47: 496, 676, 720, 729, 755, 806–807, 823, 842, 857, 987; 48: 12, 16, 22, 80, 83, 99, 135, 171, 201, 252–253, 288; 49: 643–644; 51: 276, 290, 300, 447.

is true throughout *Zhuangzi*. An interlocutor or mediator has to explain what might have been misunderstood, especially because expressing or communicating the attribute of *zhen* almost always involves flouting expectation, convention, and tradition—we recall mourners who sing instead of lament at a funeral, embodiments of truths who evade answers, thigh-slapping roamers who revel in oblivion. The interpreter is the one who names an inexplicable gesture as *zhen*. In one example, eager and respectful artisans answer the Song ruler's call for making pictures. When the Song ruler sends someone to espy the doings of a nonchalant latecomer, the latter "had taken off his clothes and sat spreading his legs, all naked" 則解衣般礴. To this the ruler responds: "This will do. This is a true picture maker" 可矣。是真畫者也.[85] The artistry of the naked man, observable in his oblivious self-containment, needs a spy and an interpreter to be known. Along similar lines, Gap-toothed 齧缺 falls asleep while Piyi 被衣 is explaining to him the mysteries of the Way, and Piyi commends this apparent indifference: "His form is like a withered corpse, his heart like dead ashes.[86] The truth is what he knows,[87] he does not hold on to explanations" 形若槁骸，心若死灰。真其實知，不以故自恃.[88]

Speaking of *zhen* always requires substitution, perhaps implying a shift of attention from *zhen* as the object of knowledge to *zhen* as a cognitive process. Such displacement defines the anecdote about Xu Wugui and Lord Wu of Wei. Lord Wu begins by expressing sympathetic concern for the material deprivation of Xu Wugui's life as a recluse. Xu counters by pitying Lord Wu's exertion, torn as he is between succumbing to desires and steering away from them—that is, between the danger of imperiling his spirit and that of diminishing his senses. When Lord Wu seems at a loss for reply,

---

85   *Zhuangzi jishi* 21.719.

86   This description of the person with "true knowledge" (sometimes in slightly different wording) also appears in chapters 2 ("Qiwu lun"), 23 ("Geng Sangchu" 庚桑楚), and 24 ("Xu Wugui").

87   Following Wu Rulun 吳汝綸 (1840–1903) and reading *shi* 實 as *suo* 所 (真其所知). Cited in *Zhuangzi jiaoquan*, 2: 815–816.

88   *Zhuangzi jishi* 22.738.

Xu Wugui regales him with his expertise in assessing dogs and horses. He enlarges on their rankings and concludes: the most superior dogs "seem to have relinquished their oneness" 若亡其一, just as the best horses under heaven "seem to have lost their oneness" 若喪其一. "Lord Wu was greatly pleased and laughed" 武侯大説而笑. Ru Shang, who facilitated Xu Wugui's audience with Lord Wu, confesses his bafflement: Ru Shang appealed to authoritative traditions as tools of political persuasion, but Lord Wu ignored him. Xu Wugui explains his success: the longer an exile has been away, the more eager he is to seize on any association with his hometown. "For a long time, there has not been one who uses the words of a True Being to chat and laugh by our ruler's side" 久矣乎。莫以真人之言，謦欬吾君之側乎.[89]

The anecdote begins with Lord Wu's concern for Xu Wugui's rustic hardships and ends with Xu comparing Lord Wu to an exile in the wilderness surprised by the joy of human contact. The underlying power struggle between the ruler and the persuader, so pervasive in Warring States writings, seems to be operative here.[90] Lord Wu's delight and laughter are part of this dynamic: they vindicate Xu Wugui but also put him in the role of entertainer. Yet "the words of a True Being" also promise to transcend the agonistic momentum underlying remonstrance. The self-forgetfulness of dogs and horses suggests a kind of true knowledge to which Lord Wu should aspire. This anecdote is followed by another exchange: Xu Wugui convinces Lord Wu to forego human intervention, even if it is for a good cause like putting a stop to wars. "Cultivate the sincerity inside yourself so that you can respond to the reality of Heaven and Earth without tampering with it" 修胸中之誠，以應天地之情而勿攖.[91] The talk of dogs and horses launches a psychological process that makes Lord Wu receptive to

---

89   *Zhuangzi jishi* 24.821.

90   On the role of paradoxes and semantic uncertainty in the power dynamic of remonstrance, see Graziani 2012; Li Wai-yee 2013.

91   *Zhuangzi jishi* 24.827. *Cheng* (translated here as sincerity) also means "(impersonal) truth": "With you I will ride the truth (*cheng*) of heaven and earth and not let things tamper with it" 吾與之乘天地之誠而不以物與之相攖 (*Zhuangzi jishi* 24.858).

the message of relinquishing subjective imposition. "The words of a True Being" bear fruit as an injunction to sincerity (*cheng* 誠).

The two iterations of remonstrance in "Xu Wugui" move between a sense of deliberate paradox in the True Being's words and an earnest lesson in sincerity. But "sincerity" in that case means the optimal state of mind that allows one to respond correctly. Defining sincerity as urgent emotions and equating it with *zhen* come to the fore in the exchange between Confucius and his interlocutor in "The Fisherman" (Yufu 漁父). The chapter begins with the fisherman being drawn to Confucius' zither music, the appreciation of which leads him to conclude that Confucius "exhausts his heart and mind, enervates his body, and therefore imperils his genuineness" 苦心勞形，以危其真. Confucius explains his endeavors and adversities, and the fisherman advises him: "Carefully cultivate your person and cautiously guard your genuineness" 謹修而身，慎守其真.[92]

> 孔子愀然曰：「請問何謂真？」客曰：「真者，精誠之至也。不精不誠，不能動人。故強哭者雖悲不哀，強怒者雖嚴不威，強親者雖笑不和。真悲無聲而哀，真怒未發而威，真親未笑而和。真在內者，神動於外，是所以貴真也。其用於人理也，事親則慈孝，事君則忠貞，飲酒則歡樂，處喪則悲哀。忠貞以功為主，處喪以哀為主，事親以適為主。功成之美，無一其跡矣。事親以適，不論所以矣。飲酒以樂，不選其具矣。處喪以哀，無問其禮矣。禮者，世俗之所為也。真者，所以受於天也，自然不可易也。故聖人法天貴真，不拘於俗。愚者反此，不能法天而恤於人，不知貴真，祿祿而受變於俗，故不足。惜哉。子之早湛人偽，而晚聞大道也。」

Confucius said with a disconsolate mien, "May I ask what is meant by 'genuine'?" The fisherman said, "The genuine is the intent of essential sincerity.[93] Without essence and sincerity, it is not possible to sway others.

---

92   *Zhuangzi jishi* 31.1025, 1031.

93   I read *zhi* 至 (fullest extent) as *zhi* 志 (intent), following Wang Shumin, *Zhuangzi jiaoquan*, 31.1242. For the connection between "essence" and "sincerity," see also *Lüshi chunqiu jiaoshi*, 9.507–508 ("Le cheng" 樂成), 17.1225–1226 ("Jubei" 具備).

That is why those forced to wail are not woeful even when lamenting; those forced to be angry are not forbidding even when being severe; those forced to be affectionate are not congenial even when smiling. Genuine lamentation is woeful without any sound; genuine anger is forbidding before manifestation; genuine affection is congenial before any smile. He who has genuineness within manifests his spirit without. That is why genuineness is valued. In terms of application to human principles, [with genuineness] one is loving and filial in serving one's parents, loyal and constant in serving one's ruler, one is joyous while drinking and grieves while in mourning. For loyalty and constancy, the main point is accomplishment; for drinking, pleasure; for mourning, grief; for serving one's parents, ease. The beauty of successful accomplishment is that it leaves no traces. Providing ease in serving one's parents, one does not debate the means. Drinking wine with pleasure, one does not choose the utensils. Grieving in mourning, one does not ask about the ritual. Rituals are what are formed by the world. The genuine is what is received from Heaven—it is natural and cannot be changed. That is why the sage models himself after Heaven and values genuineness. The foolish ones are the opposite—they cannot model themselves on Heaven and worry about people. Not knowing how to value genuineness, they are compliant and are transformed by customs. That is why they are inadequate. What a pity! From early on you have immersed yourself in human artifice and are late in hearing about the Great Way."[94]

This is a surprisingly mundane definition of *zhen*. Instead of an ineffable higher truth, it is linked to sincerity and singleness of purpose and used as an adjective to authenticate affective states. Further, its application in human affairs means eschewing conventions, ritual, and "mere form" to achieve the goal of efficacy. The goal may be effective political persuasion, especially since the context of the encounter is Confucius' woeful tale of political failure—hence the fisherman's emphasis on being able to "sway (or move) others" 動人. Despite the injunction to "follow the model of Heaven and

---

94 *Zhuangzi jishi* 31.1032.

value genuineness" and the fisherman's aura as someone beyond the world of human affairs, this is an excursus on *zhen* with broad worldly implications.

2.3 Trajectories of Notions of Genuineness *(zhen)* and Sincerity *(cheng)*

In the previous section we began with instances of *zhen* in *Zhuangzi* that refer to a tantalizing absolute, almost synonymous with the Way,[95] and concluded with its equation with *cheng* and relatively stable notions of true nature and sincere expression. The word *cheng* becomes common from late Warring States onwards, and in many cases functions adverbially to mean "truly" or "really." In ritual contexts, it refers to good faith in serving the spirits and correspondence between reverence and ritual protocols.[96] Intimations of its transcendent dimension first appear in *Mengzi*: "The myriad things are all complete within me. There is no greater joy than returning to oneself and being sincere" 萬物皆備於我矣。反身而誠，樂莫大焉.[97] "Return" is tantamount to self-examination; to ascertain sincerity in oneself is to "illuminate inward goodness" (*ming hu shan* 明乎善)—such sincerity then extends outwards as filial devotion, good faith with friends, and success in gaining recognition from those in power.[98] Xunzi describes sincerity as the paramount principle of "nourishing the heart" (*yangxin* 養心). To "fulfill the fullest potential of sincerity" (*zhicheng* 致誠) is to actualize moral principles and attain the transformative powers of "heavenly virtue" (*tiande* 天德).[99] Unlike other virtue words, *cheng* rises above specific application to particular situations

---

95   The *bei* 貝 component of the graph *zhen* is related to *ding* 鼎 (cauldron). Ji Xusheng 季旭昇 glosses *zhen* as "a spoon getting food from a cauldron." Qiu Xigui 裘錫圭 connects *zhen* to *dian* 顛 or *ding* 頂 (a person's head). Cf. http://humanum.arts.cuhk.edu.hk/Lexis/lexi-mf/search. php? Edward Shaughnessy suggests that the graph is linked to *ding* 丁, *tian* 天, *zheng* 正 (private communication).

96   *Liji jijie*, 1.9, 3A.170, 4B.292, 10B.652, 11A.670, 11A.689, 11B.707, 25.1237–1238.

97   *Mengzi yizhu* 13.4: 302.

98   *Mengzi yizhu* 7.12 : 173–174.

99   *Xunzi jijie* 3.46.

to become the guiding force illuminating inner truth and concretizing virtues, hence its crucial role in mapping the steps of self-cultivation and in underwriting social, political, and even cosmic transformation in *Daxue* 大 學 (The great learning) and *Zhongyong* (The mean).[100] Images of continuity and oneness recur in the delineation of *cheng* as a force that links the self to others and to things. By contrast, as we have seen, in some sections in *Zhuangzi*, *zhen* evokes associations with discontinuity, fragmentation, and epistemological uncertainty.

By elevating *Daxue* and *Zhongyong* as foundational texts that deserve special attention, Song Neo-Confucians confirm "sincerity" as the principle of co-incidence between self-cultivation and external order. Ming *xinxue* thinkers (and literati in their *xinxue* moments) also embrace the metaphysical dimension of sincerity. Their uses of the word *zhen*, even when it introduces Daoist and Buddhist echoes, are supposed to complement *cheng* and to augment the unity of and continuity between inwardness and transcendence. However, for many writers who articulate the quest for the true self and its expression, the preferred word is *zhen* rather than *cheng*, perhaps because the latter's valence of moral certainty does not admit of the sense of disjunction and opposition between the self and its social, political, moral, or religious contexts.

Yet it is important to remember that even in the context of literary creation and literati lives, *zhen* often does not convey anxiety. The fisherman's definition of *zhen* as "essential sincerity" and the inevitable communication of deeply felt emotions in *Zhuangzi* is not very different from the affirmation of irrepressible verbal expression of emotions and intent in the "Mao Preface" to the *Shijing*, a foundational text in Chinese literary thought. (Granted, the "Mao Preface" also focuses on remonstrance, governance, and political cohesion, which draw attention to function rather

---

100   *Daxue* 1 and 6 (*Sishu jizhu*, 3–4, 7); *Zhongyong* 20–26 and 32 (*Sishu jizhu*, 28–35, 38–39). On the role of *cheng* in socio-political order, see also *Lüshi chunqiu jiaoshi* 18.1225–1226. Cf. Sato Masayuki 2009.

than the inevitability of expression.) The rejection of artifice, convention, and external validation in the idea of "returning to the genuine" (*fan qi zhen* 反其真) in *Zhuangzi*[101] finds endless reverberations in the Chinese literary tradition. Late Ming literary thought, for example, is full of assertions about the need for emotional authentication and unmediated expression.

Zhen as fulfillment of nature, when nature is not defined in moral terms, means that such unlikely characters as Brigand Zhi in the eponymous chapter in *Zhuangzi* can denounce Confucius for failing to "preserve his genuineness" (*quanzhen* 全真).[102] As noted above, in later periods the term "True Being" (*zhenren*) often just means immortals, but it can also refer to the simple and unschooled, the sensualist, the iconoclast, the one who "follows his nature." The late Ming is particularly rich with eccentrics and counter cultural types. Pervasive fascination with the vagaries of the authentic can also be seen in fictional commentary. The commentary on *Shuihu zhuan* attributed to Li Zhi, for example, often lauds the mindlessly violent Li Kui as "true sage" (*zhen shengren* 真聖人) and "true Buddha" (*zhenfo* 真佛). The commentator seems to affirm bloodlust as the untrammeled expression of righteous anger.[103]

Most literary and cultural histories see the late Ming concern with the true self as the unproblematic iteration of the celebration of "the freedom of the spirit" in *Zhuangzi* and the Wei-Jin cultural types of wild unrestraint it inspired.[104] But perhaps the more interesting resonances are found in the contradictions of genuineness. Coherent interiority remains a question in the search for the "True Arbiter" and "True Ruler" in "The Discourse for Making Things Equal." "True knowledge" and "True Being" in "The Great and Venerable Teacher" offer the promise of absolute truth, but somewhat

---

101 *Zhuangzi jishi* 9.330, 17.590–591.

102 *Zhuangzi jishi* 29.1000. By a similar logic, Zichan's 子產 hedonistic brothers are praised as *zhenren* (*Liezi jishi*, 7.224–227). The Quanzhen sect in religious Daoism uses the term *quanzhen* differently: it is understood as "complete perfection."

103 Cf. Zuo Dongling 2010: 226–241.

104 See, for example, Song Kefu and Han Xiao 2002, Hu Xuechun 2009, Lin I-Jung 2010.

evasively. Xu Wugui, who refers to himself (by implication) as the "True Being," resorts to an excursus on dogs and horses to convey his meanings to the ruler. In general, disguise and deception are prevalent in *Zhuangzi*. The indeterminacy of reality means that expressing, communicating, or divining the truth about oneself and another can be playful and uncertain.[105]

And yet this is not how *Zhuangzi* is understood in the tradition. Later commentators see skepticism and negativity as obstacles whose raison d'être is their overcoming. It is when its "ways of being genuine" become a cultural model that questions of mediation, problematic communication, or self-division arise. Ruan Ji 阮籍(210–263), for example, wrote essays on *Zhuangzi* elucidating its transcendent ideals with no hint of irony.[106] But anecdotes about him and his biography in *Jin shu* 晉書 tell of an intriguing mixture of unrestraint and calculation. Consider the well-known example of his unconventional mourning. He feasts on a suckling pig, only to spit blood afterwards, presumably from irrepressible sadness.[107] Being true to the spirit of defying norms and flouting conventions means also going against the genuine need to express grief. *Zhuangzi* might have invented the very idea of irony, but the ironic implications of being genuine with spectators in mind (or performing genuineness) can only come into full play with the kind of social and political contexts we have for later periods. Primal Vastness 鴻蒙 "slapping his things, hopping about like a sparrow and roaming" 拊髀雀躍而遊 in *Zhuangzi* is an emblem of freedom.[108] But Li Zhi's defense of the late Ming thinker Yan Jun 顏鈞 (1504–1596), who expressed his illumination about innate knowledge by "rolling on the ground right there" 就地打滾, takes us to the treacherous boundary between the sublime and the grotesque. Yan's critics found this

---

105 This is unusual in early Chinese thought, notable for its "epistemological optimism" (Keightley 2014: 283–310).

106 Ruan Ji, "Da Zhuang lun" 達莊論, "Daren xiansheng zhuan" 大人先生傳 (*Ruan Ji ji jiaozhu* 阮籍集校注, 133–158, 161–192).

107 *Shishuo xinyu jianshu* 23.2: 728; *Jin shu* 49.1361.

108 *Zhuangzi jishi* 11.385–386.

exhibitionism absurd. Li Zhi applauded this as a sign of Yan Jun "having gained for himself the true joy of innate knowledge" 自得良知真趣.[109] How mediated or immediate is the absurd gesture deemed necessary for the joy of attaining the moment of truth? Is this also self-revelation or an act of communication? For late imperial writers, the question of the true self is compounded by belatedness, for they are in dialogue not only with *Zhuangzi* but also the cultural models it inspired through the ages, including Ruan Ji and his cohort of ostentatiously genuine characters from the Wei-Jin period.[110] Perhaps it is the self-division and potential bad faith in being consciously "genuine" or following cultural models of genuineness, in addition to simple heedless self-indulgence, that inspired Gu Yanwu's critique with which we began this essay.

Bibliography

Analects. See *Lunyu* 論語.

Chen Baoliang 陳寶良. 2014. *Mingdai shehui zhuanxing yu wenhua bianqian* 明代社會轉型與文化變遷. Chongqing: Chongqing daxue chubanshe.

Cheng Yu-yu (Zheng Yuyu) 鄭毓瑜. 2006. "Shenti biaoyan yu Wei-Jin renlun pinjian—yige ziwo 'tixian' de jiaodu" 身體表演與魏晉人倫品鑒——一個自我「體現」的角度. *Hanxue yanjiu* 《漢學研究》 24.2, 71–104.

Chunqiu Zuozhuan zhu 春秋左傳注. 1990. With commentaries compiled by Yang Bojun 楊伯峻. Beijing: Zhonghua shuju.

Chung Tsai-chun (Zhong Caijun) 鍾彩均. 2010. "Wang Longxi de benti lun yu gongfu lun" 王龍溪的本體論與工夫論. *Donghai zhongwen xuebao* 《東海中文學報》 22: 93–124.

---

109 Li Zhi, "Da Zhou Liutang" 答周柳塘 (*Li Zhi quanji zhu* 1: 218–226).

110 Sixteenth and seventeenth-century anecdotal collections tell of Ming literati who modeled their behavior on Wei-Jin prototypes (Qian Nanxiu 2001: 247–282). Extant Ming (1535, 1580, 1586) editions of *Shishuo xinyu*, including one duo-color commentary edition, testified to an abiding interest in cultivating eccentricity and discerning the continuity or rupture between surface and genuineness. Numerous late Ming and early Qing imitations of *Shishuo xinyu* confirmed the 16th- and 17th-century revival of the text as one index to the sensibility of the era. On the problem of "performing genuineness" in *Shishuo xinyu*, see Li Wai-yee 2004, Cheng Yu-yu (Zheng Yuyu) 2006.

Chuanshan quanshu 船山全書. 1988. By Wang Fuzhi 王夫之 (1619–1682). Edited by *Chuanshan quanshu* bianji weiyuan hui 船山全書編輯委員會. 16 vols. Changsha: Yuelu shushe.

Chunqiu fanlu yizheng 春秋繁露義證. 1992. With commentaries compiled by Su Yu 蘇輿. Edited by Zhong Zhe 鍾哲. Beijing: Zhonghua shuju.

De Bary, Theodore. 1999. *Sources of Chinese Tradition*. New York: Columbia University Press.

Du Lianzhe 杜聯喆. 1977. *Ming ren zizhuan wen chao* 明人自傳文鈔. Banqiao: Yiwen yinshu guan.

Fang Yong 方勇. 2008. *Zhuangzi xue shi* 莊子學史. 3 vols. Beijing: Renmin chubanshe.

———. 2015. *Zhuangzi shumu tiyao* 莊子書目提要. Beijing: Guojia tushu chubanshe.

Feng Menglong quanji 馮夢龍全集. 2007. By Feng Menglong 馮夢龍 (1574–1646). Edited by Wei Tongxian 魏同賢 et al. 18 vols. Nanjing: Fenghuang chubanshe.

Gong Pengcheng 龔鵬程. 2008 (first published 1994). *Wan Ming sichao* 晚明思潮. Beijing: Shangwu yinshu guan.

Graziani, Romain. 2011. *Les corps dans le taoisme ancien: l'infirme, l'informe, l'infâme*. Paris: Belles lettres.

———. 2012. "Rhetoric that Kills, Rhetoric that Heals." *Extrême-Orient Extrême Occident* 34, 41–77.

Handler-Spitz, Rebecca, Pauline Lee, and Haun Saussy. 2016. *A Book to Burn and A Book to Keep (Hidden): Selected Writings by Li Zhi*. New York: Columbia University Press.

Handler-Spitz, Rebecca. 2017. *Symptoms of an Unruly Age: Li Zhi and the Cultures of Early Modernity*. Seattle: University of Washington Press.

He Yuming. 2008. "Difficulties of Performance: The Musical Career of Xu Wei's *The Mad Drummer*." *Harvard Journal of Asiatic Studies* 68.2: 77–114.

Hou Hanshu 後漢書. 1997. By Fan Ye 范曄 (398–445). With commentaries by Li Shan 李善 (630–690) et al. Beijing: Zhonghua shuju.

Hu Xuechun 胡學春. 2009. *Zhen: Taizhou xuepai meixue fanchou* 真：泰州學派美學範疇. Beijing: Shehui kexue wenxian chuban she.

Huainan honglie jijie 淮南鴻烈集解. 1989. With commentaries and annotations by Liu Wendian 劉文典 (1889–1958). Edited by Feng Yi 馮逸 and Qiao Hua 喬華. Beijing: Zhonghua shuju.

Huang Zongxi quanji 黃宗羲全集. 2005. By Huang Zongxi 黃宗羲 (1610–1695). Edited by Wu Guang 吳光 and Shen Shanhong 沈善洪. 12 vols. Hangzhou: Zhejiang guji chubanshe.

Ji Wenfu 嵇文甫. 2013 (first published 1944). *Wan Ming sixiang shi lun* 晚明思想史論. Beijing: Dongfang chubanshe.

Keightley, David. 2014. *These Bones Shall Rise Again*. Albany, NY: State University of New York Press.

Kexue zhai ji 珂雪齋集. 1989. By Yuan Zhongdao 袁中道 (1570–1623). Edited by Qian Bocheng 錢伯城. 3 vols. Shanghai: Shanghai guji chubanshe.

Kwa, Shiamin. 2012. *Strange Eventful Histories: Identity, Performance, and Xu Wei's Four Cries of a Gibbon*. Cambridge, MA: Harvard University Asia Center.

Jin shu 晉書. 1997. By Fang Xuanling 房玄齡 (579–648) et al. Beijing: Zhonghua shuju.

Laozi jiaoshi 老子校釋. 1984. With annotations by Zhu Qianzhi 朱謙之 (1899–1972). Beijing: Zhonghua shuju.

Li Qiancheng. 2004. *Fictions of Enlightenment: Journey to the West, Tower of Myriad Mirrors, and Dream of the Red Chamber*. Honolulu: University of Hawai'i Press.

Li Wai-yee. 1993. *Enchantment and Disenchantment: Love and Illusion in Chinese Literature*. Princeton: Princeton University Press.

———. 2004. "*Shishuo xinyu* and the Emergence of Chinese Aesthetic Consciousness in the Six Dynasties." In *Chinese Aesthetics: The Orderings of Literature, the Arts, and the Universe in the Six Dynasties*. Edited by Cai Zong-qi, 237–276. Honolulu: Hawai'i University Press.

———. 2010. "Shuo zhen: *Mudan ting* yu Ming mo Qing chu wenhua" 説真：《牡丹亭》與明末清初文化. In *Kunqu chun san er yue tian: miandui shijie de Kunqu yu Mudanting* 崑曲春三二月天——面對世界的崑曲與牡丹亭. Edited by Hua Wei 華瑋, 448–465. Shanghai: Shanghai guji chubanshe.

———. 2013. "Riddles, Concealment, and Rhetoric in Early China." In *Facing the Monarch: Modes of Advice in the Early Chinese Court*. Edited by Garret Olberding, 100–132. Cambridge: Harvard University Asia Center.

Li Zhi quanji zhu 李贄全集注. 2010. By Li Zhi 李贄 (1527–1602). With annotations by Zhang Jianye 張建業 et al. 26 vols. Beijing: Shehui kexue wenxian chubanshe.

Liezi jishi 列子集釋. 1979. With annotations by Yang Bojun. Beijing: Zhonghua shuju.

Liji jijie 禮記集解. 1989. With commentaries compiled by Sun Xidan 孫希旦 (1736–1784). Edited by Shen Xiaohuan 沈嘯寰 and Wang Xingxian 王星賢. Beijing: Zhonghua shuju.

Lin I-Jung (Lin Yirong) 林宜蓉. 2010. *Zhong wan Ming wenyi changyu "kuangshi" shenfen zhi yanjiu* 中晚明文藝場域「狂士」身分之研究. Taipei: Hua Mulan chubanshe.

Linji lu 臨濟錄. 2001. By Yixuan 義玄 (d. 867). Edited by Huiran 慧然 and Yang Zengwen 楊曾文. Zhengzhou: Zhongzhou guji chubanshe.

Lu, Tina. 2001. *Persons, Roles, and Minds: Identity in Peony Pavilion and Peach Blossom Fan*. Cambridge: Harvard University Asia Center.

Lunheng jiaoshi 論衡校釋. 1990. By Wang Chong 王充 (27–97). With annotations by Huang Hui 黃暉. Beijing: Zhonghua shuju.

Lunyu yizhu 論語譯注. 1992. With annotations by Yang Bojun. Beijing: Zhonghua shuju.

Luo Zongqiang 羅宗強. 2006. *Mingdai houqi shiren xintai yanjiu* 明代後期士人心態研究. Tianjin: Nankai daxue chubanshe.

Lüshi chunqiu jiaoshi 呂氏春秋校釋. 2002. With annotations by Chen Qiyou 陳奇猷. Shanghai: Shanghai guji chubanshe.

Meihua caotang bitan 梅花草堂筆談. 1986. By Zhang Dafu 張大復 (ca. 1554–1630). 3 vols. Shanghai: Shanghai guji chubanshe.

Mengzi yizhu 孟子譯注. 1992. With annotations by Yang Bojun. Beijing: Zhonghua shuju.

Mudan ting 牡丹亭. 1978. By Tang Xianzu 湯顯祖 (1550–1616). With annotations by Xu Shuofang 徐朔方. Beijing: Renmin wenxue chubanshe.

Nakatani, Hajime. 2010. "Body, Sentiment, and Voice in Ming Self-Encomia (*Zizan*)." *Chinese Literature: Essays, Articles, Reviews* 32: 73–94.

Qian Nanxiu. 2001. *Spirit and Self in Medieval China: The Shih-shuo hsin-yu and Its Legacy*. Honolulu: University of Hawaiʻi Press.

Quan Tang wen 全唐文. 1976. Compiled by Dong Gao 董誥 (1740–1818) et al. Beijing: Zhonghua shuju.

Rizhilu jishi 日知錄集釋. 1996. By Gu Yanwu 顧炎武 (1613–1682). Annotated by Huang Rucheng 黃汝成 (1799–1837). Collated by Qin Kecheng 秦克誠. Changsha: Yuelu shushe.

Ruan Ji ji jiaozhu 阮籍集校注. 1987. By Ruan Ji 阮籍 (210–263). With annotations by Chen Bojun 陳伯君. Beijing: Zhonghua shuju.

Sanguo zhi 三國志. 1997. By Chen Shou 陳壽 (233–297). With commentaries by Pei Songzhi 裴松之 (372–451). Beijing: Zhonghua shuju.

Sato Masayuki 佐藤將之. 2009. "Zhanguo shidai 'cheng' guannian de xingcheng yu yiyi" 戰國時代「誠」觀念的形成與意義. In *Guannian zi jiedu yu sixiang shi tansuo* 觀念字解讀與思想史探索. Edited by Zheng Jixiong (Cheng Kat Hung) 鄭吉雄, 201–240. Taipei: Xuesheng shuju.

Shiji 史記. 1985. By Sima Qian 司馬遷 (ca. 145–90 BCE). With commentaries by Pei Yin 裴駰 (5th century), Sima Zhen 司馬貞 (670–732) and Zhang Shoujie 張守節 (7th century). Beijing: Zhonghua shuju.

Shishou xinyu jianshu 世說新語箋疏. 1984. By Liu Yiqing 劉義慶 (403–444) et al. With commentaries by Liu Xiaobiao 劉孝標 (462–521). Annotations by Yu Jiaxi 余嘉錫. Taipei: Huazheng shuju.

Siku quanshu zongmu 四庫全書總目. 1983. Compiled by Yongrong 永瑢 (1744–1790) et al. 2 vols. Beijing: Zhonghua shuju.

Sishu jizhu 四書集註. 2001. With commentaries compiled by Zhu Xi 朱熹 (1130–1200). Beijing: Zhonghua shuju.

Song Kefu 宋克夫 and Han Xiao 韓曉. 2002. *Xinxue yu wenxue lungao: Mingdai Jiajing Wanli shiqi wenxue gaiguan* 心學與文學論稿：明代嘉靖萬曆時期文學概觀. Beijing: Zhongguo shehui kexue chubanshe.

Struve, Lynn. 2019. *The Dreaming Mind and the End of the Ming World*. Honolulu: University of Hawai'i Press.

Tao'an mengyi 陶庵夢憶. 2008. By Zhang Dai 張岱 (1597–1679). Edited by Huai Ming 淮茗. Beijing: Zhonghua shuju.

Wang Ji ji 王畿集. 2007. By Wang Ji 王畿 (1498–1583). Edited by Wu Zhen 吳震. Nanjing: Fenghuang chubanshe.

Wang Yangming quanji 王陽明全集. 1991. By Wang Shouren 王守仁 (aka Wang Yangming 王陽明, 1472–1529). Edited by Wu Guang 吳光 et al. 2 vols. Shanghai: Shanghai guji chubanshe.

Wu Chengxue 吳承學 and Li Guangmo 李光摩. 2002. "Ershi shiji wan Ming wenxue sichao yanjiu gaishu" 二十世紀晚明文學思潮研究概述. In *Wan Ming wenxue sichao yanjiu* 晚明文學思潮研究. Edited by Wu Chengxue and Li Guangmo. Wuhan: Hubei jiaoyu chubanshe.

Wu Pei-yi. 1990. *The Confucian's Progress: Autobiographical Writings in Traditional China*. Princeton: Princeton University Press.

Xu Wei ji 徐渭集. 1983. By Xu Wei 徐渭 (1521–1593). 4 vols. Beijing: Zhonghua shuju.

Xunzi jijie 荀子集解. 1992. Annotated by Wang Xianqian 王先謙 (1842–1917). Edited by Shen Xiaohuan 沈嘯寰 and Wang Xingxian 王星賢. Beijing: Zhonghua shuju.

Yang Yucheng 楊玉成. 2013. "Mengyi, outu yu yiliao: wan Ming Dong Yue wenxue yu xinli zhuanji" 夢囈、嘔吐與醫療：晚明董說文學與心理傳記. In *Chenlun, chanhui yu jiudu—Zhongguo wenhua de chanhui shuxie lunji* 沈淪、懺悔與救度——中國文化的懺悔書寫論集. Edited by Li Feng-mao 李豐楙 and Liao Chao-heng 廖肇亨, 558–677. Taipei: Zhongyang yanjiuyuan wenzhe yanjiusuo.

Yuan Haowen quanji 元好問全集. 1990. By Yuan Haowen 元好問 (1190–1257). Edited by Yao Dianzhong 姚奠中. Taiyuan: Shanxi renmin chubanshe.

Yuan Hongdao ji jianjiao 袁弘道集箋校. 1984. By Yuan Hongdao 袁宏道 (1568–1610). Edited by Qian Bocheng. Shanghai: Shanghai guji chubanshe.

Yuanjue jing 圓覺經. 2010. With commentaries by Xu Min 徐敏. Beijing: Zhonghua shuju.

Zhang Dai shi wen ji 張岱詩文集. 1991. By Zhang Dai 張岱 (1597–1679). Edited by Xia Xianchun 夏咸淳. Shanghai: Shanghai guji chubanshe.

Zhang Jianye. 2013. Compiler. *Li Zhi yanjiu ziliao huibian* 李贄研究資料匯編. Beijing: Shehui kexue wenxian chubanshe.

Zhao Hongjuan 趙紅娟. 2006. *Ming yimin Dong Yue yanjiu* 明遺民董説研究. Shanghai: Shanghai guji chubanshe.

Zhao Wei 趙偉. 2007. *Wan Ming kuang Chan sichao yu wenxue sixiang yanjiu* 晚明狂禪與文學思想研究. Chengdu: Bashu shushe.

Zhou Qun 周群 and Xie Jianhua 謝建華. 2006. *Xu Wei pingzhuan* 徐渭評傳. Nanjing: Nanjing daxue chubanshe.

Zhuangzi jiaoquan 莊子校詮. 1988. With commentaries compiled by Wang Shumin 王叔岷. 3 vols. Taipei: Zhongyang yanjiuyuan lishi yuyan yanjiusuo.

Zhuangzi jishi 莊子集釋. 1995. With commentaries compiled by Guo Qingfan 郭慶藩 (1844–1896). Edited by Wang Xiaoyu 王孝魚. 4 vols. Beijing: Zhonghua shuju.

Zhuangzi zuanjian 莊子纂箋. 1957. With commentaries compiled by Qian Mu 錢穆. Hong Kong: Dongnan yinwu chubanshe.

Zuo Dongling 左東嶺. 2000. *Wang xue yu zhong wan Ming wenren xintai* 王學與中晚明士人心態. Beijing: Renmin wenxue chubanshe.

Zuo Tradition/Zuozhuan: Commentary on the "Spring and Autumn Annals." 2016. Translated and introduced by Stephen Durrant, Wai-yee Li and David Schaberg. Seattle: University of Washington Press.

Zuozhuan 左傳. See *Chunqiu Zuozhuan zhu.*

Afterword

Philological Reflections on Chinese Conceptual History: Introducing Thesaurus Linguae Sericae

Christoph Harbsmeier

Nostra, qui erat philosophia philologia facta est. (What was our philosophy has become philology).

Pierre Gassendi (1592–1655)[1]

Man wird sich daran gewöhnen müssen, in jeder Wortgeschichte eine Monographie zur Kulturgeschichte der Menschheit zu erblicken. Sprachgeschichte, Wortgeschichte, ist immer Kulturgeschichte. (One will have to get used to see, in each history of a word, a monograph on the cultural history of mankind. Linguistic history, the history of words, is always cultural history).

Fritz Mauthner (1849–1923)[2]

1. Pre-meditation on Defining Changing Concepts

Gottlob Frege (1848–1925) claimed, "What is known as the history of concepts is really a history either of our knowledge of concepts or of the

---

1 Gassendi, *Exercitationes paradoxicae adversus Aristotelem*, I.1 (Mauthner 1924, vol. 1: 74).
2 Mauthner 1924, vol. I: xv.

meaning of words."[3] Frege has a profound point here which conceptual historians disregard at their peril: concepts have structure but they themselves have no history. The invention or discovery of these concepts does of course have a history, but that is a very different story. And it may be useful to point out that Frege's remark is not just a logician's or mathematician's quibble. Nietzsche (1844–1900) noted from his own point of view the very same thing, and in terms more directly relevant to conceptual history: "*Alle Begriffe, in denen sich ein ganzer Prozess semiotisch zusammenfasst, entziehen sich der Definition; definierbar ist nur das, was keine Geschichte hat.*" (All concepts in which a whole process is semiotically bundled are beyond definition. One can only define that which has no history.)[4] Frege and Nietzsche focus on a fundamental problem with conceptual history insofar as it presumes to define historically changing concepts. I feel that we need to sort out this problem.

At an abstract level of logical analysis, concepts must be held constant and "a-historical" (though only in the sense of "unchanging"). This is not to deny that the knowledge of these concepts and the beliefs concerning these concepts do not change. Logically, a change in an abstract concept amounts to the emergence of a different, but still unchanging, new concept.

The cultural conceptions that we organize within the logical space defined by these concepts, these conceptions as envisaged by humans—and as often though not always expressed in words—do manifestly change over time, as all thoughts and feelings do, and they do vary considerably across individuals, social groups, cultures, and civilizations.

Frege, then, has a valid and important logical point, at least for some kinds of concepts: the concept of a prime number itself is unchanging and ahistorical. One may disagree whether that invariant concept is invented or discovered. But the concept itself does not have a history; there is only the history of its discovery or invention.

---

3   Frege 1926: vii.

4   Nietzsche, *Zur Genealogie der Moral*, cited from Nietzsche 1966, vol. 2: 820.

However, when Frege seems to suggest in his formulation that students of conceptual history are in fact only working with what people know about concepts on the one hand and terminological history on the other, he is profoundly misleading. For one thing, whether he likes to reflect on this or not, it makes excellent sense to investigate the historical roots of those abstract concepts that are so "a-historical": they emerge in specific cultural and historical contexts, for historical reasons, as cultural conceptions in historical contexts. For another, sound conceptual history is primarily concerned neither with the history of terminology nor indeed with knowledge about concepts. Conceptual history is primarily concerned with the historical ethnography of cultural conceptions, notions, ideas, subjective *Vorstellungen* (construals). Frege's salutary and logically hygienic insight is that these conceptions should be analytically subsumed under—or at least usefully discussed in connection with—those abstract, culturally colorless and essentially, in themselves, a-historical concepts.

Historicists have been quick to point out that this elevated logical level of abstract trans-cultural "a-historical" concepts is itself no more than a historically contingent distillation from various parochial—mostly European—notions and Vorstellungen. This, I find, was not a point that Frege took any particular interest in. Like Leibniz, Frege envisaged and aspired to "mathematics of concepts," and to a *Begriffssprache* (language of concepts), which aspired to escape as much as humanly possible from the historical and cultural vagaries of subjective conceptions, notions and construals, and to construct a logically transparent systematic framework which serves as an abstract analytic tool for a coherent analysis of these conceptions. Frege shared these aspirations with the educationalist Amos Comenius (1592–1670) and the mathematician Leibniz (1646–1716), and the many adherents of a *caracteristica universalis* (universal script) as well as a *grammatica universalis* (universal grammar). The fact that these aspirations or ideals can never quite be completely or even satisfactorily realized does not make them any less worthwhile. It is the analytic work in the pursuit of these ideals of logical transparency that is so important and that makes for intellectual progress.

I find it important that this analytic work is not only a worthy end in itself, but that in the end it serves a crucial and ultimately educational purpose: a practical aspiration which Jan Amos Comenius attempted to realize in his *Janua linguarum reserata* (An open door to the languages) as well as in his *Orbis sensualium pictus* (The totality of what is perceivable depicted) of 1659.[5] I dwell on Jan Amos Comenius in the present context because for me—as for Comenius—logical analysis must serve practicable clarification. Whether logicians like it or not: logical analysis must be made to serve the purposes of philological and historical explanation. And whether conceptual historians like it or not: explanatory transparency in conceptual history can only be achieved by the circumspect and disciplined application of logical analysis wherever possible.

2. Objections

Historians often tend to find Frege's call for logical transparency in conceptual history professionally obnoxious, methodologically naive, and historically barbaric because it establishes a non-historicized realm of logical and semantic structures: concepts.

Similarly, cognitive psychologists like the distinguished originator of WordNet, George A. Miller (1920–2012), should find the imposition of a conceptual system constructed logically, for comparative purposes, and unsupported by psychological evidence from the particular languages to which it is applied, thoroughly distasteful. Like the historians, Miller has his valid point: the ideal must be to study the cognitive system of each language on the basis of the data from that language. But in the case of psychological as well as in the case of historicist empiricism, the stubborn logical fact

---

5   Comenius 1959 and 1970, vol. 17. There is a useful bibliography of the hundreds of editions of this latter work, in various languages of the world (Comenius 1967). To this we must now add the Chinese edition that is important for the present project (Comenius 2001).

remains that the conceptual scheme language psychologists might bring to bear must be one that is logically transparent, philologically perspicuous, and generalistic in the sense that the categorical system applied to a given language must ideally be one that makes this language and its speakers systematically comparable to entirely different languages and entirely different speakers.

Unlike the colleagues in China and elsewhere who accept the English conceptions as a normative system for the description of Chinese conceptions, the project that I have initiated, *Thesaurus Linguae Sericae* (TLS), treats English as a language quite as parochial as Chinese. At the same time we are not shy to use English labels for our concepts as we work towards the conceptual part of a comparative archaeology and history of the cultural imagination. We do what we can to strip these abstract concepts of the idiomatic idiosyncrasies of parochial English semantics attached to those labels. We are convinced that we need to find a comparatist and logically well-defined abstract angle on both English and Chinese. Since we are inevitably writing in English, we try to achieve this by taking Chinese primary evidence as our point of departure for constructing a conceptual system. (On the other hand [for example, in the context of conceptual modernization and globalization], we do introduce English or European concepts, because at that historical stage these were the ones that were historically relevant.)

There are those who claim that there is no such thing as an abstract comparatist angle, only various but equally subjective and inexorably partial parochialisms. The objection is a serious one that applies across the board to all comparative studies: according to this line of thought there can be no general non-parochial angle in linguistics, only variously disguised forms of imposing one's own (typically but not necessarily English-inspired or Eurocentric) categories generally on the languages of the world. But our question is simply this: does this mean linguists should not aspire to reduce this inevitable subjective parochialism as best they can? And the answer to this question is clearly in the affirmative: linguists should do what they can to reduce their subjective parochialisms as best they can. In many ways, Western linguists have done so with some success, although it remains a deeply significant fact that their basic modern theories have tended to be developed on the basis of observations on contemporary English with a few anecdotal exotic observations from other languages thrown in for good measure.

In any case, in our project, I am determined to develop my linguistic and semantic theories on the basis of observations, *longue durée*, of the detailed Chinese linguistic evidence held up against the much more accessible and much more reliably described detailed evidence, longue durée, from Greek and Latin. In doing so I do not at all pretend in principle to avoid linguistic parochialism, only to do my very best to reduce it on the basis of the languages I know best. The justified point that subjective parochialism is in principle inevitable does not affect our duty to reduce such parochialism wherever we can, and thus to aim for abstract, non-parochial definitions of terms formulated in the light of one's intensive and sustained detailed philological experience with widely different languages.

Consider the abstract concept of H_2O, which in our system we would write as *water*, but which we could just as well—indifferently—write as *aqua* in the medieval and later European tradition, or as *shuǐ* in Chinese: our labels are arbitrary and logically irrelevant in that they are used only to remind us of the relevant stipulative and abstract formal definitions in the conceptual system.

Now it is a historical fact that pure H_2O has always been extremely rare in this world. Historically, H_2O occurs with various quantities of varying admixtures. Moreover, cultural conceptions of the nature and significance of water have varied considerably.[6] The semantic range of words for water varies very considerably across cultures: the modern Chinese word for water continues to cover liquids of many kinds. None of these historical and cultural facts affect our abstract interpretation of the analytic concept of H_2O, or the usefulness of this interpretation. The conceptual ethnography of *water* is indeed properly understood when one realizes that it involves widely different cultural conceptions (Vorstellungen) that focus on substances that consist predominantly—but not at all exclusively

---

6   For China, see Allan 1997 on the notion of water in Chinese intellectual history.

or most importantly—of H2O. No historical changes or civilizational differences, however radical they may be, will affect this basic concept of H2O, or as we have it, of *water*. And *water* is a category under which it is convenient and analytically helpful to analyze these historical changes and civilizational differences regarding conceptions of water. The very reason that we can compare the conceptual ethnography of water across history and across cultures as well as civilizations is that we have this abstract maximally transparent and explicit concept of *water* as H2O.

One may object that this model may hold for natural kinds, but that many concepts have no such solid "objective" base in the natural sciences. *Jealousy* is a case in point: here our aspiration must be to identify the conceptual *tertium comparationis* (the common semantic reference point), to make explicit a maximally transparent abstract concept of *jealousy*, which allows us to compare the complex conceputalizations that essentially involve jealousy across history and across civilizations. Essentially, this involves the kind of abstract work that has been attempted by Spinoza (1632–1677) in part III of his *Ethica more geometrico demonstrata* (Ethics demonstrated in a geometrical mode), and less successfully, I find, by Descartes (1596–1650) in his famous *Les passions de l'âme* (The passions of the soul): neither Spinoza nor Descartes was concerned with the conceptual ethnography of various speakers of Latin or French. They were concerned with the systemic conceptual underpinnings of the repertoire of human emotions or passions in general. I believe conceptual grids for emotions should be constructed in this spirit of Spinoza and Descartes.

Jost Trier's *Der deutsche Wortschatz im Sinnbezirk des Verstandes* (The German vocabulary within the semantic field of understanding)[7] marked a most inspiring philological breakthrough in the historical study of semantic fields and conceptual repertoires. His definition of the semantic field he describes as *Sinnbezirk des Verstandes* ("conceptual field of understanding") itself had to be metalinguistic and not limited to the language and the

---

7   Trier 1931 (1973).

historical period of the language with which he was concerned. Herein lies the general usefulness of Jost Trier's seminal work for the study of conceptual history. Trier's work is especially important in its emphasis on the need to study conceptual repertoires with respect to circumscribed texts and corpora: these repertoires will often vary for different authors and for different texts and text sorts even within the same period. Conceptual repertoires must be expected to vary across texts as well as idiolects investigated.

Conceptions and classifications of the emotions will vary widely across history, cultures and civilizations; even the size of these repertoires will certainly not be the same in different contexts. Yet the basic idea of philosophers like Descartes and Spinoza was to reconstruct the emotional elements from which all human emotions are built up (or indeed *not* built up, when a culture refuses to develop a terminological repertoire for a concept that is common across historical periods and different civilizations). Spinoza and Descartes used Latin and French as their points of departure. I feel it may be useful to start out with a highly sophisticated language as distant and as different from our own as possible, in order to try to avoid at least some of the crudest forms of philosophical or analytic parochialism: I choose classical Chinese as my point of departure, not because we imagine we can avoid parochialism, but in order to minimize it.

The systematicity of conceptual underpinnings, a central concern to systematic thinkers such as Leibniz and Spinoza, is best made explicit, as Plato was already aware, by specifying the conceptual hypernym for each concept, i.e. to specify for each concept what other concept(s) it is "a kind of." Thus one might try to construe a *horse* as a kind of *domestic animal*, and *jealousy* to be a kind of *dislike*, and so on. In other words, all concepts must be tentatively inscribed into a taxonomic system, very much in the spirit of the taxonomic system invented for plants by Carl von Linné (1707–1778). In practice, it turns out that in a whole range of cases it is more or equally convenient to inscribe a concept into a mereonomic (according to the now-current misspelling, meronomic) part-whole system. Anyway, for example, *finger* is best entered into a conceptual system as one of the *parts* of the *hand*. And more generally, conceptual grids, like the WordNet, should arrange their repertoire not alphabetically, but in a complex structured hierarchy.[8]

The fact that in many languages like ancient Chinese the standard word for the *finger* is the same as that for the *toe* is registered not at all as a fact of conceptual history, or a conceptual conflation of *finger* with *toe*. We never begin to imagine that the Chinese thought in terms of *finger-toes* any more than we suspect speakers of English of thinking in terms of *arm-legs* just because they do think in terms of "limbs." Rather, it is registered as an interesting fact of the natural ambiguity of Chinese terminology which in no way prevents Chinese speakers from making a neat conceptual distinction between fingers and toes, which they can make explicit as they need to.

Conversely, it is not a Eurocentric parochialist imposition to ask how the abstract concept *sibling* as explicitly opposed to "brothers" is represented in classical Chinese: I know of no obvious word or expression for this other than the unidiomatic list "elder brother, younger brother, elder sister and younger sister." In a highly family-orientated or "familist" culture like the Chinese, this vocabulary gap might seem to need an explanation, but it is far from clear whether it can ever get one.

3. Ideas behind the TLS

In light of the above considerations, a *Lexicon Grammatico-Philosophicum* in the educational spirit of Comenius and inspired by the logical-analytic spirit of Leibniz, and the philosophical/ psychological analyticity of Spinoza must operate don two levels with radically different aspirations:

Firstly, there must be a systematic philosophical attempt to define (and continually revise in the light of new evidence considered) a taxonomic and mereonomic grid of abstract concepts that aspires to be (and is

---

8   Not much needs to be said about this, because the WordNet under the direction of Christiane
     Fellbaum has elaborated this system to many people's satisfaction regarding words, not concepts.

continuously revised to become) applicable and useful across civilizations as well as across history. This web of explicit stipulative definitions of the conceptual grid must be sufficiently systematic and logically transparent to serve as a useful analytical tool and to provide an efficiently predictable browsing environment, but sufficiently flexible and underspecified to allow for a natural representation of the semantic variation and malleability among natural languages.

For philosophers of language it is important to emphasize that this conceptual grid cannot possibly aim for much subtle philosophical detail, although the inspiration from the history of analytical philosophy is obvious. The philological and philosophical detail of conceptual ethnography can only be applied to individual languages, realistically perhaps only to stages of languages and most probably only to individual writers. Our general taxonomic and mereonomic grid must aim to remain culturally underspecified and abstract if there is to be any hope for it to remain applicable in general to distant cultures.

Secondly, then, there must be a philological attempt to specify (and continually revise in the light of new evidence considered), for each abstract concept, the changing concrete repertoire of grammatically as well as semantically contrasting culture-specific and time-specific conceptions, as well as the nuances encoded in the terminologies that make up these repertoires.

Even with the caveats mentioned above, this project raises a host of obvious problems. For example, the notions of the morning star and the evening star may well come to be discussed under neither of these concepts. They may come to be discussed under the concept of *Venus* instead, under which concept it will then be noted that *Venus* is visible in certain ways in the evening and in the morning. In such cases as these one may well wish to impose a modern point of view, just as in the case of plants and animals one may well wish to opt for the organizing principle supplied by Carl von Linné, so that the whale might possibly risk having to be looked for under the mammals, and the fact that most cultures regard it as a fish manifests itself in the system as a deviant interpretation rather than as a different taxonomic classification. By taking Carl von Linné's classificatory system as a point of departure for ethno-botany and ethno-zoology, one establishes a *tertium comparationis* with reference to which all parochial systems are compared. For the convenience of retrievability and comparability, one sacrifices ethnographic bottom-up methodology. And one may well come to regret this move. That is why all taxonomic dispositions under the TLS system are technologically conceived in such a way that they are conveniently and quickly adjustable in every way.

Again, in astronomy, there will probably be no concept **Dipper* in the conceptual grid of TLS, no matter how plausible and conspicuous this constellation is in the sky. Rather, there will be a concept *constellation*, under which the Dipper will figure for those cultures that see it as a constellation. The culturally contrasting ways of subsuming the stars under different constellations must somehow be made comparable and even commensurable by the taxonomic and mereonomic system.

When we turn to psychological terminology, for example the conceptual history of *love*, we must obviously first define abstractly what we mean by love across cultures, and then—*pace* Frege—we should certainly not primarily be studying people's knowledge of this concept (they may not know what is happening to them, and they may not be interested in concepts), nor should we be primarily studying the meanings of words for love (people may be unable or disinclined to verbalize their feelings): we should concern ourselves with the changing conceptions of love, the evolution of the system of their changing amorous sensibilities themselves. It is this system of sensibilities as well as subjective cognitive practices that does have a history and that constitutes the proper primary subject of "conceptual history."

It would be a serious philosophical category mistake to think that employing a concept, living by it, is the same as knowing something about that concept. And moreover it would be a serious philological mistake to disregard the crucial evidence on this history of sensibilities that is available to us in the history of the use of words.

The crucial point brought out with such succinct elegance by Gottlob Frege has a relevance that historians often find unpalatable but which they need to take to heart: we can only study the conceptual history of love with analytic transparency insofar as we have determined what we consider an abstractly defined conceptual core of the concept of *love* that is applicable to or researchable in all cultures. Without defining this abstract concept, we have no *tertium comparationis* for our cross-historical and cross-civilizational comparisons.

Note that even in order to consider whether two words are synonymous or not, we need an abstract meta-linguistic notion of the meaning they share: only to the extent that we manage this do the two words ever begin to become semantically commensurable. We can then certainly also go on to study the history of humankind's awareness of concepts or knowledge of concepts. Indeed, at an even higher level of abstraction, we can and should consider Frege's reflections as a contingent historically conditioned event. All these things we should indeed do. But these are not the things that conceptual history itself should be primarily concerned with.

The history of the problematization of concepts must not be confused or conflated with conceptual history. The problematization of this problematization itself, as practiced by Gottlob Frege, has itself an interesting history, of course, which we can usefully discuss. And so on. But it is healthy to reflect that it makes excellent sense to study biology separately from the history of biology or physics separately from the history of biology or physics, and conceptual history separately from the history of conceptual history.[9]

To take another helpful example: *jealousy*, in children, is strong and important long before it becomes terminologically fixed in children, and even longer before it becomes an object of reflexive awareness and knowledge. What we define, when we consider the history of *jealousy*, is primarily a sensibility and secondarily the history of a changing repertoire of expressions for that sensibility.

Take even the concept of a *number*, which was not without interest to Frege. The important differences among both modern and ancient

---

9   None of which must obviously be taken to deny that in the end the study of biology and physics
     stands to gain from a self-awareness of its own history ...

languages in their conceptual practice and their terminological repertoire within this semantic field can only be studied meaningfully after one has abstractly decided what is to count as a concept of a number.

In ancient China, the relevant situation, which is of great importance for the history of science, may be summarized as follows: the notions of a number was nearly always that of a quantity or an amount (always *of something*); it was typically the idea of what the Germans call an *Anzahl*.[10] Numbers as such were not the subject of early Chinese mathematical discourse. Statements such as "the number three is prime," or indeed subjects or sentence topics such as "the number three" are notoriously absent in pre-Buddhist Chinese. This is not a matter of the Chinese failing to understand any mathematical definitions, but of changing Chinese conceptual practices within the general semantic field of *number*. Chinese knowledge and conceptions of numbers, fractions and so forth did change. The meaning of the relevant Chinese terminology has changed also. But what we are concerned with, when we do Chinese conceptual history, is primarily neither what the Chinese knew about the concept *number*, nor is it primarily, even, what their mathematical words meant: it is their changing conceptual practice, the way that the abstract concept of *number* entered their cognitive schemes, the way that concept entered their cultural activities.

In general, our concern in conceptual history must be with changing repertoires of notions, conceptions, and then also of expressions, as they are found to function in people's lives. We must deal with historical conceptual ethnography.

I must repeat the oft-misunderstood crucial point: conceptual history must classify conceptions under concepts. And the concepts must be defined as parts of an overall systemic conceptual grid. This overall grid, the *Begriffssystem*, advocated more than fifty years ago by the great scholars of French etymology Walther von Wartburg and Rudolf Hallig,[11] is not a

---

10   See Chemla and Guo 2005.

11   Wathburg and Hallig 1952.

word-net, then, but a concept-net. This taxonomic grid or "net" should ideally be a transparently and analytically defined grid of inter-defined concepts, and a grid that systematically avoids circularity in the definitions of its terms.

4. Concepts across Languages, Cultures, and Civilizations

If we are to get an objective "scientific" angle on our own varied conceptual traditions, we must focus on the deep contrasts among the European traditions. Many key concepts of modernity are currently treated as part of a common European conceptual heritage, but closer investigation reveals that a wide range of European languages have given rise to important nuances and conceptual developments that defy such a general inter-cultural, all-European treatment. Barbara Cassin provides rich food for thought and analysis on the diversity of philosophical and philosophical keywords in the major and some minor European languages.[12] Much basic analytic work still needs to be done on what is lost in translation between European languages. Barbara Cassin makes a courageous exploratory beginning.

Moreover, if conceptual ethnography is to address a modern audience of global villagers, there is an obvious need, *ideally*, for a concerted focus on the conceptual ethnography of non-Western cultures and on conceptual reception history. *Ideally*, we would need a focus on a non-Indo-European cognitive culture with an extended, well-documented, highly sophisticated history of its own, with its own advanced and autochthonous technological, scientific, politico-philosophical, historiographic, encyclopedic, hermeneutic, and lexicographic traditions, as a counter-balance to the deeply ingrained and predominant Eurocentric bias in conceptual history.

---

12   Cassin 2004.

Ideally, we should study this non-Western cognitive ethnography "bottom-up," with unflagging insistence on the non-Western primary sources as the point of departure for our conceptual schemes: for everything we say we must insist on indigenous non-European primary evidence, and explicit reference to dated chapter and verse in our non-Western primary sources accompanied by philologically argued and painfully literal translations. Moreover, everything we say about the non-Indo-European culture should ideally be based on detailed discussion with leading native-speaker specialists in that culture, and on a close study of the relevant non-Indo-European hermeneutic tradition.

Ideally this is what we all agree ought to be done. The argument against going ahead and doing it has always been disarmingly incisive: "Life is short." This is a very powerful argument. And the fact is that the task I have outlined is truly superhuman. However, G. K. Chesterton (1874–1936), inspired perhaps by Propertius's (ca. 50–15 BCE) maxim *In magnis et voluisse sat est* ("in great undertakings it is enough to have wanted [to achieve them]") was apparently of the opinion that "everything that is truly worth doing, is worth doing badly."

In *Thesaurus Linguae Sericae* I have needed the solace of Chesterton's advice. TLS defines a taxonomic and mereonomic network of abstract concepts which have completely interchangeable classical Chinese, modern Chinese and (capitalized) English *labels*. Under each of the abstract *labeled* concepts TLS summarizes the changing repertoire of contrasting Chinese words within the relevant semantic field. In addition, TLS attempts to relate the Chinese case systematically to that of Rome and Greece. This has involved more than twenty-five years of intense collaboration with leading practitioners of the art of sinology from China, Japan, the U.S. and Europe.

Alongside Carl Darling Buck's monumental *A Dictionary of Selected Synonyms in the Principal Indo-European Languages* (1949) and Émile Benveniste's legendarily inspiring *Le vocabulaire des institutions indo-européens* (1969), we badly need a *Lexicon Grammatico-Philosophicum* of "Selected Synonyms in the Principal Languages in World History." The TLS tries to make a (tentative) start on this, taking China as a point of departure to serve as an antidote against the continuing hallowed philosophical and philological conventions of European intellectual despotism.

• European intellectual despotism has led to a state of affairs where it is as if Chinese science, philosophy, and literature tend to be taken to make sense to the Chinese themselves only to the extent that they can be reduced to or subsumed under globalised English categories. What is not so reduced to Europeanized New-Speak or not so subsumed under dominant Western categories comes to look like traditionalist outdated obscurantism. Occidental despotism has been internalized by the Chinese to frightening extent, and it does appear that this enthusiastic espousal of Occidental intellectual despotism by non-occidentals is a dominant trend in large parts of the world.

Occidental intellectual despotism played an important part when it comes to China. But upon close investigation, what passes for Western concepts in the Chinese cultural environment turns out in the end to be strikingly and inexorably Chinese in many subtle ways. These conceptions often turn out to crucially contribute to the making of an ineluctably Chinese modernity.

5. The TLS Project and Its European Context

The present proposal is designed to bring together leading practitioners of the art of sinology to discuss, from a Sinological and from a comparative point of view, some of those key concepts that have shaped—and are shaping—modernity in China. The concrete aim is to produce a collaborative concise encyclopedia of Chinese keywords of modernity. The idea is to make an analytic, philological and historical contribution to comparative cognitive ethnography in a global perspective, where every contributor focuses on concepts that seem to be of special interest and importance in the formation of modernity.

Western developments have been traced in detail in the context of *Begriffsgeschichte*, or conceptual history. The transfer of modernizing concepts to other cultures has received considerable attention in the context of missionary studies and its political successors, where the West acts as a superpower imposing its ways on other weaker parties. But China constitutes a powerful and historically influential civilization of its own, as a highly articulate and sophisticated cultural superpower that has its own large sphere of influence, which is well aware of its historical strength and is emphatically emerging from its persistent political humiliations by the West since the 19th century. Thus conceptual interaction increasingly takes the form, in this case, not of reception history, but of cognitive culture clash.

Western conceptual developments inscribe themselves into a 3,000-year old, highly literate, sophisticated, articulate, and elaborate pre-existing Chinese conceptual grid which continues to inform modernizing conceptual developments in China, and where Western modern concepts have to compete. It makes no historical sense to construe Western democracy without reference to its perceived Greek antecedents, not because Greek democracy informed modern democracy, but because modern democracy was construed as a "rebirth" of that Greek tradition. Such conceptual subjectivities continue to matter even when they are full of historical wishful thinking. We need to understand such conflicting historical subjectivities if we want to understand modernization in China and in the world at large. This is why we need to take the long-term Chinese conceptual history seriously when we talk about conceptual modernization in China, and in general when we wish to reconstruct multiple modernities as multiple historical subjectivities.[13]

Here as everywhere, our main concern is to make the Chinese evidence comparable in a global and historical context and to enable the necessary, philologically based, cross-civilizational dialogue within the "vast field" of conceptual history. The purpose of this comparative study must never become the mere subsumption of the Chinese evidence under our conceptual scheme, or the tediously repetitive diagnosis of conceptual and cognitive deficiencies in the Chinese traditional conceptual system, but to tease out of the Chinese evidence the strategic schemata and the poetics of conceptual modernization that are creating in China a

---

13   For a concept of "multiple modernities," see Eisenstadt 2000.

modernity that is intensely modern, and remains in important ways irreducibly Chinese.

6. The Current State of the *Thesaurus Linguae Sericae*

Comparative conceptual history is a vast subject with a long history in Europe. The currently available TLS is inspired by *Thesaurus Linguae Graecae* (1572) and *Thesaurus Linguae Latinae* (1740), and aims to provide a reliable platform for discussion of classical Chinese philology and conceptual history, as these are relevant discussion in the humanities.

The large corpus of classical Chinese TLS texts are arranged—like poetry—by normally four to ten Chinese character lines next to their translations wherever available and publicly publishable in this form. This is designed to facilitate quick comparison of each line of text with details of the best available translation. One is thus not here faced with blocks of text next to similar-sized blocks of translations, but with short (roughly dated) lines of text with their short translations. Each of these lines is open for systematic grammatical, lexicographic and rhetorical analysis on many levels within the database. Each Chinese word in these lines can be linked to the TLS lexicon and can be annotated with regard to what exactly the words mean in the context, what rhetorical devices are present in the given line, and what systematic relations (like antonymy) are instantiated in these given lines.

The arrangement of the Chinese vocabulary in the TLS dictionary is in terms of semantic fields so that every word is placed next to other semantically related near-synonyms with which it should be compared for proper comprehension of the nuances of meaning. The detailed meanings and nuances of Chinese words (always considered within their given semantic field) are defined in the TLS synonym dictionary of classical Chinese compiled under the general supervision of Jiang Shaoyu (Peking University).

For example, TLS starts out from the assumption that one understands the English word "beautiful" exactly to the extent that one understands how exactly "beautiful" differs from "pretty," "nice," "handsome" and "sexy," and how it is opposed to antonyms like "ugly," "hideous," "unattractive," etc. Similarly for classical Chinese words like 美, 好, and 麗. A central part of TLS thus has to be a comprehensive, succinct and systematic synonym dictionary of classical Chinese. In addition, an antonym dictionary is provided that aims to capture all text passages in which antonyms are in explicit contrast with each other.

In order to give an overall account of the cognitive features of the classical Chinese lexicon, TLS provides a taxonomic system of all semantic fields (or synonym groups) in which every semantic field has its logical place in a metalinguistically construed overall taxonomic ontology of semantic fields (or concepts).

On the basis of this abstract cognitive taxonomy, the conceptual schemes of Chinese are made automatically comparable to those described in Carl Darling Buck's *Dictionary of Synonyms of the Main Indo-European Languages*.[14] All synonym groups are linked to Buck's standard handbook and are defined so as to apply to any natural language. Each semantic field (or synonym group) is attached to a bibliography/library of comparative linguistic material on the relevant conceptual schemes in different languages of the world. So far, particular attention has been paid to the comparison of conceptual repertoires of Greek, Latin, French, Russian and German.

Chinese words are notoriously polysemous, i.e. they have many distinct meanings that are often only distantly related. Our best dictionaries like the *Hanyu da cidian* 漢語大詞典 and the *Hanyu da zidian* 漢語大字典 simply number these meanings in one flat numbered series. From the point of view of cognitive linguistics and systematic lexicography, this is deeply unsatisfactory. TLS attempts—as far as possible—to explicitly derive all the meanings of a word directly or indirectly from its basic meaning(s). TLS thus constructs for each word a labelled taxonomic tree of derived meanings within different synonym groups. Every meaning attributed to a word has an explicit labelled path of derivation back to a basic meaning.

---

14   Buck 1942.

More than 1,500 such labelled taxonomic trees for the diverse meanings of given Chinese characters have been drafted so far. TLS thus attempts to show up the clearly limited but nonetheless significant extent to which the polysemy of Chinese words is systemic and predictable—and thus learnable as a coherent and transparent system, rather than as an unstructured and opaque list that needs to be blindly memorised.

The syntactic functions of Chinese words are found to differ significantly even among near synonyms. On the basis of three basic functional classes (nominals, verbals, and particles), TLS defines a systematic repertoire of syntactic functions in classical Chinese.[15] Every word in TLS is assigned a set of syntactic functions that it has so far been registered to perform, in all cases with detailed reference to the primary sources with a working translation.

Rhetoric plays a central part in the hermeneutics and the linguistics of classical Chinese texts. TLS contains a taxonomically organized system of trans-cultural definitions for rhetorical devices from Chinese and Western rhetorical traditions. It has thus become possible to compare in detail the range and frequency of rhetorical devices in different Chinese text types, and between the Chinese and the Graeco-Latin traditions.

Historical phonetics is central everywhere, but especially within the realm of rhetoric. For all characters, TLS offers *Guangyun fanqie* 《廣韻》反切 spellings, reconstructions of Old Chinese (by Pan Wuyun), Han Chinese (by Axel Schuessler), Early Middle Chinese, and Late Middle Chinese (by Edwin Pulleyblank). However, we are aware that on historical phonology more detailed online resources have become available elsewhere.

Christian Wittern (Kyoto University) is currently preparing an online version of TLS with a vastly enlarged textual corpus that will be annotatable by any number of registered users online. TLS will then make available for detailed systematic online annotation a fairly comprehensive reliable version of ancient Chinese texts.[16]

---

15   See more in Harbsmeier 2016.

16   The current state of the database may be consulted at tls.uni-hd.de.

All this is designed to make classical Chinese accessible for cooperative comparative historical linguistics, comparative rhetorical analysis, and especially comparative conceptual history in the rich tradition of German *Begriffsgeschichte* (conceptual history).[17] All of these encyclopaedic works fail to address the wealth of relevant perspectives that would arise from taking account of such major well-documented *longue durée* civilizations such as the Chinese. None of the entries in these encyclopaedias need to or deserve to be placed into a globalized perspective.

Reinhart Koselleck's *The Practice of Conceptual History* (2002) can give an idea how philological conceptual hermeneutics can become a crucial methodology for European historical studies in general. TLS aims to create an infrastructure that allows one to apply the methods of conceptual history to China. But even more importantly, it creates an infrastructure that respects Chinese perspectives and subjectivities and even encourages Chinese perspectives on the fundamental limitations of European approaches to conceptual history. Thus TLS aspires to more than placing the case of China into the purview of the great European/Western tradition of conceptual history. It aspires to do justice to Chinese subjectivities and perspectives. Extensive collaboration with leading Chinese scholars has thus been quintessential throughout.

Bibliography

Allan, Sarah. 1997. *The Way of Water and Sprouts of Virtue*. Albany: State University of New York Press.

Barck, Karlheinz et al. (eds.). 2000–2005. *Ästhetische Grundbegriffe: Historisches Wörterbuch in sieben Bänden*. Stuttgart: Metzler Verlag.

17　See the nine fat volumes on basic historical concepts edited by Brunner et al. (1972–1992), thirteen fat volumes on basic philosophical concepts edited by Joachim Ritter (1971–2007), twelve fat volumes on basic concepts of rhetoric edited by Gert Ueding (1992), seven fat volumes on basic aesthetic concepts edited by Karlheinz Barck (2000–2005), and the fifty-three volumes of the *Archiv für Begriffsgeschichte* (Archive for conceptual history).

Benveniste, Émile. 1969. *Le vocabulaire des institutions indo-européens.* Paris: Ed. Minuit.

Brunner, Otto, Werner Conze, and Reinhart Koselleck, eds. 1972–1992. *Geschichtliche Grundbegriffe; historisches Lexikon zur politisch-sozialen Sprache in Deutschland.* Stuttgart: E. Klett.

Buck, Carl Darling. 1949. *A Dictionary of Selected Synonyms in the Prinicipal Indo-European Languages.* Chicago: Chicago University Press.

Cassin, Barbara, ed. 2004. *Vocabulaire européen de la philosophie. Dictionnaire des intraduisibles.* Paris: Robert and Seuil.

Chemla, Karine and Shuchun Guo. 2005. *Les Neuf Chapitres. Le Classique mathématique de la Chine ancienne et ses commentaires,* Paris: Dunot.

Comenius Johannis A. (Komenský, Jan Ámos, 1592–1670). 1959. *Comenii Janua linguarum reserata.* Edited by Jaromír Cervenka. Praha: Státní pedagogické nakladatelství.

Comenius Johannis (Johann) Amos (Komenský, Jan Ámos, 1592–1670). 1967. *Die Ausgaben des Orbis Sensualium Pictus. Eine Bibliographie,* bearbeitet von Kurt Pilz. Nürnberg: Selbstverlag der Stadtbibliothek Nürnberg.

Comenius Johannis A. (Komenský, Jan Ámos, 1592–1670). 1970–. *Opera Omnia.* Praha: Akademia.

Comenius Johannis A. (夸美纽斯). 2001. *Tuhuazhong jiandaode shijie* 圖畫中見到的世界. Translated by Yang Xiaofen 楊曉芬. Shanghai: Shanghai shudian chubanshe.

Frege, Gottlob. 1884. *Die Grundlagen der Arithmetik. Eine logisch mathematische Untersuchung.* Breslau: Koebner.

Eisenstadt, Shmuel N. 2000. "Multiple Modernities." *Daedalus,* 129.1: 1–29.

Harbsmeier, Christoph. 2016. "A Summary of Classical Chinese Analytic Syntax: the System of Basic Syntactic Categories." In: *Problemy Kitajskogo i Obshchego Iazykoznaniia: K 90-letiiu S.E. Yakhontova,* edited by Elena N. Kolpachkova, 525–577. St. Petersburg: Studia NP-Print.

Koselleck, Reinhart. 2002. *The Practice of Conceptual History: Timing History, Spacing Concepts.* Translated by Todd Samuel Presner and others. Stanford: Stanford University Press.

Mauthner, Fritz. 1924. *Philosophisches Wörterbuch.* Leipzig: Felix Meiner.

Nietzsche, Friedrich. 1966. *Werke in Drei Bänden.* Edited by Karl Schlechta. München: C. Hanser Verlag.

Ritter, Joachim et al. ed. 1971–2007. *Historisches Wörterbuch der Philosophie.* Basel: Schwabe.

Thesaurus Linguae Sericae. http://tls.uni-hd.de/main/basic_ch_main.lasso

Trier, Jost. 1931 (1973). *Der deutsche Wortschatz im Sinnbezirk des Verstandes.* Heidelberg: Carl Winter.

Ueding, Gert, ed. 1992. *Historisches Wörterbuch der Rhetorik*. Tübingen: M. Niemeyer.

Wartburg, Walther von and Rudolf Hallig. 1952. *Begriffssystem als Grundlage für die Lexikographie. Versuch eines Ordnungsschemas*. Berlin: Akademie-Verlag (2nd ed. 1963).

Index

bureaucracy 103–104, 106, 108, 111,
113–116, 236, 272, 278, 285

Cai Ze 蔡澤 (fl. 250 BCE) 192
Canon of filial piety. See *Xiaojing*
Cao Cao 曹操 (155–220) 357
Cao Feng 曹峰 171n5–7
Cao Pi 曹丕 (187–226) 278
Cao Xueqin 曹雪芹 (1715?–1763?) xxxviii,
293, 331. See also *Honglou meng*
caracteristica universalis (universal
script) 383
Cassin, Barbara 394
Chan Buddhism xxiv, 338n12, 365n84
Chen Chun 陳淳 (sobriquet Beixi,
1159–1223) xxiii, xxiv–xxv, xxvii, 324
Chen Jiru 陳繼儒 (1558–1639) 356
Cheng Hao 程顥 (1032–1085) xxiv,
xxviin66
Cheng Yi 程頤 (1033–1107) xxiv,
xxviin66, 327n43, 329
child sacrifice 272
childlike mind 275, 277, 284, 339–342,
348, 357–358
Chu Han chunqiu 楚漢春秋 94, 96,
106, 112n78
Chunqiu 春秋 (*Spring and Autumn
Annals*) 9, 12n25, 16–17, 75, 88, 90,
93–94, 107, 111, 115–116, 172–173,
253. See also *Zuozhuan*
Chunqiu fanlu 春秋繁露 (Luxuriant
Dew of the *Spring and Autumn
Annals*) xvii, 17, 56, 59, 75, 336n4
ci 慈 (parental love, loving
compassion); *See* love, parental
Comenius, Jan Amos (1592–1670),
383–384, 389
commerce 126–127, 140, 142, 146n62,
147, 149–152, 155–156, 161n98,
163–165

conceptual history x, xxxviii 381–384,
388–389, 391–394, 396–398, 401.
See also Begriffsgeschichte
Confucius (Kongzi 孔子, 551–479
BCE) xiiin11, 3, 7–18, 26, 30–32,
89n15, 91n20, 93–95, 97, 111–112,
137, 175–178, 182–183, 190–193,
270, 276–277, 297, 302, 305,
356n59, 359n68, 368–369, 372. See
also *Lunyu*
Confucianism 8, 10, 12, 16, 27n75,
37–38, 108, 270, 276, 338n5,
cosmology, cosmological thought xix,
37, 39, 50, 53, 67, 74, 283, 324n32
Creel, Herrlee Glessner (1905–1994) 74
Cui Zhu 崔杼 (d. 546 BCE) 173n10
currency 155

Dai Zhen 戴震 (1724–1777) xxv–xxxi,
328n46, 330. See also *Mengzi ziyi
shuzhen*
Dao 道 (Way) xii, xxi–xxii, xxxn77, 7,
21, 55, 64, 65n70, 177, 179, 182–
183, 189, 205, 207, 219, 222, 238,
276, 323, 366, 370. *See also* Way
Daode jing 道德經 73. See also *Laozi*
Daxue 大學 (Great learning) xxivn54,
226, 371
de 德 (virtue) 43–45, 55, 174–175, 179,
207, 236, 370
Dewey, John (1859–1952) 9
Doctrine of Names (*mingjiao* 名教)
205, 208
Dong Hu 董狐 (fl. 607 BCE) 172
Dong Yue 董說 (1620–1686) 357
Du Weiyun 杜維運 (1928–2012) 111

economics xxxv, 24, 38, 123–166, 197, 289
Eisenstadt, Shmuel N. (1923–2010)
397n13

phonetic exegesis xv. *See also* paranomastic definition

Pietism 69

ping 平 (balancing, equability) 47, 53, 59n56, 62

population 128, 137, 138, 140, 166, 194
  control of 145, 150, 199
  demographic policy 129, 133, 135, 151–152
  edifying of 220, 288
  enrichment of 130, 143, 157
  and the state 131, 158–160

poverty 129, 145, 153, 158, 177, 179, 299

prices 148, 155, 159–163

qi (animating force, pneuma, breath) 氣 xxiv–xxv, 37, 44, 51, 59n56, 61, 64, 190–191, 338

Qi (state of) 齊 43, 96n36, 113, 125–126, 142n52, 155, 162–163, 165, 187

Qi Tai 齊泰 (d. 1402) 247–248

Qian Mu 錢穆 (1895–1990) 85, 100n47

Qian Qianyi 錢謙益 (1582–1664) 359

Qian zhong lu 千忠戮 (The slaughter of the thousand loyal ones) 221, 246–247, 251, 255, 259

Qianlong emperor 乾隆 (r. 1736–1795/1799) 289–292

Qilu deng 歧路燈 (Lantern at the crossroad) 293

Qin (state and empire of) 秦 93, 103–104, 106, 113, 115, 125–126, 147, 150, 152n75, 165, 192, 198–199, 231

qing 情 (emotions, feelings, desire, nature, actuality, truth, disposition) xxxvii, xxxviii, 304, 317–31
  and cosmic order, 322–23
  and desire (*yu*), 320
  and human nature, 317, 322

and the essential ground of being (*li*), 321–22, 330
  and *xing* (nature, latent state of being), 324–29
  as the basic condition of things, 322
  as the correct state of human behavior, 323
  as an expression of cardinal Confucian bonds, 283–84
  as the theoretical foundation of ritual, 320
  cult of, 283, 284, 294
  in opposition to ritual, 284
  See also mourning

Qing 清 dynasty (1636/1644–1912) xi, xxvi–xviii, xxxi–xxxii, xxxvii, 166, 200, 220, 258n80, 259, 273, 282–307

Qing xing lun 情性論 manuscript 319

Qingshi leilüe 情史類略 (Classification of love) 284

Qingzhong pu 清忠譜 (Registers of the pure and the loyal) 258n80

quan 權 (expediency) xviii, 153, 228, 233

Quinet, Edgar (1803–1875) 70

Quintilian (c. 35– c. 100 CE) 19

Rameau, Jean-Philippe (1683–1764) 68

Rapp, Johann Georg (1757–1847) 69

recluses 184n42, 238, 349, 366. See also *yimin* 逸民

recommendations 199

remonstrance xxxvi–xxxvii, 46, 189, 202, 226–242, 245, 367–368, 371

ren 仁 (humanity, benevolence) xvii, xxiii, 4, 55, 134, 143, 177, 193n61, 206, 275, 322, 346. *See also* benevolence

renyu 人欲 (human desires) 320